Geoffrey Blainey

Geoffrey Blainey

Writer, Historian, Controversialist

By Richard Allsop

Geoffrey Blainey: Writer, Historian, Controversialist
© Copyright 2020 Richard Allsop
All rights reserved. Apart from any uses permitted by Australia's Copyright Act 1968, no part of this book may be reproduced by any process without prior written permission from the copyright owners. Inquiries should be directed to the publisher.

Monash University Publishing
Matheson Library Annexe
40 Exhibition Walk
Monash University
Clayton, Victoria 3800, Australia
www.publishing.monash.edu

Monash University Publishing brings to the world publications which advance the best traditions of humane and enlightened thought.

Monash University Publishing titles pass through a rigorous process of independent peer review.

ISBN: 9781925835625 (paperback)
ISBN: 9781925835632 (pdf)
ISBN: 9781925835649 (epub)

www.publishing.monash.edu/books/gb-9781925835625.html

Series: Australian History

Design: Les Thomas

Cover image: Geoffrey Blainey photographed by Jacky Ghossein (Fairfax Media).

A catalogue record for this book is available from the National Library of Australia.

Printed in Australia by Griffin Press an Accredited ISO AS/NZS 14001:2004 Environmental Management System printer.

The paper this book is printed on is certified against the Forest Stewardship Council ® Standards. Griffin Press holds FSC chain of custody certification SGS-COC-005088. FSC promotes environmentally responsible, socially beneficial and economically viable management of the world's forests.

CONTENTS

Acknowledgements vii

Introduction ix

Chapter 1:   Early Influences 1

Chapter 2:   Freelance Historian 21

Chapter 3:   Academic Historian 46

Chapter 4:   Broadening Horizons 74

Chapter 5:   Progressive Historian 92

Chapter 6:   National Figure 117

Chapter 7:   The Immigration Controversy 140

Chapter 8:   Freelance Again 167

Chapter 9:   The Controversialist 182

Chapter 10:   Australian Historian 211

Chapter 11:   World Historian 238

Conclusion 261

Select Bibliography 265

Index 279

*For Julianne, James, William,
Matthew and Sarah.*

ACKNOWLEDGEMENTS

I would like to thank Nathan Hollier, former Director of Monash University Publishing, for agreeing to publish this book and Acting Director Greg Bain for his ongoing support. Monash University Publishing's referees, and copy editor, John Mahony, all provided valuable comments and suggestions, while Mei Yen Chua produced a most comprehensive index. The Monash University Publishing team of Sarah Cannon, Joanne Mullins, Les Thomas and Duncan Fardon have done a great job in preparing this book for publication. I am very appreciative of all their hard work.

Over the course of my work on this project, Mark Peel and Bain Attwood were particularly supportive and encouraging. I very much enjoyed the lively, and often challenging, discussions I had with them both. Many other individuals including Chris Berg, Peter Craven, Graeme Davison, Tim Duncan, the late John Hirst, Stuart Macintyre, Mark McKenna, Kate Murphy and John Roskam assisted by either providing specific comments on earlier drafts or giving general advice about the direction of this work. I thank them all for sharing their thoughts.

Tim Clubb and Stephen Holt assisted by drawing my attention to certain items. I am indebted to John Fetter, then an executive of Orica, who not only let me know that Orica had a copy of Blainey's unpublished history of ICAANZ, but also arranged for me to have access to it.

The staff in the various libraries and archives I have used were most helpful. I would like to thank Christian Kuhlmann and Katie Wood at the University of Melbourne Archives and Matthew Stuckings at the National Library of Australia, all of whom worked hard to ensure that archival material was delivered at the arranged times.

Geoffrey Blainey himself assisted me in the early stages of this project. He granted me access to closed archival files and generously gave me the benefit of considerable time. He encouraged me to attend the annual conference of the Australian Mining History Association which was held in Queenstown in October 2008 and acted as a most effective tour guide when I was there. While he later withdrew his support for this work, I remain grateful for his earlier encouragement.

The biggest thank you of all goes to my family, my wife Julianne and our children, James, William, Matthew and Sarah. Julianne has remained encouraging of this project through a far longer period than either of us initially envisaged. Someone with a more utilitarian bent may have suggested that I could have instead devoted more of this time to remunerative employment. I hope the finished product justifies her patience.

INTRODUCTION

On the morning of Saturday, 17 March 1984, Geoffrey Blainey flew out of Melbourne's Essendon Airport on a light plane. The chartered flight was heading to the regional city of Warrnambool on Victoria's south-west coast, where Blainey was to deliver the keynote address to a Rotary Conference.

Most of the speech Blainey delivered that day was off-the-cuff, but he had taken care to write out the conclusion. He later remarked that 'knowing that I cannot think easily in a noisy, cramped little plane, I sat down at the kitchen table at about seven that morning and thought out carefully the end of my speech'.[1] The conclusion argued that the rate of Asian immigration to Australia was 'now far ahead of public opinion'.[2]

Those words triggered a furore of such magnitude that one critic argued several months later that 'no Australian (with the possible exception of Bob Hawke) has had greater media publicity than Blainey, since his original Warrnambool speech'.[3] The controversy reached a crescendo in late June when Blainey was the target of violent demonstrations in Melbourne and Sydney. 'Wild Demo in Asia Row' screamed *The Sun*'s front page headline in Melbourne.[4] The accompanying story described events which had occurred at Blainey's own Melbourne University campus the previous afternoon, when demonstrators had attempted to disrupt an honours Australian History seminar Blainey had been conducting.

Security staff had locked and blocked all the doors into the John Medley Building, where the class was being held. It appeared for a while that the protest might just involve demonstrators chanting anti-Blainey slogans, but when some students inside the building unlocked one of the doors the situation became much more volatile. Some of the demonstrators were able to dash inside and start banging on the door of the room where Blainey and his students were. A contingent of about thirty police, who had been on standby, now became involved, managing to re-secure the doors and clear the building of demonstrators.

---

1   Geoffrey Blainey, *All for Australia* (Sydney: Methuen Haynes, 1984), 24-25.
2   Richard Goodwin, 'Immigration Policy Questioned', *The Standard* (Warrnambool), 19 March 1984, 1.
3   David Phillips, 'Blainey Critic Replies', *Look & Listen*, November 1984, 27.
4   Lynne O'Donnell, 'Wild Demo In Asia Row', *The Sun News Pictorial*, 19 June 1984, 1.

With the adrenalin now flowing on both sides, violence erupted when police chased a woman spraying slogans on the concrete outside the building, eventually arresting her and two of her comrades who fought with the police trying to get her in the van. The demonstrators temporarily changed the target of their abuse from Blainey to the police, chanting 'Cops off campus'. Realising that they were unlikely to breach the heavily-guarded Medley Building again, they launched a raid on the University's administration building, before continuing their protests in the Bourke Street Mall in central Melbourne and outside Liberal Party headquarters in Exhibition Street.[5]

The following evening, much the same thing happened in Sydney when Blainey spoke at a meeting hosted by the Kings Cross Community and Information Centre. The front page of Wednesday morning's *Sydney Morning Herald* had a large picture of him being escorted from the meeting by burly police officers, with the accompanying story describing how 'police and Special Branch members with batons' had clashed with demonstrators outside the venue.[6] Inside the hall, Blainey's words were drowned out by the chants and shouts of protestors, while others in the audience heckled those who were attacking him.

One observer thought the meeting resembled the last days of Germany's Weimar Republic 'with Communists chanting at one end of the hall and self-confessed Nazis seigheilling at the other' and with Blainey making 'a plaintive plea ... for someone to stand up and support his right to free speech'.[7] Another who was there, political journalist Peter Bowers, wrote:

> It is hard to believe that the driven, harassed figure on the stage being simultaneously abused and applauded, jeered and cheered was the distinguished academic ... Professor Blainey with his lank, wispy hair, genial manner and disarming stammer looks like the faintly absent-minded professor who finds himself in the middle of a maelstrom, as bewildered as the owl caught in a searchlight.[8]

---

5   O'Donnell, 'Wild Demo In Asia Row'; 'Protest against Blainey sparks campus violence', *The Australian*, 19 June 1984, 1; David Humphries, 'Three arrested at anti-Blainey rally', *The Age*, 19 June 1984, 5; Anna Grutzner, 'Blainey hits at demo stirrers', *The Herald* (Melbourne), 19 June 1984, 3.

6   Paul Bailey and Paul Norrington, 'Protestors confront Blainey in Sydney', *Sydney Morning Herald*, 20 June 1984, 1.

7   David Osborne, 'Men of letters, not of speech', *The Sun Herald*, 22 July 1984, 59

8   Peter Bowers, 'Blainey stirs, rather than mixes, the pot', *Sydney Morning Herald*, 23 June 1984, 13.

INTRODUCTION

The events of the week made it clear that the physical threat to Blainey was serious. As a result, Melbourne University had to adopt special measures for opening mail, security at his home needed to be stepped up and normal pleasures, such as watching football from the outer, were now inadvisable. On police advice, he gave up speaking in public.

What appeared to concern Blainey most were the claims of the Melbourne University demonstrators that they had been acting with the support of his colleagues in the History Department. Whilst subsequently assured that this was not the case, Blainey still felt that the action of many of his colleagues the previous month in writing a letter to the newspapers disassociating themselves from his views was partially responsible for stirring up this radical fringe.

In 1984, Blainey was fifty-four years old. Nothing in his previous experience could have prepared him for the degree of antipathy now being directed towards him. From the publication of *The Peaks of Lyell* (1954) thirty years earlier, Blainey's career had progressed steadily from one success to the next. Books such as *The Rush That Never Ended* (1963) and *The Tyranny of Distance* (1966) combined catchy titles with innovative interpretations and contributed significantly to his growing status. His rise to national prominence was also assisted by his steady ascent up the academic hierarchy, combined with numerous appointments to prominent government committees and a willingness to participate in the media, culminating in an eponymous television series. His stature as a public figure had been underlined when, in late 1979, he was one of six rising stars included by the ABC in its television series *Faces of the Eighties*.

Blainey had been involved in several vigorous historical and political controversies prior to 1984, but nothing he had written or said had gone close to triggering demonstrations. Debates over whether flax was a factor in the British settlement of Australia, or whether the Literature Board of the Australia Council should be allowed to have its office in Melbourne, were unlikely to provoke wild demonstrations or front-page headlines. In fact, Blainey had appeared to have a particularly good capacity to make and maintain friendships across the political spectrum, straddling felicitous relationships with everyone from conservative mining executives to communist literary editors.

The controversy of 1984 set in train events which culminated by the end of the decade in Blainey leaving the academic history profession. The schism between Blainey and much of the nation's history academy, despite some well-meaning attempts, has never been healed. Perhaps, more significantly, the rift emphasised that the history academy had little place for those who did not share its worldview on the issues its members considered important. It is striking that when Blainey expressed strong views on topics such as Australia's economic direction, his fellow historians appeared to have significantly less interest. Their intense focus on issues of race and national identity, which came to the fore in the Blainey debate, makes it an obvious starting point for any discussion of the so-called culture or history wars in Australia. The controversy was to be the first of many about race, including both immigration and Aboriginal policy, in Australia over the next few decades.

Blainey is commonly described as a 'conservative historian'. The phrase 'conservative historian' is a problematic one, for there is no recognisable school of conservative historians. Rather individual historians are given the label, sometimes due to their historical practice, but just as often because they are seen to hold conservative political views.

In 1975, Blainey published *Triumph of the Nomads*, which was almost universally regarded at the time of publication as a progressive work, correcting the long-standing exclusion of Aboriginal Australians from the national narrative. Ninety-nine per cent of Australia's human history had occurred prior to European settlement and *Triumph of the Nomads* challenged the people of Australia to recognise this fact. Blainey rejected the existing assumption that Aboriginal society had been static and argued that previous writers had underestimated Aboriginal economic success. Turning conventional thinking on its head, Blainey suggested that Aboriginal material life in 1800 could be compared favourably with many parts of Europe at the same time. The *Sydney Morning Herald*'s reviewer thought that in trying to improve the treatment of Aboriginals in history he had 'at times swung too far the other way'.[9]

Yet, within a decade, *Triumph of the Nomads* was being re-analysed to show that Blainey was conservative rather than progressive, demonstrating that there had been a radical shift in the intellectual environment, especially in what was considered acceptable comment on racial matters. The mainstream party of the Left in Australia, the Labor Party, officially supported the White Australia Policy until 1965; less than twenty years later Blainey was hounded for expressing views on immigration that were far less discriminatory.

Blainey has been ranked as one of Australia's three leading historians along with Keith Hancock and Manning Clark.[10] In the *Oxford Companion to Australian History*, Graeme Davison described him as 'the most prolific, wide-ranging, inventive, and – in the 1980s and 1990s – most controversial of Australia's living historians'. Davison also noted that there has been little

---

9 John Douglas Pringle, 'History of Australia before 1788', *Sydney Morning Herald*, 18 October 1975, 17.

10 A recent example is David Day, 'Story of a journeyman historian', *The Age*, 2 October 2010.

dispassionate analysis of Blainey's work. The few studies which had been done were 'mainly polemical in approach, reading his earlier work for signs of the emerging controversialist'.[11]

Unlike Hancock and Clark, Blainey has not previously been the subject of a comprehensive study of his work. At the time Davison was writing, the only book devoted to Blainey's work was *Surrender Australia? Essays in the Study and Uses of History: Geoffrey Blainey and Asian Immigration* (1985), written at the height of the immigration controversy. Since then, a book of essays, *The Fuss That Never Ended: The Life and Work of Geoffrey Blainey* (2003) has been published, but it only went some way towards providing what Davison believed was needed, namely 'a more mature assessment' of Blainey's work that would 'illuminate more clearly the personal and ideological dimensions of his maverick career, as well as acknowledging the sustained creativity, intellectual range, pervasive influence, and literary distinction of his writing'.[12]

This book seeks to meet that challenge. It does so by means of a detailed assessment of Blainey's prolific output, the forty books he has written, as well as the numerous articles he has contributed to journals and newspapers. It seeks to both investigate the reasons for the success Blainey achieved and explain the factors which make his works on Australian and world history different from those of the majority of professional historians in Australia.

To attempt to understand Blainey, it is necessary to go back before the beginning of his career. For by the time he turned 21, in early 1951, his embryonic career as an historian was already following an unusual path. At that time, successful Australian graduates with ambitions to pursue history as a career usually aimed for postgraduate study at a British university, particularly Oxford. Blainey showed no interest in doing that. Instead, in accepting a commission to write a company history, especially one that involved basing himself on the remote west coast of Tasmania, the young Blainey demonstrated quite different priorities. His preparedness to take on the job of researching the history of the Mt Lyell Mining Company, and the fact that, unlike the company board, he saw the potential for a book at the end of the research shows that, by his early twenties, Blainey's distinctive interests and ambitions were already well formed.

---

11   Graeme Davison, 'Blainey, Geoffrey Norman (1930-)', in *The Oxford Companion to Australian History*, eds Graeme Davison, John Hirst and Stuart Macintyre, with the assistance of H. Doyle and K. Torney (Melbourne: Oxford University Press, 1998, 2001), 74.

12   Ibid.

A number of factors had contributed to moulding the personality of the young historian who was chosen for the Mt Lyell job, and who proceeded to make such a success of it. Many of these factors have continued to influence the sort of historian Blainey has remained throughout his career. Blainey had not himself publicly analysed, or weighed, these influences on his career in great depth until the publication of a volume of delightfully written memoirs, *Before I Forget: An Early Memoir* in 2019.[13] While one critic argued that 'those looking for an exposition of Blainey's theory of history will not find a great deal in *Before I Forget*' the memoirs nonetheless provide further insights into the development of Blainey's extraordinary talent.[14] When read in conjunction with many other sources, they help identify the factors that, in varying degrees, created the writer, historian and controversialist, Geoffrey Norman Blainey.

---

13 Geoffrey Blainey, *Before I Forget: An Early Memoir* (Melbourne: Hamish Hamilton, 2019).
14 Geordie Williamson, 'Starting From Scratch', *The Weekend Australian* (Review section), 6-7 July 2019, 18-19.

Chapter 1

EARLY INFLUENCES

Geoffrey Blainey could easily have died when he was just a few weeks old. At the time of his birth, his parents Clifford and Hilda Blainey and his older brother John were living in Terang in the Western District of Victoria. However, instead of having her second child locally, as she would do with all her other children, Hilda was driven to Melbourne in the final weeks of this pregnancy because the nurse at the Terang health centre had privately advised her against the local hospital 'which she felt had a bad record'.[1]

Blainey's birth, on Tuesday, 11 March 1930, took place at Fairbank Hospital, a small private facility in Station Street, Box Hill, close to the home of Hilda's parents, the Lanyons. After taking his wife to Melbourne, Clifford had returned to Terang where, some days after the birth, he learnt the disturbing news that the infant 'showed signs of an abdominal defect for which there was at the time no certain cure'.[2]

The 'defect' was pyloric stenosis, a blockage between the stomach and small intestine, which meant that, instead of being processed, milk was vomited back up with great force. The consequences without treatment were loss of weight and death. These days the procedure to rectify the problem is routine, but that was not the case in 1930. Clifford recalled that 'six weeks of suspense followed', until the Box Hill doctor obtained the services of leading private paediatrician, Dr Kingsley Norris.

Hilda had to take her sick baby to Norris's rooms at Camberwell for a consultation, but the operation itself took place at the same hospital at which Blainey had been born. For 48 hours, Blainey's life 'hung in the balance' before 'steady improvement began, removing all trace of the serious illness, and making a strenuous normal life possible'.[3] Hilda recalled that the members of hospital staff were 'very impressed that not only did this specialist come out to Box Hill to operate, but he came out a second time to see if Geoff was

---

1   Hilda Blainey, *Hilda Blainey's Story* (Compiled by Judy Parker, unpublished, 2006), 64.
2   S.C. Blainey, *A Pastor Recalls* (unpublished, 1975), 30.
3   Ibid.

doing well enough'.⁴ She also observed that 'as by this time he was old enough to smile, the nurses fussed greatly over him so he became precocious'.⁵ The combination of the Terang nurse's advice, the ability of the local doctor to get a referral to a leading surgeon, and the success of what, at the time, was a risky operation, meant Blainey was lucky to survive. Clifford's occupation as a Methodist minister helped because it meant that Norris waived his normal fees, which otherwise would have been very difficult for the Blaineys to pay.⁶

Clifford had been born and raised at Eaglehawk, near Bendigo, on the Victorian goldfields, an area where Methodism was the dominant religion. He had begun preaching in local chapels when just 15 and, after study and service at various churches across Victoria, was ordained as a minister in 1924. It was at his first ministerial posting to Mitcham, on the eastern outskirts of Melbourne, that he met and courted Hilda. Hilda had been born in East Gippsland, but her father's job as a teacher necessitated many moves around country Victoria to places including Sugar Loaf Creek near Seymour, Corryong and Gisborne. She won a scholarship to Melbourne High School (which was co-eductaional at that time) and then became a trainee teacher.⁷ After their marriage in 1927, the Blaineys were sent by the church to Jeparit in the Wimmera (a town which was yet to receive its subsequent fame as the birthplace of Robert Menzies) where their first child, John, was born, prior to their move to Terang.

It has often been noted that many of the Australia's most prominent historians had fathers who were ministers of religion. As well as Blainey, other leading examples were Keith Hancock and Manning Clark. It has also been suggested that Blainey's upbringing in 'small-town Methodism – a religion of the lower and working classes – may have instilled an outlook more intellectually independent and socially insecure' than Hancock's and Clark's within the more middle-class Anglican Church.⁸

Not much has been written about growing up as a Methodist in Australia. In an address to members of the Melbourne Jewish community in 1997, Blainey himself noted that 'it is a reflection of the intense interest in Jewish history that in the last half century a larger number of general works of substance seems to have been written in Australia about Jews than about Methodists, a denomination which in Australia usually held some 25 times

---

4   Hilda Blainey, *Hilda Blainey's Story*, 64.
5   Ibid.
6   Blainey, *Before I Forget*, 9.
7   Ibid., 3–4.
8   Davison, 'Blainey', *Oxford Companion*, 74.

as many adherents'.⁹ Blainey made some small measure of rectification when he delivered a lecture, two years later, to the Uniting Church's Annual Synod titled 'A Methodist Childhood'.¹⁰

If Methodism engendered any social insecurity in Blainey, it was surely counterbalanced by the sense of belonging that he felt in his home state of Victoria. He has commented with pride on his eight Victorian great-grandparents and strong connections with the Victorian goldfields, an area which 'nurtured numbers of distinguished Australians out of all proportion to their population'.¹¹

An important practical consequence of Blainey's father's occupation was constant moves to various parts of Victoria. Blainey recalled in the eulogy he delivered at his mother's funeral that 'we were always moving, usually not knowing where our home would be until about a month before the move took place'.¹² In his first 18 years the family lived in Terang, Leongatha, Geelong, Ballarat and Thornbury. Blainey's father was clearly aware that, unlike the minister and his wife, the children of the vicarage had 'no such automatic place to fill' when entering a new community. It was a matter of chance whether 'the new church may abound in potential friends or there may be hardly a soul with their own interests'. Fortunately, despite 'their ages and educational interests [being] so different', things seem to have worked out as well as could be hoped for the Blaineys, partly because 'no family of five children could have received more generous treatment from the church'.¹³

There is no evidence that Blainey found the constant moves unsettling, indeed he claims to have taken them in his stride, stating that 'the frequent moving did not worry us as children: we expected it'.¹⁴ However, the fact

---

9 Geoffrey Blainey, 'Some thoughts on 200 years: The Jews in Australia', in ed. Malcolm J. Turnbull *The Australian Jewish Experience: A Colloquium, Papers presented on 26 August, 1997 to honour Rabbi Dr John S. Levi* (Melbourne, 1998), 15. In the Foreword, Rabbi Levi commented that Blainey's 'remark haunts me', and he worried whether he had gone 'over the top' in his own study of Australian Jewish history.

10 Geoffrey Blainey, 'A Methodist Childhood', *Proceedings of the Uniting Church Historical Society Synod* 6, no. 2 (December 1999): 110–118.

11 G. Blainey 'History of Victoria' in ed. G.W. Leeper, *Introducing Victoria*, (Melbourne: Australian and New Zealand Association for the Advancement of Science, Melbourne and Melbourne University Press, 1955), 11–12.

12 Geoffrey Blainey, 'A Few Words at a Funeral' in Geoffrey Blainey, *In Our Time: The Issues and The People of Our Century* (Melbourne: Information Australia, 1999), 110.

13 S.C. Blainey, *A Pastor Recalls*, 78. Blainey's birth-order of second place behind an older brother, and ahead of a sister was another similar childhood feature he shared with Manning Clark. Blainey also had two youner brothers.

14 Blainey, 'A Methodist Childhood', 116.

that Blainey claims to have not been greatly affected by the moves does not mean that they did not have a significant impact on his evolving personality. Several anecdotes about Blainey give the impression of someone who made friends easily but did not become too reliant on any individual friendship. The experience of moving to new towns as a child was no doubt a factor in the ease with which, as a young historian, Blainey entered different communities, beginning with Queenstown in Tasmania.

Blainey recalls his father as an unusually methodical man who recorded, for every week of his ministerial life, the details of the sermons he preached, together with the accompanying biblical texts and the hymns selected for the service. As Blainey has described 'he handled numbers with ease – he no doubt knew the number of every hymn in the Methodist hymnbook and the precise chapter and verse of thousands of biblical texts. He also carried in his head the exact numbers of hundreds of car number plates, and sometimes he would pass a car on the road and remark that it used to be owned by so and so in a certain country town.'[15] While the father was demonstrably 'numerate and systematic', Blainey's mother was 'more a romantic'.[16] Naturally, Hilda Blainey had to assist her husband with pastoral visits and Blainey believes his parents were 'held in affection by their various congregations'.[17]

After more than three decades of postings in country towns and lower-middle class suburbs, the Blaineys had a late-career move to the more salubrious bayside Melbourne parish of Brighton, which felt 'out of character' for Clifford, as 'neither my wife nor I had tasted the flavour of affluence' in previous locations.[18] In one sense, the Blaineys' progress symbolised a trend in Methodism. One commentator has argued that while 'Methodism has retained some of its lower middle-class characteristics up to recent times', it also became something of 'a victim of its own success'.[19] This was because 'it tended to promote those characteristics (such as reliability, responsibility, self-denial, industry) that would propel its membership up the economic and social ladder'.[20]

---

15   Ibid., 114.
16   Ibid.
17   Ibid., 111.
18   S.C. Blainey, *A Pastor Recalls*, 54.
19   Hans Mol, 'Nonconformists', in *The Australian People: An Encyclopedia of the Nation, Its People and Their Origins*, ed. James Jupp, (Cambridge: Cambridge University Press, 2001), 326.
20   Ibid.

Methodists were also recognised (often along with other Nonconformist denominations) by their opposition to activities such as drinking, gambling, dancing and the misuse of the Sabbath.[21] Clifford Blainey did not adopt a particularly hard-line position on these social issues, commenting that when dancing was permitted in a church building 'many pleasant evenings were enjoyed in the School Hall by parishioners of all ages'.[22]

Of Blainey's published reflections on his childhood the earliest relate to when he was four years old. He has described the South Gippsland floods of 1934 as 'a dramatic event for our rural district and a momentous event for me', with his recollections including seeing a washed away bridge.[23] In his 1982 television series, *The Blainey View*, Blainey used his recollections of the floods to make the point that in history there is a tendency to 'emphasise the most dramatic events' as 'we see them as the turning points in the affairs of nations or districts' but 'that flood, for all its drama and destruction, had nothing like the power of other changes which were quietly taking place'.[24] Further drama came the following year when on Monday, 2 December 1935 the body of a six-year-old girl, Jane Rushmer, with whom Blainey sometimes played, was found dumped outside the Leongatha township. Police quickly arrested local man Arthur Sodeman, who then confessed to other murders.[25] Blainey has given some insight into the less dramatic side of his young life with recollections of early Christmases or his time in the Sea Scouts.[26] He told how, as a mature adult, he could still recall all the chants by which sums, grammar, spelling and geography were taught at primary school in Leongatha.[27]

The move from Leongatha to Geelong occurred when Blainey was seven and it precipitated Blainey's lifelong attachment to the town's football club. Blainey attended his first matches at Corio Oval in 1937, being taken by his father to see Geelong's matches against South Melbourne and St Kilda.[28]

---

21 R.A. Humphreys & R.S. Ward, *Religious Bodies in Australia: A Comprehensive Guide* (Melbourne: New Melbourne Press, 1995), 108.
22 S.C. Blainey, *A Pastor Recalls*, 59.
23 Geoffrey Blainey, *The Blainey View* (Sydney: Australian Broadcasting Corporation and Melbourne: Macmillan, 1982), 125.
24 Ibid.
25 Blainey, *Before I Forget*, 24–25.
26 Geoffrey Blainey, 'Memories that last a lifetime', *The Sunday Age* (Agenda section), 22 December 1991, 4; Geoffrey Blainey, 'When distance was a tyrant', *Herald Sun*, 27 December 2007, 28; and Scouts Australia website, accessed 23 November 2011.
27 Douglas Aiton, '10 Things You Didn't Know About … Professor Geoffrey Blainey', *The Weekend Australian* Magazine, 29–30 January 2005, 10; and Blainey, *Before I Forget*, 25.
28 Blainey, 'A Methodist Childhood', 115; and Blainey, *Before I Forget*, 33–39.

Some fifty years later, he vividly described the smell of the tobacco smoke and 'the wood smoke from the fires on which the saveloys were cooking' as he and his father stood on the steep slope behind the southern goal at his first game.[29] Geelong went on to win the Premiership in 1937 and, while Blainey did not attend that year's Grand Final, he travelled up to Melbourne to see one as early as 1940. Sport, football in particular, was to remain an abiding interest for Blainey, and he was to write more about it in his general histories than most other historians of his generation.

Blainey's childhood seems to have taught him some lessons in economic self-sufficiency. According to Clifford Blainey's memoirs, it was a trait Blainey shared with his siblings. His father commented that 'they were admirable in the way they adapted and helped themselves to obtain what was beyond our limited means … in turn the boys did paper and fruit rounds, worked in radio shops, picked fruit, and did a variety of jobs in vacations'.[30] As a young child, Blainey had 'a great ambition to be a farmer', but it was in the urban setting of Geelong that he got his first actual job.[31] In 1940, he took on a newspaper round delivering the *Herald* on weekday afternoons and both the *Herald* and *Sporting Globe* on Saturday evenings, riding his bike with the newspapers balanced on the handle bar.[32]

When the family moved to Ballarat just after Easter 1941, Blainey worked every Saturday for a fruiterer. He delivered the produce in a large basket, collecting the cash and riding his bike to the next customer.[33] Blainey also grew vegetables and kept chooks, selling the eggs, and using the proceeds of the work and sales to purchase a canoe and paddle on the lake. As well as adding to his work experience, Blainey has credited Ballarat with sparking an interest in history:

> The sight of all those old buildings and the gorse coloured mullock heaps and the big cemeteries made me conscious of another era. I learned little about Ballarat's history while I was there (the relevant books were

---

29 Geoffrey Blainey, 'Score on the board sets uneasy goal for ID card', *The Weekend Australian*, 12–13 September 1987, 22.
30 S.C. Blainey, *A Pastor Recalls*, 40–41.
31 The farmer ambition is mentioned in Stuart Rintoul, 'The Essential Blainey, *The Weekend Australian*, Weekend supplement, 8–9 October 1988, 3.
32 Blainey, *Before I Forget*, 53–54
33 Geoffrey Blainey, 'Ballarat' in Blainey, *In Our Time: The Issues and The People of Our Century*, (Information Australia, Melbourne, 1999), 105.

few and out of print) but I remained curious, knowing there must be a history. I feel I owe a lot to Ballarat.[34]

An important aspect of having a minister as a father was that it meant Blainey grew up in a literary household. Blainey's father 'read widely in theology, kept a large personal library, and spent more money on books than he could afford'.[35] Childhood reading came to mind when an interviewer asked Blainey what aspect of his life he would look back on, from his deathbed, with most pleasure. He nominated his 'very happy' childhood years, specifically because 'when I was little I read so many interesting books … I thought the school readers were wonderful'.[36] In those days, most government primary schools did not have a library, but Blainey became 'an eager reader of newspapers' by the age of ten and, by twelve, he was making extensive use of the book collection of the Mechanics Institute Library in Ballarat.[37] From the age of 14 onwards, once he began at boarding school in Melbourne, he was a regular visitor to the newspaper room at the State Library, where he would 'ask for a copy of *The Argus* from 1880 or *The Age* of 1875 and read them faithfully through', an early sign of his fascination with the details of the past.[38] Another factor in his early interest in history was the influence of his maternal grandfather, Henry Maynard Lanyon, who owned several historical volumes, liked reminiscing about Australia's past and wrote a history of his local Methodist church.[39]

The historian Deborah Gare interviewed Blainey in 1997 and quoted him saying of his upbringing that 'we saw ourselves as Australians and not belonging to anywhere else'.[40] While at home and school there was respect towards Britain and the British Empire, he did not feel a 'close affinity to the British people', in part because his family 'had no connection with anyone who was English'.[41] Despite his sense of Australian identity and his love of reading, Blainey does not recall reading many books of Australian literature or history until his teenage years, when he read Walter Murdoch's biography of Deakin

---

34   Ibid.
35   Blainey, 'A Methodist Childhood', 115.
36   Doug Aiton, 'Tomorrow the world', *The Sunday Age* (Agenda section), 25 February 1996, 5.
37   Lenore Nicklin, 'Blainey is the new Chairman', *Sydney Morning Herald*, 9 July 1977, 16.
38   Geoffrey Blainey, 'Writing Australian History: A few reflections', *Stephen Murray Smith Lecture*, State Library of Victoria, 5 November 2008.
39   Blainey, *Before I Forget*, 50.
40   Deborah Gare, 'White Ghost of Empire?', *Quadrant* 43, no. 12 (December 1999): 39.
41   Ibid.

and Hancock's *Australia*. He recalls that while 'not fully understanding some of the abstractions', he was 'carried away by the excitement of various chapters and by the air of authority'.[42]

His reading of newspapers and books meant that, by the age of 18, he had what he has called an 'absurd knowledge of Australian history'.[43] It is not surprising that one of his first adult extravagances was buying the massive two-volume book about early Victoria, *Victoria and its Metropolis*. Blainey recalls that he 'paid two guineas for it and lugged it away in the tram'.[44] Yet Blainey did not just learn from the printed word. From an early age he was interested in seeing different places and was fascinated with contrasting landscapes. In *The Blainey View* he described standing on the roof of his Ballarat home, when he was 12, and wondering how the landscape north of the Great Dividing Range would differ from the one he had seen in various locations south of the Divide. The next day he cycled the twenty miles from Ballarat to Clunes to see for himself.

Blainey was a student at Ballarat High from 1941 to 1943 and then, having attended four different government schools, he completed his secondary education at Wesley College, one of Melbourne's prominent private boys' schools. His mother described the good fortune which made his education affordable:

> We entered Geoff for a newly established scholarship at Wesley and he won it. Paid for by a Geelong haberdasher, it was open to Methodist ministers' sons in country Victoria. It was a whole story in itself how we got him equipped, but he got there and we were very glad that he had the benefit of those years. He also had a junior scholarship, which covered most of the remaining regular expenses.[45]

This move to an elite city-based private school meant that Blainey's upbringing had brought him into contact with diverse elements of society – country and city, working class and establishment.

When Blainey began at Wesley in 1944 the school had just returned to its normal St Kilda Road campus, having spent the previous two years co-located at Scotch College, while the armed forces used its normal facilities. In his

---

42 Geoffrey Dutton, 'What They Read When They Were Young', *The Bulletin*, 23–30 December 1980, 169–170; and Geoffrey Blainey, 'The Hancock Express', *The Australian* (Literary Review), 1 September 2010, 6.
43 Blainey, 'Writing Australian History'.
44 Aiton, '10 Things'.
45 Hilda Blainey, *Hilda Blainey's Story*, 86.

first year, Blainey ranked only 26th in his class of 34 but, once he acclimatised to the new environment, he prospered academically, so much so that he was equal dux in his final year.[46]

Individual teachers made an impression. One was 'a fine old-fashioned history teacher, Mr Gwillim, whose head was a filing cabinet full of quotations'.[47] More significant for Blainey's future than the history teacher was the fact that his English teacher was A.A. Phillips. Phillips was subsequently to achieve lasting fame when he came up with the phrase 'the cultural cringe' to describe Australians' attitude towards the merits of their own culture.[48] According to Blainey, there was no cultural cringe at Wesley in the 1940s, observing that, in many ways, it was 'incredibly Australian in its outlook and values'.[49]

Phillips, who taught Blainey English for all four years he was at Wesley, had firm views that writing should be tight and direct, without too many subordinate clauses or unnecessary adjectives, views which clearly had an influence on his pupil. Phillips was also the teacher in charge of debating and in 1947 the team of Blainey, S.E.K. Hulme and John Stafford enjoyed considerable success.

Another Wesley teacher, Economics master Dick Belshaw contributed to a short-lived period when Blainey was supportive of left-wing ideas. Knowing that Blainey was a voracious reader, Balshaw provided him with some left-wing books and, for a period between the ages of 15 and 17, Blainey espoused some of the views he read in them.[50] Phillips provided a 'subtle influence' in a similar direction.[51]

However, this flirtation ended in the school holidays in August 1947, when Blainey cycled down to his uncle's potato farm near Colac in western Victoria. This trip took place just a couple of weeks after Prime Minister Ben Chifley's announcement of his plan to nationalise the banks. After working on the farm during the days, Blainey joined his uncle in attending local meetings on

---

46   'Schools must produce men of character', *The Argus*, 12 December 1947, 11.
47   Aiton, '10 Things'.
48   It is certainly remarkable that in one school classroom in the mid-1940s, the creators of two of the three most memorable phrases of post-war Australia ('cultural cringe' and 'tyranny of distance'; Donald Horne's 'lucky country' being the third) were together as teacher and student.
49   'Geoffrey Blainey remembers his schooldays', *Lion: The Wesley College Community Magazine*, edition 109, August 2010, 14.
50   Blainey, *Before I Forget*, 97. Blainey also notes in his memoir that his own father 'probably tended to be a Labor sympathiser' (Blainey, *Before I Forget*, 21).
51   Ibid., 111.

bank nationalisation in the evenings and saw how much anxiety the Chifley Government's plan was causing the local community.[52] Theoretical leftism suddenly seemed less attractive. It was an example of what was to be a recurring theme in Blainey's life and work: a rejection of an abstract perceived benefit to a group or class in favour of a response that appreciated the views of people he encountered. He was to favour practical economic considerations over symbolic gestures by governments.

It is certainly clear that at university, in the following three years (1948-50), Blainey demonstrated little sympathy for the attitudes of the political or cultural Left. In his own recollections, he was 'already on the middle of the political road at a time when the road travelled by most of the arts students still had a camber to the left'.[53] Although, to his own latter day surprise, on reading a notebook he kept in January 1949, Blainey discovered his own views did have one radical element. At a time when protectionism was the shared view of both sides of Australian politics, Blainey was 'snuggling up to free trade', favouring reductions in Australian tariffs on imported goods and hoping for reciprocal reductions from other countries to enable the export of more Australian agricultural products and minerals.[54]

Blainey had begun his undergraduate life at the University of Melbourne, then the only university in Victoria, in the previous autumn. Years later, when asked to reflect on his undergraduate years for a book of recollections of prominent alumni, Blainey did so with words which resonate with students from any era, not just the late 1940s:

> Intellectually and maybe emotionally, it's a time of stumbling and occasionally of defeat. It's a time of heightened enthusiasm ... most students perceptibly or quietly change during their time at university, and sixty years later or even six years later it is not easy to discover the person you once were, let alone to acknowledge publicly that lost person. More than in most phases of life, the years at university for those who take them seriously are sweet and sour ... a taste of the loneliness, awe and bewilderment of first becoming a student remains ... alongside the satisfaction and the magic.[55]

---

52   Ibid., 107.
53   Ibid., 111.
54   Ibid., 141.
55   Geoffrey Blainey, 'Foreword' in *Memories of Melbourne University: Undergraduate Life in the Years Since 1917*, ed. Hume Dow, (Melbourne: Hutchinson, 1983), viii–ix.

The immediate post-war years had been unusually stimulating times at Australian universities. The combination of the commencement of Commonwealth funding of university places in 1944, and the introduction of a special scheme to facilitate returning servicemen attending university, meant that enrolments more than doubled. The presence of many more mature-age students on campus, particularly ones with military experience, created a robust atmosphere. One book about the university suggests that part of the explanation for the stimulating atmosphere lay in the quality of teaching in the Faculty of Arts:

> A student beginning Arts in (say) 1948 might be cramped in lectures and forced by the inadequacy of the University Library to spend days in the grimy chill of the once great Public Library but ... even the mildly uninterested student could recognize an unusually concentrated excellence in teaching.[56]

Blainey commenced university thinking that he might like to become a barrister. However, he found the first-year subject, Introduction to Legal Method, 'inconceivably dull', and so he decided to concentrate on history instead.[57] In his undergraduate history studies Blainey covered a fair amount of ground including ancient, British, American and Australian history, and all within the three years, as he was among the last intakes of students who were not required to undertake a fourth year to achieve an honours degree.

The school of history Blainey entered was in the process of building its reputation as the pre-eminent history school in the nation, under the long reign of Professor Max Crawford, from 1937 to 1971. As part of the university-wide expansion, staff numbers in History increased from five in 1944 to fourteen in 1946, ushering in what historian John Poynter has suggested was 'the golden age of the school'.[58] In the eyes of some students of the time its quality reached mythic proportions. One has written:

> The golden years of Australian universities were 1946-1948, and the most Golden University was Melbourne. And the Goldenest place in

---

56　John Poynter and Carolyn Rasmussen, *A Place Apart: The University of Melbourne: Decades of Change* (Melbourne: Melbourne University Press, 1996), 93.

57　Stephen Downes, 'The Man Who Was Always Looking For Something', *The Age*, 9 August 1980, 17.

58　John Poynter, 'Wot Larks To Be Aboard: The History Department 1937–1971', in eds Fay Anderson and Stuart Macintyre, *The Life of the Past: The discipline of history at the University of Melbourne 1855–2005* (Melbourne: RMIT Publishing and Department of History, University of Melbourne, 2006), 51.

Melbourne University was the History Department — and I was there! This was the amazing era of the ex-servicemen — fellow students who have mostly gone on to brilliant careers.[59]

Writing in the early 1960s, Vincent Buckley saw the History School as the major influence on the intellectual culture of Melbourne, making it an 'earnest, do-gooding, voluble, assertive, preoccupied with "McCarthyism"' city, as opposed to 'free-thinking, libertarian, sceptical, "realist" and anti-Communist' Sydney, where the equivalent influencer was Philosophy Professor, John Anderson.[60] The status of Melbourne's history school produced a mixture of admiration and envy from outsiders, and a view that its sense of self-regard was a little overblown. All three sentiments are captured in these reflections by leading Australian historian Geoffrey Bolton:

> My perception [was] that the powerhouse of Australian historical writing was to be found at R.M. Crawford's department of history of the University of Melbourne. For years I envied contemporaries such as Ken Inglis and Geoffrey Blainey who grew up in that charmed circle, and consoled myself by observing critically that Melbourne's pre-eminence came at the cost of a certain myopia, a tendency to assume that the intellectual templates of Melbourne, the Melbourne historical experience, held good for the whole of Australia.[61]

Many history students were active in student clubs such as the Labor Club and the Student Christian Movement (SCM), both bodies attracting students who were keen to promote causes such as social change and international peace. The generally 'progressive sympathies of staff and students' in the History Department was reflected in a joke of the time which asked prospective Masters' candidates, 'Which aspect of the Australian labour movement are you going to write your MA on?'[62]

---

59   Valerie Yule, 'University Memories', The History of the University Unit on www.huu.unimelb.edu.au/memories/stories, accessed on 23 March 2010.

60   Vincent Buckley, 'Intellectuals' in *Australian Civilization*, ed. Peter Coleman, (Melbourne: Cheshire, 1962), 101–102.

61   Geoffrey Bolton, 'The Problem of History' (paper presented as the inaugural Kenneth Binns Lecture, National Library of Australia, Canberra, 29 April – 1 May 2005). Bolton had his first exposure to Melbourne when he travelled there for a conference of student newspaper editors where he met Blainey.

62   Stuart Macintyre, 'Going Down From Melbourne: Oxford, Scholarship and Journalism', paper delivered at 'Ken Inglis in History: A Laconic Colloquium', at Monash University, 24–25 November 2016.

While Blainey generally enjoyed the subjects in Crawford's History department, not all aspects of the undergraduate history syllabus impressed him. A recent graduate, Arthur Burns, who had been a leader of both the Labor Club and SCM, brought back from a spell at the University of London new historical concepts which he incorporated into a 'Theory and Method' subject. Blainey has described how 'Burns ... teaching with brilliance but at a level of abstraction that made me blink, generously let me read a selection of the great historians rather than attend his lectures'.[63] The list of historians whom Blainey read included Macaulay, Froude, Carlyle and the historian of medieval religion, G.C. Coulton. Several of these narrative historians were already considered outdated by the late 1940s, but they still resonated with Blainey. So while the rest of the students grappled with, and were examined on, topics such as the 'historian's spider-web', the examination paper also contained questions on famous historians, 'deliberately put there so that Blainey, who wasn't interested in Arthur's stuff, could write a "Theory and Method" paper in a totally different idiom and with a totally different subject'.[64] Blainey has suggested that the Melbourne History Department was 'far more sympathetic to diversity' then than a typical history department was by the end of his academic career forty years later and so were happy for him to pursue a one-student syllabus.[65] As Blainey became a prolific writer of history, one reviewer suggested that his scepticism about abstract theory was paying dividends:

> As an undergraduate at Melbourne University ... Mr. Blainey was rarely to be found at the lectures on methodology and philosophy of history which produced so much talk but so little historical writing. He was down in the Newspaper Room of the Public Library swapping gum jubes with the gentry of Gordon House and reading old newspapers.[66]

Another to reflect on Blainey's undergraduate attitudes was his former teacher Manning Clark, who wrote that he had 'showed an admirable distaste for those who prattled on about what it would be like to write a history book supposing

---

63 Geoffrey Blainey, 'The Manning Clark School of History', *Scripsi*. 6, no. 2 (August 1990): 63.

64 Ken Inglis, 'The Melbourne School of History: Memories and Reflections' in *The Fuss That Never Ended: The Life and Work of Geoffrey Blainey* eds Deborah Gare, Geoffrey Bolton, Stuart Macintyre and Tom Stannage (Melbourne: Melbourne University Press, 2003), 20.

65 Blainey, 'The Manning Clark School of History', 63.

66 J.W. McCarty, 'Prospectors and Planters', *Overland*, no. 29 (April 1964): 57. Gordon House was a building in Little Bourke Street, Melbourne (not far from the State Library), which at that time provided lodgings for homeless men.

one were to write a history book'.⁶⁷ Blainey took Clark's Australian History subject in 1949, the final of Clark's four years in the Melbourne History Department before he moved to Canberra. For his long essay in the subject Blainey chose the topic of the wheat industry in South Australia and did 'an enormous amount of work' on it, reading newspapers, royal commission reports and statistical registers, before writing an essay of about ten thousand words.⁶⁸ When Clark made positive comments about the essay, Blainey was 'delighted'. Clark also recalled the impact of the essay on him. He claimed that 'for the whole of first term' Blainey was 'absolutely silent' and then had submitted an essay 'that was by far the best in the class'.⁶⁹ Blainey found Clark 'an inspiring teacher' and appreciated how much he was able to learn about Australian history at a time when it was not widely taught.⁷⁰

Clark's description of Blainey as 'a shy boy' creates an impression that Blainey was generally quiet or a loner, an opinion which can also be found in other recollections of contemporaries who recall that 'he wasn't all that much involved in the Historical Society'.⁷¹ However, although he may have not been all that active within the History Department, he was having other experiences which contributed to his subsequent work as a historian.

First, unlike many students from more prosperous backgrounds, Blainey retained his childhood habits of pursuing paid employment in holidays, often travelling widely both in and outside Victoria. He worked in casual manual jobs in both Melbourne and country Victoria. For instance, in the summer between finishing school and starting university, Blainey and a friend hitch-hiked to Mildura to do grape-picking.⁷² Meeting workers while doing these sorts of holiday and casual jobs undoubtedly increased Blainey's ability to relate to the sort of working men he was soon to encounter, and seek to interview, at Mt Lyell.

---

67   C.M.H. Clark, 'Too Far Away', *Times Literary Supplement*, 21 November 1968, issue 3482, 1315.

68   Blainey to Stephen Holt, 11 December 1979; a copy of the letter was provided to the author by Holt in 2010; and Blainey, 'The Manning Clark School of History', 63.

69   Downes, 'The man who was always looking for something'.

70   Geoffrey Blainey, 'Geoffrey Blainey', in R.M. Crawford, Manning Clark; and Geoffrey Blainey, *Making History* (Melbourne: McPhee Gribble, Fitzroy Penguin, 1985), 69.

71   Davison, 'Blainey', *Oxford Companion*, 74; and John Poynter, 'The Melbourne School of History: Memories and Reflections', in *The Fuss That Never Ended: The Life and Work of Geoffrey Blainey*, eds Gare et. al (Melbourne: Melbourne University Press, 2003), 167.

72   Geoffrey Blainey, 'From Milk Bar to the Menu', *The Age* Extra, 8 January 1994, 2; and Blainey, *Before I Forget*, 112–115.

Further, Blainey was actively engaged in several aspects of university student life outside the History Department. One of these was Queen's College, where he resided for his three years as an undergraduate and became secretary of its student society, the William Quick Club. College historian Owen Parnaby has written of Blainey's time in charge of the club that it 'was never so popular as it was in 1950'.[73] More significant for Blainey's subsequent career was his involvement with the student newspaper, *Farrago*, of which he was co-editor of the sports section for several months in 1949, and then co-editor of the whole paper in 1949-50. It appears that, in securing these roles at this time, Blainey was the beneficiary of the work of what one participant, future Victorian Liberal Premier Lindsay Thompson, later described as a push by a group of moderate students to regain control of the Students' Representative Council from those on the political Left who had dominated it for several years.[74]

A crucial figure in the change of political environment on campus in the late 1940s was another Queen's resident and history student, Murray Groves, who in 1948 set up an ALP Club, designed to appeal to moderate Labor sympathizers and to draw them away from the Communists in the broad front Labor Club. In 1949, Queen's alone had several faculty representatives, and produced one of the two *Farrago* editors. These editors appointed Thompson and Monty Hollow (a future lawyer, best known for his role in fighting for compensation for soldiers affected by Agent Orange in Vietnam) as joint sports editors, with Blainey subsequently replacing Hollow.

Later in the year a new SRC appointed new editors, Blainey securing the role with Tony Harold. Being co-editors did not mean that Blainey and Harold worked together; rather, they produced alternating issues, using different staffs. One by-product of the shift in campus mood away from the Left was that levels of passion and activity declined rapidly, with the SRC Secretary's report of July 1950 describing the contrast between previous years when *Farrago* had been 'the subject of bitter controversy between various political groups' with all sides competing for space, and 1950 where 'the difficulty has been to get staff or contributors at all'.[75] This decline in enthusiasm meant that Blainey himself 'wrote almost entire issues, including some of the letters

---

73 Owen Parnaby, *Queen's College University of Melbourne A Centenary History* (Melbourne: Melbourne University Press, 1990), 236.

74 Lindsay Thompson, *I Remember* (Melbourne: Hyland House, 1989), 17. Liberal Club members and future Liberal MPs, Ivor Greenwood and Alan Jarman, became Presidents of the Students Representative Council in 1949 and 1950 respectively. Parnaby, *Queen's College*, 216 also referred to 'a renewed college student push into student politics after the communist dominated years of 1946 and 1947'.

75 'Secretary's Report 1949–50', *Farrago*, 19 July 1950, 4–5.

to the editor, as well as the replies'.⁷⁶ Like students of many eras active in the Union Building, the role meant that Blainey missed a lot of classes and by mid-1950, he had resigned 'through pressure of academic work'.⁷⁷

One of Blainey's Melbourne University historian contemporaries, Ken Inglis, said that 'one thing I would commend to anyone who takes on further studies of Geoff's work, on the matter of his prose, is reading the university newspaper, *Farrago*, at the time Geoff was editing it'.⁷⁸ This is not a straightforward task as many items in the paper were penned under pseudonyms, and even recollections about which writer used which name have been disputed.⁷⁹

Blainey's *Farrago* experience contributed to his desire to be a writer. The fact that, by the time he was developing the desire to be a writer, Blainey was a history student is an obvious practical reason why history became his chosen vehicle for writing. In a 1980 interview, Blainey commented that 'apart from hazy recollections', he had 'no specific notion' of why he became a historian.⁸⁰ Blainey has given some credit to Clark who, unlike any other teacher, created the impression that 'it was important to write history and to write it for an audience of intelligent laymen' and specifically 'gave me the feeling that I could write history one day'.⁸¹

Blainey's choice of history fits comfortably with Jeremy Popkin's assessment that historians choose history as their discipline, ahead of literature or philosophy, because they wish 'to engage with reality, as opposed to abstract thought or imagination' and to participate in 'the academic discipline with the closest connection to authentic human experience in all its fullness'.⁸² On that basis, history seems well suited to Blainey's down-to-earth personality. He explained his attitude to fiction, in a newspaper interview in 1988:

---

76   Nicklin, 'Blainey is the new Chairman'.

77   Blainey, 'The Manning Clark School of History', 64; 'Editor Resigns', *Farrago*, 14 June 1950, 1; and 'Secretary's Report 1949-50'. It should be noted that this was an era when student newspaper editors were unpaid.

78   Inglis, 'The Melbourne School of History', 171.

79   For instance, at a conference in 2000, Poynter and Inglis had differing views as to the identity of football correspondent, 'Old Centre', Inglis apparently correct in his view that it was not Blainey. A picture of three Melbourne University undergraduates on a trip to Sydney was published twice in *Farrago*, on the first occasion (14 September 1949) identifying one of the three as Jim Morrissey and on the second (8 August 1951) identifying him as 'Old Centre'.

80   Downes, 'The man who was always looking for something'.

81   Blainey to Holt, 11 December 1979.

82   Jeremy D. Popkin, *History, Historians & Autobiography*, (Chicago: University of Chicago Press, 2005), 149.

> I rarely finish a novel. I do a lot of my reading in bookshops. Often I'll pick up a novel and read 15 pages to see what a writer's style is, how he handles it. My wife reads a lot of novels and occasionally I will look at something she is reading, but even if I start and I'm interested, I'll never finish it.[83]

Clearly not all historians are like this. Manning Clark, for instance, wanted to write history in the manner of a Dostoyevsky novel, with grand narratives, sweeping themes and morality tales. Clark kept very emotional diaries and voluminous personal papers, even with signposts to ensure the potential future biographer did not miss anything significant.[84] Blainey in contrast is practical, grounded in the non-imagined world, commenting that he had 'trouble with abstractions unless I reach them through the concrete'.[85]

Blainey's belief that he could become a historian was reinforced by an action he took, outside the undergraduate norm, to write and get published in the journal *Historical Studies*. He wrote a reply to an established historian, Professor R.S. Parker, who had contributed an article on Federation. Parker had used voting figures in key locations in the referendum to argue that Federation had been driven by economic interests. Blainey undertook his own assessment of the figures and found what he believed to be inaccuracies in Parker's work.

Blainey argued that while Parker had handled two of the three problems in his paper with 'great success', the third, the impact of economic interests on federation, was 'astray in three ways'. First, he had not conducted any detailed electoral analysis of actual voting returns; second, he relied on electoral maps, but 'most of each map is left unexplained by the economic summary', and third, he was incorrect to use returns from the 1899 referendum in colonies where there had been a resounding 'yes' vote in 1898, because there the second referendum was not strongly contested.[86]

Parker was given the opportunity to read the manuscript of Blainey's article and to reply in the same November 1950 issue. He was polite, saying that he found Blainey's argument 'exhilarating – not only for the energy and pertinence of its criticism', but because it used 'methods of historical analysis which it

---

83 Stuart Rintoul, 'The Essential Blainey', *The Weekend Australian* Weekend supplement, 8–9 October 1988, 3.
84 Mark McKenna, *An Eye for Eternity: The Life of Manning Clark* (Melbourne: Miegunyah Press Melbourne University Publishing, 2011), 31–32.
85 Rintoul, 'The Essential Blainey'.
86 Geoffrey Blainey, 'The Role of Economic Interests in Australian Federation: A Reply to Professor R.S. Parker', *Historical Studies Australia and New Zealand* 4, no. 15 (November 1950): 224–237.

was my chief aim to recommend'.[87] While acknowledging that Blainey was correct about certain issues, such as preferring the 1898 to the 1899 figures, Parker reiterated his own position on others.

Blainey's article had a major impact within Melbourne University History Department, as John Mulvaney recalled:

> I never knew the undergraduate Geoff Blainey, as far as I know, but I recall the history tearoom gossip when his response to Parker's Federation article appeared in *Historical Studies* in 1950. Here was this young undergraduate applying departmental research techniques, complete with footnotes, to confound an authority. The department was very pleased: it was quite remarkable.[88]

The debate continued the following year when fellow history student and Queen's College resident, John Bastin investigated voting patterns in Western Australia and argued that they supported Blainey's position on the eastern states and further undermined Parker's case.[89] The same issue of *Historical Studies* which contained Bastin's piece also noted that Blainey had delivered a paper on 'Federation' at a conference held in the second term vacation of 1951 organised by Melbourne University History students and attended by others from interstate.

The significance of the Parker-Blainey exchange was reinforced by the fact that all the relevant articles were included in the first compilation of articles from *Historical Studies* in 1964.[90] One overview of Australian historiography in the 1960s commented on the flurry of journal articles reappraising the role of economic influences on Federation and highlighted how it was 'noteworthy that the immediate reply was written by an undergraduate'.[91] It can be argued that this episode had a lasting impact on Blainey's approach to history, teaching

---

87 R.S. Parker, 'Some Comments On The Role of the Economic Interests In Australian Federation', *Historical Studies Australia and New Zealand* 4, no. 15 (November 1950): 238–240.

88 John Mulvaney, 'The Melbourne School of History: Memories and Reflections', in *The Fuss That Never Ended: The Life and Work of Geoffrey Blainey*, eds Gare et al. (Melbourne: Melbourne University Press, 2003), 163.

89 John Bastin, 'Federation and Western Australia: A Contribution to the Parker-Blainey discussion', *Historical Studies Australia and New Zealand* 5, no. 17 (November 1951): 47–58.

90 J.J. Eastwood and F.B. Smith eds, *Historical Studies: Selected Articles* (Melbourne: Melbourne University Press, 1964).

91 Robin W. Winks ed., *The Historiography of the British Empire-Commonwealth: Trends, Interpretations and Resources* (Durham: Duke University Press, 1966), 166 fn.

him that the way to have an impact is to challenge received wisdom. More immediately, it added weight to the *Farrago* experience in convincing him what career he wanted to pursue.

There were some conventional options for an undergraduate, such as Blainey, completing a degree with first class honours. There was the well-beaten path to an overseas university, particularly Oxford, often undertaken before, or after, a spell as a tutor at Melbourne University. A good example of the conventional path is provided by Ken Inglis, Blainey's friend from both Queen's College and the History Department. Inglis was one year ahead of Blainey at university so finished his undergraduate degree in 1949. He then tutored in the History department in 1950 and 1951, became an assistant lecturer in 1952 and was appointed to a tenured lectureship in 1953, the same year he departed for Oxford.

In the preceding generations, Max Crawford from Sydney and Manning Clark from Melbourne had gone to Oxford and those of Blainey's own Melbourne generation to head there as well as Inglis included Geoffrey Serle, John Poynter, Hugh Stretton, Don Kennedy and Jim Main, while John Mulvaney went to Cambridge[92]. The orthodoxy of heading to Britain is also captured by John Thompson in his study of Serle, writing that 'for those with academic ambitions ... "getting away" was an integral part of an elite Australian education ... Oxford especially, but Cambridge also, were the most desirable destinations for young Australians of talent and ambition'.[93] Other future prominent historians such as Geoffrey Bolton went to Oxford from other Australian universities. Bolton has noted the uniqueness of Blainey's behaviour, stating that 'unlike nearly all the academically gifted, he did not attempt postgraduate study in Britain'.[94]

Even if heading overseas did not appeal to Blainey, there was the other obvious option of taking up a tutorship at Melbourne. There have been conflicting views as to whether Blainey was offered such a position and at what time. Manning Clark expressed the following opinion:

---

92   Stuart Macintyre has calculated that in the post-war decade 18 Melbourne history graduates went to Oxford compared to three to both Cambridge and London and a further three to the United States. Crawford provided the students with references and assistance with obtaining scholarships, while those already there furnished the next generation with information and support. (Paper delivered at 'Ken Inglis in History: A Laconic Colloquium', 24–25 November 2016.)

93   John Thompson, *The Patrician and the Bloke: Geoffrey Serle and The Making of Australian History*, (Canberra: Pandanus Books, 2006), 150.

94   Geoffrey Bolton, 'Geoffrey Blainey', in *Encyclopaedia of Historians and Historical Writing*, vol 1, ed. Kelly Boyd, (Chicago: Fitzroy Dearborn, 1999), 93–94.

Blainey's behaviour is *partly* to be explained by what happened the year after he graduated. He was not offered a tutorship. I think he felt 'left out'. He became a loner then – though I suspect that was in him from the start. He was always an individualist and not a team man.[95]

Although Clark may be correct that Blainey was not offered a tutorship for 1951, Crawford did offer Blainey one for 1952. However, Blainey declined, telling Crawford that:

At first I was inclined to accept and only this week decided otherwise … I would enjoy tutoring but I wouldn't be an academic for more than a few years, I would be marking time in a sense. I did appreciate the offer and decline it with mixed feelings.[96]

The reason Blainey declined the tutorship offer of early 1952 was because he was eager to complete a project he had begun a year earlier, a project which was to provide him with a unique opportunity to forge a very different career from that of the other products of the Melbourne History School.

---

95   Manning Clark to Kathleen Fitzpatrick, 17 October 1986, in *Dear Kathleen, Dear Manning: The Correspondence of Manning Clark and Kathleen Fitzpatrick 1949-1990*, ed. Susan Davies (Melbourne: Melbourne University Press, 1996), 94.

96   Geoffrey Blainey to Max Crawford, 9 February 1952, Max Crawford Papers (hereafter Crawford Papers), 1991.0113, File 7/87, Box 22, University of Melbourne Archives (hereafter UMA), Melbourne.

Chapter 2

FREELANCE HISTORIAN

Blainey has presented his youthful venture to Queenstown on Tasmania's remote west coast as a conscious decision on his part, saying that 'just before I turned twenty-one, I felt a great desire to write a book and went to the west coast of Tasmania'.[1] The book was *The Peaks of Lyell* (1954), a work which established Blainey's reputation as an accomplished freelance historian.[2]

However, one wonders how viable freelance history would have been as a career, or even perhaps whether it would have occurred to Blainey at all, if the opportunity to go to Queenstown had not presented itself at the time. When Sir Walter Bassett, a leading Melbourne businessman, was looking for someone to research the history of the Mount Lyell Mining and Railway Company of which he was a board member, engaging freelance historians was certainly not a commonplace event. Indeed, Blainey understood that Mt Lyell was 'the first company in Australia to make available all its records for historical research'.[3]

Bassett was probably more aware of the importance of history than most industrialists, as his wife Marnie was a well-known biographer and historian who attended seminars at the Melbourne University History Department. This connection led Bassett to seek out Max Crawford to see if he might have a candidate for the research task. Blainey's initial interview took place over Sunday lunch at the Bassetts' Armadale home, followed by a more formal one conducted by the board of the company in its Collins Street head office, an unusually rigorous process for someone about to become the firm's lowest-paid employee. The University and the company co-funded the first year of the research. Later Blainey worked as a company employee, undertaking tasks not directly related to the book, to fund his research and writing. As Blainey has recalled, he 'eagerly accepted the opportunity' to do the research and although the wage was much less than the basic wage of a labourer, for

---

1 Frank Devine, 'A Conversation with Geoffrey Blainey', *Quadrant* 50, no. 10 (October 2006), 49.
2 Geoffrey Blainey, *The Peaks of Lyell* (Melbourne: Melbourne University Press, 1954).
3 Blainey, *The Peaks of Lyell*, vi.

him it was 'ample', explaining that that he was 'being paid to do what I would almost have done for nothing' and thus felt 'on top of the world'.[4]

However, there was at least one occasion during his time at Mt Lyell when Blainey did ask for more money. He proposed to the company that he might undertake a detailed study of company records to find evidence of what previous exploration had revealed about promising or not-so-promising locations for mining on the field, knowledge which had faded from the corporate memory. After some initial scepticism from the board about the value of this task, he was given an offer in September 1952 of £16 per week to do this study, while also continuing to work on the book. Blainey responded with a counter-offer of working harder - six days per week and doing the book in his spare time - but at the significantly higher rate of £24 per week. Blainey provided a detailed explanation of the reasons for his decision to Crawford back in Melbourne, assuring his mentor that he 'need have no misgivings about inquiring of my attitude, as I don't mind stating my views'.[5] The reasons showed a young man who was confident in his own ability to undertake the task more quickly than anyone else and thus receive 'some margin for skill'. Given the potential profit to the company, he felt it reasonable 'to ask for more than the average shift worker earns here'.[6]

The coming together of Mt Lyell and Blainey was beneficial for both parties. Not only did Blainey enjoy the study of mining, so much so that he has said his second choice of career would be as a geologist, but he also enjoyed living in the local community. While based in Queenstown, Blainey finished third in Australia's longest wheelbarrow race and played for one of the local football teams, The Smelters, on the famous Queenstown oval with its gravel surface. His career finished on a high when he played in Smelters B Grade Premiership team in 1953, contributing four goals in the Grand Final Replay, after booting two in the low-scoring draw the previous week.[7] Queenstown, and even the football ground, were not completely new to Blainey when he arrived to write the company history. A year earlier, it had been included in one of his many hitchhiking holidays. Then, as well as relying on the goodwill

---

[4] Geoffrey Blainey, '"Tasmania, Tasmania!" the birth of a book', *Tasmanian Historical Studies*, vol.13, 2008: 5 (based on a paper delivered at the Centre of Tasmanian Historical Studies conference entitled 'Enterprise and Livelihood in the Tasmanian Past', October 2007).

[5] Blainey to Max Crawford, 22 October 1952, Crawford Papers, 1991.0113, File 7/87, Box 22, UMA.

[6] Ibid.

[7] 'Smelters Win Finals Replay', *Hobart Mercury*, 28 September 1953, 15; and 'Youngest, best and fairest?', *Burnie Advocate*, 7 October 1953, 11.

of motorists for free travel, he and his mate had availed themselves of free accommodation, sleeping at the back of the grandstand at the oval.[8]

The company provided employees with a weekly cigarette ration, twenty cigarettes and two ounces of ready-rubbed tobacco, and this ready availability led to Blainey, who had been an occasional smoker at Queen's College, becoming a regular smoker. He found that he enjoyed smoking while he was writing and took pleasure in the rituals around roll-your own cigarettes.

The cigarettes played a part in Blainey's relationship with the elderly Jimmy Elliott, who had moved from a Victorian goldfield to the west coast of Tasmania in 1880 and who still features in Blainey's anecdotes. Blainey spent many nights listening to Elliott's reminiscences, and rolling cigarettes for him, although Elliott always insisting on supplying his own tobacco.[9] Although happy to talk, Elliott did not like to see note taking, so immediately they parted Blainey would use a newspaper, or cigarette papers, to record as much as he could recall of the conversation.

Blainey had not been taught about oral history as an undergraduate, and yet he quickly realised that talking to old-timers was an invaluable way of learning about what had happened in the remote communities of the west coast, as he explained in 2008:

> Half a century ago the eyewitness history of events, as seen by the typical Australian, was little valued by practising historians. When I studied history at university I had not been informed that ordinary people could be precious sources. Within a few years I was to conclude that a person with little education was more likely than a professor to retain an accurate memory of events which they had actually experienced.[10]

Blainey's confidence in using this sort of material grew following the success of *The Peaks of Lyell*, as was illustrated by the fact that while he only mentioned Elliott once in the text of this specific work, he referred to him three times in his general history of Australian mining a decade later.

The Mount Lyell Mining and Railway Company had been formed in 1893, to amalgamate many smaller mining leases and, in 1903, the company merged with the rival North Lyell Mining Company. Not only did the company mine a major copper field, it operated railways, a power station and smelters. The

---

8   Geoffrey Blainey, paper presented to the Australian Mining History Association in Queenstown, 5 October 2008.
9   Blainey, 'Tasmania, Tasmania!', 9.
10 Ibid.

smelters alone employed 500 workers at their zenith and it was the sulphurous fumes from their smelting stacks which denuded the surrounding hills of almost all their vegetation. The resultant moonscape became the best-known aspect of Queenstown for other Australians, far better known than the pyritic smelting process developed on-site by metallurgist, Robert Sticht, an innovation that revolutionised copper-smelting in many countries.[11]

However, Blainey's history did not begin with the foundation of his subject company. He clearly appreciated that company and local history need to be placed in a broader context. Thus, the book has a couple of chapters setting the scene between 1642, when Abel Tasman sailed along the coast, and 1883, when the west coast contained mines ranging from the major tin mine at Mt Bischoff to the subsistence gold mining operation at King River. Blainey observed that 'western miners were now working on four fields … lying in a new moon crescent', a geographical note that becomes a literary device when Blainey concluded chapter two with the words 'down this crescent came the discoverers of Mt Lyell'.[12] The teasing conclusion is followed by an assertive opening to chapter three which states that 'the McDonoughs and Steve Karlson discovered the Mt Lyell mine'.[13]

Blainey already had the ability to evocatively describe individuals in a few words, a skill which became a feature of his work. Readers were introduced to 'Philosopher' Smith, described by Blainey as 'tall and lean, with iron-grey hair and flowing white beard. He was religious and kind, ascetic and grave.'[14] Then there was Bowes Kelly, 'a generous optimist of the Australian outback; thirty-eight years old, sixteen stone in weight, ginger-bearded and slow of speech'.[15] Significantly, there was already the standard Blainey model of the mining hero: a man with many positive characteristics for whom luck is a supplement, not a fundamental ingredient. James Crotty was an early archetype:

> Crotty, the prospector who became a mining magnate, was almost a unique figure in Australian mining. What is more he wrested his fortune from adversity enough to crush nine out of ten stout hearts. He had

---

[11] The company continued operating until 1994. After a hiatus of some years, a new operator, Copper Mines of Tasmania, recommenced mining in the late 1990s. The mine closed again in 2014 after the death of three miners in two separate incidents.
[12] Blainey, *The Peaks of Lyell*, 21.
[13] Ibid., 22.
[14] Ibid., 13.
[15] Ibid., 53.

faith, perseverance, mining knowledge, and cunning, that rare mix of qualities which, spiced with luck, bring mining success.[16]

While prominent board members of the company got passing mentions at best, Blainey focused on telling 'the story of a wild region of mountain and mines – some mines rich, many poor. It is the story of the men who found them, floated them, worked them, and died in them.'[17]

Even in his early twenties, Blainey was able to write powerful prose. A chapter telling the story of the underground fire that broke out on Saturday, 12 October 1912 and killed 42 men still makes compelling reading. Perhaps the most moving part of this narrative described rescuers seeing 'seven men clinging stiffly to the air vent of a rock drill … The searchers moved forward and then turned silently away', as the reality of the miners' deaths became clear to them.[18] In telling the story of the fire, Blainey took the opportunity to recognise the unrecognised, pointing out that, while there was a generous distribution of Royal Humane Society awards, 'two of the bravest men did not receive their honours'.[19] A controversial aspect of the book was Blainey's thesis on the cause of the fire. He revealed 'evidence that did not come before the Royal Commission' that, in his view, provided 'the only feasible explanation of the fire'.[20] He argued that a radical unionist and reputed member of the Industrial Workers of the World, whose brother had died three weeks earlier in a rock-fall, started it as a way of exposing safety flaws in the mine during a visit by inspectors. However, Blainey exhibited a desire to be fair, adding the caveat that 'the guilt of the suspect should not be magnified' as he could not have foreseen how fatal the fire would be.[21]

There had been a suggestion that the company may publish the book itself and get it printed by the *Launceston Examiner* but, by the end of 1953 when Blainey had finished writing the book, Melbourne University Press had agreed

---

16   Ibid., 118.
17   Ibid., v.
18   Ibid., 214.
19   Ibid., 221.
20   Ibid., 218. The causes of fire have remained an issue of debate. When Blainey attended the annual conference of the Australian Mining History Association in Queenstown in October 2008 a paper was given by Peter Schulze, a retired engineer and MP, arguing that the fire was caused by an electrical fault, an explanation specifically rejected by the original Royal Commission. See Peter Schultze, 'North Mount Lyell Disaster – A Miscarriage of Justice', *Journal of Australasian Mining History* 9 (September 2011): 94–116.
21   Blainey, *The Peaks of Lyell*, 220.

to publish it.[22] The title was suggested by Melbourne University Press publisher Gwyn James, who picked the phrase out of the narrative. *The Peaks of Lyell* was published in late 1954, one of just 36 books to be published in Australia that year.[23] In those days, there was no book launch; in fact, Blainey first saw the book on public display in the Robertson & Mullens bookshop window. The dust-jacket depicted a range of sepia coloured peaks in an unusual style for the time. Blainey recalled years later that he 'thought it was tremendous'.[24]

Despite the lack of new titles being published, Blainey believes that in those days writers were 'in clover' as any book that was published was guaranteed to be reviewed in the newspapers.[25] Reviews of his debut work did not appear immediately, but from February to May 1955 the book was covered in major metropolitan daily newspapers around the country, not surprisingly getting more extensive coverage in Victoria and Tasmania than elsewhere. Although only making the 'Reviews in Brief' column of the *Sydney Morning Herald*, it was described as a 'well-produced book' and its author praised for having drawn 'much interesting material'.[26] The *Adelaide Advertiser* said Blainey had told his story 'very ably and entertainingly' and 'produced a book of considerable interest and historical value'. In Perth, the *West Australian* thought it was the way he brought characters to life and produced 'the atmosphere of human struggle' that elevated the book 'out of the rut and makes it something more than a well-documented history of a great industrial venture'.[27]

The Age produced a lengthy review, written by stockbroker K. McCaughan, as the lead item in its literary supplement. The majority of the review told the Mt Lyell story, not passing comment on the quality of the book until the final three paragraphs. It concluded that Blainey had 'done a difficult job extremely well' and that the book was 'very readable, well put together and authentic'.[28] This review contained one of the rare criticisms in the newspaper reviews, a suggestion that the book lacked humour.

As well as the recognition it received in the newspapers, the book was reviewed in the academic history journals. *Historical Studies* chose a Tasmanian,

---

22   Blainey to Crawford, 9 February 1952, Crawford Papers.
23   Blainey, 'Writing Australian History'.
24   Rintoul, 'The Essential Blainey', 3.
25   Blainey, 'Writing Australian History'.
26   'Reviews in Brief', *Sydney Morning Herald*, 21 May 1955, 11.
27   'Great Australian Mine Enterprise', *Adelaide Advertiser*, 7 May 1955, 11 and 'From Bonanza To Open Cut', *West Australian*, 7 May 1955, 25.
28   K. McCaughan, 'A Great Australian Copper Field: The Mt Lyell Discovery', *The Age*, 19 March 1955, 17.

the Marxist Ken Dallas, Senior Lecturer in Economic History at the University of Tasmania, to review the book.[29] Dallas commented that Blainey had 'achieved a successful, not to say triumphant outcome', delivering 'the most stimulating contribution we have to our industrial history, more exciting reading than many historical novels'.[30] In a tribute to how deeply Blainey had immersed himself in the local community, Dallas believed that he wrote 'as if he were himself a West Coaster ... blending the narrative of the survivors with his own experience'.[31] However, to Dallas, *The Peaks of Lyell* was more than just a local history. It also made 'a valuable contribution to trade union history' and its investigation of how distance affected investment decisions meant that the book had 'point and value to scholars in other parts of the world'.[32] Dallas' recommendation was reinforced in the next edition of *Historical Studies* by L.F. Fitzhardinge, who described *The Peaks of Lyell* as one of the year's three local histories of 'outstanding quality'.[33]

A more critical review by Jules Ginswick of the Economics Department of Sydney University was published in the inaugural edition of *Bulletin of the Business Archives Council of Australia* (later *Business Archives and History* and then *Australian Economic History Review*).[34] Ginswick acknowledged that the book presented an 'interesting story, written in a vigorous style ... considerably enriched by the wide personal knowledge of the region displayed by the author', but argued that the work also contained 'weaknesses that cannot be overlooked'. These weaknesses included not properly considering marketing arrangements, metal prices, or the effects of wars on demand. Ginswick argued that Blainey overstated the importance of the company's relatively efficient management, placing too heavy a weighting on individual personalities in the success or failure of companies. Ginswick was to establish a pattern for the journal. Five different reviewers, reviewing six books, across a period of thirty years display a remarkable consistency in their attitudes to Blainey's work: praise for his writing style and readability, juxtaposed with criticism

---

29 K.M. Dallas, review of *The Peaks of Lyell*, *Historical Studies Australia and New Zealand* 7, no. 25, (November 1955): 101–102.
30 Ibid.
31 Ibid., 101.
32 Ibid., 102.
33 L.F. Fitzhardinge, 'Writings on Australian History, 1955', *Historical Studies Australia and New Zealand* 7, no. 26 (May 1956): 222.
34 J. Ginswick, review of *The Peaks of Lyell*, *Bulletin of the Business Archives Council of Australia* 1, no. 1 (May 1956): 30–33.

of his historical method and failure to emphasise those factors that his critics thought significant.

The Peaks of Lyell was published in Britain and the United States by Cambridge University Press and this led to some reviews in overseas journals, including *The Journal of Economic History*, *The Business History Review*, *The Pacific Historical Review*, and the *Times Literary Supplement*. *The Journal of Economic History* review followed the pattern of its Australian equivalent: praise for writing of 'unusual clarity', which provided an 'exceptionally vivid picture', but concern that the author was 'too eager to uphold the stand of the Company on important issues'.[35]

Of the Australian books published in 1954, *The Peaks of Lyell* was the only one that remained in print fifty years later. It still attracted comment. In 2007, journalist and author Nicholas Rothwell described *The Peaks of Lyell* as 'one of the purest achievements of Australian literature, even though it was tossed off in a wild vernacular style in his early 20s, and is concerned solely with a mining province in remote west Tasmania'.[36] Dallas had identified one vernacular feature when he playfully concluded his review with a one sentence paragraph: 'But I wish he would not begin sentences and even paragraphs with "But"'.[37] Of more concern to many contemporaries was the fact that the book did not contain footnotes. At the start of the book's bibliography, Blainey provided the following explanation for their absence:

> Most of the evidence, on which this story is founded, comes from the private records of the Mt Lyell Company. As these records are not open to public perusal, and as this history is written for popular rather than academic tastes, I have not inserted footnotes on each page. To compensate for their absence I have made the bibliography of public sources as detailed as possible.[38]

One overseas reviewer, Kenneth Wiggins Porter, accepted Blainey's argument for not providing specific references to private company records, but believed he should have done so with public sources such as the providers of

---

35 Colston E. Warne, review of *The Peaks of Lyell*, *The Journal of Economic History* 16, no. 2 (June 1956): 250–251.
36 Nicholas Rothwell, 'Continental Drift', *The Australian* (Literary Review), 1 August 2007, 3.
37 Dallas, 102.
38 Blainey, *The Peaks of Lyell*, 293.

the anecdotes that were used to provide colour to the story.[39] Clearly, Blainey enjoyed being released from the academic shackles and, as described by Stuart Macintyre, produced a work that 'had a freshness and authority that could not have been achieved within the confines of a research thesis'.[40]

As the university co-funded the exercise, Blainey needed to produce an academic version. Reversing the accepted practice of submitting the thesis and only later attempting to get it published, Blainey inserted footnotes into the first half of the book and submitted it for an MA. The thesis was awarded first-class honours and the Ernest Scott Prize, an award presented for the best work published on Australian or New Zealand history.

By the time the book was published, Blainey had a firm desire to pursue a career as a freelance historian and thus the success of the book was more important than the academic recognition the project had delivered. His publishers regarded the book's success as strong enough to write on the blurb of his next major work that it was written by 'a young graduate whose reputation as a writer and historian was firmly established with *The Peaks of Lyell*'.[41] In the months between his completion of the book and its publication, Blainey had quite a lengthy period without securing further commissions but its success meant that other opportunities began to arise.

One of the first was writing a short centenary history of the structural steel and lift manufacturers, Johns & Waygood.[42] He also secured an offer to write the historical chapter for *Introducing Victoria*, a book produced by Melbourne University Press for delegates attending the meeting of the Australian and New Zealand Association for the Advancement of Science (ANZAAS) held in Melbourne in August 1955, which was the major Australian academic conference of the era.[43] As part of his research, Blainey looked at census and Year Book statistics, and calculated that, whereas the population of New South Wales had grown faster than that of Victoria in every census period between 1861 and 1947, the reverse had happened in the most recent seven years. Blainey has claimed that the fact that nobody else had done this simple calculation demonstrates how little research was being undertaken at that

---

39 Kenneth Wiggins Porter, review of *The Peaks of Lyell*, *Business History Review* (December 1955): 371.
40 Stuart Macintyre, 'The Making of a School' in *Making History*, R.M. Crawford, Manning Clark and Geoffrey Blainey (Melbourne: Penguin, 1985), 28.
41 Geoffrey Blainey, *Centenary History of University of Melbourne* (Melbourne: Melbourne University Press, 1957).
42 Geoffrey Blainey, *Johns and Waygood Limited: one hundred years, 1856-1956* (Melbourne: Johns and Waygood, 1956).
43 Blainey, 'History of Victoria', in *Introducing Victoria*.

time in Government departments or universities, recalling 'the sensation it caused even in Parliament House'.[44] The publicity no doubt increased the status of his work. The *University Gazette* commented on *Introducing Victoria*:

> Where all is excellent, it may be invidious to select. Nevertheless mention should be made of the first essay by Mr. Geoffrey Blainey, who is establishing a considerable reputation as an historian of our Australian institutions. The book is worth reading for this article alone.[45]

Despite being a freelance historian, Blainey continued to enjoy the sense of security provided by being something of a joiner. It has already been noted how he was a joiner as an undergraduate at University and in Queenstown, and the trend continued in his freelance period. He served on the committee of the Fellowship of Australian Writers with his former teacher A.A. Phillips, and other friends such as Stephen Murray-Smith and Judah Waten. In less formal ways, Blainey also maintained friendships, for instance, in May 1955 attending a Carlton versus Geelong football match at Princes Park with his former lecturer, Manning Clark.[46]

Another factor which assisted Blainey was the fact that several key Melbourne institutions had been founded in the 1850s, and were thus celebrating their centenaries in the 1950s, felicitous timing for the freelance historian. The Johns & Waygood job was followed by commissions for more substantial centenary works on the University of Melbourne and the National Bank.

As with *The Peaks of Lyell*, Crawford played an important role in securing Blainey the commission to write the history of the university, which resulted in the publication of two books, *The University of Melbourne: A Centenary Portrait* (1956) and the *Centenary History of University of Melbourne* (1957).[47] It was a striking vote of confidence in the intellectual maturity of the young historian that he should be given such as prestigious commission. Blainey was technically based in the History Department.[48] He had morning tea there

---

44   Blainey, 'Writing Australian History'.
45   'New Publications', *University of Melbourne Gazette* 11, no. 5 (27 September 1955): 72.
46   Aiton, 'Tomorrow the world'.
47   Arranged and illustrated by Norman H Oliver, narrative by Geoffrey Blainey, *The University of Melbourne: A Centenary Portrait* (Melbourne: Melbourne University Press, 1956); and Geoffrey Blainey, *Centenary History of University of Melbourne* (Melbourne: Melbourne University Press, 1957).
48   He was given the title Senior Research Fellow of the University of Melbourne, *Historical Studies Australia and New Zealand* 7, no. 25 (November 1955): 120.

quite often and the recollections of others certainly portray Blainey as a lively presence in the history staff room:

> Another observer remarked on the difference in style between Serle and his younger contemporary Geoffrey Blainey – the 'two Geoffreys' as they were sometimes called. Where Serle seemed po-faced, lugubrious, stolid, the young Blainey sparkled. He would roll his own cigarettes and giggle. In conversation, he was amused and amusing. With a keen eye for the curious and unusual connections in history and in the world at large, Blainey was endlessly enlightening and refreshing.[49]

The history of the university again demonstrated a striking feature of the young Blainey: his preparedness to criticise established authority, a trait no doubt emboldened by the Professor Parker experience. The previous principal history of the University of Melbourne had been written by Ernest Scott, Crawford's predecessor, and Blainey cited many inaccuracies in Scott's book.[50] A more recent historian of the university, Richard Selleck, was also critical of Scott's work, arguing that his book 'does not conform to his policy of working from contemporary records' and writing that 'it compares poorly with Geoffrey Blainey's *A Centenary History of the University of Melbourne* which remains as sharply observed, incisive and lively as it was when written nearly fifty years ago'.[51]

Blainey's presence around the university led to another smaller job: writing a biographical sketch to introduce a collection of addresses by Sir Samuel Wadham. Wadham was retiring at the end of 1956 after a thirty-year stint as the University's Professor of Agriculture, a job he combined with extensive journalism and public commentary, plus service on numerous government bodies. Blainey noted that while Wadham had received 'tributes from the graduates and public men', the impact he had outside the academy was more significant, citing 'the countless letters which he has received from country people and the goodwill which his name evokes from hundreds of farmers who have handed him their problems and found a friend'.[52]

---

49 James Griffin quoted in Thompson, *The Patrician and the Bloke*, 2.
50 Ernest Scott, *A History of the University of Melbourne* (Melbourne: Melbourne University Press, 1936).
51 R. J. W. Selleck, *The Shop: The University of Melbourne 1850-1939* (Melbourne: Melbourne University Press, 2003), 638.
52 Geoffrey Blainey, 'Biographical Study' in Sir Samuel Wadham, *Selected Addresses* (Melbourne: Melbourne University Press, 1956), 16.

Blainey also made critical comments about the work of other historians in *Gold and Paper: A history of the National Bank of Australasia Limited* (1958).[53] For instance, while referring to Edward Shann as a 'distinguished historian', he doubted Shann's argument that bankers were lending on city land.[54] Blainey challenged popular views on the inevitability of the 1893 crash, citing Shann and A.G.L. Shaw as examples of historians who 'viewed the bank crash as a moral or economic punishment which, because it seemed just, was bound to come'.[55]

Another noteworthy feature of *Gold and Paper* was the weight that Blainey gave to social and general history compared to economic history, a fact W.A. Sinclair commented on in his review in the premier economic history journal, *Bulletin of the Business Archives Council of Australia*. As an example, Sinclair pointed out that the impact of the severe British depression on the Australian economy in 1878-79 received less treatment than the exploits of the Kelly Gang in those years.[56] However, for the general reader, the descriptions the book provided of bushranging in the 1870s, or the social impact of the bank crash of the 1890s, was probably a positive aspect, rather than a weakness.

Reviewers raised similar doubts about Blainey's next published work, *Mines in the Spinifex: The Story of Mt Isa Mines* (1960).[57] Economic history journal reviewer, Boris Schedvin, emphasised that Blainey's desire to reach a wide audience and thus to 'dispense with the elaborate paraphernalia and dry pedantry of the academic' presented 'a number of dangers'.[58] In Schedvin's assessment Blainey had succumbed to some of them, by passing over or incompletely answering difficult questions, and omitting facts which might disrupt 'the continuity and rhythm of the story'.[59]

An example of Blainey's ability as a storyteller was his description of John Campbell Miles, the discoverer of the Mt Isa field. Miles was the archetypal

---

53 Geoffrey Blainey, *Gold and Paper: A history of the National Bank of Australasia Limited* (Melbourne: Georgian House, 1958).

54 Ibid., 132. However, he defended Shann in the bibliography remarking that *An Economic History of Australia* was 'more accurate on banking history than is often acknowledged'.

55 Ibid., 162.

56 W.A. Sinclair, review of *Gold and Paper, Bulletin of the Business Archives Council of Australia* 1, no. 6: 64–65.

57 Geoffrey Blainey, *Mines in the Spinifex: The Story of Mt Isa Mines* (Sydney: Angus and Robertson, 1960).

58 C..B, Schedvin, review of *Mines in the Spinifex Business Archives and History* 2, no. 1 (February 1962): 82.

59 Ibid.

Blainey character, a man exhibiting 'a degree of persistence and perception shared by few prospectors'.[60] Miles' father had not married until he was 49 but had then fathered nine children. Unlike his father, Miles had not married at all, indeed 'he had not even attended a wedding as a guest, though he did recall once seeing a bridal party emerge from a church in Cloncurry'.[61] Miles lived into his eighties, ascribing his good health to shunning fresh fruit! To the lay reader, the absence of weddings and fruit in Miles' life was memorable colour; to the academic reviewer it was perhaps a distraction from the purpose of a serious work.

Mines in the Spinifex was one of two works in this period of Blainey's career where there was a significant time lag between writing and publication. Blainey largely completed the work after spending the first half of 1957 in Mt Isa, but it took another three years before it finally appeared. The other delayed work was his commissioned history of the eastern Melbourne municipality of Camberwell, which he researched around 1960 but which was not published until 1964 as *A History of Camberwell*.[62] This work was often bracketed with, or just behind, Weston Bate's history of Brighton, as the best local history published in Australia at that time. When Blainey produced an updated version in 1980, local historian Janet McCalman was effusive in her praise, saying that 'this little book represents the acme of the historian's craft, its apparently effortless narrative belying the intellectual sophistication and depth of scholarship that makes it all possible'.[63] Blainey was a strong defender of the significance of local history. He argued that its critics tended to be subscribers to the 'outdated creed' that history should tell the story 'of important people or people who held power'. Blainey's view was that history was 'also the story of the average person, how he lived, what work he did, and how he spent his leisure'.[64]

As well as Blainey's quick and slow publications, there was also a third category: an instance where Blainey researched and wrote a company history that was never published. The Imperial Chemical Industries Australia & New Zealand (ICIANZ) gave Blainey a one-year contract, running from November 1958 to November 1959. Blainey submitted the work on time, but

---

60 Blainey, *Mines in the Spinifex*, 87.
61 Ibid., 88.
62 Geoffrey Blainey, *A History of Camberwell* (Brisbane: Jacaranda Press, 1964).
63 Janet McCalman, 'Community Spirit', review of *A History of Camberwell*, *Australian Book Review* 29 (April 1981): 16–17.
64 Geoffrey Blainey, 'Problems of Interpretation (II)', *The Victorian Historical Magazine* 37, nos. 2 and 3 (May and August, 1966): 124.

the company never published it, nor provided an explanation as to why they did not, although they did pay Blainey the full amount owed under the contract.[65] The text contained numerous comments which may have contributed to its non-publication. Blainey argued that company management had shown a lack of initiative in entering new areas.[66] There was also the issue of tariff protection, which saw the company 'as well guarded as a gridiron player in its commercial contests, with the Tariff Board and the Commonwealth quick to offer protection'.[67]

Just as Blainey was commencing work on the ICIANZ commission he gave a talk at a conference on Australian Business History, held at Melbourne University in October 1958.[68] One point he made was that it was understandable that companies would not commission historians who were hostile to them. Given this attitude, it is probably not surprising that Blainey seems to have been neither surprised nor aggrieved by the decision of the ICIANZ management not to publish his work. Perhaps the fact that Blainey already had several books to his name by this time and was confident in his own ability made him less concerned than others might have been in the situation, as most writers rank getting published with getting paid as equally important to their esteem and well-being. Nor did the rejection prevent Blainey forming a lifelong friendship with the company's public relations manager, and future head of Melbourne University Press, Peter Ryan.

The climax of the first freelance period (1951-61) of Blainey's career was getting a commission to write a general history of Australian mining, published as *The Rush That Never Ended: A History of Australian Mining* (1963).[69] Writing a general mining history had been on Blainey's agenda for several years. From the mid-1950s there are references to this being a project on which he was working.[70] By 1960, the project had shifted from personal interest to commissioned work as a result of the patronage of Mt Isa Mines Chairman,

---

65 Blainey did not retain a copy of the work, but fortunately Orica (the modern successor to ICIANZ) was prepared to reverse the decision of 1959 and allow the manuscript to be released when approached by the author.

66 Geoffrey Blainey, *History of ICIANZ* (unpublished, 1959), 199.

67 Ibid., 174.

68 A summary of the talk was published in *Bulletin of the Business Archives Council of Australia* 1, no. 5 (1959): 12–15.

69 Geoffrey Blainey, *The Rush That Never Ended: A history of Australian mining* (Melbourne: Melbourne University Press, 1963).

70 For instance, in both February 1956 and February 1957 the Tasmanian History Research Association *Papers and Proceedings* contained references to Blainey working on 'The rise and fall of Australian Mining 1880-1955'.

George Fisher, and the Professor of Metallurgy at the University of Melbourne, Howard Worner. Both men were on the council of the Australasian Institute of Mining and Metallurgy, an influential professional body which formed a syndicate to sponsor the work.

The first point to make about *The Rush That Never Ended* is that it was not actually a history of all aspects of Australian mining. As one reviewer commented, it 'might more precisely be described as a condensed history of Australian non-ferrous metal mining'.[71] Blainey himself acknowledged in the Preface that his book is actually 'a history of Australian metal mining', and explained the exclusion of coal-mining on the grounds that it was 'a less speculative industry, was not an outback industry, had no metallurgical problems; its industrial tensions differed, and it was not such a dynamo of Australia's growth'.[72] Much later, Blainey explained that, having gone down all the big underground mines, he found that 'the metal mines appealed to me more than did the coal mines which conveyed at least to me a slightly gloomy air'.[73]

Having already written two mining histories, and with his background knowledge of Victoria's goldfields, he was well placed to undertake the task. Furthermore, having experienced an industrial company's lack of sympathy for his views, there was the added attraction that the mining industry, whose values had more in common with his own, was more likely to appreciate what he had written. Certainly, when writing about mining, Blainey did not have to pander to the protectionists as he was able to write that 'undoubtedly many Australian gold mines would have survived the 1920s but for Australia's policy of protecting urban industry at the expense of primary industry'.[74]

It was not just the prevailing economic orthodoxy of protectionism that Blainey was rejecting. One reviewer noted that Blainey was making 'many important revisions of accepted doctrine on Australian history', while another commented that he was 'challenging popular theory and belief on a number of points, and in some instances to a startling degree'.[75] To some this was inherently good; others, such as Geoffrey Bolton, warned that Blainey's delight in putting forward contrary opinions created a tendency towards oversimplification. Bolton believed that Blainey's painting of the nineteenth-century

---

71 Maurice Vintner, 'Mining for Wealth', *Sydney Morning Herald*, 9 November 1963, 15.
72 Blainey, *The Rush That Never Ended*, v.
73 Blainey, 'Tasmania, Tasmania': 8.
74 Blainey, *The Rush That Never Ended*, 289–290.
75 J.W. McCarty, 'Prospectors and Planters', 56; and Stuart Sayers, 'An Australian History of Mining and Miners', *The Age*, 2 November 1963, 21.

miner as 'a political moderate, interested only in safeguarding his working conditions' was an example.[76]

As the economic historian John McCarty put it, Blainey rejected 'the traditional honest solid workers versus wicked capitalists' interpretation of Australian labor history'.[77] Blainey stated in the Preface that he thought others had exaggerated the importance of class struggle on the metal fields, but acknowledged that, because of this view, he 'may not have written enough on trade unionism'.[78] His reluctance to write about industrial conflict may also go some way to explaining his aversion to writing about coal, an industry that played host to some of the nation's most bitter industrial disputes.

Of course, lack of interest in trade unionism and class conflict does not mean lack of interest in workers. Stephen Murray-Smith noted in the *Australian Book Review* that 'in Blainey we have that rare specimen, a democratically inclined historian who cannot be classed as ideologically a left-winger'.[79] The mindset that Murray-Smith described was captured in a paragraph which Blainey began by noting that 'gold checked and for a time reversed Australia's tendency to become a land that favoured the big man'. He concluded the paragraph with a eulogy to the place and time, writing that 'the hope of gold was shared by every man, and Australian society became more optimistic, individualist, and fluid than it ever was in the eras of jailers and pastoralists'.[80] Optimism was certainly an important theme of the book and Blainey wrote that 'it is easy to forget from the remoteness of the years that mining fields can never be created without optimism, even if such optimism seems absurd after a field has failed'.[81] The optimism helped create societies such as the Bendigo of the 1860s and 1870s, 'a dusty democracy in which the wealthy capitalists sometimes worked underground and humble miners owned mining shares'.[82]

Blainey lamented the decline in speculation in mining stocks as 'workingmen and shopkeepers in the mining towns found two-up and horse-racing and lotteries safer and more exciting'.[83] He sheeted the blame home to governments

---

76   G.C. Bolton, review of *The Rush That Never Ended*, *Historical Studies Australia and New Zealand* 11, no. 42 (April 1964): 280.
77   McCarty, 'Prospectors and Planters', 56.
78   Blainey, *The Rush That Never Ended*, vi.
79   Stephen Murray-Smith, 'Paydirt in plenty', review of *The Rush That Never Ended*, *Australian Book Review* 2, no. 12 (October 1963): 194.
80   Blainey, *The Rush That Never Ended*, 62.
81   Ibid., 140.
82   Ibid., 73.
83   Ibid., 289.

'prowling for easy revenue encouraged public lotteries that fed like parasites on a gambling instinct that had once flowed to a socially useful form of gambling'.[84] These comments placed him firmly within a strand of pragmatic Methodism which he had identified earlier in the book, saying that 'the dissenting chapels denounced gambling on cards and racehorses but were wisely lenient to a form of gambling that was industrially essential'.[85]

Given the prominence of the Eureka Stockade in 1854 in Australian history, chapter four of the book, 'Ballarat's Ditch of Perdition', attracted significant attention. According to Blainey, other historians had been wrong about both the causes and consequences of Eureka. In *The Fuss That Never Ended*, Graeme Davison usefully placed Blainey's assessment of the causes of Eureka in a historiographical context, explaining that Blainey 'approached the problem from an entirely different angle' from his predecessors, noting that 'while other historians were interested in what political ideas were in the air, he was investigating what was happening under the ground'.[86]

A supplement commemorating the centenary of the Eureka revolt in *Historical Studies* in 1954 had seen contributors weighing the influence of 'Chartist ideology, Irish rebelliousness, American republicanism and working class grievances'.[87] None of those factors carried much weight with Blainey. For him the key explanation for Eureka was not abstract ideas, but concrete technological and economic changes that had taken place on the Ballarat field. Other historians had overlooked the fact that Ballarat was quite different from other fields by 1854. No longer were miners working individually on the surface, but instead they were forming into groups to pursue deep lead mining. Blainey asserted that these 'new methods of mining and organization' were 'the key to understanding the armed rebellion of Ballarat miners in 1854'.[88] While Blainey's revisionist position credited technology and economics with providing the underlying causes of the rebellion, he also believed that a key factor was the weather. Government officials chose to raid for licences on a day with a hot northerly wind, which made mining difficult and frayed tempers.[89]

---

84 Ibid.
85 Ibid., 181.
86 Graeme Davison, 'Half a Determinist', in *The Fuss That Never Ended: The Life and Work of Geoffrey Blainey*, eds Gare et. al. (Melbourne: Melbourne University Press, 2003), 20.
87 Ibid.
88 Blainey, *The Rush That Never Ended*, 46.
89 Ibid., 54.

In Blainey's view, the tendency to impose an ideological framework on the causes of Eureka was similarly evident in the consideration of its consequences:

> In Australia's quiet history Eureka became a legend, a battlecry for nationalists, republicans, liberals, radicals, or communists, each creed finding in the rebellion the lessons they liked to see. Collectively their fascination magnified the effects of the episode.[90]

Blainey acknowledged that 'the Ballarat riot probably quickened political democracy in Victoria' and made subsequent politicians 'alert to the democratic spirit of the goldfields', but he argued that overall 'the colonies' political constitutions were not affected by Eureka'.[91] The key democratic impact was on the goldfields themselves. It created a situation where 'the miner in moleskins, for long hunted and herded, was lord of his own goldfields', the new structure being exemplified by the establishment of a new court of mines.

Davison has noted how Blainey's literary skill made the chapter 'a tour de force of historical interpretation, in which narrative, analytical and descriptive elements are brilliantly combined'. Davison explained that 'its power derives in part from the way in which the imagery of depth and digging, which explain the action of the miners, reinforces the role of the historian in excavating the subterranean causes of the revolt'.[92]

Given later discussions of the degree to which Blainey was a historical determinist, a believer that all events are determined by existing causes, it is important to note that at this time he was critical of other historians for being overly determinist, writing critically of the prevailing view that the gold rush had to take place in the early 1850s. In one of two articles he contributed to *Historical Studies* foreshadowing elements of the book, Blainey discussed the historiography of gold and explained that 'we can trace the maturing of the present interpretation of the gold rushes to the arrival of academic historians in the field of Australian history'.[93] He explained that:

> This interpretation seems wrong in main themes and details, but it possibly survived so long because of three frailties in our trade. First, we like to see an orderly pattern in a wing of history where chance traditionally seems to hold sway; the ruling interpretation satisfies this

---

90   Ibid., 56.
91   Ibid., 57.
92   Davison, 'Half a Determinist', 20.
93   Ibid.

wish. Second, in Australian history we tend to be isolationalists, so we ignore the nature of the Californian gold discoveries that are said to be so relevant to our own. Third, we are uneasy outside the old triad of political, and social and religious history, and so we accept the evidence of technical witnesses who had convictions for bias and even perjury in the court of nineteenth century historians.[94]

Blainey triggered another controversy with his argument that 'whenever the price of wool was low, and colonies were depressed, gold always revived to stimulate the economy' and that major metal fields generally opened during or just after recessions.[95] This position generated what can only be described as anger from one reviewer, Alan Barnard of the Australian National University. Just months earlier, Blainey had penned an uncomplimentary review of Barnard's biography of nineteenth century businessman Thomas Mort for *The Australian Journal of Politics and History*, asserting that 'both the research and the interpretation have strange gaps', and noting many 'discrepancies'.[96] Barnard returned fire with an even less favourable review of Blainey's work. He took issue with Blainey's thesis that mining booms from the 1860s onwards followed stock exchange booms in mining scrip, which, in turn, tended to occur when the Australian economy was depressed and there were few other outlets for investment. He stated that 'I, for one, can't believe that Blainey ... could himself be satisfied with this as anything more than a preliminary hypothesis designed to suggest possible lines that an investigation might take'.[97]

Felicitously, the pattern of discovery of gold and other metals in Australia meant that, in part, Blainey's narrative was able to be simultaneously chronological and geographical, a feat made possible by the spread of mining in an anti-clockwise direction, from the gold rushes in the south-east corner in the 1850s, through later rushes in Queensland, the Northern Territory and Kimberley before, in the 1890s, Kalgoorlie becomes the mining field of the moment. Blainey subsequently described this structure as evidence that he has 'always been fascinated by arrangements of space' for, as he explained, 'the shape of that book, the sequence in which events unfold, is influenced

---

94   Geoffrey Blainey, 'Gold and Governors', *Historical Studies Australia and New Zealand* 9, no. 36 (May 1961): 337–338.
95   Blainey, *The Rush That Never Ended*, 61, 138.
96   Geoffrey Blainey, review of *Visions and Profits: Studies in the Business Career of Thomas Sutcliffe Mort* by Alan Barnard, *The Australian Journal of Politics and History* 9, no. 2 (November 1963): 271–272.
97   Alan Barnard, review of *The Rush That Never Ended*, *Business Archives and History* 4, no. 1 (February 1964): 86.

more by a sense of place than a sense of time; and that's probably unusual in a narrative history'.[98]

However, as Stephen Murray-Smith pointed out, 'the story is not one of consecutive development: mining in Australia has been characterised by long periods of relative inanition'.[99] This potential difficulty was overcome by the fact that Blainey was 'a masterly narrator' with a style that was 'lucid, fast-moving, satisfyingly personal and pleasantly ironic'. Murray-Smith expanded on his praise, describing the book as 'an irresistible story, all the more absorbing in the telling by reason of Blainey's alchemical skill at blending a precise delineation of technological and financial development with a human commitment and interest of a high order'.[100] Hence, the reader learnt about Alfred Deeming, who cemented the bodies of two wives and four children in the floors of homes in London and Melbourne before taking up a position at Southern Cross, a remote Western Australian mining town. Deeming's presence illustrated that Southern Cross had become 'one of those quiet dead-end towns to which men escaped from wives and debts and murders'.[101]

This was the first occasion that literary journals, *Meanjin* and *Overland*, reviewed one of Blainey's works. Blainey's writing style was sufficiently distinctive to prompt *Meanjin* reviewer, Philip Brown, to comment that it had become 'well known, and would set a fashion if others could imitate it'.[102] McCarty, who was the historian of the Western Australian goldrush, in *Overland* proclaimed it Blainey's 'best book so far' and suggested that taking on a larger subject had given 'full scope to his brilliant narrative skill and ability to evoke the spirit of times past'.[103]

Bolton in *Historical Studies* had an extensive list of criticisms of Blainey's interpretations. Notwithstanding this, he commented that Blainey's decision to write the book has 'paid off triumphantly' and noted his joy that 'a book of such seminal importance should also be a pleasure to read'.[104] This pleasure

---

98   Blainey correspondence, 5 January 1972, Geoffrey Blainey Papers (hereafter Blainey Papers), MS 9225/4/12 Box 23, National Library of Australia (hereafter NLA), Canberra.

99   Murray-Smith, 'Paydirt in Plenty'.

100   Ibid.

101   Blainey, *The Rush That Never Ended*, 172.

102   Philip L. Brown, 'Victoria's Golden Decade', *Meanjin Quarterly* 22, no. 4 (December 1963): 433.

103   Brown, 'Victoria's Golden Decade', 453; and J.W. McCarty, 'Prospectors and Planters', 56.

104   G.C. Bolton, review of *The Rush That Never Ended*, 279.

was tempered by his feeling that, at times, the writing was a little too close to journalism, albeit 'high-grade journalism':

> Much of the time his style is good by the most exacting standards: subtle, moving and showing that felicitously sympathetic insight into character and situation that seems to be the distinctive gift of a Melbourne training. More's the pity that he sometimes pretends that he isn't an academic, and refrains from plying his readers with footnotes and statistics. Such apparatus, if kept tidy, seldom scares the general reader, and it implies no distrust of Blainey to suggest that *The Rush That Never Ended* would have been an easier book to evaluate if one were enabled to locate the source of some of his statements.[105]

Barnard also complained about the absence of footnotes and argued that Blainey's desire to tell a good story had got in the way of examining the major themes posed by the work. He claimed that 'in achieving success at the market level, Blainey has made considerable sacrifice to scholarship and the study of history'.[106] However, Barnard was prepared to acknowledge that Blainey's prose was 'spirited, forcible, and colourful… a phrase creates a picture; an anecdote epitomizes complex trends in a changing situation; homely words and similes painlessly unravel the mysteries of metallurgy', resulting in 'a huge vivid canvass, crammed with excitement, movement and tension, full of life'.[107]

The book was also reviewed internationally, most notably in the prestigious *The Economic History Review* by K.H. Burley, who described it as a 'valuable work' and commented that 'the author's eye for the colourful remains keen'. However, he also noted that 'on company mining the book is slightly disappointing' and lacked statistical data.[108]

The Rush That Never Ended was prominently reviewed in major Australian newspapers. As had happened with *The Peaks of Lyell*, there was a difference in the length of the reviews *The Rush That Never Ended* received in the major broadsheet newspapers in Melbourne and Sydney.[109] It was nowhere near as extreme this time, one being approximately double the length of the other. However, whereas in 1955 the subject matter was a factor, here the topic was

---

105 Ibid.
106 Barnard, review of *The Rush That Never Ended*, 86.
107 Ibid.
108 K.H. Burley, review of *The Rush That Never Ended* in *The Economic History Review* (second series) 17, no. 1 (August 1964): 184–185.
109 Vintner, 'Mining for Wealth'; and Sayers, 'An Australian History of Mining and Miners'.

genuinely national, and so the origins of the author and publisher were the more likely causes of the different treatment. The book sold well. A Melbourne University Press advertisement of April 1964 boasted that 'the second impression is now printing, only six months after publication'.[110]

It was a good time to be writing books about Australia, one review placing *The Rush That Never Ended* in the context of a 'flood of Australiana' that publishers were getting out to meet demand.[111] Forty years later, Bolton made a more specific point as to why the timing of Blainey's work was felicitous: it appeared at a time when minerals were about to replace wool as Australia's major export. Bolton contrasted Blainey's picking of this trend with the contemporary multi-disciplinary work of Keith Hancock and Barnard on the subject of wool. While Hancock and Barnard did not even get to release their planned second volume on wool, *The Rush That Never Ended* has been updated several times. Bolton concluded that 'Hancock could be seen as the voice of the past and Blainey of the future'.[112] More recently, the freelance Canberra historian Stephen Holt has made the same point viz-a-viz Blainey and Barnard:

> In the 1960s, minerals decisively replaced wool as Australia's main export and focus of investment. With the comparative decline of the wool industry, students of Australia's economic history switched their attention to other aspects of Australia's economic past, such as transport, urbanisation and, even more topically, mining. In 1962, Barnard was Australia's premier wool industry historian, but the ever-more triumphant mining industry already had its own laureate in the person of the slightly younger Geoffrey Blainey. Of the two, Blainey was more attuned to the future economic destiny of Australia.[113]

And although business history might not have appealed to all Blainey's fellow writers and historians, there is no doubt it was something of a boom area at the time. In 1960, Merab Tauman of the University of Western Australia gave a paper commenting on how the past decade had seen a greater interest in the writing of business history in Australia, citing Blainey as a key

---

110   *Overland*, no. 29 (April 1964): 40.

111   M.H. Ellis, 'Golden Days', *The Bulletin*, 9 November 1963, 47.

112   Geoffrey Bolton, 'The Tyranny of Distance Revisited', in *The Fuss That Never Ended: The Life and Work of Geoffrey Blainey*, eds Gare et.al (Melbourne: Melbourne University Press, 2003), 35.

113   Stephen Holt, 'The home-town historian whom history forgot', *The Canberra Times* (The Public Sector Informant section), 5 June 2012, 23.

example.[114] This followed similar developments in both the United States and United Kingdom, where business history was becoming an important part of economic history. Blainey's status as a leader in the field was underlined by John La Nauze, who said that Blainey had 'shown that business history may be both intellectually respectable and readable'.[115] One American study of Australian historical writing noted that *The Peaks of Lyell* 'marked the opening of a new phase in the writing of Australian history' where Australian companies had become more inclined to both open their archives and provide funds for historical research.[116]

Another critic, Peter Coleman, placed Blainey's work in business history as part of a broader counter-revolution in the study of history that saw topics such as the middle class, religion, and business being belatedly studied in Australia.[117] Coleman identified 'the standard radical-leftist interpretation of Australian history which is given in nearly all the textbooks', including works by V.G. Childe, H.V. Evatt, Brian Fitzpatrick and the *Cambridge History of the British Empire*, all of which tried to cement 'the unfolding of Social Progress and the increasing initiative of the working class' as one of Australian history's overriding themes.[118]

In a paper delivered at the ANZAAS conference in the same year that Coleman's book was published, historian Allan Martin considered whether the 'radical-leftist' history described by Coleman could be considered a comprehensive 'Whig view of Australian history'. Martin doubted that it could, but thought there were identifiable Whig interpretations, with some similar elements to the ones Herbert Butterfield had identified in English historiography. Martin took more issue with Coleman's concept of counter-revolutionaries, of which Martin was considered one, as they were 'a rather mixed bunch' who, as well as not having a lot in common, were also rarely engaged in explicitly overturning Whig interpretations.[119]

---

114   Merab Tauman, 'A Critical Comment of Australian Business Histories' (paper presented at the University of Melbourne, 6 February 1960 and published in *Bulletin of the Business Archives Council of Australia* 1, no. 9 (August 1961)).
115   J.A. La Nauze, 'The Study of Australian History', *Historical Studies Australia and New Zealand* 9, no. 33 (November 1959): 4. The article was first presented as a talk to ANZAAS conference, Section E in Perth, August 1959.
116   Ed. By Robin W. Winks, *The Historiography of the British Empire-Commonwealth: Trends, Interpretations and Resources* (Durham: Duke University Press, 1966), 168.
117   Peter Coleman, 'Introduction: The New Australia', in *Australian Civilization*, ed. Peter Coleman, (Melbourne: Cheshire, 1962), 8.
118   Ibid., 6.
119   A.W. Martin, *The 'Whig' View of Australian History and other essays*, ed. J.R. Nethercote (Melbourne: Melbourne University Publishing, 2007), 1–27.

With hindsight, what looks particularly odd is that the designated leader of the counter-revolution described by Coleman was none other than Manning Clark who 'did more than anyone else to release historians from the prison of the radical interpretation and to begin the systematic study of the neglected themes in our history, especially of religion'.[120] By the time Coleman's book was published, Childe was dead and Evatt seriously ill which left only Fitzpatrick able to respond which he did, not only to Coleman, but also to Clark's 1954 inaugural lecture at Canberra University College, when he too had attacked the radical-nationalist tradition. Fitzpatrick argued that there was no such tradition and that nowhere in his writing had he described any golden age of the labour movement in Australia.[121]

A different contemporary perspective was provided by author W.A.P. Phillips who bracketed Clark with Russel Ward as writers of versions of Australian history that were too parochial. By contrast, he argued that Blainey was one of only two post-war Australian historians (Margaret Kiddle was the other) 'to write history fit to stand on the world market' and speculated that it must be more than a coincidence that 'these two historians have worked only on the fringe of the academic world'.[122]

The rapid development of the mining industry in the 1960s meant that by the end of the decade there was demand for a new edition of *The Rush That Never Ended*. The second edition, published in 1969, saw Blainey expand the final chapter, 'New Age', from six to 25 pages. Blainey was naturally keen to include the recently discovered oil, natural gas and phosphate fields, but in doing so he had to acknowledge that his definition of 'metal mining' had become too narrow. The new resources gelled nicely with the old minerals because the resource fields 'clearly fit into the theme of search and discovery' which dominated the book.[123]

In his 1979 book, *The Manufacture of Australian History*, Rob Pascoe identified a significant development in Blainey's approach to writing history between the 1963 and 1969 editions of *The Rush That Never Ended*. The original was 'a lively readable book' which concentrated 'more on formist

---

120 Coleman, 'Introduction: The New Australia', 7.
121 Brian Fitzpatrick, 'Counter-Revolution in Australian Historiography', *Meanjin* 22, no. 93, 200–204. Also see Stuart Macintyre, 'The Radical and the Mystic: Brian Fitzpatrick, Manning Clark and Australian History', in eds Stuart Macintyre and Sheila Fitzpatrick, *Against the Grain: Brian Fitzpatrick and Manning Clark in Australian History and Politics* (Melbourne: Melbourne University Press, 2007), 12–36.
122 W.A.P. Phillips, 'Art of Writing History', *The Age*, 13 April 1963, 13.
123 Blainey, *The Rush That Never Ended*, v.

detail than mechanistic pattern'.[124] However, the revised edition contained a general theory of mineral discovery in 'the form of a law: "if a mineral has not been vigorously sought, it is not logical to argue that the mineral is rare in a country"'.[125] Once historians start identifying patterns and laws, they usually also begin making predictions and greatly increase their chances of becoming involved in political controversy. Indeed, in the same year that the second edition of *The Rush That Never Ended* appeared, it was Blainey's mineral discovery law that got him embroiled in his first significant political controversy (see chapter 3).

Pascoe pondered what prompted the shift that saw Blainey's works 'gradually take on a more analytic character' and made him redefine 'his purpose as the search for regularity and pattern, in the mechanistic tradition'. His answer was that 'it was probably his decision to return to academe', which produced this significant change of outlook.[126]

The decision to return to the academy was to have larger consequences.

---

124 Rob Pascoe, *The Manufacture of Australian History*, (Melbourne: Oxford University Press, 1979), 130.
125 Ibid.
126 Ibid.

Chapter 3

ACADEMIC HISTORIAN

In the early 1960s Blainey decided there would be advantages in becoming an academic historian. This move to a university was to have significant impacts on Blainey and his work. It opened up a range of new opportunities to become a significant public figure, gave him the freedom to write about what interested him, and significantly altered some key aspects of his perspective on writing history. Yet many other aspects of Blainey's methods, style and attitudes remained constant. The interaction of the old and new elements was to play a part, in the 1980s, in his ultimate severance from the academy.

The initial move to take up an academic appointment was not the result of any profound change of heart on Blainey's part. Rather it was a more prosaic sequence of factors which revealed to him that having the secure income of an academic might be beneficial.

The financial viability of his chosen career as a freelance historian had not been an issue for most of the 1950s. Further, for most of the decade Blainey had the freedom of being young and single. However, marriage, parenthood and property ownership all occurred within three years near the end of that decade. On 15 February 1957 Blainey married the 21-year-old Ann Heriot and the couple became parents of a daughter, Anna, in September 1959. In the meantime, they had moved into their new home at 262 The Boulevard, East Ivanhoe. Designed by the architect Don Hendry Fulton, the house had several of the typical stylish features of the 1950s, including open plan living, a complete wall of glass to maximise the Yarra view and roof glazing over the kitchen and study.[1]

These life changes meant that earning a steady income became more important. For most of the time this was not difficult, as Blainey's reputation as a

---

1   Museum Victoria website, http://museumvictoria.com.au/collections/themes/1257/blainey-house-ivanhoe-1957, accessed 11 January 2010. Further description of the house was included in an article by James Mulholland, 'Living with History', *Herald Sun* (Home section), 10 April 1999, 14–15. It described a 'lovely simple design that suited its time, but a little under 200 sq m in size'.

business historian had grown sufficiently for him to have a constant flow of work and, indeed, a higher income than an academic of his age could expect to earn.[2] The credit squeeze of 1960-61 is best remembered for almost bringing about the defeat of the Menzies Government in the December 1961 election, but it was also an important factor in turning Blainey from a freelance historian into an academic historian. Not only did it slow approaches about potential new commissions, but even the funding for his research on the mining history had been paid slowly by the mining companies, with Blainey noting early in 1961 that this had made him 'a bit broke'.[3] Fortunately, a more reliable funding source had been the University of Melbourne's Economic History Department, whose Professor Bill Woodruff was a supporter of the mining history project and had provided a £1,050 research grant for the year to 28 February 1961.

Although the research grant subsidised his mining research, the credit squeeze made Blainey more receptive than normal to an academic offer. He was getting those quite regularly as universities were expanding and they did not yet have large pools of graduates from whom to choose. Blainey accepted an offer from the University of Adelaide for the third term of 1961, filling in for Ken Inglis who was away at Brown College in the United States. Blainey taught Australian history for a term, but still found time to work on *The Rush That Never Ended*. He thus realised that he would still have time to work on his own projects even if he became an academic. This led him to accept an offer from the Melbourne Department of Economic History to become a Senior Lecturer in 1962.

Having joined the Commerce faculty, Blainey was promoted to a Readership in 1963, but only after some quite spirited lobbying by Woodruff as it was unusual for an individual to be promoted so quickly. One of the references Woodruff sought was from Max Crawford, who commented:

> We have occasionally persuaded him to do a little teaching for us and found him completely first-rate; but we have not been able to hold him. Adelaide would have done so if it could have succeeded. It would be a great pity if the University did not hold him as he is a very distinguished practising historian. I have no experience of him

---

2   Geoffrey Blainey to Bill Woodruff, 2 August 1961, Geoffrey Blainey Papers (hereafter Blainey Papers), Acc. No. 89/145 Box 12, University of Melbourne Archives (hereafter UMA), Melbourne.

3   Blainey to Woodruff, 1 March 1961, Blainey Papers, Acc. No. 89/145 Box 12, UMA.

in administration, but I would expect well from his good sense, good humour and good judgment of people. I can confidently support the proposal for his promotion.[4]

Like many other academic fields within universities, economic history experienced something of a boom in post-war Australian universities. The largest increase was at the Australian National University (ANU), which also came to be seen as the location of the orthodox school of economic history, following the lead of Noel Butlin. The Melbourne department also grew, but its members, including Blainey, generally followed a different methodological path to the ANU. *The Oxford Companion to Australian History* entry on Economic History observed that Blainey's work charted 'a different course from the mainstream', being 'less quantitative and not overtly founded on formal economics'.[5] A recent study of the relationships between economic historians in this period confirmed that Blainey was an outlier, along with fellow Melbourne graduate John McCarty, in adopting a deductive approach to economic history, as opposed to 'the orthodox school's inductive methodology of building a narrative around the quantitative evidence'.[6]

Blainey's early years as an academic saw him teaching only Australian history. He did so in his term in Adelaide, and in his first year at Melbourne he taught Australian Economic History to second-year students for half the year and took some tutorials for honours students. From 1963, the Australian economic history subject was made into a full year course, known as Economic History B, and Blainey both lectured and tutored in this subject for several years. The numbers taking the subject grew rapidly, and because these included many part-timers, the two lectures each week were repeated in the evenings, plus there were six to eight tutorials each week. Some notes Blainey made for the first lecture of a new year mainly relate to procedural matters but also give something of an insight into what he saw as the purpose of the subject:

---

4   Max Crawford to George Paton, 21 December 1962, Blainey Papers, Acc. No. 89/145 Box 12, UMA.

5   W.A Sinclair, 'Economic History', in *Oxford Companion to Australian History*, eds Graeme Davison, John Hirst and Stuart Macintyre, (Melbourne: Oxford University Press, 1998, 2001), 201–203

6   Claire Wright, 'The formation of Australia's economic history community 1950–1970: A multidimensional network analysis'. A paper prepared for the Digital Humanities 2016 Conference, Krakow 2016, published at www.uow.academia.edu, accessed 27 September 2017.

1. Reading list not issued because you're encouraged to specialise and read about the things that interest you, and there are no books on a lot of these things.

...

8. Australian syllabus. Main emphasis 1851-1920.

9. Aim of the course is not necessarily to impart a body of knowledge or a series of interpretations. No right answer to a lot of these problems.

    1. Try and cultivate a curiosity about the past.

    2. A knowledge of the attitudes to evidence.

    3. The complexity of motivation, the role of the economic motives and conditions in Australian history, and in places the relation of economic theory to economic history.[7]

One of Blainey's early students was the journalist Les Carlyon, who was completing an economics degree part-time. In a profile of Blainey he wrote in the 1990s, Carlyon recalled that students were keen to go to Blainey's lectures, unlike those of some of his colleagues, because he knew that if you wanted students' attention 'you must first learn to entertain them'. According to Carlyon, Blainey lectured in the same style as he wrote, as a 'storyteller' who 'presented history not as a series of stops and starts but as a flow'.[8] In his memoir, Blainey explains that all he took into lectures was a single sheet of white paper with some headings and 'if the lecture went well in the opening ten minutes, and the students were immersed, I consulted no further notes as a rule'.[9] Literary critic Peter Craven has commented that Blainey's 'lectures dazzled everyone with the mask of ignorance he would assume'.[10]

Blainey also provided opportunities for his students to hear from others with interesting backgrounds and perspectives. Throughout the 1950s and early 1960s, socialist historian Brian Fitzpatrick had struggled to secure academic appointments due to a combination of his radical ideology and heavy drinking. However, in 1964 Blainey arranged for Fitzpatrick to give a series

---

7   Blainey course notes, Blainey Papers, Acc. No. 89/145 Box 4, UMA.
8   Les Carlyon, 'A Curious Man – Geoffrey Blainey', *The Independent Monthly*, April 1995, 13-19.
9   Blainey, *Before I Forget*, 259.
10 Peter Craven, 'The historian masters his art and craft', *The Age* (Spectrum section), 29 June 2019, 20-21.

of guest lectures and take two seminars for honours students, which proved to be his last academic engagement before his death the following year.[11] In the same period, Blainey was a guest at a dinner held in Fitzpatrick's honour, sharing a table with Fitzpatrick's daughter Sheila, who was keen to sit as far from the head table as possible.[12] There were tributes to Fitzpatrick from a range of figures from across the political spectrum, including then Liberal Federal Treasurer Harold Holt who told an anecdote about debating Fitzpatrick at Geelong Grammar on the merits of socialism and private enterprise, a debate organised by then student Rupert Murdoch. Blainey wrote a tribute to Fitzpatrick in *Business Archives and History* and the following decade was one of the examiners of Don Watson's thesis on Fitzpatrick.

Another feature of Blainey's lecturing was that once or twice a year he would organise for his students to go on excursions to country Victoria to see first-hand 'the deserted goldfields and waning towns' that straddled the Great Dividing Range. As Blainey describes in his memoir:

> The eyes of the students lit up when, at the end of a lonely bush track, they found a small gold stamp-mill at work, or the remains of a blast furnace that had once glowed at night, or even an ancient arrangement of large Aboriginal stones in a circle … Some students, who became colonels of commerce, remember the excursions more than the lectures.[13]

Despite the fact that one of the key attractions of becoming an academic had been that it allowed plenty of time to pursue his own historical interests, Blainey always seems to have been prepared to take on extra responsibilities. He was one of seven members of a committee, chosen at a general meeting of five hundred academic staff on 12 May 1964, whose role was to document staff difficulties and grievances and submit them to the university administration. The committee produced what one history of the university calls 'the famous "Red Book"' detailing the academics' concerns.[14]

The opportunity also arose for Blainey to take up other significant committee appointments. He became a member of the Board of Directors of Melbourne University Press (M.U.P.) at the meeting on 29 October 1962 and

---

11. Macintyre, 'The Radical and the Mystic' in eds Macintyre and Fitzpatrick, *Against the Grain*; and Blainey, *Before I Forget*, 259.
12. Sheila Fitzpatrick, *My Father's Daughter: Memories of an Australian Childhood* (Melbourne: Melbourne University Press, 2010), 192.
13. Blainey, *Before I Forget*, 258.
14. Poynter and Rasmussen, *A Place Apart*, 275.

remained on it for several years. The Board met ten times a year on Monday afternoons with meeting lengths varying between 45 minutes and over two hours. The responsibilities covered publishing, printing and retail (M.U.P. being responsible for the campus bookshop, The Bookroom). Blainey seems to have taken an active interest in all aspects of the business, and clearly felt at ease with financial statements, balance sheets and consultants' reports. The Chairman when Blainey joined was William Macmahon Ball who, twenty years later almost to the day, was to appear on TV screens around the nation as a key interviewee in the first episode of *The Blainey View*.

Earlier in 1962, M.U.P. had appointed a new Director, Peter Ryan, the man whom Blainey had met some years earlier at ICIANZ. Ryan would sometimes ask Blainey to provide advice about manuscripts that had been submitted, for instance offering him five pounds to provide an assessment of a history of Cobb & Co.[15] Blainey's responses usually covered not just the historical and literary merits of the books in question, but also gave an assessment of their commercial prospects. On the Cobb & Co manuscript he wrote back to Ryan within three days expressing concern that 'as it stands I imagine it would be a dicey financial proposition, as people might not come at 35s or so for such a small book'.[16]

Another activity Blainey continued to pursue was book reviewing, including for the fledgling *Australian Book Review*.[17] He appeared in the first issue of November 1961, reviewing L.F. Crisp's biography of Ben Chifley, which he neatly summarised by saying that as a biography it was 'too heroic' but as political history it was 'valuable'.[18] Marjorie Barnard, the author of *A History of Australia*, had read 'too few of the books and historical journals published since the war' and thus, on many topics, the book reflected 'the state of historical knowledge in 1930 or earlier'.[19] On the other hand, he praised the 'vividness and sympathy and fluency of some of her writing' and was pleased that she had focused on 'themes which most general histories of Australia skimp or ignore: the aborigines, the judiciary, civil service, the daily round

---

15 Peter Ryan to Blainey, 13 December 1965, Blainey Papers, Acc. No. 81/9 Box 3, UMA.
16 Blainey to Peter Ryan, 16 December 1965, Blainey Papers, Acc. No. 81/9 Box 3, UMA.
17 This publication was published monthly from 1961 to 1973. The current publication of the same name first appeared in 1978.
18 Geoffrey Blainey, 'Abe Lincoln and Ben Chifley', *Australian Book Review* 1, no. 1 (November 1961): 8.
19 Geoffrey Blainey, 'Wanted: Publisher's Reader', *Australian Book Review* 1, no. 7 (June 1962): 98.

of convicts and shepherds and explorers, surfing and flying, and many facets of economic and social change'.[20]

Blainey's teaching responsibilities, committee work, and reviewing did not reduce his writing output. In his first four years at Melbourne University he completed *The Rush That Never Ended*, wrote *The Tyranny of Distance*, and accepted assorted other commissions from friends in the mining industry and his old school.

Even if being an academic was not dominating his life, it was having a significant influence on the content of his work. Several commentators have written of the impact that the move to the academy had on Blainey's historical writing. One of these, as already noted, was Rob Pascoe who tracked Blainey's 'transition from the empiricism of his company histories of the 1950s to a mechanistic sociological approach' by the early 1970s. Pascoe based his categorisation of historians on a model developed by Stephen C. Pepper, mechanist being one of the four different ways of thinking, the others being contextualist, formist and organicist.[21]

In the Australian context, the mechanists were considered in a chapter titled 'The search for laws', the first half of which dealt with sociological historians who included Blainey, Ken Inglis, A.W. Martin, Weston Bate and Hugh Stretton, while the second half featured the New Left historians, such as Humphrey McQueen and R.W. Connell. Although appreciative of Pascoe's effort, Blainey only partially accepted his conclusions:

> I respect very much what he tried to do and what he achieved. I'm not sure if his theoretical framework comes off. I see I'm down as a 'mechanist' or a searcher for general laws. This is true of some topics I write about but probably not about others. It's true of one of my approaches but it's not my only approach. I wonder whether I and many others straddle too many of his pigeonholes to be safely placed in one.[22]

Blainey's scepticism about the Pascoe model of classifying Australian historians was shared by others and it has not had a continuing influence on the nation's historiography. However, Pascoe's observation that Blainey was becoming more interested in general laws had some merit. Others would describe this search for laws as a form of historical determinism, the view that events are

---

20 Ibid.
21 Pascoe, *Manufacture*, 5.
22 Blainey correspondence, 16 March 1983, Blainey Papers, MS 9225/4/23 Box 24, NLA.

largely determined by factors, most often material ones, which are beyond individual human agency.

Blainey has acknowledged that he was 'half a determinist', this middling status being arrived at by a 'tendency to be a determinist', matched by a counterbalancing effort to correct himself.[23] He claimed not to like determinism, but 'somewhere in my background, in my training or in my makeup, I have a preference for hundred to nought answers'.[24] Graeme Davison picked up the phrase 'half a determinist' for an essay he wrote about Blainey in the early 2000s. He argued that Blainey's move into the academy made him more receptive to determinism. According to Davison, Blainey benefited from not being weighed down by the theories that Burns had taught in his Theory and Method course in 1950 and thus 'could respond without the philosophical inhibitions of those who had wrested with the dense logic of Hempel and Popper'.[25] Davison also placed significant weight on the fact that Blainey moved into the 'very different intellectual environment' of the Faculty of Commerce:

> His new students were intellectually able but they looked for knowledge that was practical rather than speculative. History had to compete with the confident claims of the social sciences, especially economics. By applying the positivist model of science with its pursuit of general models and rigorous mathematical proofs, economists promised knowledge that was not only useful but predictive. Could history do the same? Blainey wondered. First in his teaching, and then in his writing, he began to explore the possibility of a history that could illuminate the present and shape the future.[26]

Without the shift in intellectual outlook precipitated by the move into the Commerce Faculty, the book Blainey worked on between 1963 and 1965 would have been quite different; and one of the most famous Australian historical and literary phrases may never have been coined. Even before his history of Australian mining was published in September 1963, Penguin Books had commissioned Blainey to undertake a similar task with another important aspect of the Australian economy: a history of Australian transport. The finished product was neither published by Penguin nor, by any standard

---

23 Blainey in *Making History*, 75.
24 Ibid.
25 Davison, 'Half a Determinist', 17.
26 Ibid., 19.

expectation, a history of Australian transport. Blainey had sketched on a far larger canvas.

His completed work, *The Tyranny of Distance: How Distance Shaped Australia's History* (1966), challenged sufficient truisms of Australian history to generate plenty of controversy; its initial publication as a paperback made it immediately affordable; its readability saw it leap onto school curricula; and, perhaps most importantly of all, its title was so catchy that it entered the popular vernacular.[27]

In identifying distance as an encompassing feature of Australian history, *The Tyranny of Distance* presented an all-embracing theory of Australian exceptionalism that Blainey claimed was comparable to Frederick Jackson Turner's 'frontier thesis' in North American history.[28] Turner first enunciated his theory in a landmark 1893 speech 'The Significance of the Frontier in American History', arguing that that the constantly westward-moving frontier had been the creator of distinctive American character of independence and resourcefulness. Although contested by many historians during the twentieth century, it has endured as a frame of reference for consideration of American history. University of Western Australia historian Fred Alexander had written an essay in 1948 in which he attempted to apply Turner's thesis to Australia. Other Australian historians had noted the absence of an Australian equivalent of Turner's theory. For instance, in 1959, John La Nauze had observed 'it has been clear that there has emerged no dominating or general theme, to stimulate original minds and become a catchword for others, comparable to Frederick Jackson Turner's interpretation of American history to the end of the nineteenth century in terms of the moving frontier'.[29]

Thinking and writing about transport, Blainey surmised that distance might make him the antipodean Turner. Geography had always been an interest of his and distance was perhaps the element of the subject which most intrigued him. Reflecting on the issue of distance in 1983, Blainey commented that 'right from the start my mind seems to have been attracted to historical themes in which spatial relationships – geography if you like – was important'.[30] He expanded on this by explaining that distance was an important factor as far back as the Parker article in 1950 and continued to be in books such as *The Peaks of Lyell* and *Gold and Paper*.

---

27   Geoffrey Blainey, *The Tyranny of Distance: How Distance Shaped Australia's History* (Melbourne: Sun Books, 1966).
28   Blainey, *The Tyranny of Distance*, ix
29   La Nauze, 'The study of Australian History'.
30   Blainey correspondence, 14 July 1983, Blainey Papers, Acc. No. 89/145 Box 4, UMA.

Blainey's first attempt at using distance more generally was in a journal article he wrote in the mid-1950s on population movements in Tasmania; and to prove that distance could be a vertical as well as a horizontal factor, he had deployed it as a key part of his explanation for Eureka in *The Rush That Never Ended*. In *The Tyranny of Distance*, distance moved to centre stage. Pascoe deployed a neat metaphor to describe what Blainey did in singling out distance as the progenitor of a pattern in Australian history:

> He took one card out of the historian's pack, the one labelled 'distance' and played it off against the others. Essentially, he argued that the vast distance within Australia, and between it and Europe, shaped the pattern of European settlement in Australia to a much greater extent than historians had previously recognized ... at the outset of the project his aim was, strictly speaking, empiricist but by the inclusion of an abstract explanatory factor the cause and effect relationships of transport innovation formed a pattern.[31]

For Pascoe, Blainey's use of distance reflected the change in his intellectual outlook precipitated by the move into the academy, specifically in economic history. *The Tyranny of Distance* was 'the mid-point in Blainey's transition from the empiricism of his company histories of the 1950s to a mechanistic, sociological approach' and demonstrated Blainey's new belief that his purpose as a historian was 'the search for regularity and pattern, in the mechanistic tradition'.[32]

However, grand theories and abstract explanatory factors were not what Penguin Books had commissioned. They expected an illustrated history of just 45,000 words. Blainey has described what happened:

> Brian Stonier was then the head of Penguin and full of go. We signed the contract in 1964. The book changed direction and in the end grew to more than 100,000 words. Brian Stonier and I used to lunch occasionally in Carlton (in the days when hardly anybody ate in Carlton) and he was happy with the book's change in direction. He then left Penguin to start Sun Books. Sometime later I finished the book and submitted it to Penguin ... and the book was rejected. I don't think they gave a reason. Stonier was happy to take it for Sun Books, and they published

---

[31] Pascoe, *Manufacture*, 131.
[32] Ibid.

it in 1966. It didn't worry me that Penguin said no; I knew – or thought I knew – that the book would find a market.[33]

The co-founder of Sun Books was Geoffrey Dutton, who later wrote the history of Penguin Books in Australia in which he comments that '*The Tyranny of Distance* certainly did find a market, and Brian and I, at our fledgling Sun Books, were delighted that Penguin said no'.[34]

One way for a book to have an impact is for the author to attack the positions previously put by others. There are numerous places in *The Tyranny of Distance* where Blainey attacked the sins of both omission and commission of previous unnamed historians. Not unexpectedly, this precipitated a reaction. One reviewer, Gordon Rimmer, noted that 'on at least six occasions, he draws attention for the benefit of his readers to the fact that he is taking issue with most historians' but then, 'having taken up the cudgels against his colleagues, Mr Blainey fails to put forward his revisions in the proper manner', neither presenting enough evidence, nor footnoting it adequately.[35]

Not naming the historians with whom one was taking issue was clearly an unusual practice for an academic historian. Blainey attempted to justify his approach by explaining that 'because the main interpretations with which I disagreed are so widely held – and often unanimously held – that interested readers wishing to make up their own minds can easily find examples of them in standard histories of Australia'.[36] The lack of names was noted by the unnamed. A.G.L. Shaw commented that 'as one of the many "former historians", rarely specified but often criticized, may I plead that we are not so ignorant as Blainey suggests, nor did we *always* ignore those factors upon which he would have liked us to have laid more stress'.[37]

While many historians are referred to in the endnotes, interestingly, the only two historians mentioned in the narrative were not mainstream historians. One was a camel teamster, Herbert Barker, who wrote a 'fine book' on the history of camels in the Australian outback; the other was Marxist economic historian, Ken Dallas, who 'brilliantly probed' why Britain decided

---

33 Geoffrey Dutton, *A Rare Bird: Penguin Books in Australia 1946-96* (Melbourne: Penguin, 1996), 79-80.
34 Ibid.
35 Gordon Rimmer, review of *The Tyranny Of Distance*, Australian Economic History Review 7, no.. 2 (September 1967): 194–196.
36 Blainey, *The Tyranny of Distance*, 340.
37 A.G.L. Shaw, 'New Explanations in Australian History', *Meanjin Quarterly* 26, no. 2 (June 1967): 221.

to send convicts to Australia 'in a lecture to a small, sceptical audience in Hobart in 1952'.[38]

It was the specifics of Blainey's extension of Dallas' ideas, more than his general thesis, which made the publication of *The Tyranny of Distance* a seminal moment in Australian historiography. Blainey's arguments about the reasons for Britain establishing a colony in New South Wales, contained in chapter two of the book, stimulated such significant debate that, in 1997, Humphrey McQueen claimed that 'no article or chapter by any historian of Australia has provoked so much extensive and detailed rebuttal'.[39]

Including consideration of the motives for settlement was something of an afterthought for Blainey, who only decided to go back as far as 1788 when he was well advanced on the project. Blainey saw merit in Dallas' theory that Britain wanted to establish an alternative sea route to China and provide a basis for trading in the Pacific and argued that, if the sole objective was a convict colony, there were other suitable locations for the British Government much closer to home. Hence, there must have been other reasons for the choice of New South Wales. Blainey suggested an economic explanation, the availability of flax and timber, vital raw materials for the ship-building industry. Their absence from documents could be explained counterintuitively, as Blainey argued that 'in letters in which British politicians explained their reasons for selecting Botany Bay they did not have to emphasize that flax and timber were vital to their country; it was too obvious to be spelled out'.[40]

The main debate about the plausibility of Blainey's argument began early in 1968 when Geoffrey Bolton in the *Australian Economic History Review* and A.G.L. Shaw in *Historical Studies* produced two very similar critiques published within a month of each other.[41] Both Bolton and Shaw disagreed with Blainey's theory regarding flax and pine. The similarity of their argument extended to the choice of titles – 'The Hollow Conqueror: Flax and the Foundation of Australia' and 'The Hollow Conqueror and The Tyranny

---

38   Blainey, *The Tyranny of Distance*, 24–26; 291. See also Gideon Haigh, 'The History Boy', *The Weekend Australian* (Review section), 16–17 July 2016, 8–9. Blainey explains more about Barker in Blainey, *Before I Forget*, 261–264. Dallas' talk was reproduced in Dallas, K.M., 'The First Settlement in Australia; considered in relation to seapower in world politics', *Papers and Proceedings of the Tasmanian Historical Research Association*, 3 (1952): 1–12.

39   Humphrey McQueen, *Suspect History*, (Adelaide: Wakefield Press, 1997), 190.

40   Blainey, *The Tyranny of Distance*, 28.

41   G.C. Bolton, 'The Hollow Conqueror: Flax and the Foundation of Australia', *Australian Economic History Review* 8, no. 1 (March 1968): 3–16; and A.G.L. Shaw, 'The Hollow Conqueror and the Tyranny of Distance', *Historical Studies: Australia and New Zealand* 13, no.50 (April 1968): 195–203.

of Distance'. In a subsequent article, Bolton was even forced to deny that they had collaborated. Blainey replied to the former in the next issue and to the latter in the same issue, his relish for the debate being captured by the title 'A reply: I Came, I Shaw…'. The exchange unsettled Bolton, who often compared his own career with that of his contemporary Blainey, and found it hard seeing 'his own expertise in the period and knowledge of the British archives brushed aside by the Melbournian's irreverent iconoclasm'.[42]

Blainey seemed to wish to provide as large a contrast as possible between his own views and those of other historians. His recently acquired position as a tenured academic perhaps gave him greater freedom to be controversial. The lesson Blainey had been taught in 1950 from challenging Parker's views in *Historical Studies* was being re-learnt on a bigger stage. Challenging the views of others on historical matters was both intellectually stimulating and career affirming. Yet, within this debate, there was also the typical Blainey mix of vigorous argument and self-effacing manner, evident when he wrote of Shaw that 'in my opinion his article helps my interpretation as much as it hinders it, but my opinion could be wrong'.[43]

Finding new reasons for British Settlement at Botany Bay was not the only challenge to conventional views that Blainey presented in *The Tyranny of Distance*. He took issue with the orthodox assessment that the colonial officials who had allowed rail gauges to differ between jurisdictions were guilty of gross stupidity. He had accepted this view himself until he began researching the nation's transport history. Then he discovered that there was no contemporary criticism when the two colonies' different gauges met at Albury in 1883 and realised that 'we were ridiculing them because they had failed to foresee changes that came about half a century later'.[44] The nineteenth century economic reality was that products needed to be brought from the interior to coastal cities. As Blainey commented:

> The building of railways to the interior, rather than railways which linked coastal cities, was the goal and main achievement of Australian governments, and those radial routes had no broken gauges. That simple

---

42   Stuart Macintyre, 'Geoffrey Bolton: A Lifetime of History', in eds Stuart Macintyre, Lenore Layman and Jenny Gregory, *A Historian For All Seasons: Essays for Geoffrey Bolton* (Clayton: Monash University Publishing, 2017), 1–39.

43   Geoffrey Blainey, 'A reply: I Came, I Shaw…', *Historical Studies: Australia and New Zealand* 13, no. 50 (April 1968): 206.

44   Geoffrey Blainey, 'Antidotes for History', in *Historical Disciplines and Culture in Australasia* ed. John A Moses, (Brisbane: University of Queensland Press 1979), 84.

fact made the break of gauge a mild nuisance rather than a barrier for two generations.[45]

As Blainey commented in a journal article around that time, if 'you do not know a lot of the obvious things about the past you find that when you come to interpret history that the past is full of fools'.[46] Blainey was not saying that the break of gauge did not eventually create problems, but that earlier generations should not be condemned for their lack of foresight. Hence, it is hard to agree with Noel McLachlan when he complained that it was 'a little perverse (of Blainey) not to deplore them'.[47]

Blainey subsequently wrote, in a 1979 historiographical collection edited by University of Queensland historian John Moses, on the subject of challenging conventional views, or as he called them 'stock responses', to historical problems, a failing which he defined as 'the willingness to see only one side of a many-sided problem'.[48] An example of a stock response that particularly annoyed Blainey was the growing favour of what he termed the 'great fool theory' (as opposed to the previous great man theory). He observed that 'it is easy in studying technology, for example, to argue that any decision that proved to be a blunder in its long-term effects must have been the work of a fool'.[49]

The rationale for British settlement and the history of rail gauges were but two of a long list of Blainey reinterpretations in *The Tyranny of Distance*. The reader was invited to share his shock at how wrong other historians had been. Commenting on his discovery that the most popular early sea route from Sydney was via New Guinea, he observed that 'this fact has been so long forgotten that one's first impression, on realizing it, is incredulity'.[50] Similarly perplexing was that, while research showed that the existence of Bass Strait had been identified by the unnamed master of the ship 'Sydney Cove' in 1797, this reality 'has since eluded dozens of historians', who incorrectly credited the discovery to the later explorers, Bass and Flinders.[51] Another stock response Blainey rejected was the conventional view that the Blue Mountains formed a barrier to inland settlement. Instead he argued

---

45 Blainey, *The Tyranny of Distance*, 257.
46 Blainey, 'Problems of Interpretation (II)', 128.
47 Noel McLachlan, 'Our Choice for the week', *The Age*, 5 November 1966, 21.
48 Blainey, 'Antidotes for History', 84. The term 'stock responses' was earlier used by literary critic I.A. Richards to describe a reader bringing previously established judgements to the reading of a poem.
49 Blainey, 'Antidotes for History', 84.
50 Blainey, *The Tyranny of Distance*, 51.
51 Ibid, 74.

that in the first quarter century after British Settlement there had been little economic incentive to seek a crossing, a prime example for one reviewer of how Blainey, by analysing particular factors relating to transport, destroyed 'many shibboleths of Australian history'.[52]

According to Blainey, another forgotten aspect of Australian history was its inventiveness and he delighted in pointing out that an important contributor to the efficiency of steam turbines was 'the ingenuity of a young Melbourne engineer, A.G.M. Michell'.[53] Yet, his mention of Michell obviously did not have the desired impact on the public consciousness as, in his histories of Victoria published two and four decades after *Tyranny of Distance*, he lamented that Michell's name was 'virtually forgotten in his own city'.[54] *The Tyranny of Distance* also introduced its readers to 'an ingenious Scot named James Harrison' who designed and operated one of the world's first artificial ice works; pastoralist F.Y. Wolseley, creator of a sheep shearing machine; and Lawrence Hargrave who 'contributed much to the theory and technique of flight'.[55]

The fact that the reasons for Settlement contained in Chapter Two of *The Tyranny of Distance* created so much controversy tended to crowd out discussion of other sections of the book. One other front was opened up by Australian-born, American-based historian Samuel Clyde McCulloch in a review in *American Historical Review* in 1969, who argued that Blainey had failed to emphasise the decline of distance in the second half of the twentieth century.[56]

A broader critique finally came almost a decade after publication when historian John Hirst challenged different aspects of the work.[57] Hirst believed that the first section which had 'attracted the most attention from reviewers and has since been the subject of scholarly dispute' was actually 'the more satisfying section of the book'.[58] On the other hand, while accepting the detail of much of Part Two, Hirst argued that what Blainey actually demonstrated was how easily and rapidly the inland plains had been settled and integrated

---

52   Charles Bateson, 'Wrecked – And far from Home', *Australian Book Review* 6, no. 2 (December 1966–January 1967): 22.
53   Blainey, *The Tyranny of Distance*, 267–268.
54   Geoffrey Blainey, *Our Side of the Country: The Story of Victoria* (Sydney: Methuen Haynes, 1984), 177 and *A History of Victoria* (Melbourne: Cambridge University Press, 2006), 180.
55   Blainey, *The Tyranny of Distance*, 271–272, 293, 298.
56   Samuel Clyde McCulloch, review of *Tyranny of Distance*, *American Historical Review* 5, no. 74 (June 1969): 1692–1693.
57   John Hirst, 'Distance in Australia – Was It a Tyrant?', *Historical Studies* 16, no. 64 (April 1975): 435–447.
58   Ibid.

into the colonial economy. He argued that not only were Australians much more mobile than the typical residents of British villages, they moved more easily than inhabitants of other settler societies. Hirst concluded:

> From the beginning, goods, people and information have been highly mobile. Blainey's chapters speak of this movement, and it may seem churlish to object to the introductory sections and the title. However, it is my impression that the title of the book has an influence apart from the book itself. It diverts attention from the mobility which has made the Australian experience distinctive.[59]

Another to query the impact of distance has been the economic historian Ian W. McLean who noted that wool was able to be successfully exported from New South Wales from 1820 onwards, with distance from the market 'no barrier to the colonial producer'. Australia has continued to sell products worldwide and McLean argued that 'at least in this important example there is no hint that the "tyranny" of distance shaped the country's economic development'.[60]

The continuing debate about various aspects of the book was a boon for the publisher. Stonier regarded it as crucial to the early success of Sun Books, commenting that 'we were extremely fortunate that Geoffrey Blainey offered it to us in our very first year – we published it in 1966 and it has been in print ever since – surely some sort of record'.[61] The book was available to school teachers and their pupils in very quick time. Bolton has made the point that the fact that 'from the very beginning the book was available in paperback' may have been a factor in its success.[62] Its cheap price made the book highly attractive for inclusion on school syllabuses, sometimes in English instead of History.

The book's sales were also assisted by significant publicity in the newspapers. It was *The Age*'s 'Choice for the Week' and, while its review was still longer than that of the *Sydney Morning Herald*, there was a much smaller difference than there had been with previous Blainey books, indicating that he was becoming more of a national figure.[63]

---

59 Ibid.
60 Ian W. McLean, *Why Australia Prospered: The Shifting Sources of Economic Growth* (Princeton: Princeton University Press, 2013).
61 Brian Stonier, speech at the launch of an exhibition on Sun Books, Monash University library, 31 May 2005. http://monash.edu/library/collections/exhibitions/sunbooks/opening-address.html, accessed 12 August 2009.
62 Bolton, 'The Tyranny of Distance Revisited', 28.
63 McLachlan, 'Our Choice for the week'.

One factor that should not be underestimated in an assessment of the book is the title. Indeed, one could certainly mount a case that the title has had a greater impact than the arguments contained within the book. There is no doubt that the phrase 'tyranny of distance' ranks with 'the lucky country' as the phrase from the 1960s which has continued to be most constantly used, and misused. Blainey came up with the title, explaining that 'at first the feel of the words – the T juxtaposed against the D, and the repetition of the letters "n" – appealed to me more than anything'.[64] In the Preface to the 2001 edition, Blainey described the phrase as 'hyperactive' and observed that 'some people take the phrase further than it should be taken'. A few years later he expanded on this:

> When I coined the phrase ... I did not foresee how the pithy phrase would travel. The phrase had a looseness, a slightly abstract air, and that looseness enabled it to be used widely, serving all kinds of purposes. On the other hand, the imprecision in the phrase led easily to misunderstanding, and sometimes the phrase or slogan was misused.[65]

The phrase rapidly became ubiquitous, being used in a vast variety of contexts in both serious literature and popular culture, the latter best exemplified by its use in Split Enz's 1982 hit *Six Months In A Leaky Boat*, a song which has now been passed on to another generation of Australians by its inclusion on a Wiggles DVD. In 2018, Qantas CEO Alan Joyce described the purpose of the national airline as 'overcoming the tyranny of distance' and the possibility of the airline flying direct from Sydney or Melbourne to London as 'one last tyranny of distance, one last frontier in aviaation'.[66]

In Blainey's view, the concept of 'the tyranny of distance' still says something important, not just about his country's history, but about Australia in the twenty-first century, despite many commentators proclaiming its having been conquered, including English writer Frances Cairncross in her 1997 work, *The Death of Distance*. Cairncross argued that the communications revolution was rapidly reducing the influence of distance as a factor in both commercial and personal spheres. In turn, Blainey used her argument as the basis of his own reappraisal of the ongoing influence of distance in a new chapter in the

---

64   Blainey correspondence, 23 July 1979, Blainey Papers, Acc No. 80/66 Box 3, UMA.
65   Geoffrey Blainey, 'A Key to Australia's Economic Distance Dilemma', *CEDA Growth*, no. 58, July 2007, 7.
66   Patrick Hatch, 'In for the long haul', *The Age*, 22 December 2018, 14.

2001 edition of the book, titled 'Is Distance Dead?' The answer he gave was a qualified 'no':

> While distance, by some definitions, has died for Australians, it would be unwise to sign too early a certificate of death and to write the obituary. Each generation, perhaps from the 1850s onwards, was entitled to think that distance had virtually died within its living memory.[67]

Blainey explained how, at the start of the twenty-first century, distance was influencing Australia's growing services sector. However, a few years later he noted that his views on the topic were 'hardly commented on publicly by anybody in the next couple of years'.[68]

Although his recent reflections might not have cut through, the original work certainly went closer than any other Australian historian has gone to providing the sort of 'dominating or general theme' that La Nauze had sought in 1959. Historian and Prime Ministerial speech-writer, Don Watson, reflecting in 2002 on the impact of the book, argued it was 'unquestionably *one* of the half-dozen most influential of *our* last century... It is the equivalent in Australian historiography of Fred Williams or Sidney Nolan's landscapes.'[69] A couple of years later, Donald Horne coupled *Tyranny of Distance* with the first two volumes of Manning Clark's *A History of Australia*, as works which gave 'intelligent general readers their break', continuing that 'both of these successes - impelled by two quite different imaginations - achieved what had seemed previously unachievable: they encouraged people to read Australian history'.[70]

Blainey explains in his memoirs how *The Tyranny of Distance* also saw a change in his manner of providing references to his source material. He has always maintained that 'footnotes at the foot of the page were a deterrent, an intrusion, for the average reader'. Following a suggestion from historian Kathleen Fitzpatrick, from *The Tyranny of Distance* onwards, he instead began providing brief notes at the back of the book and thus 'thanks to her, mine was one of the first Australian books to display a method that now is commonplace'.[71]

---

67 Geoffrey Blainey, *The Tyranny of Distance: How Distance Shaped Australia's History* (Sydney: Pan Macmillan, 2001), 361.
68 Blainey, 'A Key to Australia's Economic Distance Dilemma', 8.
69 Don Watson, 'The untamed tyrant', *Sydney Morning Herald* (Spectrum section), 16-17 February 2002, 4. Italics in original.
70 Donald Horne, 'We should be so lucky', *Sydney Morning Herald*, 21 August 2004, 47.
71 Blainey, *Before I Forget*, 302.

At the same time that Blainey was producing major works such as *The Tyranny of Distance* he still felt obligated to accept certain commissions. With its centenary approaching, his old school Wesley College wanted its history written and, unsurprisingly, approached Blainey. To reduce the size of the task, Blainey enlisted two fellow old boys and friends, James Morrissey ('Old Centre' from Blainey's *Farrago* days) and S.E.K. Hulme, as co-authors. Their qualifications were as barristers 'with strong literary interests'.[72]

Blainey wrote the four chapters relating to the nineteenth century, which made up approximately forty per cent of the book and was assigned the role of general editor. As he had previously demonstrated when writing about the University of Melbourne, Blainey was no sycophant himself when it came to his alma maters. A mildly anti-authoritarian tone pervaded much of his four chapters. Blainey recognised that the sources for writing school history are likely to emphasise those for whom school was a successful experience. He commented that it is not possible for the modern historian to 'gauge today what influences, for good or bad' the school had on its students.[73] Blainey was keen to avoid his work being just a tribute to the obviously successful, but it was hard to assess 'what the average boy thought of [headmaster] Irving and what he gained from him and his school remain partly a mystery'.[74] Similarly, the everyday details of school life evaded the modern historian partly because things that, at the time, seemed commonplace were not recorded. Deprived of the crucial information of how students experienced their school life, Blainey believed 'most histories of schools describe the bottle rather than its contents'.[75] He clearly had a preference for the school's early years when 'successive headmasters tried to make the energetic scholar rather than the champion sportsman the idol of the school'.[76] Over-emphasising the importance of school sport was highlighted by the story of former Wesley sports star, Harry Hughes, working in 1903 as a bank clerk in Darwin, 'one of the most isolated and dreary places in Australia', who received school sporting results by costly telegram and proudly pinned them on the noticeboard.[77]

---

72   Geoffrey Blainey, S.E.K. Hulme & James Morrissey, *Wesley College: The First Hundred Years* (Melbourne: Wesley College in association with Robertson & Mullens, 1967), 5.
73   Ibid., 27.
74   Ibid., 53.
75   Ibid., 27.
76   Ibid., 70.
77   Ibid., 79.

While it is understandable that Blainey felt an obligation to take on a job such as the Wesley one, it is harder to see what prompted him to accept a commission to write a history of Jaques Limited, a Melbourne-based company, established in 1885, that made crushing equipment for the mining and quarrying industries. The facade of the building that Jaques operated from in inner-suburban Richmond remains as a testament to the history of Jaques, but the only known copy of the draft of Blainey's history, which he forwarded to the company in January 1964, is hidden in his papers at the University of Melbourne Archives.[78] Given this comment from Blainey in the Preface, it is perhaps understandable that the company decided against publishing:

> A large part of this history had to be compiled from meagre evidence, and for these reasons it is impossible to say a lot of things that should be put in a historical record. Likewise I've put down a lot of things that are of sparse interest to anyone outside the firm; if those things were not put down, there would have been little else to write about in long periods of the history.[79]

Blainey has acknowledged that he was too willing to accept the offers which came his way:

> Looking back I can see now that I made a serious mistake. I responded too often to invitations from publishers and editors to write this book or that article. Instead I should have been blazing my own track in the direction that I wished to travel.[80]

Loyalty to friends in the mining industry, prompted Blainey to write other books in the 1960s, such as a biography of former BHP boss Essington Lewis, published as *The Steel Master: A Life of Essington Lewis* (1971) and a detailed study of another major Australian mining field, Broken Hill, *The Rise of Broken Hill* (1968).[81]

Blainey made no attempt to hide the fact that he experienced difficulties writing Lewis' life story, confessing in the Acknowledgements that he 'found it difficult to write this book'. However, he was more circumspect about why it had been difficult and what caused a lengthy delay between 1968, when

---

78 Unpublished manuscript, Blainey Papers, Acc. No. 89/145 Box 17, UMA.
79 Ibid.
80 Blainey, *Before I Forget*, 260.
81 Geoffrey Blainey, *The Steel Master: A Life of Essington Lewis* (Melbourne: Macmillan, 1971); and Geoffrey Blainey, *The Rise of Broken Hill* (Melbourne: Macmillan, 1968).

it was almost complete, and its 1971 publication. According to Humphrey McQueen, the reason was a dispute between BHP and Blainey. McQueen alleged that the company did not want any mention of Lewis' womanising, but that Blainey believed that this was an important aspect of Lewis' personality which helped explain his business career.[82] Blainey emphatically denies that any such dispute occurred.[83]

Writing about Lewis the man was certainly a difficult task for, although his 57-year involvement with BHP was well documented, material relating to the life of Lewis himself was hard to find, largely because Lewis avoided publicity and rarely reminisced.[84] The most significant non-BHP activity in Lewis' life was holding the position of Director-General of Munitions during the Second World War. Blainey set the scene for Lewis' appointment to this position by highlighting some of his pre-existing views about the role of government. Thus, the reader can appreciate the irony of Lewis' role as the supremo of 'big government', having traced his views on the evils of government economic intervention.

Another section of BHP had engaged their own senior economist, Neville Wills, to write a history of the company and, while he failed to do this, he did review *The Steel Master*.[85] Wills had several complaints about Blainey's work, including that he was too respectful of Lewis and his reputation. However, one can hardly sustain the accusation of sugar coating Lewis when Blainey presented 'the unbiased opinion of Walter Duncan and other friends that Lewis was the rudest man they had ever met', or the implicit criticism of a daughter who said that being the wife of Lewis was like living on the edge of a volcano.[86] Further, Blainey criticised certain aspects of Lewis' handling of the company, such as his failure to invest in research.[87] One of Blainey's most perceptive comments about Lewis' personality came when he observed that 'the characteristic which stood out was his certainty about how much he could accomplish'. Blainey continued:

> This led some friends to say he was an optimist, and in one sense he was. He was not optimistic in his view of human nature and he was not

---

82 McQueen, *Suspect History*, 192.
83 Note supplied to the author by Geoffrey Blainey, 7 June 2012.
84 Blainey, *The Steel Master*, 201.
85 Neville Wills, review of *The Steel Master*, The Australian Quarterly, no. 46 (December 1974): 105.
86 Blainey, *The Steel Master*, 183–188.
87 Ibid., 80.

optimistic that events would work in his favour, but he was remarkably assured in handling any problem of construction or production.[88]

It was typical Blainey to try to seek to point out contradictions; in contrast, a critic like Wills seemed to want black or white characterizations. Combine this Blainey ability to draw nuanced character sketches with what even Wills acknowledged as a 'great gift of style' and one clearly has significant potential as a biographer.[89] And, within the limitations imposed, Blainey had produced a highly readable biography. However, *The Steel Master* has remained a one-off, with the only subsequent Blainey book getting close to biography being his 2008 *Sea of Dangers* about the voyages of Captain Cook.

Those who read Blainey's books and enjoy his ability to capture the appearance and character of a person with a handful of pithy words may wonder why a writer with an apparent interest in individuals, and an acute ability to describe them, has only written one full-length biography, and a small number of shorter biographical works, in his prolific writing career.[90]

Asked in 1968 why he tended to avoid writing biography he replied that he was 'not so intensely interested in the man that I want to know in full detail why and how, over the years, he developed into the kind of man who was predisposed to behave this way or that'.[91] He saw himself as 'more competent at seeing and trying to explain changes in a society, than in a particular individual' and believed that 'the two tasks seem to require different techniques and talents'.[92]

Blainey's attitude towards biography highlights an important part about his approach to history. It is a long way removed from 'great men' style history; it is a history where material factors of landscape, geography and climate are emphasised, and individuals tend to have cameo roles where they make transitory impacts (more lasting if they invent new technology) and whose main contribution to the text is often their literary colour as much as their historical significance. Blainey is much more concerned with his characters actions, than their motivations. As already noted, Blainey has stated that he rarely read novels and his aversion to biography seems to stem from a similar lack of interest in exploring people's inner lives. It has also been notable in

---

88   Ibid.
89   Wills, review of *The Steel Master*.
90   An example of the latter is a chapter on Patrick Hannan which Blainey contributed to a 1979 book called *Westralian Portraits*, one of only three of over 40 chapters to be penned by non-Western Australians.
91   Stuart Sayers, 'A Vivacious Writer', *The Age*, 22 June 1968, 11.
92   Ibid.

his reflections on his own life, which rarely stray into the realm of his feelings or emotions.

In 1966, Blainey queried why a biography of a significant individual such as Governor Macquarie or Alfred Deakin was often considered a bigger topic than a history of 'a small community spread over six generations and perhaps embracing a total of 5,000 people'.[93] He reinforced the point two years later, saying that 'broad forces affect our destinies more than individuals'.[94] They are revealing comments for, as Stuart Macintyre has explained, those historians who in this period were rejecting biography's 'exaggeration of human agency' were often Marxists or followers of the *Annales* school.[95]

The *Annales* school was an influential French school of history, founded by Lucien Fevre and Marc Bloch, and continued by Fernand Braudel, which promoted the detailed study of ordinary peoples' lives and the impact of geography and climate, rather than the actions of leaders, and certainly there are similarities between it and Blainey, both in choice of topics and analysis of historical causation.

While the Lewis biography remained 'in manuscript', the Australasian Institute of Mining and Metallurgy commissioned Blainey to write a history of Broken Hill to commemorate the seventy-fifth anniversary of the organisation's founding on that field in 1893. The resultant work, *The Rise of Broken Hill*, was a shorter book than Blainey's earlier mining histories and he commented that 'it is perhaps more a volume of essays than an orthodox history'.[96] The focus was on the period until the 1920s; subsequent events are summarised in an eight-page epilogue.

Shortly before the First World War, Broken Hill, with a population of close to 35,000, was the tenth largest city in Australia. Its impact on Australians was perhaps even greater than that figure would indicate as, due to its high itinerant population, many more citizens had some experience of it.[97] To indicate the range of men who worked the field Blainey listed a diverse foursome of future politician Ted Theodore, poet C.J. Dennis, industrialist Essington Lewis and Mt Isa founder Campbell Miles.[98] Another visitor to the field was

---

93   Blainey, "Problems of Interpretation (II)", 124.
94   Sayers, 'A Vivacious Writer'.
95   Stuart Macintyre, 'Biography' in *The Oxford Companion to Australian History*, eds. G. Davison, J. Hirst & S. Macintyre, with the assistance of H. Doyle and K. Torney,(Melbourne: Oxford University Press, 1998, 2001), 71.
96   Blainey, *The Rise of Broken Hill*, 9.
97   Ibid., 122.
98   Ibid., 112–113.

future US President, Herbert Hoover.[99] By the time Blainey wrote this book, the population was just over 30,000 and growth elsewhere had seen it slide down the rankings. Moreover, it had a far more stable population and careers were more specialised, so its alumni were less likely to rise to prominence in other locations and occupations.

A distinguishing feature of *The Rise of Broken Hill* was that it gave greater weight to industrial relations than Blainey's previous mining histories, and there was quite a degree of sympathy towards unions and more than the usual quota of criticism of mining companies. This led McQueen to describe it as 'the book which does most to confirm the Left's pre-1984 view of Blainey as a democrat, though not a radical'.[100] However, Blainey was critical of the methods of others in the field as he believed that 'Australian historians so far have studied more the politics of trade unionism and industrial conflicts than the living and working conditions from which these conflicts often emerge'.[101] Blainey summed up his position at the end of his lengthy chapter 'The Fight', which considered the sequences of strikes culminating in the 'Long Strike' of 1919-20:

> The forces working for friction at Broken Hill were strong and unusual and in the context and attitudes of the times, were difficult to remedy. It is therefore unwise to apportion too much blame on the leaders of either the unions or the mines for the industrial unrest and the ultimate solution.[102]

Blainey asserted that, in the years leading up to the 'Long Strike', it would have been 'in the companies' interests to be more generous' and regretted that 'the genius which the companies had displayed in solving their metallurgical and marketing problems was invisible when they faced labour problems'.[103] Militant unionists who were members of the Industrial Workers of the World should be treated tolerantly by history on the grounds that 'there was more shine on socialism then … [and] there were also more scars on capitalism'.[104]

On the other hand, Blainey continued to display some sympathy for the forces of capital, pointing out that in the first thirty-five years of operation

---

99 Ibid., 73. Blainey does not actually mention Hoover becoming President, being content to refer to his entry to 'public life in World War I'.
100 McQueen, *Suspect History*, 196.
101 Blainey, *The Rise of Broken Hill*, 88.
102 Ibid., 152.
103 Ibid., 133.
104 Ibid., 125.

in Broken Hill only twenty per cent of the 106 million pounds of production went into dividends to shareholders. The other eighty per cent went into the pockets of workers and secondary suppliers. He was also keen to stress the broader role of the Broken Hill mining companies in the Australian economy and in particular the economy of South Australia.[105] Blainey made perceptive observations about factors which distinguished the silver miners of Broken Hill, who did not settle there, from the gold miners of Ballarat who did.[106] Hence, the founders of Broken Hill played no role in beautifying the city or providing civic infrastructure. 'The Broken Hillionaires' were not philanthropists, did not join exclusive clubs and were never knighted. Instead they were big spenders with earthy interests. Blainey defined them as 'entrepreneurs, not capitalists'.[107]

The Rise of Broken Hill was not just a mining history but a social history of the broader Broken Hill community. Blainey's consideration of living conditions was aided by a list of weekly expenses submitted by the wife of a miner to Justice Higgins' Arbitration Court in 1909 and he eagerly reprinted the list of individual grocery items. Reeling off a list was a regular Blainey device. Earlier in the book, Blainey had informed readers that in April 1886 Broken Hill had '30 tents, 23 houses, 15 huts, 3 hotels, 2 blacksmith's shops, 1 general store, and a few sheds and humpies'.[108]

Blainey also never missed the chance to deliver a colourful description, even if it was somewhat tangential to the main purpose of the book. The adventures of the widow of one of the founders of BHP, Charles Rasp, were irrelevant to what was happening in Broken Hill at the time, but only the most churlish reader would have felt aggrieved at Blainey's consideration of the question of 'how this colonial woman of fifty-five, once pretty but now massive, gained entry to the highest society of Europe ... even allowing for her willingness to pay'.[109] Places could be described as evocatively as people. The range of hotels in newly settled Broken Hill in 1888 stretched from ones with delusions of grandeur which had 'dining room menus written in French – though not the French of Paris' through to hotels made from corrugated iron which 'sold warm beer and displayed shorter menus in English – though not the English of Oxford'.[110]

---

105   Ibid., 46–47.
106   Ibid., 43.
107   Ibid., 45.
108   Ibid., 27.
109   Ibid., 35.
110   Ibid., 27.

Although busy on assorted commissions in the mid to late-1960s, Blainey continued to contribute to economic history journals. The fact that he included contemporary public policy in his writing meant that he had the potential to enter political debates, and this happened after he penned an article titled 'The Cargo Cult in Mineral Policy' for the *Economic Record* in 1968.[111] It detailed how the ban on iron ore exports imposed by successive Australian Governments had constrained mineral discoveries and explained that a similar policy was now affecting uranium.

Blainey's journal article was cited in a *Financial Review* editorial in February 1969, sparking a lively exchange in the paper's letters page between the responsible Gorton Government Minister, David Fairbairn, and Blainey. Fairbairn did not share the newspaper's belief that Blainey exhibited 'a refreshing talent for searching for the reasons behind history and behind policy'. Instead, he described Blainey's article as a 'quite fallacious attack' and denied that the Government's policies were failing.[112] In turn, Blainey responded that Fairbairn had 'sincerely reaffirmed his belief that a mineral discovery was often a mysterious cargo falling from the sky'.[113] Blainey said that the policy options were either to search vigorously for new mining fields, or to hoard the existing known deposits. He argued that if the Government really believed in the latter policy, it should also be applied to industries other than mining.

Apart from his books and articles on economic or general history, one piece of Blainey's writing from the period stands out. In 1966-67, *Meanjin* commissioned prominent Australian intellectuals to write a series of articles entitled 'Godzone', described by the journal as a 'series of commentaries on the reality of present-day life and living in God's own country'.[114] Blainey was the last of seven writers, the others having been Ian Turner, Owen Webster, Allan Ashbolt, Noel McLachlan, J.D.B. Miller and Geoffrey Serle. Blainey believed that the others had been too pessimistic:

---

111 Geoffrey Blainey, 'Mining – And Undermining', *Economic Record* 44, (December 1968): 470-479.

112 David Fairbairn, 'Cargo cult that works', *Australian Financial Review*, 18 February 1969, 3. As an aside, it is amusing for an observer of politics in the 21st century to note the leisurely pace of the media cycle in the 1960s. The Minister's letter appeared twelve days after the editorial and began with the words that 'my attention has been drawn to your editorial'. Today, a Minister who was not aware of an editorial in a major newspaper, critical of a policy in his or her portfolio, by 7 a.m. on the morning of publication, would be regarded as slack.

113 Geoffrey Blainey, 'Mr Fairbairn and the cargo cult' (letter to the editor), *Australian Financial Review*, 27 February 1969, 3.

114 *Meanjin Quarterly* 25, no. 2 (June 1966): 133.

The pessimists fired most of the rounds; bursts of inspired accuracy were followed by sacrificial shots at their own feet. It was almost as if they wished to be whisked away to those utopias which they vaguely glimpsed in the future or saw more confidently in the past. Indeed their belief that the times had once been more promising seemed to make the 1960s even more disillusioning, and their pessimistic view of the present seemed to gild the past. At least I assume that their age of gloom and their age of gold were linked, for I'm not sure that I have lived in the Australia of the 1960s and I do not recognize the golden ages which they safely enshrined in the past.[115]

Blainey pointed out that whatever were the faults of modern industrial society its citizens were likely to work for shorter hours, have greater certainty of food supply, better family planning and were more likely to be literate than their pre-industrial forebears. Similarly, there was far more political freedom in 1966 than in 1766.

Several of the previous contributions had been notable for their anti-Americanism. This was something which Blainey felt could be useful in small doses but, when exaggerated, was as irrational as the actions of the slavish followers of American culture. Blainey analysed in some detail the arguments of Serle that Australia was becoming a satellite of the United States, arguing instead that 'Australia is more independent than at any time in its history', and that 'in the last generation Australia's *economic independence* ... has probably advanced at a swifter pace than in any other generation of Australian history'.[116]

Blainey took issue with the glib assumption that material progress for working men can only come from the struggles of organised labour, noting that 'many followers of the legend are slightly incredulous that the Menzies era should have been accompanied by increasing comfort for workingmen'. Blainey did not particularly ascribe credit to Menzies or his Government as 'no single governing party in Australia has had a monopoly of material progress, partly because the economic policies of successive governments have had too many similarities, but more because the scientist and the technologist have been more creative than the politicians'.[117]

Although Blainey was far more optimistic than the other contributors in the 'Godzone' series, there was one slightly pessimistic note that came near

---

115   Geoffrey Blainey, 'Godzone: 7) The New Australia: A Legend of the Lake', *Meanjin Quarterly* 26, no. 4 (December 1967): 365–366.
116   Ibid., 368–369.
117   Ibid., 378.

the conclusion of his article, when he suggested that 'democracy could be a more flourishing plant in Australia'.[118] He argued that while the Vietnam War was an attempt to export democracy overseas, there had been no attempts to add to democracy at home. Unlike choice in consumer goods, which had grown enormously in the twentieth century, there had been no attempts to add to the democratic gains of the nineteenth century. In contrast to some of the other contributors, Blainey appreciated the federal system, arguing that it gave electors a wider choice and provided citizens with twice as many elections as a unitary state. Additionally, Blainey suggested a major reform proposal of his own, arguing that 'the most practicable, immediate remedy for the antiquated form of democracy we practice is probably the initiative referendum'.[119]

While there is a touch of pessimism in his view of the state of democracy in 1967, and about the prospects for reform, the stance that Blainey was taking was an optimistic and liberal one. However, within a few years, Blainey's position seemed to be evolving more towards pessimism and conservatism. A key factor was his growing interest in global rather than purely Australian matters.

---

118   Ibid.
119   Ibid., 379.

Chapter 4

BROADENING HORIZONS

Blainey was overseas when *The Tyranny of Distance* first appeared in the bookshops in the second half of 1966. This might surprise some readers. After all, Blainey had shown no interest in joining his contemporaries in postgraduate study at a British university and, since then, had shown little inclination to head overseas, or to contemplate non-Australian historical topics.

Beginning his academic career in the early 1960s, Blainey remained a historian largely focused on Australia. His direct academic responsibilities did not immediately alter this. It was not until he became Professor of Economic History in 1968 that he first taught anything other than the economic history of his own country. However, becoming an academic did play a role in pushing Blainey's interests beyond his own nation. Firstly, it prompted Blainey to not just write more journal articles but to begin doing so for overseas journals in the economic and business history fields.

Initially, he wrote on Australian topics, such as reviewing Sydney Butlin's history of the ANZ Bank for the American journal, *The Business History Review*.[1] However, before long, Blainey published his first article on a non-Australian topic. It was prompted by his attending a lecture on imperialism in South Africa at the University of Adelaide in late 1961. When the lecturer referred to the Jameson Raid, a failed attempt to gain control of the Transvaal goldfields, Blainey's own exploration of the factors which contributed to the Eureka Stockade immediately came to mind. He wondered if similar reasons could be found for what made miners either supporters or opponents of Jameson's action. So he spent some time in the summer of 1963-64 doing research in the National Library in Canberra, which had the relevant South African newspapers from 1895-96. Normally, Blainey would want to see the physical landscape and assess its impact on historical events but, as he could not see the Transvaal, he 'read geological maps very carefully and tried

---

1   Geoffrey Blainey, review of *Australia and New Zealand Bank: The Bank of Australasia and the Union Bank of Australia Limited 1828–1951* by S.J. Butlin, *The Business History Review* 37. No. 3, (Autumn 1963): 300–302.

to imagine the surface terrain and the geological terrain', although such imaginings were 'no substitute for a visit'.[2]

'Lost Causes of the Jameson Raid', published in the English journal *The Economic History Review* in 1965, proposed a radically different interpretation of an important event in South African history.[3] The aim of the December 1895 raid, led by Leander Starr Jameson, was to overthrow the Boer Government of Kruger in the Transvaal and replace it with one more amenable to Jameson's close associate, the Prime Minister of the Cape, Cecil Rhodes, and the new ultra-imperialist British Colonial Secretary, Joseph Chamberlain. Most historical discussion of the Raid had concentrated on political causes but, according to Blainey, important economic factors had been overlooked. The causes that earlier historians had 'lost' were the different economic interests of outcrop and deep-level miners, these interests producing loyalists and rebels respectively, with Blainey asserting that earlier historians had not recognised the significance of the large investments that were being made in the deep level mines in 1894 and 1895.[4]

When one made a large investment, one was likely to be upset if that investment was placed in jeopardy. Blainey identified a range of grievances that affected the deep-level miners more than the outcrop miners, some due to the inherent differences in their mining practices, and some due to explicit discrimination. Grievances identified by Blainey included the high costs of dynamite and coal, the supply and cost of native labour, restrictions on where deep-level mines could be sunk, and taxation. Blainey presented a very similar argument to the one he was making at the same time about the reasons for British settlement of Australia, arguing that 'there were many facts and assumptions that were so obvious to the mining leaders of 1895 that they did not write or speak about them; and the obvious facts were often the important ones'.[5]

Blainey's article has maintained a place in South African historiography. The Melbourne-based crime writer, Peter Temple, who grew up in South Africa, once described how 'history students in South Africa used to spend hours arguing about what was known as the "Blainey thesis" on outcrop & deep

---

2 Blainey correspondence, 12 October 1979, Blainey Papers, Acc. No. 80/17 Box 6, UMA.
3 G. Blainey, 'Lost Causes of the Jameson Raid', *The Economic History Review* 18, no. 2 (August 1965): 350–366.
4 Ibid., 355.
5 Ibid., 361.

level mining interests'.[6] Despite its impact, Blainey's article was very much a one-off contribution. One South African historian, Richard Mendelsohn has noted that 'it is ironic that the most suggestive and influential contribution of the past decade to the historiography of the late nineteenth century Transvaal has been that of an Australian filibuster who made a lightening sortie into the territory and then retreated into silence'.[7]

While some South African historians have found merit in Blainey's argument, others have strongly criticised it. Donald Denoon, later a professor at the Australian National University, wrote to Blainey from his post in Uganda, enclosing a copy of an article he had submitted to the Cambridge *Historical Journal*. The article noted his 'direct obligation' to Blainey for having provided 'the essential clue which made it possible to reconcile apparent contradictions in the available evidence'.[8] In the covering letter, he expressed his 'indebtedness to you, for the ideas and information you published in "Lost Causes"', adding that 'without that article, I doubt I would ever have made sense of my own subject'.[9] A few years later, Denoon co-authored a book called *Southern Africa since 1800* (1972, 1984) which, in discussing the Jameson Raid, set out the clear difference in the economic interests of surface and deep level miners. The book argued that the deep level miners could not admit that they were overthrowing the Government out of financial self-interest, and so had to dress their rationale up with a lot of political rhetoric, which other scholars had taken at face value.[10]

On the other hand, in 1995 Elaine N. Katz used the same journal in which Blainey sparked the argument thirty years earlier to try to demolish his theory, asserting that 'the abandonment of the Blainey thesis is long overdue: the "outcrop/deep level theory" has no validity at the level of either ownership or production'.[11] In 2000, the then 35-year-long debate was summed up in a general history of South Africa with the comment that 'Geoffrey Blainey set

---

6   Peter Temple to Blainey, 25 July 1983, Blainey Papers, Acc. No. 89/145 Box 35, UMA.
7   Richard Mendelsohn, 'Blainey and the Jameson Raid: The Debate Renewed', *Journal of Southern African Studies* 6, no. 2 (April 1980): 157.
8   D.J.N. Denoon, '"Capitalist Influence" and the Transvaal Government During the Crown Colony Period, 1900–1906', *The Historical Journal* 11, no. 2, (1968): 301–331.
9   Donald Denoon to Blainey, 17 January 1968, Blainey Papers, Acc. No. 89/145 Box 11, UMA.
10 Donald Denoon with Balam Nyeko and the advice of J.B. Webster, *Southern Africa since 1800* (London: Longman, 1972, 1984), 101.
11 Elaine N. Katz, 'Outcrop and deep level mining in South Africa before the Anglo-Boer War: re-examining the Blainey thesis', *The Economic History Review* (second series) 48, no. 2 (May 1995): 326.

in motion a debate which has helped to clarify the motivation and tactics of individual Randlords'.[12]

As with his foray into South African history, Blainey's first trip overseas to undertake historical research (indeed, his first trip out of the country for any reason) arose from his role as historian of the Australian mining industry. W.S. Robinson, a leading Australian businessman with interests in mining companies, died in September 1963 leaving behind partially completed memoirs. Robinson's literary executors, who included Maurie Mawby, asked Blainey if he would complete them.

Thinking the task would be reasonably straightforward, Blainey agreed to do it, but after a year he had to explain to Mawby that the task was bigger than he had anticipated.[13] The extent of the ghosting made Blainey reflect that the book may have been better written as a biography.[14] The choice of title was also an issue. Blainey objected so strongly to the publisher's proposed title of 'The Friendly Force' (on the grounds that it was inconsistent to use a third-person description on memoirs) that he wrote to his friend Mawby and said that, if the title was used, he would not allow his name 'to be publicly associated with the book'.[15] In the end, the title used was the one which Robinson himself had intended, *If I Remember Rightly: The Memoirs of W.S. Robinson*.[16]

As part of his Robinson research, Blainey travelled overseas for the first time, going to Europe and the United States in the Australian summer of 1964-65 to interview people who had known Robinson. In the middle of the following year he used a period of sabbatical leave to again head overseas, choosing the most unconventional method of travelling to London of flying to

---

12 Rodney Davenport and Christopher Saunders, *South Africa: A Modern History*, (Basingstoke: Macmillan, 5th edition, 2000), 98. There is an Australian connection to the genesis of this work, the first edition of which was published in 1977. The author wrote in the Acknowledgements to the 5th edition that 'this *History* was originally conceived in 1966 when Sir Keith Hancock, who held a visiting fellowship at Rhodes to work on the second volume of *Smuts*, regretted the absence of an up-to-date twentieth century History of South Africa to provide a back drop for his own work'.

13 Blainey to Maurie Mawby, 28 September 1965, Blainey Papers, Acc. No. 89/145 Box 11, UMA.

14 Blainey to Barton Maughan, 24 March 1966, Blainey Papers, Acc. No. 89/145 Box 11, UMA.

15 Blainey to Maurie Mawby, 9 and 27 May 1967, Blainey Papers, Acc. No. 89/145 Box 11, UMA.

16 W.S. Robinson, *If I Remember Rightly: The Memoirs of W.S. Robinson 1876–1963*, ed. by Geoffrey Blainey (Melbourne: Cheshire, 1967).

Hong Kong, and then travelling by train across Communist China and the Soviet Union.

Traversing mainland China was a rare venture for a westerner to do in 1966. It was the height of the Cultural Revolution and there were very few foreigners visiting. Typically, Blainey decided that he should write about what he had seen, but unusually for him, he was a little slow in getting the writing job done. Instead, he spent several months travelling round Britain and Europe, when getting the book written and published quickly may have increased its impact. In the end, *Across a Red World* did not appear until 1968.[17]

Writing up one's own travels is a different exercise to writing a work of history or biography. It allows more scope for a writer to include the personal, which Blainey did:

> When a passenger was kind to me or tried to communicate I felt for an instant inexpressibly sad. I doubt if this was a high-minded feeling, a sadness at the barriers erected to prevent human contact. It was echoingly like the memory of a trivial incident of childhood, such as not receiving, by an oversight, a cake or prize when every other child got one. [18]

Reflecting on the book a few years after its publication, Blainey believed that this intrusion of the personal meant that this book 'probably reveals more about me than anything I've written ... you can't keep yourself out of a travel book even if you try'.[19] Blainey appreciated that personal experience can all too easily shape opinions of a country (he cites rude New Yorkers or cheerful Italians) and that it becomes 'dangerously easy' to equate one's own degree of enjoyment as a traveller with what it would be like to live in a particular country. It was a particular problem in China, which was 'a paradise for those allowed to visit it'.[20] By contrast, some of the logistics in Russia left Blainey lamenting that 'mishaps of man and nature seemed unusually common in Russia'.[21]

Blainey's style was well suited to the travelogue. In its review, the *Times Literary Supplement* praised Blainey for 'acute observation and a broad-minded outlook ... thought-provoking reflections ... graphic and delightfully written

---

17   Geoffrey Blainey, *Across a Red World* (Melbourne: Macmillan, 1968).
18   Ibid., 135.
19   Blainey correspondence, 5 January 1972, Blainey Papers, MS 9225/4/12 Box 23, NLA.
20   Blainey, *Across a Red World*, 89.
21   Ibid., 125.

descriptions'.[22] There were endless opportunities for one-paragraph descriptions of people and places. He was skilfully able to link physical and personal descriptions to make political points, such as when he wondered 'where else in the world the inner streets of a city of two million people could be swept so clean of stray leaves and stray people'.[23]

Blainey also appreciated that it is easy to go along with a crowd and feel empathy for a political crusade. He described a rousing speech before the ballet at a theatre in Peking (Beijing), writing that he had 'no idea what the slogans were that they chanted so briskly, and yet the atmosphere was so electrifying that one's reaction was a slight unease at being unable to join in and a feeling of exhilaration such as idle spectators must have felt when Hitler spoke in Berlin or the evangelist Moody spoke in New York'.[24]

There often appeared to be a battle taking place throughout the book between Blainey's desire to be fair and his belief that democratic capitalism was a better system than communism. Unlike many supporters of democratic capitalism, he did not automatically assume that, offered greater freedom, the residents of authoritarian communist countries would necessarily embrace it. He commented that 'one could not be certain that, if rival parties were suddenly tolerated in Russia, a communist party in one form or another would not win a free election'.[25] Blainey's 'even-handedness' certainly appealed to some reviewers. The *Times Literary Supplement*'s critic commented that 'unlike many detractors of communism's so-called democratic practices, Mr Blainey does not resort to exaggerated praise for parallel practices in the capitalist West'.[26] While it was true that Blainey queried the degree of freedom of choice provided by the democratic system in the West, he did also recognise that, when it came to economic freedom, the West did better:

> Trust in the people's judgement in Britain, the United States, and many parliamentary democracies tends to be extended more freely in shops than in polling booths, more freely in commodities than ideas. Similarly the dishonoured promise of a politician is viewed much less seriously than the dishonoured promise of a salesman.[27]

---

22 G.E. Wheeler, 'From East to West', *Times Literary Supplement*, Issue 3497, 6 March 1969, 224.
23 Blainey, *Across a Red World*, 18.
24 Ibid., 68.
25 Ibid., 120.
26 Wheeler, 'From East to West'.
27 Blainey, *Across a Red World*, 121.

Across a Red World contained the unusual suggestion that there could be value in conducting 'a massive, international investigation by sociologists and psychologists' to determine whether Russian Communism was really delivering on objectives 'to increase contentment or personal fulfilment, to reduce emotional ailments and personal tensions and to make life more satisfying'.[28] Blainey argued that there had been much debate about the two systems' relative abilities to produce material wealth, but little on the 'human effect' and believed that it was a waste to have an 'enormous laboratory' and then conduct 'no independent tests'. However, as part of this discussion, Blainey also argued that the differences between the West and Russia have been exaggerated:

> So many apologists for Russia and for western democracies see themselves standing on opposite ends of a deep gorge, with only the slenderest plank bridge crossing the gap. In fact the gap is more a valley than a gorge and the bridges are many, and the slope is so gentle that no bridge is needed.[29]

This seems to have been a period of Blainey's life when he felt that differences between seemingly polar opposite political views could be overcome. Written at a similar time, his biography of Essington Lewis described how many Labor politicians who had attacked Lewis in the lead-up to the Second World War came to admire him when they got to know him through the war effort and similarly he came to appreciate their qualities.[30]

Reprising one of his favourite themes, Blainey suggested that geography ('a vast area containing a large population') was an important factor in why the Communists succeeded in coming to power in Russia and China, rather than elsewhere. He argued that 'the interplay of size with other factors may well have been decisive in achieving communist rule in the two large countries of the communist zone'.[31] This being only Blainey's second overseas trip, it was probably understandable that geographic comparisons with his own homeland came to his mind, such as a surveillance tower on the Chinese-Mongolian border which was 'like a fire-spotting post in the Australian countryside'.[32]

Geographic analogies were not the only stylistic device Blainey used. He also inserted humorous asides. When he crossed the border from Hong Kong

---

28   Ibid., 182–183.
29   Ibid., 183.
30   Blainey, *The Steel Master*, 177.
31   Blainey, *Across a Red World*, 187.
32   Ibid, 92.

to China and saw two Chinese soldiers standing 'very casually', he suggested that 'if they had been actors in a film the producer would have denounced them for their apathy'.[33] Another device Blainey deployed was the self-deprecatory comment such as when his inquisitive English-practising Chinese guide asked for the English name of various trees and shrubs in the park and Blainey observed that 'my ignorance soon cut that line of conversation'.[34]

Several writers have drawn comparisons between *Across a Red World*, and Manning Clark's *Meeting Soviet Man*. Some have observed the differences; for instance, Graeme Davison commented that Blainey described 'a bleaker, more rigid society than Manning Clark had found a decade earlier'.[35] Others have been keen to stress similarities. Given the nature of some of the allegations made after Clark's death about his closeness to the Soviet regime, attempts were made to use *Across a Red World* as an exhibit in Clark's defence. Hence, Humphrey McQueen wrote in 1997:

> Implicit in the *Courier-Mail*'s treatment of Clark is the assumption that to visit the Soviet Union between 1917 and 1991 was improper, indeed sinister... By the *Courier-Mail's* reckoning, Blainey should not have gone on this expedition. While he was in China and the USSR, their governments were competing with each other to supply the Vietnamese with weapons to kill Australian troops.[36]

McQueen made the point that, although no one 'would mistake him for a fellow traveller or a dupe', Blainey also 'did not colour incidents to pander to prejudices about the repressiveness of the regime'.[37] On the other hand, it would be easy for a reader coming from a less left-wing perspective than McQueen to worry that the book provides too little acknowledgement of the repressive nature of Mao's regime and the widespread famine induced by government policy, although admittedly the full details of this horror took some years to emerge.

While re-reading Blainey for ammunition in later debates became a popular pastime, there were also more subtle guides to shifts in his intellectual outlook in the works of this period. *Across a Red World* contained some of the first seeds of the pessimism about the direction of western society that, as the 1970s

---

33　Ibid., 12.
34　Ibid., 19.
35　Davison, 'Blainey', *Oxford History*, 75.
36　McQueen, *Suspect History*, 91–92.
37　Ibid., 92.

progressed, was to force its way into Blainey's outlook at the expense of his fundamental optimism. He was concerned that 'the stagnation, even decline, of democracy in many of its traditional strongholds during a long period of rising education and startling improvements in communicating ideas and knowledge may someday be seen as far more regrettable than the fact that in some nations communism had taken over from another form of autocracy'.[38]

Clearly, Blainey felt something troubling was taking place in Western societies. The West was certainly entering a period of rapid social change and the epicentre of the change was university campuses. Blainey's Melbourne University did not see the sort of violent confrontation that took place on some campuses in the United States, nor did it quite match the radicalism displayed at the newer Monash University in Melbourne's south-eastern suburbs, but the changes were dramatic and sudden. A Liberal student of that period recalled that a prevailing mood of student tolerance of the Vietnam War, and affable relations between student politicians across the political divide, ended abruptly as 'the mood changed dramatically within a few months in 1967'.[39] The change was reflected in lecture theatres as well as in the Union building, for while opposition to the Vietnam War was the focus of student activism, an important subsidiary demand by radical students was for greater input into what, and how, they were taught.

Theories were being expounded around campus about how capitalism caused wars and many economic history students were keen to examine whether there was such a link. Responding to this, Blainey introduced a half-year course on war and economic history in 1970. He also decided that he would write a book on the topic, which was published as *The Causes of War* (1973).[40]

In a letter Blainey wrote to Robert Cross, the Managing Director of Macmillan, in 1969 to propose the book, he made it clear that the theory which the book would contain distinguished 'sharply between causes of rivalry and causes of war – perhaps that is its essence'.[41] This distinction is crucial to understanding *The Causes of War*. Blainey was not considering the causes of dispute between countries, but the causes of actual war. Given the significance of this point to his thesis, it was odd that Blainey did not highlight it at the outset. His clearest statement of it does not come until the 24th of 33 conclusions at the end of the book:

---

38 Blainey, *Across a Red World*, 121.
39 History of Melbourne University Liberal Club in Club Information Booklet in author's collection.
40 Geoffrey Blainey, *The Causes of War* (London: Macmillan, 1973).
41 Blainey to Robert Cross, 16 May 1969, Blainey Papers, Acc. No. 89/145 Box 19, UMA.

Most of the popular theories of war – and the explanation by historians of individual wars – blame capitalism, dictators, monarchs or other individuals or pressure groups. These theories, however, explain rivalry and tension rather than war: rivalry and tension can exist for generations without producing war.[42]

The explanation was not completely ignored in the text, with Blainey at one point noting that 'the explanations that stress aims are theories of rivalry and animosity and not theories of war'.[43] His theory required readers to accept that rivalry and tension between nations were a given. Readers have continued to grapple with this feature of the work ever since. For instance, Professor Julian L. Simon, most famous for his bet with biologist Paul Ehrlich on the direction of metal prices in the 1980s, wrote to Blainey saying 'the only reservation I have about the book is that you said so little about the causes of conflict'.[44]

Naturally, both contemporary and subsequent critics also commented on this feature of Blainey's thesis. Hugh Stretton described Blainey's position as being that one should accept 'as data that disputes exist, and should concentrate on why some of them issue in war and others do not'.[45] Graeme Davison made a similar point, writing that *The Causes of War* was 'confined very largely to a discussion of the circumstances under which rivalry is likely to assume the form of armed conflict' and that 'its presuppositions are of calculative self-interest and balances of power'.[46]

According to Blainey, accepting that rivalry between countries is a given meant that students of war should not seek to make moral judgements about which side of a conflict had unreasonable ambitions:

> Indeed nearly all explanations of war which overwhelmingly stress ambitions are propaganda. They are designed to pin the blame on one group, class or institution. Their selection of the target of blame rarely comes from a study of war but from deep convictions about behaviour in a wider context.[47]

---

42 Blainey, *The Causes of War*, 248.
43 Ibid., 150.
44 Julian L. Simon to Blainey, 3 July 1986, Blainey Papers, MS 9225/3/15 Box 10, NLA.
45 Hugh Stretton, 'Review Articles: The Causes of War', *Historical Studies* 16, no. 62 (April 1974): 105.
46 Davison, 'Half a Determinist', 23.
47 Blainey, *The Causes of War*, 154.

One can certainly understand why L.C.F. Turner of Royal Military College Duntroon commented that sometimes Blainey 'seems to come close to denying the existence of morality in international affairs'.[48] The most used example of a moral war is the fight against Hitler. A few years before Blainey wrote his book, British historian A.J.P. Taylor had created quite a stir with his revisionist attitude to Hitler's culpability for the Second World War. Blainey endorsed the Taylor view, describing Hitler as an 'alert opportunist who tempered his objectives to the available means of achieving them'.[49]

Reviewers certainly noticed the similarities with Taylor. Another Duntroon lecturer, Brian Beddie, reviewing the book in *Quadrant*, called them 'striking parallels'.[50] The similarities with Taylor created difficulties in pinning an ideological label on *The Causes of War*. Other than both having reputations as mavericks, it was hard to find an ideological label that covered both Taylor, generally seen as being on the political Left or at least a radical liberal, and Blainey. Both Stretton and Davison painted Blainey's stance on war as 'conservative', as did two American academics, Keith L. Nelson and Spencer C. Olin, who saw Blainey as one of the leading proponents of a conservative (as opposed to liberal or radical) view:

> One of the most brilliant and thoroughly developed versions of conservative analysis has been developed by the Australian historian, Geoffrey Blainey. Devoting himself specifically to the question of what causes war, Blainey explores the history of conflict over the last three centuries in great detail. His conclusion is that, though wars would not occur without longstanding disputes over issues vital to the contending countries, wars do not begin until two nations disagree as to their relative strengths.[51]

Further muddying the ideological waters was the suggestion by another reviewer, D.E. Kennedy, that Blainey had similar perspectives to Engels and Lenin, reflecting the pessimism of the former and the latter's approval of Clausewitz's argument that was was a continuation of politics by other means, writing that Blainey's book started 'from a similar premise'.[52]

---

48   L.C.F. Turner, 'Review Articles: The Causes of War', *Historical Studies* 16, no. 62 (April 1974): 106.

49   Blainey, *The Causes of War*, 151.

50   Brian Beddie, 'The Cause of War', *Quadrant* 17, no. 5–6 (September-December 1973): 62.

51   Keith L. Nelson and Spencer C. Olin, *Why War? Ideology, Theory and History* (Berkeley: University of California Press, 1979), 31–32.

52   D.E. Kennedy, 'Review Articles: The Causes of War', *Historical Studies*, 16, no. 62 (April 1974): 109.

While identifying the ideological basis of Blainey's argument was not straightforward, what was clear was the ideology that the book explicitly rejected – the laissez-faire liberalism of the Manchester School. Ironically, it is the ideology to which Blainey himself had previously been sympathetic, as he explained in a letter a few years after the book's publication: 'I do not like the taste of my conclusions – I am by upbringing and sympathy a Manchester liberal – but the evidence of my mind does not support my prejudices'.[53] In the book itself, Blainey argued that overturning a theory on the basis of evidence was an unusual trait, observing of one individual who weighed up contrary evidence against a theory that 'like most of us in a similar quandary he plumped for his theory'.[54] This positioning as an individual prepared to face up to unpalatable realities, as opposed to liberal theory, was to become a feature of Blainey's views in the 1980s. Davison drew the analogy, linking the need in writing *The Causes of War* 'to subdue his own peaceful instincts in order to confront the brute realities of war' with his subsequent taking of a personally unpalatable position in the immigration debate.[55]

Blainey was particularly harsh in his assessment of the idealism of the Manchester School, arguing that 'to many of its adherents [it] was a dogma; and so contrary evidence was dismissed'.[56] Where Blainey normally avoided sneering at attitudes held by others in the past, here he ridiculed the entry written on peace for the *Encyclopaedia Britannica* in 1911 as hopelessly idealistic and, as it was written by an MP representing the Lancashire mill town of Blackburn, used it as evidence against the Manchester School.

In fact, key members of the Manchester School, from Richard Cobden and John Bright onwards, were not naive optimists who thought that there would not be further wars, but rather individuals who believed that the risk of future wars would be greatly reduced if their policies were implemented. Followers of the Manchester School would argue that it was the failure to pursue the sorts of policies they advocated that produced the smaller conflicts that occurred in their era of strength in the mid nineteenth century (e.g. the Crimean War), and that it was their decline in the influence of their views in the early twentieth century that led first to protectionism, then militarism, and finally war. Yet Blainey saw their policies prevailing, even after the First World War (in the two decades of the past two centuries when free trade

---

53   Blainey to A.W. Marshall, Office of the Secretary of Defence, Washington, 20 February 1978, Blainey Papers, Acc. No. 89/145 Box 19, UMA.
54   Blainey, *The Causes of War*, 8.
55   Davison, 'Half a Determinist', 26.
56   Blainey, *The Causes of War*, 22.

ideas were least in favour). He asserted that 'versions of the creed survived' and 'indeed that creed may even have been partly responsible for the outbreak of another world war only two decades later'.[57]

The amount of space Blainey devoted to attacking Manchester liberals is perhaps best understood if one considers them as a proxy for the anti-Vietnam protesters of his own time of writing. Blainey saw a direct link between the Manchester School and 'much of the criticism of the Vietnam War'.[58] Yet, in linking the Manchester School and New Left peace activists, Blainey did not seek to explain why the latter adopted the peace idealism of the former, but jettisoned their views on free trade and capitalism. As the peace activists of the late twentieth century moved further down the path of anti-globalisation, a position that would have completely bemused Cobden and Bright, the analogy between the two movements became even more problematic.

The Causes of War took Blainey's aim to be a historian of trends to a new level. He looked at almost one hundred international wars from 1700 to 1971 and tried to establish whether trends could be discerned. Davison described the book as 'the most daring of Blainey's ventures into the logic of historical causation', observing that it was 'a curious book, both for the boldness of what it attempts and the limits within which it attempts it'.[59]

Blainey appreciated that he was entering an area 'already crowded with entrenched assumptions about why nations fight', but he believed that by examining the minutiae of the causes of particular wars, historians had missed trends.[60] Besides, as Blainey had argued in *The Tyranny of Distance* a few years earlier and reinforced more than once in this work, relying solely on the documentary record can be misleading.[61]

In his search for trends to explain the causes of wars, Blainey resuscitated a 'forgotten observation' from Alec Lawrence Macfie that the upswing in the business cycle was more likely to lead to wars than the downswing.[62] Blainey noted that only 'one member of the many disciplines studying the causes of war had offered any judgement or comment' on Macfie's 1938 article on the connection between certain economic conditions and the outbreak of war. The one comment came in 1948 and was delivered by historian Sir George Clark, who 'assured his listeners that the historians who had contributed the most

---

57 Blainey, *The Causes of War*, 26.
58 Ibid., 29.
59 Davison, 'Half a Determinist', 23.
60 Blainey, *The Causes of War*, vii.
61 Ibid., 4, 41.
62 Ibid., 91–96.

to an understanding of war had not traced economic trends but rather had "minutely dissected treaties and dispatches"'. Blainey observed that Clark's statement 'was not surprising, for the historians of treaties outnumbered the historians of trends by one thousand to one'.[63] It is important to point out that, although Blainey praised Macfie, he found that many other economists, and economic historians, were as culpable as mainstream historians. In fact, he used Macfie's thesis to batter them, writing that 'Macfie's observation offers an additional reason for suspecting the dogmas, beloved of many economists, that economic pressures and ills were the main stirrers of wars'.[64]

Rob Pascoe saw *The Causes of War* as the culmination of Blainey's new-found desire to develop general laws of history.[65] In an interview he granted Pascoe, Blainey acknowledged how his approach to history had changed, commenting that 'if he had written *The Causes of War* in the 1950s, for example, it would have evoked the sights and sounds of warfare, concentrating less on the general pattern of causation'.[66]

So what trends did Blainey identify? The most important related to the expectations of the combatants. Blainey explained that 'expectations – and particularly expectations in the short term – seem a crucial clue to the causes of war and peace'.[67] Unrealistic optimism was a trigger both for action and timing as 'international wars tended to come during the more optimistic months of the more optimistic years'.[68] On top of this, 'the seizing of a favourable opportunity to wage war … seems to be part of the very decision to go to war rather than the aftermath of the decision'.[69] The optimism that Blainey described was optimism about the relative strength of one nation's forces compared to a potential opponent.

Blainey argued that 'wars occurred only when both rivals believed that they could achieve more through war than through peace'.[70] This position ignored the fact that one nation can be sole aggressor, invading another country without even offering negotiation as an alternative, and thus making surrender the alternative. It does not recognise the possibility that an aggrieved country might think there was a greater risk of losing than winning an imminent war,

---

63   Ibid., 94.
64   Ibid., 96.
65   Pascoe, *Manufacture*, 130–131.
66   Ibid., 128.
67   Blainey, *The Causes of War*, 55.
68   Ibid., 103.
69   Ibid.
70   Ibid., 125.

but because of principle, or honour, might still believe that it was duty bound to fight rather than surrender.

The most cited case of excessive optimism was prior to the start of the First World War. Blainey argued that, while in this case it has been recognised, there was nothing exceptional about it, as optimism was a recurrent prelude to war.[71] Blainey acknowledged that, in the lead-up to war, there were always some pessimists, however, in Blainey's eyes, this only proved that 'the optimistic threads must have been far thicker to weave the prevailing mood'.[72] The optimism theory was immediately disputed. Turner devoted more than half his review to arguing that 'not all great wars have been inaugurated in a spirit of optimism'.[73] He used numerous examples of pessimism from the lead-up to the Napoleon's war with Britain, the American Civil War and the First World War to make his case.

Another trend which Blainey found 'astonishing to discover' was how many wars had been preceded by serious internal conflict in one of the warring nations: the one which had been attacked by the other country.[74] Blainey's argument on this point has remained part of the literature on war causation. In 2007, he was cited in a new American work as the source of the theory the authors dub the 'kick 'em while they're down war', with the comment that 'although the diversionary war theory argues that states with internal conflicts seek wars, it is also possible that such states are the *targets* of attacks by others'.[75] They further suggested that Saddam Hussein's opportunistic invasion of Iran in 1980 was a good illustration of Blainey's concept.

There were constant suggestions in *The Causes of War* that others, particularly the acknowledged experts, have not studied the subject with an open enough mind and hence Blainey was surprised by what he discovered when he investigated. One of the few well-known historians to get a positive mention was Barbara Tuchman who, in her writing about the enthusiasm at the start of the First World War, was in Blainey's opinion 'one of a small band of historians who saw it as part of the atmosphere that caused the war rather than an ironic but irrelevant example of folly'.[76]

---

71 Ibid., 40–41, 53.
72 Ibid., 36–38, 47.
73 Turner, 'Review Articles: The Causes of War', 107.
74 Blainey, *The Causes of War*, 70.
75 Greg Cashman & Leonard C. Robinson, *An Introduction to the Causes of War: Patterns of Interstate Conflict from World War One to Iraq* (Washington: Rowman & Littlefield, 2007), 11.
76 Blainey, *The Causes of War*, 39.

There were several obscure, but perceptive, writers whose work Blainey wanted to bring back to public view. One was John Frederick Maurice who, in the 1880s, had observed that most wars began with fighting rather than a declaration of war. Blainey argued that this was 'one of the most valuable investigations ever made of a facet of war', but regretted that, after 'a short period of influence', it had 'slowly floated away from the mainstream of knowledge'.[77]

The need to reclaim the neglected, and overthrow the accepted, on such an important topic left Blainey in no doubt that *The Causes of War* was an important work. It was clearly a work of worldwide relevance and so, in this instance, success in Australia was not going to be sufficient. Nobody could dispute the significance of the topic, and none could argue that Blainey had not made an original contribution. Yet, the grand temporal and geographic scale of *The Causes of War* meant that it was going to be harder for an 'Australian iconoclast' to make the sort of impact he had made via an entry into South Africa with a new interpretation of a single event, or with a descriptive work such as *Across a Red World*.

Even in Australia, publisher Macmillan felt *The Causes of War* needed something of an unorthodox launch to stimulate interest and sales. A plan was developed to launch the book at the Tullamarine Airport Travelodge on a Sunday afternoon, with a group of war games enthusiasts playing their games as a backdrop to provide some colour.[78] Regardless of gimmicks, by 1973 Blainey had achieved sufficient stature that any new book of his was guaranteed to receive major reviews in Australian broadsheet newspapers. *The Australian* found his arguments 'subtle, profound and immensely readable', although the review also argued that Blainey had pursued 'an idiosyncratically third course' between the traditional approaches of historians and sociologists.[79]

Some of the critical comments of Stretton, Turner and Kennedy in *Historical Studies* have already been noted, but it is important to recognise that all three historians praised the book. Stretton believed that Blainey had done an excellent job showing 'that our general beliefs about the causes of war have the simplest possible shortcoming: they are not true' and described it as an 'absorbing, tough and wonderfully original study'.[80] Turner also mixed

---

77 Ibid., 170. Maurice showed that declaring war was a rare exception rather than the norm, a point Blainey made in relation to Pearl Harbour.
78 Roger Henry at Macmillan to Blainey, 16 May 1973, Blainey Papers, Acc. No. 89/145 Box 19, UMA.
79 John Coates, 'Over-confident into battle', *The Australian*, 23 June 1973, 19.
80 Stretton, 'Review Articles: The Causes of War', 105–106.

compliments with his reservations, saying that 'when all criticisms have been made, it cannot be denied that Blainey has produced a most stimulating book and has made an outstanding contribution to the study of war'.[81]

The book has tended to divide Blainey sympathisers. In 1990, Les Carlyon wrote that *The Causes of War* was Blainey's 'masterpiece: original, cool, never distorted by dogma, stylishly written', a view he reiterated a few years later. On the other hand, Peter Ryan mentioned without specifying his reasons that *The Causes of War* was Blainey's 'least satisfying' book.[82] A more recent Australian critic, Ian Hodges, the historian at the Australian War Memorial contributed a chapter on Blainey's treatment of war to *The Fuss That Never Ended*. He noted the mixed reception of *The Causes of War* and argued that, while Blainey 'countered many commonly held views with deft arguments and skilful analysis', when some of those arguments were 'held up against alternative evidence his claims can appear dubious'.[83]

Outside Australia, there was a significant difference between how the book was inially received in its two major potential markets: Britain and the United States. Blainey was quite disturbed at how British reviewers failed to appreciate the book's arguments, writing in October 1973 that 'not one reviewer of the book in England has so far comprehended even a fraction of what I was trying to say'.[84] In the United States, *The Causes of War* was 'very popular with students' and indeed it remains on curriculums at a wide variety of North American universities.[85] It continues to be cited in various modern contexts. In 2006, American public intellectual and author of his own book on war, Michael Walzer listed *The Causes of War* as one of his two recommended books on war, commenting that it was 'a fine piece of historical analysis'.[86] The *Britannica Online* described it as 'the best short modern introduction to

---

81 Turner, 'Review Articles: The Causes of War', 108.

82 Les Carlyon, 'Carlyon', *Business Review Weekly*, 14 December 1990, 16; Carlyon, 'A Curious Man – Geoffrey Blainey'; and Peter Ryan, 'Tyranny of the trivial', *The Weekend Australian* (Review section), 15-16 March 2003, 10.

83 Ian Hodges, 'From the Frontier to the Gulf' in *The Fuss That Never Ended: The Life and Work of Geoffrey Blainey*, eds Gare et al. (Melbourne: Melbourne University Press, 2003), 120.

84 Blainey to Robert Gibbons, 1 October 1973, Blainey Papers, Acc. No. 89/145 Box 19, UMA.

85 James Jupp, 'Blainey, fashionable old-fashioned historian', *Australian Book Review*, no. 70 (May 1985): 12–14. North American universities where the book has been on the syllabus in the twenty-first century include Cleveland State, Notre Dame, Rutgers, Toronto and Yale.

86 Rachel Donadio, 'War: A Reader's Guide', *New York Times* (Sunday Book Review), 17 December 2006.

the origins of wars, and two twenty-first century contributors on the topic described it as a 'landmark study' in 'a longstanding research program linking overconfidence and war'.[87] On the other hand, Blainey maintains that professional historians have generally not studied the topic properly, making the point in 2008 that 'history departments in the United States are lackadaisical in their approach to war', being 'not very interested in its causes, apart, maybe, from signing petitions or writing letters to the editor about Iraq or whatever is the current war'.[88]

Yet while *The Causes of War* was taking time to achieve the recognition Blainey felt it deserved, he was working on another book which would, at least in Australia, have an immediate impact.

---

87   *Encyclopaedia Britannica Online*, entry on 'Strategy – Bibliography', accessed 6 February 2013; and Dominic D.P. Johnson and Dominic Tierney, 'The Rubicon Theory of War: How the Path to Conflict Reaches the Point of No Return', *International Security*, 36 no 1 (Summer 2011): 7–40.

88   Geoffrey Blainey, 'Diminishing returns', review of *Castles, Battles & Bombs: How Economics Explains Military History* by Jurgen Brauer and Herbert van Tuyll, *Australian Book Review*, no. 303 (July-August 2008): 35.

Chapter 5

PROGRESSIVE HISTORIAN

If Blainey harboured any doubts about the impact his books could have following the initial response to *The Causes of War*, the weeks after the publication of *Triumph of the Nomads* in late September 1975 quickly dispelled them.[1] The book received extensive, favourable reviews across the nation's newspapers and quickly became a bestseller.

It was hardly surprising that the book stimulated great interest. After all, what could be more thought provoking for the 'average educated Australian' than to be told that in 1800 a typical Aboriginal Australian had a higher standard of living than a typical European of the time? Reviewers immediately highlighted the potential of such radical arguments to change Australian attitudes. The rapid sales showed that many Australians were receptive to change.

The use of the word 'triumph' in the title of the book indicated that Blainey was presenting a case that Aboriginal Australians had lived in a successful society. In mounting his case, Blainey described how early white settlers and commentators misunderstood Aboriginal society and how, despite a growing accumulation of new evidence, much of the misunderstanding still persisted in 1975. Not all settlers had misunderstood. Blainey's sources included the testimony of certain 'old settlers', who spoke Aboriginal languages and 'quietly watched them on their own hunting grounds'.[2] The key value of these particular settler recollections of Aboriginals was that 'they neither romanticized them nor belittled them'.[3] Those seven words summed up the perspective Blainey attempted to bring to his own writing in *Triumph of the Nomads*, as he explained:

> It is tempting to praise or condemn the practices used by aboriginals. The nomadic life of aboriginals was so different that to apply there the system of values culled from a society of settlements would be irrelevant.

---

1 Geoffrey Blainey, *Triumph of the Nomads: A History of Ancient Australia* (South Melbourne, Macmillan, 1975).
2 Ibid., 78.
3 Ibid.

> Their values and our values ... are not eternal and therefore not to be indiscriminately imposed but are in part ephemeral because they arise from the necessity and background of different societies.[4]

There was a definite desire to normalise Aboriginal society and, wherever possible, to show that it had the same mixture of strengths and weaknesses as that of any other people. For instance, he stated that 'the aboriginals probably treated old people as favourably as white Australians treat their old today – a mixture of concern and neglect'.[5] In 1975, such a position was seen as unusually sympathetic to Aboriginal society; by 1985 it was seen at best as conservative, if not reactionary, and even racist. This change meant that Blainey no longer received credit for being one of the first academics in the country to teach Aboriginal history as part of a general Australian history subject. The fact that *Triumph of the Nomads* had its genesis in an economic history subject contributed to the fact that it emphasised the Aboriginal economy and not other aspects of their society.

An important influence on Blainey was the archaeologist John Mulvaney, a long-standing friend. Blainey had gone on an archaeological expedition with Mulvaney to Fromm's Landing, near Mannum in South Australia as far back as 1956. He had been included in the party for the somewhat prosaic reason that he owned a car, taking six in his smallish Jowett. Once there, while others dug, Blainey assumed responsibility for chopping wood and in the evening provided entertainment by reading aloud Howard Spring's historical novel *Fame is the Spur*.[6] Years later, Mulvaney queried why Blainey, along with all other historians, excluded Aboriginal history from his courses. Blainey reflected:

> I used to begin a course on Australian economic history in the accepted manner with the European explorations of the eighteenth century until one day the archaeologist, John Mulvaney, in conversation enquired what I said about the earlier 99 per cent of time embraced by the human history of Australia. He pointed out that the ancient and recent history of Australia had continuous as well as broken threads, and he pointed to some of the threads, and so the book owes much to his original comment and his later encouragement.[7]

---

4   Ibid., 121.
5   Ibid., 100.
6   John Mulvaney, *Digging Up a Past* (Sydney: UNSW Press, 2011), 99; and Geoffrey Blainey 'A digger who made history', *The Weekend Australian* (Review section), 2–3 April 2011, 20.
7   Blainey, *Triumph of the Nomads*, viii.

The anthropologist L. R. Hiatt commented that 'a lesser scholar would have ignored the remark ... Blainey reacted (some might say overreacted) by mastering the subject and writing a book on it'.[8] Hiatt predicted that 'prehistorians and ecologists working in Aboriginal studies will properly subject it to critical scrutiny, and ask their students to do the same, but I hope they will not allow the fact that the author is an outsider to inhibit decent expressions of gratitude'.[9] Ross Campbell in *The Bulletin* commented that Blainey liked 'making audacious sorties into the fields of other specialists ... in this case he relies heavily on the work of archaeologists and anthropologists'.[10]

A few years elapsed between Blainey first teaching Aboriginal history and writing the book. One of the triggers for converting the material from the course into a book was Blainey's work on a Federal Government inquiry into museums [see Chapter 6]. He visited many museums in Australia and overseas and saw lots of exhibits about Australian Aboriginals, New Zealand Maoris and Native Americans. Blainey appreciated that artefacts had their limitations as a source for history, particularly for appreciating a skills-based society rather than an object-based one. He noted that museums had an inherent bias to 'display objects' and thus there was a tendency to 'place too much emphasis on the instruments and weapons and not enough on the techniques and tricks'.[11]

As well as Mulvaney and the museum visits, another influence on the nature of the book was 'an Aboriginal student who, knowing what I was writing, enquired why so many academic writing on past Aboriginals treated them as scientific specimens rather than as people – "Can't the history of Australia before 1788, he asked, be written in the same style as the history of Australia after 1788?"'[12]

Triumph of the Nomads was part of a growing awareness of Aboriginal Australia in the 1960s and 1970s. Evidence of this trend included the 1967 Referendum and Bill Stanner's 1968 Boyer Lectures when he coined the term 'the Great Australian Silence' to describe the treatment of the Indigenous population. Despite this growing awareness, it was still only a minority who could categorise Blainey's book as 'demolishing old shibboleths many of us thought already disposed of'.[13] For the majority, the book meant that

---

8   L. R. Hiatt, 'Dreamtime archaeology', *Quadrant* 20, no. 3 (March 1976): 54–55.
9   Ibid.
10 Ross Campbell, 'Fair living from a hard land', *The Bulletin*, 18 October 1975, 63.
11 Blainey, *Triumph of the Nomads*, 125–130.
12 Geoffrey Blainey, 'Triumphs of a race reviewed', *The Age*, 2 October 1979, 35.
13 Ronald M. Berndt, review of *Triumph of the Nomads*, *Historical Studies* 17, no. 69 (October 1977): 531.

for the first time 'the ordinary Australian, untutored in the language of archaeologists, anthropologists, prehistorians, anatomists, marine scientists, geologists, botanists, zoologists and linguists' accepted the length and nature of the Aboriginal occupation of the continent and 'the acceptance of that simple truth might prove the most significant development yet in Australian historiography'.[14]

The first point Blainey emphasised was the epic nature of the original human habitation of the continent. He underlined the point throughout Chapter 2, describing it variously as 'one of the great events in the history of man', 'one of the momentous events of world history' and 'one of the great treks in the history of the human race'.[15] Further weakening the hold of the founding of Sydney in 1788 as the seminal event in the nation's history, Blainey also asserted that 'the first decade of the trepang [sea cucumber] industry on the northern coast had greater influence on the aboriginals than did the first decade of British settlement (1788-98) on the Pacific coast'.[16]

Nor did the Aboriginal settlement of the continent mean the imposition of a static society, an unchanging Aboriginal Australia from the time of human arrival on the continent, through to British colonisation in 1788. As Blainey observed, 'we are accustomed to thinking, erroneously, that aboriginal Australia had static population, static resources, and static ideas'.[17] The customary thinking about a static society was 'still the belief of the average educated Australian' in the 1970s, despite the fact that it had been challenged as early as 1930.[18] One source of change in the Indigenous culture was the changing environment. Blainey emphasised that the physical environment of Australia changed 'violently and dramatically' in the period of Aboriginal occupation, in turn forcing radical change on the lifestyle of the continent's human inhabitants.[19] The changes to the landscape at the end of the most recent Ice Age far outweighed the environmental changes produced 'in the short history of white men in Australia'.[20]

Another source of environmental change was the Indigenous people themselves, particularly through their mastery of fire, something which 'should still

---

14   Stuart Sayers, 'Australian Historiography: A Layman's View', *Victorian Historical Journal* 48, (1977): 294.
15   Blainey, *Triumph of the Nomads*, 15, 23, 30.
16   Ibid., 248.
17   Ibid., 105.
18   Ibid., 13.
19   Ibid.
20   Ibid., 14.

be ranked as the greatest of man's conquests'.[21] The mastery of fire was just one of the justifications for Blainey's arresting title and the memorable opening line that 'long before the rise of Babylon and Athens, the early Australians had impressive achievements'.[22]

One of Blainey's major focuses was the comparative standards of living of Europeans and Aboriginals. He argued that 'when aboriginal commerce is dissected it no longer appears so different from modern commerce'.[23] Turning conventional thinking on its head, Blainey suggested that 'by the standards of the year 1800 … the aboriginals' material life could be compared favourably with many parts of Europe'.[24] Indeed, 'they probably lived in more comfort than nine-tenths of the population of eastern Europe'.[25] To emphasise his point, in particular in relation to diet, Blainey constantly made comparisons with Europe at the time of colonisation and beyond. For example, he wrote that 'Orwell's average coalminer in Lancashire could not afford to buy in a month as many pound of cooked poultry and as many eggs as these primitive hunters were eating in a day'.[26] Even contemporary Australians suffered by comparison as 'in a normal year the aboriginals in many parts of the continent ate a variety of plant foods such as no present greengrocer or fruiterer in an Australian city could hope to display'.[27]

The failure of settlers to appreciate the material quality of the Aboriginal way of life was demonstrated by the fact that two alleged benefits of European civilization – shelter and absence of famine – were illusory, the former being less necessary in Australia and the latter actually worse in Europe.[28] Settlers also failed to appreciate how 'ample leisure was indeed one of the signs of the aboriginals' favourable standard of living', a point he underlined by observing that 'the aboriginals, moreover, probably obtained their food with less effort than was spent in 1861 by the average Londoner or Berliner'.[29]

While Blainey argued that 'Aboriginals in most parts of Australia appear to have had an impressive standard of living at the time of the European invasion', he did not condemn settlers who failed to recognise it, because

---

21 Ibid., 71.
22 Ibid., v.
23 Ibid., 212.
24 Ibid., 225.
25 Ibid.
26 Ibid., 149.
27 Ibid., 157.
28 Ibid., 226.
29 Ibid., 222.

the Indigenous society they encountered was so different from their own in Europe.[30] As he argued, 'the contrast between nomadic and settled peoples was so vast that neither could easily understand, nor assess, the standard of living of the other'.[31] Settlers failed to appreciate the land as well as the people, often concluding that 'the land was mean and hungry, not realizing that some regions in the course of four seasons provided a wider variety of foodstuffs than a gourmet in Paris would eat in an extravagant year'.[32]

In several other ways, Blainey attempted to show that Aboriginal Australia was the equal of what others took to be civilised Europe. Indigenous Australians had complex social structures, developed ingenious technology, spoke several languages and engaged in trade.[33] While all these reflected Aboriginal Australia in a positive light, another comparison was less complimentary.

Aboriginal Australia was, according to Blainey, a violent place. Chapter 7, 'Birth and Death', discussed the role of abortion and infanticide in Aboriginal society, together with attitudes to the old and lame, and espoused theories about the toll that inter-tribal war took on population numbers. It was to become the most controversial chapter in the book. On the issue of war, Blainey used figures suggested by escaped convict William Buckley and American anthropologist Lloyd Warner to compare the percentage death toll in Aboriginal battles to that in the Second World War.[34] He recognised that his views on 'these episodes of fighting in Aboriginal Australia run counter to the beliefs of most anthropologists'.[35] There were some criticisms of Blainey on this point, the anthropologist Ronald Berndt arguing that 'there is little evidence of intensive and extensive fighting'.[36] Acknowledging Berndt as a 'distinguished scholar', Blainey responded:

> Now my view could be mistaken but I based it on my own calculations of the likely mortality rate of Aboriginal warfare, using the patchy evidence. It is slightly hazardous for scholars to reply that the Aboriginal population was not much affected by warfare if they refuse to reveal the calculations or hunches on which their conclusion was based.[37]

---

30   Ibid., 217.
31   Ibid., 218.
32   Ibid., vi.
33   Ibid., 29–30, 31, 152, 203. Blainey does make the point (214) that 'not every tribe engaged in trade'.
34   Ibid., 108–111.
35   Ibid., 111.
36   Berndt, review of *Triumph of the Nomads*, 533.
37   Blainey, 'Triumphs of a race reviewed'.

Blainey has maintained his position until the current day, lamenting in his 2015 book, *The Story of Australia's People: The Rise and Fall of Ancient Australia* that 'the tribal warfare now tends to be denied or completely ignored in certain academic circles' and reiterating his own view that warfare in tribal Australia was probably 'dislocating and deadly'.[38] Predictably, academic critics still remain unconvinced.[39]

Another view spreading in the 1970s was that Aborigines had lived in harmony with a pristine and unchanging environment. To Blainey, this attitude was a classic example of the 'static society' concept he was challenging. He pointed to the introduction of the dingo and advanced his theory that this triggered the arrival of the bush fly to suggest that this was 'one of those sequences that defy the simple idea that aboriginals were living in harmony with a static environment'.[40] A few pages later he ridiculed how tourist literature in Tasmania described 'impenetrable forest, parts of which have never been explored', when he claimed that in Aboriginal times the area was grassland regularly burnt by fire.[41] In short, Aboriginals were neither better, nor worse, than European settlers; they were neither passive custodians, nor victims, of their environment.

The call for greater recognition of the achievements of pre-1788 Aboriginal Australia fitted with a significant theme of many other Blainey works, that those of us in the present should never feel too superior to the people or events of the past because, when we study them, we often find that they stand up very well in terms of both importance and success.

Most reviewers were sympathetic to Blainey's aim, but some questioned it. John Douglas Pringle in the *Sydney Morning Herald* thought 'Professor Blainey, in his desire to restore the balance between white man and black man and to make up for our scandalous neglect of the Aboriginal heritage, has at times swung too far the other way'.[42] A more extreme version of this position came in *The Economist*, whose reviewer thought Blainey had attempted the impossible with his 'learned and ingenious plea for greater respect and knowledge of

---

38 Geoffrey Blainey, *The Story of Australia's People: The Rise and Fall of Ancient Australia* (Melbourne: Penguin Viking 2015, 119–120).
39 John Maynard, 'A culture to celebrate', *The Age* (Spectrum section), 21 March 2015, 26–27.
40 Blainey, *Triumph of the Nomads*, 65.
41 Ibid., 79.
42 John Douglas Pringle, 'History of Australia before 1788', *Sydney Morning Herald*, 18 October 1975, 17.

the aboriginal peoples'.[43] Normally, 'rehabilitating lost reputations' provided 'a healthy corrective to western man's ridiculously triumphalist view of his place in the scheme of evolution', but not in the case of the Aboriginal population as 'nobody else, anywhere, seems to have been so submissive to the environment'. Totally unconvinced by any of Blainey's evidence about Aboriginal living standards, the reviewer commented that 'the question that arises, and which Professor Blainey does not attempt to ask, is why these peoples for so long took nature as their master not their servant'.[44]

However, the majority of the reviews in Australian newspapers were sympathetic both to Blainey's purpose and his execution.[45] The reach of Blainey's work was captured by the range of places, outside the daily newspapers, where it was reviewed. One striking example was the *Women's Weekly* whose review commented:

> When you were at school I bet you fell for the standard line about pre-Captain Cook Australia – an empty, timeless, place inhabited by Stone-Age men who'd just been drearily doing the same old things, without variation or innovation, for countless thousands of years. Geoffrey Blainey makes nonsense of these ideas. His *Triumph of the Nomads* I found as engrossing as a whodunit... It's easy to read, and very hard to put down, because it opens up the imagination to new feelings about Australia.[46]

Even the Communist Party liked it, commenting that 'if you like to read the fascinating 40,000 year history of the Aborigines in simpler language than that of pre-historian and archaeologist D.J. Mulvaney, then this is the book for you'.[47] Visiting *Guardian* journalist, Martin Woollacott, in one of a series of articles on Australia, wrote that 'in many a Christmas stocking this year will be Geoffrey Blainey's *Triumph of the Nomads* which can best be described as a book about how the blacks used Australia more wisely than the

---

43 This quote is included on the back of the Sun Books edition and seemingly referencing it alone, rather than the full article, meant Tim Rowse presented a somewhat misleading impression of *The Economist*'s view in his chapter in *The Fuss That Never Ended*.

44 *The Economist*, 28 February 1976, 107.

45 Examples include Noel Hawken, 'The proud people who ruled a continent', *The Herald* (Melbourne), 4 October 1975; Alex Harris, 'Our Oldest Immigrants', *West Australian*, 18 October 1975, 15; and Peter Corris, 'Australia's first occupation', *The Australian*, 6 December 1975, 28.

46 Margaret Sydney, 'At home' column, *Women's* Weekly, 10 December 1975.

47 *Tribune*, 14 July 1976.

whites'.[48] That was not Blainey's intention, but Woollacott's reading of the work certainly was not uncommon. Blainey commented on this phenomenon in a piece written for the Education section of *The Age* in 1979:

> Some reviewers saw the book as a strong affirmation of the idea that Aboriginals lived in harmony with their environment; other reviewers saw the book as affirming that the Aboriginals, like us, were polluters. Some saw the book as indirectly a condemnation of western society and an affirmation of the superior virtues of a nomadic society. I myself don't see the book as a rejection of western society.[49]

Not everyone found *Triumph of the Nomads* fully sympathetic to Aboriginal Australia. There were inklings of those negative views that were to gain much greater force in the 1980s. The reviewer in the radical weekly *Nation Review*, Peter White, argued that the 'subtitle [A History of Ancient Australia] removes most of the force carried by the somewhat trendy *triumph* of the main title and reveals Blainey's ambivalent and somewhat defensive attitude about aborigines'.[50] Having run a wholly positive review in early October, *The Age* ran a second review some weeks later which asserted that 'from an academic point of view the central weakness of the book is the complete lack of any theoretical perspective'.[51] This reviewer, the anthropologist Nicolas Petersen, acknowledged 'these criticisms do not detract from the value of the book for the general reader... Blainey's misconceptions and factual errors are infinitely preferable to the gross levels of misinformation in the community at large'.[52]

Historical Studies also published two reviews. One was by historian and future crime writer Peter Corris, who believed that Blainey had produced 'a convincing and moving portrayal of people subject to nature's tyranny'.[53] The other was by Ronald Berndt from the University of Western Australia, whose views on mortality rates have already been noted. He was quite critical, arguing that while 'in some respects this is an interesting and thoughtful book

---

48 Martin Woollacott, *The Guardian*, 28 December 1975.
49 Blainey, 'Triumphs of a race reviewed'.
50 Peter White, 'Forager among the archaeologists', *Nation Review* 6, no. 3, 31 October – 6 November 1975, 75.
51 Nicolas Peterson, 'Racy ancient history', *The Age*, 22 November, 1975. Peterson had worked with Edward Woodward on the Gove case and Royal Commission on NT land rights.
52 Ibid.
53 Peter Corris, review of *Triumph of the Nomads*, *Historical Studies* 17, no. 69 (October 1977): 533. Corris had also reviewed the book for *The Australian*.

... it is also an irritating and thoughtless one ... its broad, often unsupported generalisations, attractive in some respects, are sadly in need of re-examination and reconstruction'.[54]

Reflecting on the book four years after its publication, Blainey acknowledged that it 'should have said more about the social and religious beliefs of Aboriginals'.[55] This picked up a point made by William Kerley in the inaugural issue of the *Journal of Australian Studies* that 'the book suffers from a lack of balance because there is little examination of kinship and social structure except in the most general terms'. Kerley also regarded Blainey's use of a lower case "a" for Aboriginals as one of the book's 'minor annoyances'.[56]

To best understand the place of *Triumph of the Nomads* in the historiography of its time it is worth quoting from a lecture given, in 1977, by Michael Roe, then Professor of History at the University of Tasmania, in which he considered the growing challenge to the Whig view of Australian history, as 'out-groups' such as women, convicts and particularly Aboriginals were written back in:

> Revisionists in this area have stressed first and foremost that the very existence of European Australia, and its apparent success in territorial-economic terms, has diminished a whole race of humanity. In this light – particularly in Tasmania – our history might appear as a fearful tragedy, a grotesque exemplar of that European ethnocentrism which has cursed the modern world. Many writers have written to this effect, but none – inevitably – with the wit and skill of Geoffrey Blainey. This is the more striking because Blainey's earlier work fitted pretty close to the Whig pattern. But *Triumph of the Nomads* (1975) presents the traditional Aboriginal life-style in glowing, as well as scintillating, terms. The Australians' vast and varied skills enabled them traditionally to enjoy a standard of living higher than the ordinary European knew until recently. In this, Blainey infers, rather than in anything that has happened since 1788, lies the great achievement of humanity in Australia.[57]

---

54 Berndt, review of *Triumph of the Nomads*, 533.
55 Blainey, 'Triumphs of a race reviewed'.
56 William Kerley, review of *Triumph of the Nomads*, *Journal of Australian Studies*, no. 1 (June 1977): 93-94.
57 Michael Roe, 'Challenges to Australian Identity and Esteem in Recent Historical Writing' (paper delivered as 1977 Eldershaw Memorial Lecture), published in *Tasmanian Historical Research Association Papers and Proceedings* 25, no. 1, (March 1978): 9.

The next historian considered by Roe in apparent continuity with Blainey in 'the "aboriginal" chapter in anti-Whig historiography' was Henry Reynolds. Yet, within a decade, Blainey and Reynolds were to be seen as key figures on opposing sides in the debate about Aboriginal history. Reynolds acknowledged that *Triumph of the Nomads* had 'presented in a highly readable manner the discoveries of both recent Australian archaeology and prehistory and new international assessments of hunter gatherer societies', and due to the fact that 'little of this material was generally accessible the book played a major role in changing Australian perceptions of traditional Aboriginal society'.[58]

On the other hand, Reynolds commented that 'literary panache and a reputation as a gadfly have disguised just how conservative and conventional much of his writing is'.[59] Reynolds drew attention to the fact that Blainey's views on the death rates in internecine Aboriginal conflicts were being used by those attacking the Aboriginal land rights movement. He discussed this aspect of the work, and only this, on the basis that it was 'the aspect of the work relevant to the present discussion ... the political implications of which have already been picked up by Hugh Morgan and other opponents of land rights'.[60] Focusing on the areas which could be considered critical of Aboriginal society provided a distorted picture of the work as a whole. Just as Reynolds disagreed with some aspects of the book, so those opposing Aboriginal land rights in the 1980s may have found disturbing Blainey's use of the word 'invaders' and 'invasion' to describe British colonisation.[61] The use of the word 'tragically' in the context that 'tragically, the largest region of nomads in the world was now face to face with the island [Great Britain] which had carried to new heights that settled specialized existence that had arisen from the domestication of plants and animals' may have also surprised them.[62]

In the context of 1975, Blainey had written a sympathetic work. For instance, he ascribed common human emotions to Aboriginals in scary situations, writing that 'how volcanic eruptions affected the few aboriginals in the vicinity can be easily supposed' and that 'no record is needed to sense

---

58 Henry Reynolds, 'Blainey and Aboriginal history', in *Surrender Australia? Essays in the Study and Uses of History: Geoffrey Blainey and Asian Immigration*, eds Andrew Markus and M.C. Ricklefs, (Sydney: George Allen & Unwin, 1985), 84–85.
59 Ibid., 82.
60 Ibid., 85.
61 Blainey, *Triumph of the Nomads*, 194, 217, 223, 229.
62 Ibid., 253.

the frequent terror of the voyage' which had brought them to Australia in earlier millenia.⁶³ The shift in the intellectual climate which saw judging Aboriginals like Europeans being generally considered 'progressive' in 1975, but being more widely seen as 'regressive' by the 1980s, is summed up in comments made by anthropologist Barry Morris in 1990:

> Blainey ... mobilizes psychological and economic categories which reduce Aborigines to reflections of ourselves. In his historical account, pre-colonized Aborigines make choices, react to dangers, etc. as 'anyone' would. It is this reduction of the 'Other' to an equivalence, a psychological facsimile of ourselves which underpins Blainey's reading of Aboriginal pre-history.⁶⁴

Gradually, a little more nuance has returned to the discussion. In a chapter in *The Fuss That Never Ended* titled 'Triumph of the Colonists', Tim Rowse's consideration of *Triumph* also focused largely on the 'Birth and Death' chapter, but more descriptively and less critically than Reynolds did. Rowse commented that 'the subjectivity of early Australians eluded Professor Blainey', but 'we can see him trying to evoke it, as the limitations of the evidence with which he was dealing challenged his humanism'.⁶⁵ Rowse concluded by saying that '*Triumph of the Nomads* was both a celebration of the adaptive success of Aboriginal civilisation and a warning against turning descriptions of its moralities and sensibilities into essays in "progressive narcissism"'.⁶⁶

Rowse's description is accurate. Blainey challenged ignorance about Aboriginals from what might be considered the Right and the Left. He rejected both 'unjustified contempt for the aboriginals and ignorance of their civilizing achievement', while also asserting that there was 'no justification' for the growing assumption that 'the aboriginals lived in complete harmony with the natural environment'.⁶⁷

The fact that any issue involving Blainey and race became so sensitive in the 1980s has tended to obscure how influential the book was in changing attitudes in the 1970s. In November 1975, it entered *The National Times*

---

63   Ibid., 13, 18.
64   Barry Morris, 'Making Histories/Living Histories' *Social Analysis*, no. 27 (April 1990): 85.
65   Tim Rowse, 'Triumph of the Colonists', *The Fuss That Never Ended: The Life and Work of Geoffrey Blainey*, eds Gare et al., (Melbourne: Melbourne University Press, 2003), 41.
66   Ibid., 45.
67   Blainey, *Triumph of the Nomads*, 58, 109.

non-fiction best-sellers list at number two, remaining third in December, an excellent result, especially considering that, unlike the $1.95 paperback *Tyranny of Distance*, *Triumph* was a $9.95 hardback, which, even allowing for the high inflation of the era, was a significant price rise.[68]

Hoping to capitalise on the commercial success of *Triumph of the Nomads*, Blainey's publisher, Macmillan, asked him to write a single volume history taking up the Australian story from where he had concluded in *Triumph*. Blainey found that he had too much material for a single history, so Macmillan suggested he do two volumes. The first took the national story up to 1900 and was published in August 1980 as *A Land Half Won*.[69] The volume on the twentieth century never appeared. Any chance of such a book being published was reduced when, in 1982, Macmillan packaged *A Land Half Won* with *The Tyranny of Distance* and *Triumph of the Nomads* in a deluxe edition, based on the somewhat dubious notion that they were a trilogy.

The ending that Blainey gave to 1900 not only provided *A Land Half Won* with its title, but also reflected a crucial double ambivalence. There was not only the explicit ambivalence of nineteenth-century Australians to their country of residence, but also the implicit ambivalence in Blainey's attitudes towards this generation of Australians. In the book he explained how, by the end of the nineteenth century, it was still not common to find Australians of European origins becoming emotionally attached to the Australian landscape. The Heidelberg School and Dorothea Mackellar were exceptions – 'Most Australians did not love a sunburnt country'.[70] He concluded with two short sentences: 'Most Australians were still strangers in a new land. The land was only half won'.[71]

Blainey himself was never a stranger in the land. From his youth he had appreciated the Australian landscape, evidenced by his cycling venture as a 12-year-old across the Divide to see how the scenery differed. Yet, ironically, the late nineteenth century Australians, who had not seen Australia through his fascinated eyes, were the same Australians who had moulded the Australian society he most admired - the Australia from the gold rushes to the 1880s. Blainey was later to further examine the attitudes of the late nineteenth century

---

68 'November's Best Sellers', *National Times*, 1–6 December 1975, 25 (Number 1 was actor David Niven's autobiography); and 'December's Best Sellers', *National Times*, 5–10 January 1976, 19.

69 Geoffrey Blainey, *A Land Half Won* (Melbourne: Sun Books, 1980). Macmillan had become the owner of the Sun Books imprint in 1971.

70 Ibid., 361.

71 Ibid.

in *A Shorter History of Australia*, making more explicit how the 1890s was a turning point in the country's history, a turning point for the worse. In that sense, *A Land Half Won* provided a foretaste of Blainey's later preoccupations, although the continuity with his earlier works is an equally strong feature.

In the first chapter of *A Land Half Won*, Blainey returned to the reasons for European settlement that had become so controversial when *The Tyranny of Distance* had been published 14 years earlier. The intervening years had only strengthened his view that the traditional interpretation, reiterated by Bolton and Shaw in 1968, needed to be overturned:

> In the debates since 1966 ... no *new* evidence has been found to support the old interpretation but new evidence has been found to support other interpretations. Many supporters of the old interpretation have since quietly abandoned their views. Early this year a lecturer at La Trobe University [Alan Frost] found in London another document of 1786 which undermines the traditional interpretation.[72]

Blainey clearly admired Frost's research on the topic and commended him for 'the sheer volume of evidence, the untangling of it and the reweaving of it'.[73] However, he also suggested that there was another aspect of the historian's craft which Frost needed to embrace more and, in letting him know, Blainey provided an important insight into his views as to how historical debates should be conducted:

> Your history of the history misses what seems to me a crucial point. In any slow tortuous revision of a traditional interpretation the campaign really consists of two separate fronts, often linked, but each separate. One is the harvesting of new evidence and the putting up of new hypotheses (which you describe in chapter one). The other – and almost as essential – is the knocking down, the assault on the traditional interpretations by probing their weaknesses. Your account perhaps ignores the latter. I suspect the debate between Shaw, Bolton, and me in 1966-69 etc. was useful not because it raised much new evidence that had been overlooked (you have found ten times as much), but because it began to persuade many historians that the traditional interpretation was in trouble even if they could not be sure what interpretation should replace it.[74]

---

72 Blainey correspondence, 15 May 1975, Blainey Papers, Acc. No. 80/66 Box 7, UMA,
73 Blainey to Alan Frost, 21 November 1977, Blainey Papers, Acc. No. 80/66 Box 7, UMA.
74 Ibid.

There was sufficient interest, and sufficiently diverse contributions, to the debate about the reasons for colonisation for Ged Martin to be able to compile a book on the topic, *The Founding of Australia: The Argument about Australia's Origins*, in 1978.[75] Two years later, in *A Land Half Won*, Blainey updated his own position. In addition to his *Tyranny* reasons of flax and naval stores, he now added a third: the British need for a port of call in the region, and a fourth, an erroneous view that the climate was more favourable for a colony than it proved to be in reality. He used a note to explain that 'since 1966 the evidence for the third reason has so accumulated that it must be regarded as beyond dispute'. In regard to the fourth reason, he commented that 'delusions of climate, I believe, must now be regarded as a fourth vital cause of the settlement'.[76] Blainey made a tentative prophecy that, rather than considering why colonisation happened, 'in years ahead perhaps the most controversial issue in early Australian history will … be … why they did not abandon it or deliberately prevent it from growing'.[77] The argument about the reasons for British Settlement proved to be not so easily settled.

The interpretation that Blainey put forward in *The Tyranny of Distance* and *A Land Half Won* was considered in subsequent histories but, generally was not accepted by other historians. As well as the critiques by Bolton and Shaw, later historians, such as Alan Atkinson, rejected it in their works in the 1980s and 1990s.[78] The most widely read work on the founding of the British colony was art critic Robert Hughes' *The Fatal Shore*, in which he wrote that 'the "strategic" arguments for Botany Bay do not seem to have impressed Pitt … his concern was getting rid of convicts'.[79] Summing up three decades of debate Stuart Macintyre commented in *The Oxford Companion to Australian History* that 'the settlement debate remains remarkably polarised, no closer to resolution than it was during the spirited argument over Blainey's *Tyranny of Distance*'.[80]

---

75 Ged Martin ed., *The founding of Australia: The argument about Australia's origins* (Sydney: Hale & Iremonger, 1978).
76 Blainey, *A Land Half Won*, 18.
77 Ibid., 26.
78 Alan Atkinson, *The Europeans in Australia 1: The Beginnings* (Melbourne: Oxford University Press, 1997), xv.
79 Robert Hughes, *The Fatal Shore: A History of the Transportation of Convicts to Australia 1787–1868* (London: Collins Harvill, 1987), 64.
80 Stuart Macintyre, 'Settlement', in *Oxford Companion to Australian History*, eds Graeme Davison, John Hirst and Stuart Macintyre, (Melbourne: Oxford University Press, 1998, 2001), 586.

In 2011, Frost released two books which brought together his 35 years of scholarship on the topic.[81] His conclusion was that naval supplies were the major motive, and they were actually part of 'a much larger plan ... to expand British commerce throughout the Indian and Pacific Oceans'.[82] In a review in *The Australian*, Blainey commented that 'it is almost certain that Frost knows more than anybody else about the early maritime history of this land' and expressed confidence that his work 'will surely alter the way Sydney sees its history'.[83] Given the tenacity with which others have held to the traditional view that settlement was predominantly about convicts, despite so much evidence to the contrary, it would be surprising if Frost's latest work had now settled the debate.

Just as there was continuity with *The Tyranny of Distance*, many of the themes of *Triumph of the Nomads* were also continued in *A Land Half Won*, in particular in the two specific chapters on Aboriginal dispossession titled 'White Ghosts Ride By' and 'War on the Grasslands'. The inclusion of Aboriginal Australia in a short history was recognised as a landmark moment by one reviewer who commented that this was 'the first short history to give significant space to Aborigines and to do their history in the period of white settlement anything like justice'.[84]

Historian John Molony, writing in the *Sydney Morning Herald*, liked much about the book, describing Blainey's treatment of Aboriginal history as 'superb', as he saw 'the tragedy and the wonder of it all'.[85] Tom Stannage lauded the fact that 'the Aborigines are in' and, although he had some quibbles on details, he recognised that the description of them defending the grasslands was 'a welcome turnaround in a general history'.[86] This aspect of the book was given even greater emphasis in the introduction to extracts published by *The Age* under the heading 'How the Aborigines lost the great guerrilla war'.[87]

---

81   Alan Frost, *Botany Bay: The Real Story* (Melbourne: Black Inc, 2011) and Alan Frost, *The First Fleet: The Real Story* (Melbourne: Black Inc. 2011).
82   Frost, *Botany Bay*, 13.
83   Geoffrey Blainey, 'New Take on Old Sydney', *The Weekend Australian* (Review section), 18–19 June 2011, 22–23.
84   John Merritt, review of *A Land Half Won*, *Victorian Historical Journal* 52, no. 3 (August 1981): 199.
85   John N. Molony, 'Australia: Survival or Greed', *Sydney Morning Herald*, 13 September 1980, 20.
86   Tom Stannage, review of *A Land Half Won*, *Historical Studies* 20, no. 78 (April 1982): 115.
87   Geoffrey Blainey, 'How the Aborigines lost the great guerrilla war', *The Age*, 6 September 1980, 21.

Blainey's trail-blazing role was acknowledged by Tim Rowse in *The Fuss That Never Ended*, who noted that Blainey was 'one of the earliest of recent historians to make a substantial topic of that violence'.[88]

One aspect of Blainey's treatment of the Indigenous population which had changed in the five years since *Triumph of the Nomads* was that the word Aboriginal was now given a capital, but otherwise there was continuity between the two books. Blainey maintained the twin positions that 'the lands were not static' and that 'the Aboriginals, even on the eve of the industrial revolution, were amongst the more prosperous people of the earth'.[89] One area of Aboriginal accomplishment highlighted in *A Land Half Won* was their understanding of botany, for both food and medicinal purposes. Blainey blamed the fact that so many Aboriginals died so quickly, and their nomadic lifestyle, for the failure of their botanical knowledge to be passed onto Europeans. However, there were examples where it was put to good use. Many of the troops involved in the D-Day landings in 1944 did not suffer seasickness due to taking a drug, the hyoscine from the Australian corkwood tree, the beneficial properties of which had been discovered by Indigenous Australians.[90]

Blainey still called the arrival of British settlement an 'invasion'.[91] He also expressed the belief that a treaty between the Indigenous population and the British would have been useful, writing that 'in many regions both the invaders and defenders would have gained from the kind of treaty signed in other lands'.[92] In discussing the interaction of Aboriginals and settlers, Blainey strove to avert collective condemnation of the latter, describing them as 'both enemies and friends' and 'the carriers of the wanted and the unwanted', and also observing that 'the Aboriginals received many kindnesses but many acts of meanness'.[93] Although sympathetic to the plight of Aboriginal Australians who were the victims of the expansion of white settlers across the nation, Blainey did not believe that sympathy for Aboriginals should extend to condemnation of the settlers:

> In Victoria where the Aboriginals by the 1880s were few, they received more generous help than the poor whites. Indeed the recent burst of

---

88 Rowse, 'Triumph of the Colonists', 45.
89 Blainey, *A Land Half Won*, 98, 305.
90 Ibid., 137.
91 Ibid., 62.
92 Ibid., 87. It is unclear whether he felt such a treaty would have any value in 1980 or whether the time had passed.
93 Ibid., 70, 251.

fierce criticism of colonial ministries of a century ago and of their 'racist' policies towards the blacks is not always fair, for it neglects to say how those same ministries treated the destitute members of their own race.[94]

There are several comments of this sort in *A Land Half Won*. For the first time one can see the battle lines being formed for what in the subsequent decades became the History Wars. While the term was not coined until much later, by the late 1970s settler Australians who, in earlier generations were seen as blameless, were being criticised for many failings. In a talk, soon after the launch of the book, Blainey noted that 'too often today people looking back at the 19th century think it would have been a simple matter for these two people to live in harmony… it wasn't a simple matter and it's still not a simple matter'.[95] He spotted a similar attitude towards Chinese immigrants, noting how 'it was the custom more than a century ago to place all the blame on the Chinese but now, as if in guilt, it is increasingly the custom to place no blame on the Chinese'.[96] Likewise, 'since 1890 academic explanations of poverty have tended to swing from the extreme position of placing virtually all the blame on the poor and unemployed to the other extreme of placing all blame on society'.[97]

Blainey's concern about modern judgments of past actions also arose in relation to several other issues. One example was that, while Eureka was now often seen as a symbol of Australian independence, at the time 'many saw the rebellion in 1854 as an uprising by outsiders who were exploiting the country's resources and refusing to pay their fair share of taxes'.[98] Similarly, while in the nineteenth century 'an English domestic servant who migrated here would probably have noticed a relative lack of visible wealth amongst the very rich and – to her eyes – a surprising number of possessions held by the poor', modern observers 'are more inclined to see the opposite'.[99]

Most historians concluding a book on Australia to 1900 would finish with the movement towards Federation. In Blainey's work, it was hardly mentioned. One learnt as much of his attitude to Federation in a lecture he gave the following year in which he observed that increasing nationalism had made

---

94   Ibid., 251.
95   Bill Birnbauer, 'How explorers died in blacks' land of plenty', *The Age*, 10 September 1980, 4.
96   Blainey, *A Land Half Won*, 165.
97   Ibid., 248.
98   Ibid., 158.
99   Ibid., 238.

people retrospectively consider 'the creation of the Commonwealth in 1901 as inevitable' whereas, at the time, 'it was as much a surprise as a foregone conclusion'.[100] Blainey was always prepared to consider political events such as Federation when someone else's arguments, such as Parker's, needed correction, or when asked to give a lecture on the topic, but when given a blank page he was more inclined to fill it with economic, social, technological and increasingly climatic issues. Thus, a far more significant 1890s event in *A Land Half Won* was the onset of drought, a drought that 'showed how little the Europeans, as distinct from the Aboriginals, had so far learned about the erratic climate'.[101]

Climate was an important feature of the work in other regards too, from its role as a factor in the British decision to settle at Botany Bay onwards. Blainey observed that 'many times the moods and motivations in Australian history had been strongly influenced by climate'.[102] He argued that attitudes towards the Australian climate ebbed and flowed:

> The attitude to Sydney's climate in 1800 seems to have been more favourable than it was two generations later. The mental attitudes to climate sometimes change, though we do not know much about those changes. Climate is more than a physical and measurable fact: its geniality or harshness depends much on how people adapt their minds and habits.[103]

The 'unexpected drought' of the 1890s was an antidote to the optimism about the climate that had been the normal mood in the 1870s and 1880s and, coming in conjunction with the bank crashes, it shattered the confidence of the colonies and 'the movement to federate the colonies into the Commonwealth of Australia was in part the result of that humbling'.[104] It was common to see Federation as a sign of growing Australian confidence and optimism. For Blainey it was the opposite.

One is generally inclined to think of Blainey as being a historical optimist. However, in *A Land Half Won*, there are warnings against being overly optimistic; for instance, he commented that 'a surfeit of optimism was to be

---

100 Geoffrey Blainey, 'Interstate Rivalries – A Historian's View' (paper delivered as the 1981 Alfred Deakin Lecture, University of Melbourne, 23 September 1981), 3.
101 Blainey, *A Land Half Won*, 348.
102 Ibid., 359.
103 Ibid., 141.
104 Ibid., 352, 359.

one of the dangerous legacies of the 1850s'.[105] Yet, at other points, he wrote approvingly of the optimism of men like Henry Parkes, who failed repeatedly at business but kept persisting.[106] The issue of optimism and pessimism had been on Blainey's mind in the period leading up to his writing *A Land Half Won*. He had begun work on a book on the topic before abandoning it (this was to re-emerge a decade later as *The Great Seesaw*). *A Land Half Won* perhaps marked something of a turning point in Blainey's outlook. Writing in 1985, Graeme Davison observed a 'growing pessimism' in Blainey's attitudes and hinted that there were some embryonic signs in *A Land Half Won*:

> His vision of Australia's history has hitherto been shaped by a strong sense of the country's material and social advance. The rush for wealth and progress had never seemed likely to end. In his *Land Half Won*, it is true, he pondered the adverse, as well as the favourable, results of the European conquest of Australia.[107]

As well as framing Federation as a result of material pessimism, rather than political optimism, *A Land Half Won* contained reminders that the reader should not overestimate the importance of political changes. Blainey argued that 'the main instruments of change had been less the political philosophers than telegraph operators, postmen, railway men, coach-drivers and ostlers, lighthouse keepers and steamship captains'.[108] Politicians often believed that they were powerful, or that legislation was the principal method of achieving change, whereas Blainey often pointed to their ineffectiveness compared to other players or sheer happenchance.

Blainey did hold the politicians accountable for some key failures, writing that 'the crash of the banks in 1893 could almost certainly have been averted by sound government polices'.[109] However, there was one aspect of Australian politics that pleased Blainey: the fact that 'many Australians were proud that their land was a political laboratory'.[110] A key democratic reform was the secret ballot, which was not introduced in the United Kingdom until 1872,

---

105   Ibid., 168.
106   Ibid., 239.
107   Graeme Davison, 'Unemployment, race and public opinion: reflections on the Asian immigration controversy of 1888', in *Surrender Australia? Essays in the Study and Uses of History: Geoffrey Blainey and Asian Immigration*, eds Andrew Markus and M.C. Ricklefs (Sydney: George Allen & Unwin, 1985), 102.
108   Blainey, *A Land Half Won*, 198.
109   Ibid., 330.
110   Ibid., 224.

some sixteen years after some Australian colonies had initiated it.[111] Blainey charted the arrival on the scene of the early Labor Party and highlighted the influence of the ideas of Henry George. He noted that Labor first rose to prominence in New South Wales where 'the ruling ideology of free trade, once a radical ideology, now seemed tame because radicalism in Europe was increasingly expressed more in collectivist and less in individualist terms'.[112] According to Blainey, Labor became a major party because living standards stopped rising from the 1890s onwards. However, he noted that the arrival of the Labor Party did not improve living standards, as prosperity did not improve over the next fifty years.[113]

Just as it was a pioneer in politics, Australia was a leader in many other fields in the nineteenth century, a fact Blainey highlighted. Australian newspapers were the first to be free from both taxes and censorship and Blainey quoted a contemporary observer who believed that the main newspapers in Sydney and Melbourne were the most powerful in the world.[114] He ran through what became his regular roll-call of Australian inventors, Harrison, Brennan, Hargrave and Michell and said that 'Australians contributed the most' to the combined harvester.[115] Blainey also gave Australia credit for arguably the most important scientific and intellectual development of the nineteenth century – the theory of evolution. Having described the visits of Charles Darwin, Thomas Huxley and others to Australia, Blainey asked whether it was 'merely a coincidence, at a time when only a handful of the natural scientists of Europe had visited Australia or its adjacent islands, that most scientists who were foremost in formulating and promoting the new theory of biological evolution had made such a visit?'[116]

It was not just the famous, or those he argued should-be-famous, who attracted Blainey's attention. He recognised that 'hundreds of long-forgotten men and women must have made those numerous small discoveries – how to make a better damper, how to make the handle of a stockwhip – which eased the daily burdens'.[117] He claimed that 'the mighty men were those who prospected in rain forest or desert'.[118] One reviewer, the labour historian John

---

111   Ibid., 222–223.
112   Ibid., 272.
113   Ibid., 275.
114   Ibid., 231–234.
115   Ibid., 215, 294.
116   Ibid., 151.
117   Ibid., 139–140.
118   Ibid., 169.

Merritt from the Australian National University, commented that while 'Karl Marx might not have liked Blainey's history (class and struggle are seldom present) ... he would have approved of the priority Blainey gives to the Australian people's material conditions of existence'.[119]

The economic historian W.A. Sinclair praised Blainey's 'sympathy for his characters' and how he was 'interested in what people were trying to do, not in making judgments as to whether they should have done it'.[120] Though sympathetic to the achievements and travails of early Australian settlers, Blainey's ambivalence about the period can be found in his delight in recounting the misadventures when northern hemisphere solutions were applied to the new environment. He listed a catalogue of poor decisions in agriculture, mining, railways and other facilities that undermined a lot of the progress that was being made, arguing that while 'risks were inevitable in the process of opening new natural resources ... many of the risks taken were extravagantly risky'.[121]

A classic poor decision was the introduction of rabbits. Blainey believed that the negative impact of the introduction of rabbits probably outweighed the benefits of the innovation of refrigerated ships, or even the discovery of the Broken Hill mining fields. He explained that historians had perhaps not given sufficient emphasis to rabbits because 'the written history of a new land is, understandably, so centred on applauding the innovations that lead to swift material progress that the innovations retarding progress are overlooked'.[122] Blainey also presented the interesting argument that rabbits 'indirectly were a form of welfare legislation' as the labour-intensive battle against them 'transferred money from wealthy squatters to rural labourers'.[123] Another apparent failure was William Lane's utopian socialist New Australia settlement in Paraguay, which Blainey saw forming part of a pattern:

> In failing as utopians they possibly became more a part of Australian folklore than if they had succeeded; and New Australia has quietly taken its place with Eureka, Cooper's Creek, Glenrowan and Gallipoli as a tantalizing failure, as a nationalist legend appealing to an unexpectedly wide range of people.[124]

---

119 Merritt, review of *A Land Half Won*, 200.
120 W.A. Sinclair, review of *A Land Half Won*, *Australian Economic History Review* 22, no. 1 (March 1982): 79–80.
121 Blainey, *A Land Half Won*, 297.
122 Ibid., 314.
123 Ibid., 313.
124 Ibid., 343.

Blainey has always maintained a particularly poor regard for the value of many of the trips undertaken by inland explorers, commenting that 'the courageous expeditions travelling far into the centre rarely had much effect on our history'.[125] He noted of an enthusiastic reception for John and Alexander Forrest that 'this welcome was for bravery ... the Forrests had found nothing'.[126] However, as always trying to appear balanced in his writing, Blainey also noted that 'we remember only the failure' of these journeys undertaken by inland explorers and 'forget the enthusiasm with which they commenced and the optimism which survived their return'.[127]

One aspect of *A Land Half Won* which raised some critical eyebrows was the use of a counterfactual time line of 'events which might have happened' if a separate colony had been founded in North Queensland in the 1880s.[128] This went through to the silver jubilee of the 'colony' in 1938, thus containing the only twentieth century 'events' in the book. Blainey justified its inclusion as follows:

> To set out a chronology of events that did not happen hardly seems appropriate in a history book. And yet we easily forget that every statement we make of why events happened is in part speculation. In looking at history we have to ask: what might have happened? ... In writing history we concentrate more on what did happen, but many of the crucial events are those which almost happened.[129]

Sometimes whether something happened, or failed to happen, came down largely to luck. Words related to luck figured often in Blainey's language. He referred to 'the casino of transportation' and uses the word 'lottery' three times to describe individuals' chances in Australia.[130] In contrast to Europe, 'even a feckless misfit of a migrant' had reason to have some optimism about his prospects as 'the unexpected event influenced the distributing of wealth in a new land'.[131]

Reviewers noted the absence of women from the book. Merritt thought it strange that 'one who has done so much to restore aborigines to mainstream

---

125 Ibid., 132.
126 Ibid., 177.
127 Ibid., 132. In his 2016 book *The Story of Australia's People: The Rise and Rise of A New Australia*, Blainey adopts a more charitable tone towards the land explorers; see 29–30.
128 Blainey, *A Land Half Won*, 201–203.
129 Ibid., 203.
130 Ibid., 43, 210, 239, 315.
131 Ibid., 238.

Australian history should remain insensitive to the equally justifiable claims of Australian women, black and white'.[132] John Rickard suggested that the neglect of women could be explained by Blainey's 'lack of interest in personal relationships', but recognised that 'an excellent little chapter on nineteenth-century feminists ... seems to reflect an awareness of this gap'.[133] When later in the book Blainey considered women's exclusion from the early period of democratic reform, he noted a 'now forgotten obstacle' which was the fact that members of the army, navy, police and clergy were often excluded from the rolls so women were not the only group to be excluded.[134] Another forgotten factor which, in Blainey's view, made women's political participation more difficult was that prior to the invention of the microphone the ability to project one's voice to the back of a large hall was a necessity for those seeking office.[135]

Another intriguing issue the book's approach raised was the potentially conflicting roles of the generalist and specialist historian. Sinclair, while generally praising the work, noted that he expected 'specialist readers to wish for more documentation of the ideas expressed'.[136] Merritt argued that contemporary general historians of Australia had a harder task than their predecessors because there were now specialists in many more fields.[137] Merritt foresaw that the specialists would attack, but warned them:

> Specialist critics, if they wish to be taken seriously, will need to do more than assert 'He has forgotten the churches' (or whatever their fancy may be). They will need to argue that Blainey's priorities are wrong and that other themes should dominate a short history; otherwise they will be criticising him for failing to write an encyclopaedia.[138]

Blainey's own specialty, economic history, was well represented in the book, with many acute observations and comparisons. For instance, he noted that the fact that the first two capitals, Sydney and Hobart, were furthest from mineral deposits altered the pattern of economic development in the country, and pointed out that inflation during the gold rush was five times higher than

---

132   Merritt, review of *A Land Half Won*, 200.
133   John Rickard, 'In Dialogue with the Environment', *Australian Book Review*, no. 28 (March 1981): 44.
134   Blainey, *A Land Half Won*, 258.
135   Ibid., 285.
136   Sinclair, review of *A Land half Won*, 79–80.
137   Merritt, review of *A Land Half Won*, 199.
138   Ibid., 200.

during the Korean War or the 1970s.[139] He provided a summary of the country's taxation history, noting the oddity that hardly anything had yet been written on the growth of new taxes.[140] Blainey hedged his bets somewhat on the influx of British capital into Australia. He coupled it with Australian ingenuity as one of the two most important factors in economic development from 1850 to 1890 but, when it came to the 1890s crash, he argued that 'Australia could not hope to absorb sensibly so much capital so quickly'.[141]

A Land Half Won was perhaps the highpoint of economic history's impact on the writing of general Australian history. Writing in 1979, Boris Schedvin said that 'over the past fifteen years economic history has grown in status and importance in most Australian universities, and there has been a transformation in our knowledge about many aspects of Australian material life'.[142] Subsequent decades have not been so kind to the subject. And while, when writing *A Land Half Won*, Blainey may still have been thinking like an economic historian, he was no longer officially working as one, having moved across campus at Melbourne University to join the general historians.

---

139 Blainey, *A Land Half Won*, 134, 164.
140 Ibid., 254–256 and note on 372.
141 Ibid., 198, 294–295, 319.
142 C.B. Schedvin, 'Midas and the Merino: A perspective on Australian Economic Historiography', *The Economic History* Review 32, no.4 (November 1979): 542.

Chapter 6

NATIONAL FIGURE

Between the early 1960s and the mid-1970s, Blainey advanced from being a well-known figure amongst historians, associated intellectuals, and parts of the business community, to being a national figure. The publication of such popular works as *The Tyranny of Distance* and *Triumph of the Nomads* were key factors in this. Another was his continued success in the academy as he secured appointment as a Professor, first of Economic History, and then of History at the University of Melbourne.

Since joining the Commerce Faculty in 1962, Blainey had received suggestions that he should apply for other positions. For instance, when he was in England in 1966, he received an aerogramme from Manning Clark proposing he apply for a role at the ANU, a move which Clark claimed 'Ken Inglis, John La Nauze and Ron Barassi insist will be'.[1]

However, when Blainey did move it was to the Arts Faculty of his own university to assume the title of Ernest Scott Professor of History, a slight irony considering his forceful critique of aspects of Scott's work on the history of the university two decades earlier. The professorship in Scott's honour had been created in the mid-1950s, when the University decided that many departments needed two professorial positions. In the period since the position's creation, it had been held by La Nauze and John Poynter, the latter vacating it to take up a role as Deputy Vice-Chancellor. The original selection of La Nauze provided two precedents for Blainey's appointment. Both men were Professor of Economic History at the time and both were on the selection committee for the position. In Blainey's case, part way through the selection process the Vice-Chancellor, David Derham, approached him and asked him to put his name forward. His appointment was announced in March 1976.

---

1   Manning Clark to Blainey, 1 August 1966, Blainey Papers, MS 9225/4/7 Box 23, NLA. At this time, Ron Barassi was in his second season as captain-coach of Clark's football team Carlton (after a dramatic move from Melbourne), and therefore the highest authority (albeit a spurious one in this context) that a football-loving former Melburnian could invoke. He later progressed to signing off postcards as with the name of Alex Jesaulenko, a Carlton champion in the 1970s (Blainey, *Before I Forget*, 216).

Although the distance between the Commerce Building on the western side of campus and the John Medley Building near the southern entrance from Grattan Street was not that great, there were differences between Blainey's old colleagues in Economic History and his new ones in History, which ended up making the latter a less congenial working environment for Blainey. Yet this did not manifest itself for several years. Stuart Macintyre, who joined the History Department in 1980 and has written its history, has commented that Blainey 'adapted readily to its collegial forms, and when he served as head of department he conducted business with a remarkable dexterity: staff meetings were rarely so harmonious or expeditious'.[2]

Blainey lectured and tutored in a mixture of Modern European and Australian History subjects, constantly updating his material and trying to convince others to do likewise, as one observer described:

> Blainey exercised leadership by example and encouragement – he took a warm personal interest in the work of even the most junior members of the Department – and served just one term as Head of Department. This was remarkable for resolving the lengthy prior arguments over the curriculum with his own proposal that no subject should be offered for more than five years. Since it was his habit to teach from his current research, and his teaching invariably attracted overflow numbers, the traditionalists were shamed into endorsing the proposal – and while some carried on regardless, his point was made.[3]

Not only was Blainey popular with undergraduate students, when he spoke to final year high school students as part of the Baillieu Library HSC Lectures, the university's Public Lecture Theatre was invariably full, with students bringing copies of his books to be signed.

Blainey brought to Arts from Economic History firmly held views about thesis supervision and examination. Supervision was something he thought should be done with a light touch. He explained that 'my practice ... is to find out whether the candidate is competent, and if so, to leave him largely alone... a thesis is a useless form of examination if it calls for too

---

2   Stuart Macintyre, 'Blainey and the Australian Historical Profession', in *The Fuss That Never Ended: The life and work of Geoffrey Blainey*, eds Gare et al. (Melbourne: Melbourne University Press, 2003), 12.

3   John Salmond, 'Adapting to Change: The History Department, 1970-2004' in *The Life of the Past: The discipline of history at the University of Melbourne, 1855-2005*, eds Fay Anderson and Stuart Macintyre, (Melbourne: RMIT Publishing, 2006), 104.

much supervision'.⁴ And when it came to examination, his most strongly held view appears to have been in favour of giving weight to students who pursued ambitious topics. He praised one candidate for being 'intellectually adventurous ... high praise, given the band-aid strip of territory studied by the average postgraduate thesis'.⁵ His opinions often seem to have clashed with those of other examiners. In one 1979 case, he said of an essay given an H1 by another examiner that he felt that 'parts of her work were not up to pass standard'.⁶

While early in his tenure in Economic History Blainey had been sufficiently in step with his colleagues to be one of the authors of the Red Book of academic grievances, by the time he moved to History he had developed a more jaundiced view of their work. In 1980, he expressed scepticism about his colleagues' campaign seeking more government funding for research, outlining a number of ways in which the actions of various academics had undermined their own case, including ill-advised attacks on science and too much focus on expanding numbers of staff. He also pointed out that he had 'never applied for ARGC money ... nor even for University research money, short of small change, so I don't feel the pinch in the same way'.⁷ He suggested that instead of focusing on their own funding, academics should be pushing for more generous awards for postgraduates.

One other difference between Blainey and most of his colleagues was that Blainey had a much broader focus than just his academic career. Between 1967 and 1984, he was a member, or chair, of several Commonwealth Government committees or boards. These were a significant factor in his rise to national prominence. The roles brought him into contact with many other prominent Australians and saw him become embroiled in issues which generated media controversies. Of course, the time commitment of these committee roles meant that even someone with as strong a work ethic as Blainey ran the risk of being drawn away from writing history.

Blainey's first appointment came in September 1967 when he was invited to join the Advisory Board of the Commonwealth Literary Fund (CLF). The fund had been established in 1908 to provide pensions to impoverished authors and expanded in the late 1930s to provide grants to facilitate the writing of

---

4   Note from Blainey contained in letter from R.A. Cumming to Dr Herman, 26 January 1973, Blainey Papers, Acc. No. 89/145 Box 4, UMA.
5   Report on a thesis 1979, Blainey Papers, Acc. No. 89/145 Box 4, UMA.
6   Report on a thesis 1979, Blainey Papers, Acc. No. 89/145 Box 7, UMA.
7   Blainey to Peter Darvall, President, Federation of University Staff Associations, 20 December 1979, Blainey Papers, Acc. No. 89/145 Box 29, UMA.

new works and the conducting of lectures to stimulate interest in literature. The decision-making body was a committee comprising the Prime Minister, the Leader of the Opposition and the Leader of the Country Party, with the politicians' advice coming from an advisory committee of literary experts which, in 1967, comprised the geographer Archie Grenfell Price (Chair since 1953), the poets Douglas Stewart and Kenneth Slessor, novelist and critic Kylie Tennant, and academics Tom Inglis Moore and A.R. Chisholm.

It was Price who pushed to get Blainey on the Board. He decided that Blainey should replace the aging Emeritus Professor of French at the University of Melbourne, Chisholm, who often did not make it to the Sydney meetings. The CLF official, Valda Leehy, recalled what happened:

> Sir Grenfell wanted by hook or by crook to have Blainey on that board instead of Chisholm, because he was an historian. He said, 'It's going to be Geoffrey Blainey or nobody', and he won, although it took the powers-that-be about three months to make up their minds. That was Geoffrey Blainey's introduction to various boards of the Establishment...
> Sir Grenfell was terribly fond of him. He brought him out into the world, shall one say.[8]

Years later, Blainey wrote the foreword to Price's biography and recalled their first meeting 'at a history conference at Easter, 1965, near the sand dunes at the mouth of the Murray', and how they talked about 'old-time whaling ships, and we could hear the waves pounding the beach as we talked'.[9] While the rest of the board's 'exceptionally talented members' usually called Grenfell Price 'Archie', Blainey who was 'half his age ... did not call him "Archie" [as] he seemed too venerable'.[10]

When Blainey joined the Advisory Board, it was usually meeting four times a year, nearly always in Sydney or Canberra, and he was the only Victorian on it. From the time he joined the Board, Blainey was 'struck by the board's fierce tradition of independence in the face of political pressures'.[11] For most of his long Prime Ministership, Robert Menzies had taken a keen personal interest in the committee, but the less intellectual Harold Holt delegated the role of assessing the works and attending the meetings to Billy Snedden, a practice

---

8   Colin Kerr, *Archie: The biography of Sir Archibald Grenfell Price*, (Melbourne: Macmillan, 1983), 212.
9   Blainey, 'Preface', Kerr, *Archie*.
10 Ibid.
11 Geoffrey Blainey, 'Government patronage and literature', *Overland*, no. 57 (Summer 1973–1974): 40. The article was based on a talk Blainey gave in November 1972.

also followed by Country Party Leader, John McEwen (to Philip Lucock). However, the Opposition Leader, Gough Whitlam, attended the meetings in person and he made the committee more overtly political when he leaked to the press the details of a meeting held in late 1968. At that meeting the advisory board recommended that the Communist Frank Hardy should be awarded a literary fellowship; however, Snedden and Lucock voted against it. Chairman Price was more upset by the leaking than by the overturning of his Board's recommendation, and at its next meeting the Board made the following statement:

> The Board expressed alarm at the leakages which had occurred in connection with the refusal of a Commonwealth Literary Fund fellowship to Mr. Frank Hardy, particularly as discussions between the Committee and the Advisory Board had always been regarded confidential.[12]

Whitlam could not claim that he believed in the principle of following the Advisory Board's recommendations, because when the Advisory Board proposed a grant to *Quadrant* he voted against it.[13]

Having been stable for many years, the membership of the Advisory Board changed dramatically in 1971, most notably with the retirement of Price. Blainey ended up succeeding him, but only after the responsible Minister, Peter Howson, had to deal with the fact that recently departed Prime Minister (and at this stage still troublesome Deputy Prime Minister) John Gorton 'had apparently made half a promise' to the former National Librarian, Harold White.[14] A discussion on the telephone with Blainey, whom his department had recommended, led Howson to decide that he 'should proceed to appoint him chairman as soon as possible'.[15]

At 41, Blainey was almost twenty years younger than the next youngest member of the Board, but despite, or perhaps because of, this he leapfrogged

---

12   Minutes of meeting of Advisory Board of CLF, 31 January 1969, Blainey Papers, Acc. No. 75/38 Box 2, UMA.

13   *Quadrant* sought a grant of $4,000 to match that received by *Meanjin*, however the Advisory Board concluded that it did not merit it, due to its being more a political than a literary journal, however because it provided some service to Australian literature it should receive $1,500.

14   Peter Howson, *The Howson Diaries: The Life of Politics* (Melbourne: Viking Press, 1984), 737, entry for 21 June 1971.

15   Howson, *Diaries*, 750, entry for 16 July, 1971. Howson does not explain what impressed him about Blainey. The appointment was approved by Prime Minister, Billy McMahon, on 6 September 1971.

the older and more experienced members to the chairmanship. The change of Chair was not the only change to the Committee in 1971 as Moore, a member of the board since 1945, retired and Slessor died. In addition to replacing them, a further new member was required when membership was increased to seven.

In Blainey's first year as Chair, the CLF budget was raised from $171,000 to $300,000, which not only enabled more fellowships to be given but saw their value increase from $6,000 to $8,000. One critic who had written a series of negative articles about the Fund in 1971 had altered his tune by late 1972, noting that 'in the past year or so the fund has changed radically', evidenced by the fact that 'its membership has altered, the money has increased, and its thinking has changed'.[16] The Board also met in more diverse places, adding Perth and Melbourne to a schedule that had previously only left Sydney and Canberra for a bi-annual visit to Adelaide at Festival time.

More radical change followed the election of the Whitlam Labor Government in December 1972. The CLF was abolished and replaced by a Literature Board which, instead of being answerable to a political committee, became a committee of the Australian Council for the Arts, a body chaired by H.C. 'Nugget' Coombs with Jean Battersby as its chief executive. The new structure was announced on Australia Day 1973. Whitlam had originally intended not to allow any members of previous boards to have a role in his new structure, but Coombs convinced him to retain a third of them.[17] In the case of Literature, this led to Blainey's confirmation as Chair and to former CLF members, Geoffrey Dutton and A.D. Hope, joining him on the new body, whose new appointees included Manning Clark, Judah Waten and Nancy Keesing. Waten suggested Michael Costigan as an administrator and Costigan has described how all the members of the new board 'arrived at the early meetings full of ideas for fresh approaches to the task'.[18]

The new structure meant a greatly increased workload for Blainey. The Literature Board met twenty-eight times between March 1973 and June 1974, in addition to which there were the meetings of the Council and meetings of a sub-committee overseeing a competition to choose a new national anthem. As a result, Blainey was averaging two days per week interstate on government

---

16   Maurice Dunlevy, 'Eating some words about grants', *Canberra Times*, 11 November 1972, 12.

17   Gough Whitlam, *The Whitlam Government 1972–1975* (Melbourne: Viking Penguin, 1985), 558.

18   Michael Costigan, 'My decade at the Literature Board', *Southerly* 56, no. 2 (Winter 1996): 150.

business.[19] However, at least initially, Blainey welcomed the new arrangements. Firstly, there was no interference in the Literature Board, with Blainey noting in late 1973 that 'none of the decisions made at its first twenty meetings have been overruled or amended by the council'.[20] Secondly, having almost doubled in the final year of the Coalition Government, funding for literature now increased fourfold. The increased budget enabled the Board to give more twelve-month fellowships and provided the flexibility to take more risks with young writers, knowing that this speculation was not at the expense of an established writer.[21]

The massive increase in funding meant that Blainey was often required to address the principle of why taxpayers should support writers. During his time on the CLF he had already given the matter considerable thought, at one stage commenting that he supported funding writers, not for the good of writers, but for the good of the nation:

> If a competent writer cannot make a living from freelance work or books he can certainly make a living by writing for a salary… It seems that there is only one justification for government aid to a writer: aid is justified when someone, by spending the best hours of the day on creative writing, gives much more to the nation than if he spent the time writing recipes and speeches or doing other work.[22]

By 1972, he had developed an analogy to justify funding writers, an analogy that he deployed regularly as the attacks on the quantum of funding grew:

> The case for government aid for writers is at least as strong as the government aid for teachers; and that's why I used teachers' salaries by way of comparison. If teachers had to depend on the free market – on the fees received from children – few would make a reasonable living; accordingly just on a century ago in Australia the state began to take over the sole responsibility for teachers' salaries in most schools. The similarity between the writer and the teacher is much closer than we usually realize. A talented author is a teacher, a very special teacher… He is therefore entitled to his reward.[23]

---

19   Blainey to Michael Zifcak, 30 May 1973, Blainey Papers, Acc. No. 75/38 Box 6, UMA.
20   Blainey, 'Government patronage and literature', 42.
21   'Providing State Salary for Fiction Writers', *National Times*, 9–14 July 1973, 58.
22   Blainey to W.R. Cumming, 25 November 1969, Blainey Papers, Acc. No. 75/38 Box 2, UMA.
23   Blainey, 'Government patronage and literature', 41–42.

Blainey continually used his comparisons with teachers and compared the arguments against writers' fellowships to those used a century earlier against free lending libraries, free primary schools and paying salaries to members of Parliament.[24] As well as the principle of funding authors, there were also complaints about specific grants, including the suggestion that one had been given to a woman whose husband was a highly paid professional. Blainey argued that rare examples like this did not justify the setting up of a bureaucracy to search out such matters, adding that for all he knew the woman in question might 'be taking the opportunity to give up that professional man and his high salary'.[25] The extra funding increased the output of writers, with the numbers of Australian novels published annually increasing from 19 in 1972 to over 200 by the mid-1980s.[26]

Another important issue was Public Lending Right, a proposal to recompense authors and publishers for the lending of their books from public libraries. In 1974, Australia became the ninth country in the world to legislate for such a scheme and, in order to avoid imposing costs on libraries or borrowers, the taxpayer picked up the tab. Previously, Blainey had considered more funds for authors via the CLF a higher priority than subsidising a PLR scheme.[27] However, under the Whitlam Government there appeared to be sufficient money to fund authors directly, and also provide support to publishers, introduce the PLR and contribute to other more radical ideas to stimulate interest in Australian books. Under Blainey's chairmanship, the Literature Board initiated the world's first dial-a-book and dial-a-poem services; developed a scheme for handing out coupons in shopping centres which could be redeemed on Australian books; and investigated the setting up of an Australian bookshop in London.

The Literature Board also ventured into both state and international spheres. Blainey provided some colourful comments to the press when the NSW Government introduced a new Indecency Law, suggesting that, if the proposed law had been in force in the 1890s, magistrates 'would have decreed "Waltzing Matilda" an indecent publication'.[28] In June 1974, on the

---

24 Geoffrey Blainey, 'The Hazards of Handing Out a Million', *The Australian*, 12 September 1973, 14.
25 Blainey, 'The Hazards of Handing Out a Million'.
26 Thomas Shapcott, *The Literature Board: A Brief History* (Brisbane: University of Queensland Press, 1988), 9.
27 Blainey to W.R. Cumming, 2 February 1970, Blainey Papers, MS 9225/4/6 Box 23, NLA; and Blainey to Cumming, 12 February 1970, Blainey Papers, Acc. No. 75/38 Box 3, UMA.
28 'Pornography bill "will do grave harm"', *Sydney Morning Herald*, 20 March 1973, 2.

first day of a two-day Board meeting at the Embassy Motel in Canberra, Blainey reported on a trip he had made to the Soviet Union, where a meeting with four officials of the Writers' Union had reached an agreement which would see three writers going each way between Australia and the Soviet Union every year. The Board endorsed this proposal, the only contrary view coming the following morning, when Richard Walsh (who had not been present on the first day) asked that his dissent to the scheme be formally recorded (since he did not think the Board should accord recognition to the Soviet Writers' Union).[29] Blainey clearly believed in engagement with communist countries, just as he had done with his 1966 trip.

That Canberra meeting was Blainey's last as Chairman of the Literature Board, his departure the result of friction with Battersby. From the start, there was a dispute over office location, triggered by Blainey's recruitment of Joan O'Donnell, former private secretary to the recently retired Arthur Calwell, to be secretary to the board. As she lived with her elderly mother, O'Donnell had to be Melbourne-based, which was acceptable to Blainey and his board, especially once O'Donnell, through her public service connections, quickly secured an office in Treasury Place. However, this independent behaviour did not please the centralising Battersby who complained to Whitlam about it.[30] The influence of Battersby and Coombs was underscored by the fact that when Labor was still in Opposition, the pair had prepared a confidential briefing for Whitlam on how arts bodies should be structured under a future Labor Government.[31]

Blainey's friend Stephen Murray-Smith was in no doubt that 'Blainey was rolled by Battersby and Coombs' due to his being 'too independent a chairman of the Literature Board'.[32] Murray-Smith believed that the rapid turnover of board members was allowing more power to accrue to the bureaucracy and that therefore 'the say of artists and writers in their own affairs has diminished very rapidly in the last eighteen months … no Liberal Government ever overrode its arts boards as this government has done'.[33] His own Labor partisanship in 1972 increased Murray-Smith's disappointment at these events, and also made him feel entitled to write directly to

---

29   Minutes of Meeting no. 28, Blainey Papers, Acc. No. 75/38 Box 13, UMA.
30   Costigan, 'My decade at the Literature Board', 149. Costigan described O'Donnell as 'a wonderfully experienced, shrewd and unflappable public servant, who stood in awe of nobody'.
31   Whitlam, *Whitlam Government*, 557.
32   Stephen Murray-Smith, 'Swag', *Overland*, no. 58 (Winter 1974): 37.
33   Ibid.

the Prime Minister enclosing a copy of his critical article. Whitlam wrote a witty response saying that he had read the article 'with interest, captious and caustic as much of it was'.[34] He reiterated his support for rapid turnover of Board members, despite the fact that 'I yield to none in my admiration of Geoffrey Blainey and his work for the Board'.

The Murray-Smith version of events seemed to become the accepted wisdom. It was quickly endorsed in a feature article in *Nation Review* which argued 'that somewhere in the incestuous upper layers of the public service an opinion was formed that Geoffrey Blainey was too independent and conscientious and that the board might, as a result, escape the vassalage that the mandarins of the public service demand'.[35] It remained the standard interpretation. A press article three years later commented that it was 'widely believed' that the reason Blainey and other members of the board were not reappointed was because 'they had tended to be outspoken and clashed with the council executive'.[36]

Ironically, the board finally moved to Sydney in December 1975, just after the demise of the Whitlam Government. Years later, Whitlam commented in his memoirs that 'Geoffrey Blainey resisted the whole idea of a Literature Board, preferring that the responsibility for assisting writers be retained by the Commonwealth Literary Fund, preferably based in Melbourne; for him the tyranny of distance to Sydney was intolerable'.[37] Blainey responded in a newspaper column explaining that:

> Mr Whitlam's long account does not really need the bursts of high partisanship, the loaded figures, and the inaccurate tilt at those politicians who came before and after him. His records in the arts largely speaks for itself, and his willingness to promote the arts, both with eloquence and money, will be remembered long after most of his failures and his other successes are forgotten.[38]

---

34 Prime Minister Gough Whitlam to Stephen Murray-Smith, 17 September 1974, Blainey Papers, Acc. No. 75/38 Box 7, UMA.

35 Edward Kynaston, 'Australia's Little Literary Watergate', *Nation Review*, 13–19 September 1974, 1541.

36 Wendy Owen, 'Historian takes the helm', *The Age*, 9 July 1977, 21.

37 Whitlam, *Whitlam Government*, 558.

38 Geoffrey Blainey, 'Gough Whitlam and the arts', *The Australian*, 29 November 1985, 15. Reprinted as 'Mr Whitlam loads the dice' in Blainey, *Eye on Australia*, 51–55.

Blainey's term as Chairman built his status, with one newspaper article noting that 'he had made many friends and won much respect; he was honest, unegotistical and an eloquent persuader in argument'.[39]

Blainey's time on the Literature Board reinforced the friendship he had with the novelist Judah Waten. Being the only Victorians on the board the pair travelled everywhere together. The communist Waten could be considered an unlikely friend for Blainey. Waten was so hardline in his pro-Soviet stance that he criticised Manning Clark's *Meeting Soviet Man* (1960) for being too critical of the Soviet Union and later quit the Communist Party of Australia (CPA) after it moved away from the Soviets in the wake of the 1968 invasion of Czechoslovakia. By the mid-1970s, Waten had joined the pro-Soviet Socialist Party of Australia (SPA), writing a column in the party newspaper.[40] At his 1985 funeral, those delivering eulogies included a representative of the SPA and Blainey. Describing the rich social interaction between the Blaineys and Watens, Blainey observed that 'it did not seem to matter' that the couples had such divergent political views as Waten's 'warmth and personal tolerance coped easily with such differences'.[41]

The termination of Blainey's role on the Literature Board did not bring an end to his involvement in national committees under the Whitlam Government. In 1974, Blainey was included as a member of a Committee of Inquiry into the Development and Co-ordination of Museums and Collections, the Government having secured his part-time leave from the University.[42] The committee was chaired by Sydney businessman, Peter Pigott and, while it had nine members, it seems that much of the intellectual load fell on Blainey, who became vice-chairman, and John Mulvaney, both of whom had lobbied for such an inquiry to be set up.

As well as receiving over 400 submissions, members of the committee travelled to every state in Australia, visiting museums and meeting with interested parties. In early 1975, Blainey headed a delegation which undertook an extensive trip to Europe and North America, visiting forty major museums. The Committee's officials did much of the drafting of the committee's final report, but Blainey also undertook some of this task, as well as taking prime

---

39   Nicklin, 'Blainey is the new chairman'.
40   David Carter, 'Waten: Judah Leon (1911-1985)', *Australian Dictionary of Biography*, National Centre of Biography, Australian National University, http://adb.anu.edu.au/biography/waten-judah-leon-14884/text26074, published first in hardcopy 2012, accessed online 24 September 2017.
41   Geoffrey Blainey, 'Judah Waten', *Overland* no. 100 (September 1985): 97–100.
42   Special Minister of State, Lionel Bowen, to Vice-Chancellor, David Derham, 14 March 1974, Blainey Papers, Acc. No. 77/3 Box 6, UMA.

responsibility for redrafting and editing. The total time commitment was estimated by Blainey at '110 or 120 working days solely or overwhelmingly on the committee's business'.[43]

The Committee's report was tabled on 5 November 1975, just six days before the dismissal of the Whitlam Government. Its recommendations included the establishment of an Australian Museums Commission to determine needs and priorities for museums throughout the nation for both preservation and further acquisition, a national fund to facilitate emergency acquisitions, the establishment of a Museum of Australia in Canberra, and the regulation of exports of items of significance. Given the political situation at the time, the recommendations did not generate much media interest, but the committee itself did become an issue in the final week of the campaign for the 13 December election. Richard Farmer wrote a piece in *The Australian* titled 'Like Topsy the committees just never seemed to stop growing', highlighting that the museums' committee had cost taxpayers $202,476.[44] Pigott wrote a spirited defence of the value of his committee's work and its report 'which was the combined effort of nine dedicated people and was finely edited by the highly regarded author and historian Professor Geoffrey Blainey'.[45] Pigott's letter appeared on Thursday, 11 December 1975; two days later the voters of Australia delivered their own judgement on the value of the spending of the Whitlam Government.

It was not only the Commonwealth Government which used Blainey on committees in the 1970s. In 1973, the Hamer Government in Victoria appointed him to the inaugural Public Records Advisory Committee, a group designed to guide the newly created Public Records Office. He also chaired the judging panel for the inaugural awarding of *The Age* Book of the Year in 1974. Blainey and his panel assessed 54 books before selecting joint winners – Manning Clark for volume three of the *History of Australia* and the novelist David Ireland for *The Pure Land*.

There was only a hiatus of a few months when Blainey was not on a Commonwealth committee. He returned to active duty in mid-1976 when the Fraser Government appointed him as one of six inaugural commissioners of the Australian Heritage Commission (AHC). This statutory authority

---

43   Notes of Blainey's address to Museums Association of Australia Annual Conference in Ballarat, 23–24 October 1975, Blainey Papers, Acc. No. 77/3 Box 9, UMA.

44   Richard Farmer, 'Like Topsy the committees just never seemed to stop growing', *The Australian*, 8 December 1975, 9.

45   Peter Pigott, 'National treasures being lost' (letter to the editor), *The Australian*, 11 December 1975, 12.

had been established in Whitlam-era legislation, to act as the Government's policy advisory and administrative body responsible for the National Estate. Matters of the National Estate considered by the AHC in its first year included sand-mining on Fraser Island, wood-chips, nature reserves, Aboriginal places, Ayers Rock, Norfolk Island, Hanging Rock, and municipal buildings.

Blainey resigned from the AHC after just over a year when he was offered the Chairmanship of the Australia Council for what proved to be a four-year term, succeeding Peter Karmel, who had held the position since Coombs' retirement in mid-1974. Karmel had kept a low profile, but one newspaper article commented that, while Blainey gave 'the impression that he finds publicity a little bothersome', he nonetheless believed that his job was 'to articulate what the council is trying to do'.[46]

Fraser himself was Arts Minister, but appointing Blainey to the position seems to have been at the initiative of the Minister Assisting, Tony Staley. Having been Fraser's numbers man in his party room victory over Billy Snedden, Staley presumably had more clout than most junior ministers and so it is plausible that, as journalist Phillip McCarthy put it a few years later, 'both the appointment of Blainey as chairman and the appointment of John Cameron as general manager – a post Staley created in 1976 to wrest control from the chief executive officer Jean Battersby – were Staley's ideas'.[47] The article explained that Blainey and Cameron were consistent with Staley's 'pointedly liberal, consensus approach to politics' and that the two appointees were 'impeccably polite, proper, reserved and undogmatic'.[48]

However, the relationship between the Australia Council Chair and the Fraser Government did not prove to be an entirely happy one, particularly after the 1977 election when Bob Ellicott took on a Home Affairs portfolio that included the arts. Ellicott was more interventionist than Staley, for instance objecting in 1978 when the Theatre Board of the Australia Council took a controversial decision to defund Sydney's Old Tote Theatre.

While specific decisions, such as the Old Tote, attracted attention, the main way in which the arts community judged the Government was by the overall quantum of the funding. There were none of the big increases of the early Whitlam years, but neither was funding cut severely. Three years into Blainey's tenure, one observer noted that the consensus was that he had done

---

46   Owen, 'Historian takes the helm'.
47   Phillip McCarthy, 'Malcolm as Medici: Just Getting By', *National Times*, 27 December 1981–2 January 1982, 15.
48   Ibid.

'all that was diplomatically possible to minimise an erosion of arts funding'.[49] In his memoirs, Whitlam criticised the Fraser Government cuts to arts funding. It prompted a response from Blainey, who pointed out that the boom times had ended with Labor's own economically more rational 1975 budget, which delivered a twelve per cent reduction in real terms, a larger cut than any under the Fraser Government.[50]

During Blainey's tenure the Industries Assistance Commission (forerunner to today's Productivity Commission) recommended that all funding to publishing, other than copyright protection, be removed. Asked for a comment, Blainey called the report 'bone shaking'. Returning to his familiar refrain about the relative importance of writers and teachers, he stated that he 'could draw up a long list of important Australian books which would never have been published without a subsidy' and asserted that 'some of these books have possessed more influence educationally than a dozen teachers in our subsidised school system'.[51] Blainey also added another analogy to his repertoire. He argued that 'there's a mighty difference between wasting public money and risking public money', comparing a grant to a writer who failed to produce the promised novel with a tertiary student who dropped out of a science course part way through.[52]

Part way through his term, Blainey summarised his view of the state of the arts for a newspaper overview of the topic, saying 'I think you have to say that the arts are reasonably healthy in Australia now, but it's hard to know if they touch more than about 10 per cent of the population – if that'.[53] In another interview, he suggested that one of the reasons for the narrow reach of the arts was that 'our definition of the arts is too narrow', arguing that football was also 'an art form'.[54] He explained that he attended the majority of Geelong's home and away games, catching the train to games in Geelong, generally standing in the outer by himself, and commenting that he got 'more pleasure out of watching a good football match than almost anything else'.[55]

A further Fraser Government appointment, which Blainey accepted, was as the inaugural Chairman of the Australia-China Council, a position he held from 1979 to 1984. Originally the Government had planned to

---

49 Downes, 'The man who was always looking for something'.
50 Blainey, 'Gough Whitlam and the arts'.
51 Jennifer Byrne, 'Cut book aid: report', *The Age*, 20 November 1978.
52 Owen, 'Historian takes the helm'.
53 Peter Ward, 'No business like show biz', *The Australian*, 6 February 1979, 10.
54 Downes, 'The man who was always looking for something'.
55 Ibid.

appoint former Ambassador to China, Stephen FitzGerald, to the role, but he was vetoed after a revolt by Government backbenchers, who objected to Fitzgerald's strongly pro-China stance. In part of his discussions before accepting the role, Blainey suggested that Fitzgerald should be asked to be Deputy Chair, a role he accepted.

The Council was set up to encourage business, cultural and sporting contacts between the two countries. As his support for contact with Soviet writers when he was Chair of the Literature Board had already demonstrated, Blainey believed that engagement with Communist countries was a better approach than isolation.

Annual trips to China, commitments when Chinese delegations came to Australia and quarterly meetings of the Council only added to Blainey's workload. At times, his multiple roles meant he found himself overwhelmed by the volume of work, writing to his friend Ken Inglis in 1978 that 'I seem to be overwhelmed by this and that, mostly trivial things… they seem to be the more overwhelming'.[56] The sum of Blainey's responsibilities meant that there were only a few days a year on which he did not work. Thus, it is no coincidence that the period from 1975 to 1980 was the longest gap between books in Blainey's career. He noted in a 1977 newspaper interview that it was the first time in 25 years that he could not say that he was actively writing a book.[57]

Another development in Blainey's career during the 1970s was getting the opportunity to write newspaper opinion pieces, a growth area for historians and other public intellectuals in the 1970s. His departure from the Literature Board in 1974 was the trigger for his first regular newspaper column, which appeared fortnightly in *The Australian* in 1974-75. He wrote on topics including the risks of ever higher inflation, attitudes to Aboriginal Australia, and the decline of small rural towns. One of his strongest objections was to metrication. He queried 'whether in the history of Australia any major reform – any reform affecting every day of every life – has been adopted on the basis of so many spurious arguments and so much mangled evidence'.[58] The opposition to metrics reflected the tone of many of the columns, a dislike of certain aspects of contemporary life. This was well captured in one of his final columns, in early 1975, when he lamented the growth of gratuitous

---

56 Blainey to Ken Inglis, 17 November 1978, Blainey Papers, Acc. No. 89/145 Box 4, UMA.
57 Nicklin, 'Blainey is the new Chairman'.
58 Geoffrey Blainey, 'Time for a rethink on metrics', *The Australian,* 13 November 1974, 8. Blainey's friend Stephen Murray-Smith headed an anti-metric association.

noise produced by motor mowers, jet aircraft, freeways, transistor radios and pop music at parties. He proposed a piece of political progressivism by suggesting that each State Government should set up 'an environment ministry capable of assessing and regulating novel engines before – not after – they devastate the peace'.[59]

The Australian column proved short-lived but within a year Blainey had negotiated a deal with the editor of *The National Times*, Max Suich, to write articles and book reviews. From the start of the discussions with Suich, one of the topics under consideration was the 'Origins of the Pacific War' and, by January 1976, Blainey had produced an article.[60] It was not published until July but, when it appeared, it generated significant controversy.[61] The article pointed out that a very different standard had been applied to Japan annexing territory than to the countries of the British Empire when they did the same. Further, the failure to appreciate the potential strength of Japan made Australia respond in a bellicose manner towards the threat and therefore increased the likelihood of war. And Australia's role was significant because, unlike many others, Blainey believed that Australia was influential in deciding British imperial policy towards Japan.

Many Australians who had always considered Japan totally to blame for the war in the Pacific wrote in anger to the paper. Suich reported that 'most letters have contained the touch of the ratbag' but also noted that, after discussion with Blainey, 'where you suggested that even ratbag letters may be of use to future historians, I plan to publish a couple'.[62] The article formed the basis for a new chapter in an Australian-only new edition of *The Causes of War*, published in 1977.

Another position Blainey expressed in the pages of *The National Times* was support for the supersonic jet, the Concorde, being allowed to operate to Australia, an aircraft which many in the community were opposing on environmental grounds. In a formulation very similar to the one he had used to link opponents of literary grants in the 1970s to opponents of state education in the 1870s, Blainey argued that the main line of argument of the Concorde's opponents 'if applied as fervently in the last century to the

---

59   Geoffrey Blainey, 'Invasion of noise', *The Australian*, 3 February 1975, 8.
60   Blainey to Max Suich, 19 December 1975, Blainey Papers, Acc. No. 89/145 Box 13, UMA.
61   Geoffrey Blainey, 'Origins of the Pacific War', *National Times*, 26–31 July 1976, 26–31.
62   Max Suich to Blainey, 9 August 1976, Blainey Papers, Acc. No. 89/145 Box 13, UMA.

new steamships and railway lines, could easily have prevented steam from revolutionising transport and from helping to ease poverty in many lands'.[63]

A further activity which both reflected, and reinforced, Blainey's profile was the delivery of public lectures or addresses to conferences. These were sometimes published in booklets or reproduced in edited form in newspapers. As well as exploring some of the historical themes Blainey had long pursued, they tended to include some form of prediction. Melbourne Cup Day 1976 found Blainey in Canberra delivering the Annual Lecture of the Academy of the Social Sciences in Australia on the topic 'The Politics of Big Business: A History'. It included some comments about the rise of managerialism, about which Blainey observed that 'in time to come historians will probably single out the increasing power of the professional manager – whether in big business, the civil service, the government corporation or trade unionism – as one of the significant events in Australian history in the twentieth century'.[64]

In March 1978, Blainey spoke to a lunch of Australia-Japan Bilateral Conference of Editors and Publishers in Canberra, which, unsurprisingly given the nature of the audience, received significant coverage in the following day's press. *The Australian* reported that Blainey had predicted more Japanese capital, migrants, tourists and technology, while also issuing the caveat that increased contact would not necessarily produce greater harmony.[65] A few years later in Tokyo, Blainey gave a talk, an edited version of which was published in *The Australian*, with the evocative title, 'How to sterilise the golden goose', assessing how the future prosperity of the Australian mining industry could be adversely affected by poor public policy.[66] Blainey believed that mining economics was 'little understood', lamented that few Australians realised how much it had contributed to contemporary prosperity, and worried that 'a democracy which does not understand the economics of its main export industry is likely, in good faith, to make occasional decisions of crippling stupidity'. He argued that some of the anti-mining sentiment 'reflects a current ideological fashion – a reaction against technology and material progress'.

By the late 1970s Blainey's profile was sufficiently high for television channels to consider him for a variety of roles. There were various proposals about

---

63 Geoffrey Blainey, 'Concorde: Aviation's Albatross of the 70s Shouldn't Be Killed', *National Times* 23–28 February 1976, 11–12.
64 Geoffrey Blainey, 'The Politics of Big Business: A History' (paper presented at the annual lecture of the Academy of the Social Sciences in Australia] Canberra, 2 November 1976), 6.
65 'More Japanese migrants forecast', *The Australian*, 7 March 1978, 4.
66 Geoffrey Blainey, 'How to sterilise the golden goose', *The Australian*, 30 April 1982, 16.

screening his own works, but his first significant role came in the summer of 1977-78, when Channel 7 used him to introduce a series of documentaries about the Hapsburgs called 'Fall of Eagles'. A couple of years later he was one of the six 'Faces of the Eighties' interviewed by Bob Moore for the ABC and presented to viewers across the summer of 1979-80.[67]

The high point of Blainey's television career was *The Blainey View*, a series of ten half-hour documentaries about aspects of Australian history, several of them replicating the arguments of his major works. The series was conceived and produced by the unit within the ABC Rural Division responsible for the long-running 'Big Country' series, which told stories of regional life. This was perhaps not the most likely source for such a history documentary and may have made management look askance at the series, for it was programmed at 9.30 on Sunday nights, rather than at a more viewer friendly 7.30 or 8.30. Blainey took up the cudgels publicly on behalf of his producers and had a lively discussion with ABC Chairman, Leonie Kramer, about the scheduling. He thought that the ABC was in part suffering from cultural cringe in scheduling BBC programs in better timeslots, and that it had a conservative view of what constituted history:

> Is it possible that the Controller has an outdated or narrow idea of what is history? Nearly all the historical documentaries imported by the ABC concentrate on kings, generals, great painters and architects, wars and revolutions; and there are valid reasons no doubt for that emphasis. But it is also legitimate – and in Australia it is essential – to look at other kinds of history, especially a mixture of social, economic and political. Are people really less interested in that kind of history? And is it a less legitimate kind of history, especially in a new country?[68]

Some reviewers, such as Dennis Pryor in *The Age*, praised Blainey's performance.[69] Others including the *Sydney Morning Herald*'s television critic Harry Robinson, had many complaints.[70] His 'chief objection' was that Blainey seemed to be 'musing inwardly rather than using a prepared script – a fine technique for some occasions but not when we look to a scholar to define

---

67 The other five were Sir Roderick Carnegie, Philippa Smith, Michael Kirby, Ranald Macdonald and Simon Crean.
68 Blainey to Leonie Kramer, 30 March 1982, Blainey Papers, Acc. No. 89/145 Box 36, UMA.
69 Dennis Pryor, *The Age* (Saturday Extra section), 23 October 1982, 16.
70 Harry Robinson, *Sydney Morning Herald*, 30 October 1982, 16.

our history'.[71] When Blainey said the 'ordinary person was the superstar', Robinson accused him of 'trying to speak the lingo of a tabloid magazine' and, as for comparing a small bush monument to the Statue of Liberty, this was 'confusing a large symbol of an ideal with a small symbol of luck and material wealth'.[72] Yet, for Blainey, luck and material wealth were clearly not small things. Indeed, several episodes of *The Blainey View* gave great weight to social history, using the reminiscences of 'old timers', together with archival footage of Australians going about the now forgotten routines of earlier decades. Blainey also used the occasional expert, usually ones to whom he had a previous connection, such as MacMahon Ball and John Mulvaney.

A book accompanied the series. There, the chapters were arranged chronologically, but on television the episode which was most likely to generate controversy ran first. Predictably, 'Invasion', which reiterated Blainey's thesis about the origins of the Pacific War, stirred up the same sort of complaints as the *National Times* article had in 1976. One correspondent to the *Sydney Morning Herald*, who had spent four years as a prisoner of war, complained that 'the whole thing could not have pleased Japan better had it been designed and made in Tokyo… [and] is a mockery to the memory of the thousands of Australians and Americans who died to keep this country free'.[73]

Blainey was not in the country when the series went to air in late 1982. He was in Boston where he was Visiting Professor of Australian Studies at Harvard. This position had been established in 1976 and already had been held by such prominent historians as John La Nauze, Manning Clark and Ken Inglis, as well as other prominent academics such as Blainey's recent combatant, Leonie Kramer. At Harvard, Blainey taught a subject called History 1801 (Australian) in the Fall Term of the 1982-83 US academic year. He gave lectures at noon on Mondays and Wednesdays, with occasional discussion sessions on Fridays. The requisite reading for the course included two of his own works, plus those of Clark, Inglis and Walter Murdoch.

The young Americans he encountered were very interested in Australia; indeed, for them, it had an 'unusual glamour', was perceived as 'a land of opportunity' and provided something of an antidote to their feelings that America was no longer a spacious land.[74] His students may have been

---

71 Ibid.
72 Ibid.
73 Reg Mahoney, Letter to the editor, *Sydney Morning Herald*, 22 October 1982, 6.
74 Geoffrey Blainey, 'How Americans See Australia – and Thus Themselves', *Christian Science Monitor*, 4 February 1983, and reproduced in Blainey, *Blainey: Eye on Australia*, 16–18.

'looking for the old America', but rather than just salving their nostalgia Blainey was clearly trying to get them to consider different ways of thinking about history. Included on the exam paper at the end of the term were a couple of quintessentially Blainey questions, which also show that the questions he had posed to Leonie Kramer a few months earlier were still very much on his mind:

> 1A "What I like most about Australia's history is that nothing ever happened." (Joe Derita) How much do we gain in studying the history of a land, by concentrating on the infrequent dramatic events such as wars and revolutions and how much do we gain by examining the quieter, slower, changes?
>
> IB "Australia's history since the 1780s has been moulded to an unusual degree by economic rather than by political events and factors." Discuss.

Some students appreciated his teaching sufficiently to write to him, with one commenting that 'the course you taught at Harvard not only provided excellent instruction of history but gave a vivid picture of the values, lifestyle and people of Australia'.[75] Another wrote to Blainey saying that he was 'the finest professor' the student had had in his four years at Harvard, explaining that others lacked 'the personal touch, that real concern and care for his work and for his students' which Blainey had exhibited.[76]

The stint at Harvard came in the latter part of Blainey's first year as Dean of the Faculty of Arts at Melbourne. After his election in 1981, he was to hold the role for six years (two three-year terms). The role of Dean meant that Blainey was officially relieved of all teaching duties although, in his usual conscientious manner, he continued to give some lectures and take tutorials. From the moment his election was announced, he was inundated with supplications from departments opposing mergers, individuals seeking redress for alleged unfair treatment, and the like.

In his early 50s, Blainey had compiled an impressive curriculum vitae: an opus of successful books, academic eminence, an eponymous TV series and chairmanship of major government committees. The media coverage he received tended to paint him in an attractive, down-to-earth light. In 1982, journalist Tom Duggan was struck by the fact that, despite being Dean of Arts, Blainey still made tea and coffee for his visitors and 'even more curiously, he boils up

---

75   Letter to Blainey, 30 May 1984, Blainey Papers, Acc. No. 89/145 Box 24, UMA.
76   Letter to Blainey, undated, Blainey Papers, Acc. No. 89/145 Box 24, UMA.

the water in a small electric kettle which sits on the carpeted floor beside his desk [and] resourcefully, and not unlike some of the tribal elders he so much admires, he sits on the carpet jiggling a tea bag in its cup'.[77]

With his only child now an adult, Blainey could have chosen to become more selective about the tasks he undertook. Occasionally he did say no, for instance declining a request from the National Bank to update his 1958 edition of *Gold and Paper*.[78] However, there was no suggestion that he was going to rest on his laurels. Indeed, as the winter of 1983 progressed, he was getting up earlier and earlier to get some writing done, as he mentioned in letters to Rob Pascoe and Peter Temple in June and August respectively:

> I am over-burdened with this and that. It's years since I've got any research done at the University. I squeeze in time by getting up at 6 but that doesn't get one far.[79]

> I have promised my publisher I will finish a history of Victoria well before the end of the year; and that takes all my spare moments – I got up at 5.15 this morning: such virtue.[80]

He appears to have just about met his deadline, with the endnote of *Our Side of the Country: The Story of Victoria* being dated January 1984 and the book being published in April 1984. However, although generally well received, more than one reviewer noted errors, with one speculating that 'perhaps the book was written in a hurry: punctuation strays, sentences don't add up and once or twice the stories from his own life come close to mere whimsy'.[81]

One activity Blainey had largely forgone by the early 1980s was writing journal articles and book reviews. One of his last attempts at a journal article was an interesting departure from the Blainey norm. Titled 'Slaves of the ten-fingered hand?' it argued that 'Keynesians over-emphasized aggregate demand and virtually reversed Say's Law'. It had three unusual features for Blainey – it

---

77 Tom Duggan, 'Land Rights and Future Wrongs', *The Age*, 29 May 1982, 2.
78 Instead journalist, Geoffrey Hutton, wrote up the bank's modern history which was added to an abridged version of Blainey's 1958 edition.
79 Blainey to Rob Pascoe, undated but in reply to letter from Pascoe dated 9 June 1983, Blainey Papers, Acc. No. 89/145 Box 55, UMA.
80 Blainey to Peter Temple, 31 August 1983, Blainey Papers, Acc. No. 89/145 Box 35, UMA.
81 Edmund Campion, 'Everything in its place in the garden state', *The Bulletin*, 29 May 1984, 98.

was more pure economics than economic history, it had a co-author (Peter Jonson) and no journal would agree to publish it.[82]

Blainey had also lost the desire to write book reviews, telling one journal editor in 1971 that 'I try to evade book reviewing... whether it is the belief that I don't review well enough or whether I think writers of books should shut up occasionally I'm not sure'.[83] A decade later his opinion against reviewing had further hardened. In a covering letter, apologising for declining to review a book he had been sent, he wrote that he had 'no desire to review it ... I find I like reviewing less and less unless I strongly like the book'.[84] He did make an exception in 1982 when he reviewed volume 5 of Manning Clark's *History of Australia* for the Australian-Asian magazine *Hemisphere*. The review certainly came to Clark's attention. He noted that 'Geoff Blainey has written a decent one' - a pleasant contrast for him to a 'scurrilous' review written elsewhere.[85] Blainey was effusive:

> Manning Clark is our Carlyle and Macaulay. A narrative historian now rarely found even in Europe he writes history on the grand scale ... He has the eye for detail that helps him give to readers the sense that they too were there when the great or trivial events took place ... his skills in constructing a narrative and in spinning the threads of his story are probably unrivalled amongst Australian writers of fact or fiction.[86]

The praise was balanced by gentle chiding for occasional lapses in historical accuracy, noting that Clark's 'books should not necessarily be invoked as a court of appeal in detailed debates about the past', and for pessimism, saying he was 'too gloomy'. Clearly, Blainey still saw himself as the optimist and Clark as the pessimist. While in some ways this was true, in others Blainey was himself becoming gloomy.

Around the same time he was writing this review Blainey provided a revised ending for a new edition of *The Tyranny of Distance*, which gave evidence of that pessimism about Australia's place in the world compared to his perspective

---

82 Copy of article and various rejection letters, Blainey Papers, Acc. No. 89/145 Box 31, UMA.
83 Blainey to Gordon Rimmer, 17 February 1971, Blainey Papers, Acc. No. 89/145 Box 13, UMA.
84 Blainey letter, 7 April 1984, Blainey Papers, Acc. No. 89/145 Box 35, UMA.
85 Manning Clark to Dymphna Clark, 8 September 1982, reproduced in *Ever Manning; Selected Letters of Manning Clark 1938-1991*, ed. Roslyn Russell, (Sydney: Allen & Unwin, 2008), 427.
86 Geoffrey Blainey, 'Towards Today', *Hemisphere* 27, no. 2 (September/October 1982), 98.

in 1966. He drew an analogy between contemporary Australia in the early 1980s and Aboriginal Australia in 1788, both being 'unable to defend their land adequately' if their isolation ended. It was a different sort of pessimism from Clark's, but it was one which was about to contribute to his becoming at least as controversial a figure as Clark was. As Blainey pointed out in his review of Clark, controversy could be a problem for a historian:

> He has been, since 1975, a focus of political controversy, and many partisans in the daily press and parliament intemperately condemn or praise him as a historian in the light of their own political views. He is too fine a historian to have his life's work judged by the boos and cheers of a kangaroo court.[87]

Within two years of writing these unwittingly prescient words, Blainey was to find that his own work as a historian, like Clark's, would henceforth be judged by a similar kangaroo court.

---

87 Blainey, 'Towards Today', 99.

Chapter 7

THE IMMIGRATION CONTROVERSY

In July 1983 Blainey wrote to Rotary representative, Ian Soulsby, declining an invitation to speak at a Rotary Conference in Warrnambool on a Saturday in the following March.[1] He already had a commitment in Melbourne that evening and explained that it would be impossible to make the round trip of more than 500 kilometres to the town on Victoria's west coast by road. However, Soulsby was very keen to secure Blainey's services. He proposed that Rotary hire a light plane. So Blainey flew out of Essendon Airport on a chartered Shaywood Air flight at 8.45 am on Saturday, 17 March 1984 and was in Warrnambool in time to deliver his address straight after the conference's morning tea break.

As delegates resumed their seats in Warrnambool's Capitol Theatre, they had no inkling that the speech they were about to hear was to spark one of the most heated political controversies in Australian history.[2] Most of the speech Blainey delivered that day was uncontroversial, but he concluded by asserting that 'the pace of Asian immigration is now far ahead of public opinion, especially the public opinion in those suburbs and workplaces to which many of these Vietnamese and Kampuchean refugees will go'.

Warrnambool was not the first occasion Blainey had raised Asian immigration. In ABC TV's *Faces of the Eighties* at the start of the decade, he had made comments about the presence of Asian migrants which echoed the way he had discarded his own liberalism in *The Causes of War*. Blainey said that as a good liberal university academic with a secure job, it was easy for him to support more migrants from Asia, but 'if I lived in Footscray or out beyond Parramatta, or somewhere where my job was to be challenged, I think I would think twice'.[3]

---

1   Blainey to Ian Soulsby, 13 July 1983, Blainey Papers, MS 9225/3/32 Box 12, NLA.
2   The conference was attended by representatives from 46 Rotary clubs (covering an area stretching from Ocean Grove, near Geelong, to Millicent across the border in South Australia).
3   Robert Moore, *Faces of the Eighties: Interviews by Robert Moore* (Sydney: Australian Broadcasting Commission, 1980), 62.

Blainey had also discussed Asian immigration when addressing the National Press Club in November 1983 on the topic of Australia's relations with China, a speech 'based partly on my experience as Chairman of the Australia-China Council since 1979 and partly on my own attitudes as a historian'.[4] In this Press Club speech, Blainey speculated about whether Australia might become a major destination for refugees from Hong Kong in the lead up to the Chinese takeover in 1997. He argued that the arrival of Vietnamese 'boat people' had created 'very serious tensions' in some suburbs and a larger influx from Hong Kong 'could well create widespread tensions'.[5] He also expressed concern that in the following 25 years Australia might be unable 'to regulate the arrival, the peaceful arrival, of Asian refugees' and argued that 'we should continue to welcome a variety of Asian immigrants, but they should come on our terms, through our choosing, and in numbers with which our society can cope'.[6]

As the post-Warrnambool controversy raged, the fact that Blainey had raised the issue before without generating controversy was one of the few things Blainey and his critics agreed upon. This worried some people, such as the editors of the critique *Surrender Australia*, who observed that 'there has yet been no satisfactory explanation of why Warrnambool should have attracted such press attention and public reaction when similar previous observations by Blainey had not'.[7] There appear to be two factors which made Warrnambool different to his previous comments. One is that while Blainey had expressed concern about Asian immigration before, his remarks in Warrnambool had gone further in one crucial aspect: he singled out the Hawke Government for criticism, claiming that it was 'jeopardizing the remarkable gains in tolerance and understanding slowly built up in Australia in the last third of a century'. The other half of the explanation is the one which is so often underrated: luck.

Blainey's Warrnambool comments would not have run in the media at all, if not for the presence, and news sense, of Richard Goodwin, a senior journalist with the local daily newspaper, *The Standard*. Goodwin was wearing two hats that day. He was doing some freelance work for Rotary, recording the conference, and also looking for something newsworthy for his paper. A retrospective article in *The Standard* in 2008 described the day from Goodwin's perspective:

---

4   The speech was reproduced as Geoffrey Blainey, 'Our Relations With China: A Backward and Forward Glance', *The Australian Journal of Chinese Affairs*, no. 11 (January 1984), 104.
5   Blainey, 'Our Relations With China', 101–102.
6   Ibid., 103.
7   Andrew Markus and M.C. Ricklefs, 'Introduction' in *Surrender Australia? Essays in the Study and Uses of History: Geoffrey Blainey and Asian Immigration*, eds Markus and Ricklefs (Sydney: Allen & Unwin, 1985), 2.

I had sat through a few speeches that day, taking notes and recording it on tape. I found Blainey's speech particularly interesting and during a break I talked with him outside the theatre next to Flaherty's shop which was where we took the photo that appeared on the front page. It wasn't until I returned home a few hours later that it struck me that what he said was highly significant.[8]

Standard editor Jim Clarke remembered Goodwin returning to the newsroom with a certain eagerness to report on what he rightly anticipated to be a story that would gain national attention. The story dominated the front page of the *Standard* on the Monday under the headline 'Immigration policy questioned' with a sub-heading of 'Too Many Asians'. Goodwin won a Walkley Award for the story and, in reply to a letter of congratulations from Blainey, commented that, 'like you, I had no idea at the time that your reported remarks would trigger such a sustained and passionate debate'.[9]

The first step on the path to the story's explosion was the fact that *The Standard* was not the only paper with the story on Monday morning. The *Standard* was owned by *The Age* and, in an attempt to get a contact phone number for the Immigration Minister to seek his comment, Goodwin alerted *Age* Canberra bureau journalist, Ken Haley, to the story. *The Age* ran it on the front page under the headline 'Asian entry threatens tolerance: Blainey', albeit on the bottom half of the page below a story on the increasing likelihood of Budget tax cuts and a big picture of Australia's first national triathlon championship held at Frankston the previous day.[10] It was certainly prominent enough that whatever other plans Blainey had for the day had to be largely put on hold as he responded to a flurry of media calls.

Blainey had to take a fundamental decision that Monday. There were three options open to him. He could play down his remarks, point out that he had said something similar a few months earlier and decline to do further media.

---

8   Alex Sinnott, 'Blainey's speech still proves to be the fuel of much fiery debate', *The Standard* (Warrnambool), 20 September 2008, 9.

9   Richard Goodwin to Blainey 23 October 1984, Blainey Papers, MS 9225/3/10 Box 9, NLA.

10 Ken Haley, 'Asian entry threatens tolerance: Blainey', *The Age*, 19 March 1984, 1. The article included the statement that it might be better to give '$1000 to each of these refugees to go to a place further away'. Blainey wrote to *The Age* (Geoffrey Blainey, letter '$1000 confusion', 22 March 1984, 12) to say he had not made that comment. The point he was making was that costs of transporting refugees were small compared to costs of resettlement, so there was no reason that geographic proximity be a key determinant of final destination. However, despite the correction, the false statement continued to resurface in the debate for the next year.

If he had adopted that response the story would probably have died fairly quickly. The second option would be to actively do media, but in a conciliatory way in an attempt to disarm his critics. However, Blainey chose the third option: digging in and expanding on his views, including writing an opinion piece for the following day's issues of *The Age* and *Sydney Morning Herald*.[11] If his words on Saturday had unintended consequences, his actions on Monday were taken with a clear appreciation of what might lie ahead as 'by the end of that day I was sure the controversy would last for some time, and I sent a cheque to one of those firms that specialize in news clippings, asking for anything relevant that would be published on the immigration controversy in any Australian newspaper'.[12]

As a Rotary conference in Warrnambool was not an obvious location for someone with Blainey's access to high profile outlets to start a campaign, it can be argued that on this specific occasion he was not seeking controversy. However, it was equally clear that Blainey considered it was an important issue as he had been raising it in speeches whenever he deemed it appropriate. Thus, when the media interest came, he was prepared to actively defend his position. The choice he made that Monday led him to be, for the next decade, arguably a public policy commentator first and a historian second, although his prodigious work-rate still delivered significant historical output. Blainey became one of the foremost critics of the Hawke and Keating Labor Governments, not just in regard to immigration, but in other areas, such as economic policy.

Before the Asian immigration controversy, Blainey was largely seen as being near the centre of the political spectrum. Conservative political commentator Gerard Henderson later observed that until this point Blainey had been 'remarkably non-political' and a 'genuinely swinging voter', who voted more on the basis of his perception of the competence of the parties rather than ideology.[13] Indeed, Henderson went as far as to implicitly criticise Blainey for his failure to 'take an open stand against the anti-intellectual behaviour that was a hallmark of much of the student radicalism' of the late 1960s and early 1970s. As the controversy raged in mid-1984, Blainey explained to a journalist that, as a firm believer in the secret ballot, he had never even told his wife how he voted, although he confirmed that he had voted for a variety

---

11 Geoffrey Blainey, 'The Asianisation of Australia', *The Age*, 20 March 1984, 11; published as 'Prisoners of our past', *Sydney Morning Herald*, 20 March 1984, 9.
12 Blainey, *All For Australia*, 26–27.
13 Gerard Henderson, *Australian Answers*, (Sydney: Random House Australia, 1990), 60–61.

of parties including Labor.[14] The article described him as 'essentially a fence-sitter when it comes to politics'; someone who believed in private enterprise but also 'saw many Labor social policies as attractive'.[15]

There seem to have been several factors underlying Blainey's decision on that March Monday to take the controversial rather than the conciliatory road. First, there was his long-held lack of esteem for many politicians and his belief that they tended to jeopardise the good work of ordinary Australians. While Blainey claimed that his time on government committees had given him greater respect for politicians, that gain had been more than offset by the fact that the same period had seen Australia in constant economic difficulty. It was easy to think that contemporary politicians did not have the answers. Thus, the inclusion in Monday's story of statements by Immigration Minister, Stewart West, was significant. A few months into the debate, Blainey commented that he was 'so astonished' at Mr West's remark that 'the Asianisation of Australia was inevitable' that 'on the Monday, I set out in pursuit of him'.[16]

Responding vigorously to a Minister was not new for Blainey; he had done so to David Fairbairn's comments about iron ore in 1969. No harm had come to Blainey from that dispute and indeed, until this point in his life, controversy had tended to serve Blainey well. Whether it was taking on Professor Parker while still an undergraduate, overturning long-established ideas about the reasons for British settlement in *The Tyranny of Distance*, or falling out with the Whitlam Government over the Literature Board, the ensuing controversies had generally assisted his career. There had never been a reason for him to fear controversy.

However, perhaps the most important reason for not backing down on Monday 19 March 1984 was the same one that had led him to take all the government committee positions and to become the Dean of Arts at the University of Melbourne. If a job presents itself, you do it. The nonconformist sense of responsibility was still strong.

The job became big enough that later in the year Blainey felt the need to write a book, *All for Australia*, in an attempt to clarify and promote his position. A key reason for setting out his views in book form was that he felt his views were being misrepresented in elements of the media. He was upset that *The Age* and the *Sydney Morning Herald* constantly claimed that he opposed Asian immigration, and he was exasperated enough with the former that after

---

14 Russell Robinson, 'Witch-hunt, says Blainey', *The Sun News Pictorial*, 25 July 1984, 2.
15 Ibid.
16 Tim Duncan, 'Blainey sees a threat emerge to free speech', *The Bulletin*, 3 July 1984, 26.

a while he refused to write opinion articles for it.[17] However, he regarded SBS Television as an even worse offender, claiming that every time he 'uttered a sentence in favour of Asian immigration they deleted it'.[18] The ABC, in his view, was a mixed bag with the *AM* and *PM* programs being 'fair and perceptive', but longer programs, such as *Background Briefing* and *Four Corners* were 'incredibly one-sided' and 'sheer government propaganda' respectively.[19]

The debate was given further impetus in May 1984, when it became an issue of partisan debate in federal politics, largely because of some provocative comments from Shadow Minister for Immigration, Michael Hodgman. This development meant that Blainey was no longer the sole driver of the debate, though he remained its key figure. He was overseas in May, but rejoined the fray soon after his return and outlined a policy prescription:

> I think we've got a period of settling down to do before we decide what the new immigration policy should be. But given that, I think it should be halved and there should be a lower percentage of Asian people in that half.[20]

An important aspect of Blainey's stance, at least in the early stages of the debate, was his claim that his was a moderate position. He chided the Anglican Dean of Brisbane for giving the impression 'I was polarising the debate when I was objecting to polarised positions'.[21] Just as he had observed shifts in attitudes on several matters in *A Land Half Won*, Blainey claimed that immigration policy had 'virtually turned a somersault', leaping from one side of his position to the other in the process.[22] He explained that 'in the past thirty years the Government has moved from the extreme of wanting a white Australia to the extreme that we want an Asian Australia'.[23] In contrast, Blainey claimed to be advocating 'a middle-of-the-road immigration policy, which was 'not the one the strong pro-Asia lobby would like, and it's not the one the relics of the White Australia people would like, but it is somewhere in the middle'.[24]

---

17   Henderson, *Australian Answers*, 57; and Blainey to Creighton Burns, 8 October 1984, Blainey Papers, Acc. No. 89/145 Box 7, UMA.
18   Henderson, *Australian Answers*, 57.
19   Blainey, *All for Australia*, 28.
20   Alan Tate, 'Blainey defends Asian views', *The Herald* (Melbourne), 8 June 1984, 4.
21   Blainey to Robert Butterss, 27 April 1984, Blainey Papers, MS 9225/2/4 Box 1, NLA.
22   Blainey, *All for Australia*, 6.
23   Blainey, 'The Asianisation of Australia'.
24   Tate, 'Blainey defends Asian views'.

However, his views were regarded by many as being closer to one end of the spectrum. In *All for Australia* he expressed surprise that these opinions 'aroused such intense feelings' because 'my views are not on the extremes, but sit very much in the middle ground, and such views do not usually arouse redhot reactions'.[25]

Blainey was correct to identify how quickly policy had altered. Perhaps, more importantly, the accepted parameters of what could be said about a topic like Asian immigration had changed rapidly in Australia. Until 1965, White Australia remained the official policy of the Labor Party and even when in that year the party notionally changed the policy, the substance was expected to remain, as Leader, Arthur Calwell, wrote in his autobiography:

> For political and diplomatic reasons, the 1965 Federal ALP conference removed the words 'White Australia' from the Labor Party platform. We certainly did not try to water down the policy nor take the ideal of a White Australia from the hearts and minds of the Australian people. Nobody will ever be able to do that.[26]

Even as late as 1971, Calwell's successor as Labor Leader, Gough Whitlam, had to sack his Shadow Immigration Minister, Fred Daly, for still supporting aspects of a White Australia policy. In that same year one critic observed that, while Liberal Governments had taken steps to unravel the White Australia policy, the Labor Party remained 'largely a crucible of yesterday's prejudices, its conservatism on the question of immigration much more entrenched than that of the Liberal Party'.[27] The Whitlam Government confirmed this truism by slashing immigration numbers.

The Hawke Government was different. In similar vein to its economic policies, which were designed to internationalise the Australian economy in a way which would have been anathema to previous Labor Governments, this Government also had a strong commitment towards an outward-looking and non-discriminatory immigration policy. As one commentator claimed the month before Blainey's Warrnambool speech, 'the unabashed aim of the Government is to create as culturally diverse a population as possible through its policy of total non-discrimination'.[28] Given this radical change,

---

25   Blainey, *All for Australia*, 31.

26   Arthur Calwell, *Be Just and Fear Not* (Melbourne: Lloyd O'Neil, 1972), 120.

27   Maximillian Walsh, 'The Politics of it all' in *How Many Australians? Immigration and Growth*, ed. John Wilkes (Sydney: Angus and Robertson, 1971), 180.

28   Jane Dargaville, 'Government stirs the immigration melting pot', *The Weekend Australian*, 4–5 February 1984, 14.

it is perhaps understandable that someone like Blainey, who had grown up in an Australia where a key policy of the party of the Left was maintenance of a White Australia, might find it surprising that his own expression of a position, far more moderate than Labor's own previous one, might lead to vehement criticism by members of a Labor Government.[29]

Blainey's intellectual outlook had developed when the views of the Old Left were dominant. Indeed, some of his best friends were Communists and he knew how to disagree with them without causing offence. One New Left historian, writing in the Marxist journal *Arena*, put this down in part to the fact that although Blainey differed from the Old Left in his enthusiasm for capitalism, he shared with them 'broad sympathy for the honest working man', plus 'the easy egalitarianism of his personal style' had made him 'a little mate and drinking companion of the Old Left ideologues'.[30]

Blainey had managed to write about Communist China and the Soviet Union while studiously avoiding polemic; indeed, some saw him as being soft on communism. Robert Manne, who at that time was on the political Right, criticised Blainey's remark that he saw 'merits in communism for certain kinds of societies', commenting that it showed Blainey had 'little feeling for the totalitarian reality of communist revolution'.[31] Yet, when it came to the positions held by younger generations of the Left, Blainey displayed less sympathy. There were signs of this in his criticism of anti-war activists in *The Causes of War* and was to come more to the fore as, in the 1970s and 1980s, the Left became more concerned about issues such as race, gender and the environment.

It was not just the views of the Australian Left which had shifted. Blainey had also changed. In *The Tyranny of Distance*, he came across as a strong supporter of immigration, describing post-war immigration as 'a vital ingredient of the longest span of prosperity' in the nation's history.[32] In 1967, while playfully lampooning those on the Left who combined support for the arrival of foreign people in Australia with objections to the arrival of foreign capital, he argued that the contribution of both new people and new capital had been

---

29 Not everyone in the labour movement had caught up with the policy change. Blainey received a letter from the Toowoomba Trades & Labour Council expressing 'comradely support for your moral and intellectual integrity'. Letter to Blainey, 20 August 1984, Blainey Papers, MS 9225/2/18 Box 3, NLA.
30 Marian Aveling, 'The History Debate: A False Dichotomy', *Arena*, no. 75 (1986): 151.
31 Robert Manne, 'The Blainey Affair: All for Australia?', *Quadrant* 29, no. 3 (March 1985): 19.
32 Blainey, *The Tyranny of Distance*, 334.

'impressive'.³³ At this time, Blainey had appreciated that nostalgia for aspects of an older Australia should not be a basis for public policy:

> I was a disappointed to see a British company take over Mt Lyell ... yet the real test of this transaction is ... will the new owners contribute far more ... than they take away in dividends. If they pass this test, then my only defence is nostalgia, the invoking of a golden age with which to tarnish the present.³⁴

At this time, his liberalism extended to the increased presence of Asians in Australia. He wrote approvingly of the fact that the restrictive policy was being 'administered more liberally, and the public favoured even more liberality than the Commonwealth Government conceded'.³⁵ Yet, by 1984, Blainey no longer held the same liberal views on either the economics, or the social impact, of immigration. He acknowledged in *All for Australia* that 'I can see now that my views on immigration were changing without my realizing'.³⁶

On the economics, he noted that, although in the 1960s he supported the view that immigrants created employment, he now believed this was no longer clear even in prosperous times and that, in times of high unemployment, it was clear that immigrants would 'aggravate' the situation.³⁷ However, it was not just the jobs of older Australians that Blainey was keen to see preserved; he increasingly argued that they had the right to have the suburbs in which they lived remain recognisable to them. He also concluded that reducing the resentment of older Australia would also make life easier for newer arrivals, writing that 'there should be positive steps taken to make two groups of aggrieved people feel at home here: the old Australians who have lost their jobs and find their neighbourhoods disrupted and also the new migrants from Indo China who believe they are under public attack'.³⁸

Where initially Blainey's argument emphasised economic factors, he gave greater weight to cultural aspects, such as neighbourhood disruption, as the

---

33   Blainey, 'Godzone: 7', 365.
34   Ibid.
35   Blainey, *The Tyranny of Distance*, 336.
36   Blainey, *All For Australia*, 21.
37   Ibid., 138. The topic of whether immigration is positive or negative in an economic downturn remains controversial. Economic studies tend to support the positive argument. For instance, it has been argued that the arrival of 300,000 migrants at the height of the Global Financial Crisis in 2008-09 offset a fall in per capita consumption and 'stopped mass lay-offs', David Uren, 'We are indeed exceptional, but it's no accident', *The Australian*, 20 December 2018, 10.
38   Tate, 'Blainey defends Asian views'.

debate progressed. This shift in emphasis led commentators to remark that Blainey 'hardened his position' or made 'stronger assertions'.[39] A key factor in strengthening his resolve was undoubtedly the large amount of correspondence he received, 600 or 700 letters in the first few months alone. The letters were often triggered by hostile interviews with Blainey, such as one conducted by Huw Evans on the ABC TV current affairs program 'Pressure Point', which reinforced the view of many of Blainey's correspondents that if the 'silent majority' expressed their view they would be howled down by the media.[40] Blainey himself was less concerned about Evans' approach, telling him a few weeks later that, while many had complained, he had personally been unperturbed.[41] There were also several opinion polls which generally showed around sixty per cent support for Blainey's position, compared to thirty per cent who were happy with the current migration composition and ten per cent undecided.[42]

Blainey clearly felt he was speaking on behalf of those whom he believed were otherwise being denied a voice, the sort of people who sent him a 'handwritten letter … two pages torn a little roughly from a pad', or those unable to participate through fear for 'in a climate where the campaign against racism is partly a moral crusade, those who do not believe in the crusade find the pressures acute, especially if they occupy lower and more vulnerable positions in government, business or industry'.[43] A left-wing critic such as ABC producer Allan Ashbolt was able to dismiss Blainey's attention to these people as him 'hearing strange voices from dead and dying generations'.[44] This was a debateable proposition given evidence that many younger Australians also supported Blainey. For example, a phone-in poll on iconic Melbourne rock music station 3XY had the biggest response of any topic, with well over ninety per cent supporting Blainey.[45]

---

39 Paul Kelly, *The End of Certainty: The Story of the 1980s* (Sydney: Allen & Unwin, 1992), 125; and Geoffrey Bolton, *The Oxford History of Australia volume 5, The Middle Way 1942-1995* (Melbourne: Oxford University Press, second edition 1996), 287.

40 Examples of the correspondence that the Evans interview generated, Blainey Papers, MS 9225/2/15 Box 3, NLA.

41 Blainey to Huw Evans, 7 June 1984, Blainey Papers, MS 9225/2/17 Box 3, NLA.

42 Joe Payne, '62pc of Aussies say "no"', *Sun Herald*, 20 May 1984, 1–2; and '60pc worry on migration', (Melbourne) *Herald*, 27 August 1984, 3.

43 Blainey, *All for Australia*, 47 and 124.

44 Allan Ashbolt, 'Historian Speaks for Dead and Dying', *Sydney Morning Herald*, 18 May 1985, 42.

45 S.M.L. Guilfoyle (Managing Director of 3XY) to Blainey, 21 March 1984, Blainey Papers, MS 9225/2/4 Box 1, NLA. In the hour long poll between 7am and 8am, there were 515 recorded calls with 488 agreeing with Blainey and 27 disagreeing.

An astute observation that Ashbolt made was to draw attention to the fact that Blainey was pitching to an audience that felt a growing sense of belonging to this land.[46] In *A Land Half Won*, Blainey had described the lingering ambivalence of Australians in the 1890s towards the Australian land in which they lived; in *All for Australia* their descendants had been won over. He described how 'most Australians who have lived here for years are quietly proud of this land' and noted 'the increasing sense of national pride that has become so vivid since the Whitlam era ... the enthusiasm for the past and for the harsh landscapes and unpretentious heroes'.[47] However, his correspondents reported that the land was changing; that Cabramatta was 'becoming more and more like an Asian town'.[48]

In the late 1940s and 1950s, Blainey's youthful optimism and liberalism had perhaps made him less aware of the degree of resentment older Australians felt as European immigration changed neighbourhoods. Throughout the controversy of 1984-85, he maintained that the massive post-war immigration, far higher in percentage terms, had been a success, and despite a bit of name-calling older Australians accepted it:

> Back in the 1950s and 1960s the typical Australian had believed that immigration was vital for the country ... No matter what nicknames the old Australian had used then against the new Australian, he believed that immigrants in general were good for the country.[49]

In reality, the available evidence indicates that 'the typical Australian' of the 1950s opposed non-British migration. Public opinion polling in the 1950s revealed that those who thought there were too many immigrants to Australia outnumbered those who believed there were too few by margins of over 30 points, before a move to a more favourable attitude towards immigrants in the 1960s.[50] One striking feature of post-war polling was that the Chinese were found to be the most favoured type of migrant, apart from the English

---

46 Ashbolt, 'Historian Speaks for Dead and Dying'. The observation was somewhat spoilt by Ashbolt's attempt to give this affection sinister overtones by comparing it with the attachment of the Afrikaans to South Africa.
47 Blainey, *All for Australia*, 153–155.
48 Ibid., 125.
49 Ibid., 15.
50 Ian McAllister, 'Immigration, bipartisanship and public opinion' in *The Politics of Australian Immigration*, eds James Jupp and Marie Kabala (Canberra: Australian Government Publishing Service, 1993), 161–180, in particular figure 9.4 on 171.

and Irish, in a list of eight options provided to respondents to a 1948 survey, well ahead of Greeks, Italians and Jews.[51]

A key part of Blainey's argument was that post-war migration had been accepted because the economy was strong and there was full employment, whereas now the migrants were coming into a less robust economy. Unlike the situation in the 1890s and 1930s where immigration had almost ceased in depressions, he pointed out that in the 1980s people were 'arriving in unprecedentedly large numbers for a time of depression'.[52] The recession of 1982-83 was the worst since the Depression, with unemployment peaking at 10.4 per cent in February 1984 before slowly beginning to fall. The Government had responded in a typical manner by cutting the skilled migration intake, but immigration continued at a higher level than in previous downturns, because family reunion was now a major component of the program.

Blainey also argued that by supporting the Government's immigration policy, 'the trade union movement in Australia has drifted into becoming an indirect but formidable opponent of the unemployed'.[53] This perhaps underlined Blainey's previous political centrism. Many on the political Right would have argued that the actions of the union movement had been hurting the unemployed since the 1890s. By contrast, entrepreneurial immigrants from diverse cultures could prove to be more beneficial to the Australian economy than Australian unions had traditionally been.

While it was common to argue that immigration was a threat to jobs, Blainey also broadened the debate by claiming that immigration of people without a democratic heritage could undermine democracy in Australia. He also claimed that there was a 'secret room' in the Immigration Department where policy was determined, the sort of statement which prompted leading political commentator Paul Kelly to observe that 'Blainey proved to be his own worst enemy'.[54]

Blainey was on safer ground when he pointed out some of the inherent contradictions in the official policy of multiculturalism, querying why 'if the people of each minority should have the right to *establish* here a way of life familiar to them, is it not equally right – or more so, in democracy – for the majority of Australians to *retain* the way of life familiar to them'.[55]

---

51   H.I. London, *Non-White Immigration and the 'White Australia' Policy* (Sydney: Sydney University Press, 1970), 148.

52   Blainey, *All for Australia*, 160.

53   Ibid., 142.

54   Kelly, *The End of Certainty*, 132.

55   Blainey, *All for Australia*, 124.

However, there was no reason why opposing multiculturalism, as defined by the ethnic lobby, should preclude support for a high rate of immigration, or a higher Asian component of that immigration. One who made this point was Manne, who observed that while 'the emergence of multiculturalism and the beginning of large-scale Vietnamese immigration both occurred in the late 1970s the coincidence was accidental' and, moreover, 'those who became enthusiastic multiculturalists were not in general interested in the plight of the Vietnamese'.[56] Similarly, Blainey was correct when he asserted that even a 'non-discriminatory' policy can be arbitrary, although of course it did not follow that, because the policy was arbitrary, it was also wrong.

Despite the concerns of Blainey and the change of official policy from assimilation to multiculturalism, Indochinese immigration in the late 1970s and 1980s has probably had the same degree of success as the wave of European migrants from the late 1940s to the late 1960s. The earlier influx had been described by Blainey himself in the original edition of *The Tyranny of Distance*:

> In encouraging massive migration, Australians could foresee some sacrifices – perhaps a weakening of their social security, perhaps unemployment, and perhaps the importing of racial and national tensions ... The main fears have so far been unfulfilled.[57]

Blainey had clearly moved some distance from his optimism in the 1960s on the topic of immigration, but 1984 revealed something far more concerning for the future of serious discourse in Australia than a bit of misplaced pessimism. The fact that Blainey was too pessimistic about the likely outcomes of high levels of immigration ended up being almost incidental to more fundamental issues around freedom of speech, academic independence and the use of historical authority.

There had been ideological battles involving academics previously in Australia, on both sides of the Cold War divide. These included instances such as the left-wing historian Russel Ward, who was vetoed for a position at the New South Wales University of Technology in 1956 and the psychologist and philosopher, Frank Knopfelmacher, denied a position at Sydney University in 1965 because of his strident anti-communism. Nonetheless, the debate about Blainey's views marked a key turning point in the intellectual and political discourse in Australia. Indeed, it is hard to disagree with the observation

---

56   Manne, 'The Blainey Affair', 20.
57   Blainey, *The Tyranny of Distance*, 334.

made in 2000 by political journalist Michael Gordon that 'the Blainey affair was the first of Australia's "culture wars" of the 80s and 90s'.[58]

It need not have been this way, but the triumph of a new orthodoxy in many intellectual circles meant that, rather than a sensible debate about immigration, there was something more akin to a moral crusade waged against Blainey by some politicians, elements of the media and by many of his fellow academics. The irony of the situation was that the nature of the attacks on Blainey meant that many who would otherwise have opposed the position he was taking on immigration ended up defending him, because they felt the assault on his right to express his views was far more pernicious than his stand on immigration.

Prominent member of the Old Left and friend of Blainey, Stephen Murray-Smith, lamented 'the fanatical intolerance of the New Wave in history and the fear they hold of freedom of debate'.[59] He believed that younger radicals were trying to control acceptable topics for debate more tightly than their 'conservative grandfathers' had two generations earlier.[60] Even within the New Left some individuals, such as the editor of the radical journal *Arena*, wrote to Blainey saying that 'unlike some left wing people we are keen to keep in view a distinction between your right to speak out and our attitudes to what you have to say'.[61] The desire to prevent Blainey speaking became a lasting impression of what happened. A few years later, the retired academic historian Sandy Yarwood described how in 1984-85 many of Blainey's 'academic colleagues and erstwhile friends seemed to be denying his right to state a view of the immigration question that challenged the new Australian orthodoxy'.[62] Blainey himself saw calling someone 'racist' was a 'new McCarthyism, a stifler of discussion, and trampler of freedom, and that this new McCarthyism is the favoured weapon of a section of the intellectuals'.[63] Right from the start of the debate, Blainey believed that academics were the most inclined to want the debate shut down:

---

58   Michael Gordon, 'Geoffrey Blainey comes in from the cold', *The Age* (News Extra section), 18 November 2000, 1.

59   Kristin Williamson, 'Geoffrey Blainey's Year of Living Dangerously', *National Times*, 22-28 March 1985, 7.

60   Ibid.

61   Geoff Sharp to Blainey, 25 June 1984, Blainey Papers, MS 9225/2/22 Box 4, NLA.

62   Sandy Yarwood, 'Who will take up the mantle of Manning Clark?', *The Bulletin*, 22 October 1991, 84–85.

63   Blainey to Jeremy Long (Commissioner for Community Relations), 12 June 1984, Blainey Papers, MS 9225/2/18 Box 2, NLA.

> I was under strong pressure the first week that I spoke and the pressure – from individuals – was overwhelmingly from academics. They said it was wrong to raise the subject. Various politicians ... made strong statements. But I don't think they (politicians) challenged my right to free speech as much as academics did.[64]

The role of the outspoken academic was one which Blainey had previously considered when he had written his history of Melbourne University. Blainey had observed that, in its early days 'the university was never intended to be primarily a forum of independent thought and intellectual liberty'. However, beginning with the case of G.W.L. Marshall-Hall, dismissed as professor of music in 1900 after community outcry over his production of blasphemous and risqué poetry, and furthered when Guido Baracchi was sanctioned in 1917 for condemning participation in the First World War, the view began to take hold that the university should be a bastion of free speech.[65] Throughout his history of the university, Blainey took the side of the individual academic against the majority, for instance, he expressed sympathy for German academics expelled because of their nationality during the First World War. In the lively campus environment in the aftermath of World War Two, the radicalism of students 'was distortedly reflected in down-town newspaper controversies', and there developed the 'myth' that the university was 'a citadel of communist influence'.[66] Changed attitudes to freedom of speech by academics meant that, when the press ran 'noisome and ill-informed criticism of the university as a home of communist influence', the council defended its staff, with Vice-Chancellor, John Medley, arguing that 'unless every member of staff had freedom to discuss and investigate and publish 'anything and everything under the sun' the university would be false to its ideals".[67] Yet, whereas in the late 1940s, defending free speech was seen as progressive notion, by the 1980s, there was a new type of intolerance of diverse views within universities. Blainey himself was reluctant to classify this as left-wing dominance:

> I think that within the universities, within the social sciences, there are small but influential groups who believe that the truth comes with

---

64   Duncan, 'Blainey sees a threat to free speech', 25–26.
65   Blainey, *Centenary History of University of Melbourne*, 117–118. Blainey's view of the Marshall Hall case was challenged by Joe Rich, 'Liberalism, Expediency and the Schoolmaster Interest at the University of Melbourne: The Blainey View Reconsidered', *Journal of Australian Studies*, no. 38, September 1993, 62–77.
66   Blainey, *A Centenary History of the University of Melbourne*, 183.
67   Ibid., 198.

only one brand name and that they own that brand name. I don't know whether you would call it left. The left is predominant but it is not solely the left.[68]

While Blainey received criticism from academics in various faculties and in various universities, the attack that made the most lasting impact was the one from members of his own department. Twenty-three members of the History Department at Melbourne University wrote a letter to the editors of several newspapers in mid-May 1984, reading as follows:

> As historians at the University of Melbourne we wish to disassociate ourselves entirely from the widely-publicised attacks which Professor Geoffrey Blainey, an eminent member of our profession and a professor in our department, has recently made on the Government immigration policy in regard to Asians. Professor Blainey speaks and writes on this issue as an individual and not as a representative of historians at this university.
>
> We are particularly aware of the dangers of trying to channel debate on immigration policy into consideration of the suitability of certain ethnic and national groups as immigrants. We are also aware, from many historical precedents, that raising such an issue in racial terms (however much it is couched in the language of reason) becomes an invitation to less responsible groups to incite feelings of racial hatred. Framing debate in such racial terms can become a potent weapon to rouse public fears and prejudices and to direct hostility at certain groups in our society.
>
> We do not wish to limit debate and discussion by Professor Blainey or anyone else on such issues of public concern. But to raise discussion of immigration in terms of race will inevitably draw in and encourage racist groups to come forward and claim legitimacy from what has been said.[69]

An initial version of the letter had been written at a meeting in the staff room a week before publication and circulated to others in the following days. The driving forces in the Department appear to have been South African-born British historian David Phillips and medieval and early modern European

---

68   Henderson, *Australian Answers*, 62.
69   The letter was published in *The Herald* (Melbourne) (18 May), in *The Age* (19 May) and in *The Australian* (24 May). The *Sydney Morning Herald* declined to publish it. Eighteen of the signatories had signed in person while a further five had given consent by telephone.

historian Charles Zika.[70] The signatory who has gone on to achieve the highest profile in the historical debates of the subsequent quarter century, Stuart Macintyre, has acknowledged that the second sentence was 'unfortunate', as 'the fact that the twenty-three signatories themselves wrote as members of the History Department suggested either inconsistency or even the imposition of a collective orthodoxy'.[71]

Not all those whose names were included were happy. Alison Patrick, historian of the French Revolution and sister of former Victorian Liberal Premier Dick Hamer, wrote to Blainey saying that her name had been added despite some stipulations she made not being included in the text and assured him that 'I don't think you are in any sense a racist, and never will'.[72] Even before the letter appeared one former staff member, Norman Harper, complained to Department Chairman Ian Robertson about the Department's attitude:

> I was surprised to learn from you over lunch today that the History Department was publicly disassociating itself from Geoffrey Blainey's views. I told you that I supported him on the question of the speed of Asian immigration ... I haven't any doubt that he is not a racist in any sense of the term. I assure you that I am not either and that I am not unfamiliar with problems of immigration.[73]

Harper saw himself as a liberal on issues of race, having quickly incorporated issues such as civil rights and Black Power into his American History courses when lecturing, and having spent time living and working close to black neighbourhoods in Chicago. A reflection on Harper's life and work observed that 'there was a feeling of incomprehension from Harper about the alignments of the 1980s' for, having investigated and written about race relations for decades, he 'was obviously somewhat surprised and indignant to find himself out of step with younger colleagues by 1984'.[74] There were also numerous dissidents from other departments and faculties, who wrote

---

70 Memo signed by C. Zika and D. Phillips, 14 May 1984, History Department Papers, Acc. No. 100/59, University of Melbourne Archives, (hereafter UMA).

71 Stuart Macintyre and Fay Anderson, 'History in the Headlines', in *The Life of the Past: The discipline of history at the University of Melbourne, 1855–2005*, eds Fay Anderson and Stuart Macintyre, (Melbourne: RMIT Publishing, 2006), 370.

72 Alison Patrick to Blainey, 19 June 1984, Blainey Papers, MS 9225/2/20 Box 3, NLA.

73 Norman Harper to Ian Robertson, 17 May 1984, History Department Papers, Acc. No. 100/59, UMA.

74 David Goodman, '"There is no-one to whom I can talk" – Norman Harper and American History in Australia', *Australasian Journal of American Studies* 23 (2004): 15–16.

privately to Blainey, attacking his History colleagues. An example came from an academic who, although not agreeing with all Blainey's views, bemoaned the fact that, instead of promoting 'open, sensible, discussion … these privileged members of our University have hastened to reassure the community that they are not tarred with any controversial opinions'.[75] Another strong support for Blainey was the Sub-Dean of the Arts Faculty, Dinny O'Hearn.

As well as the dubious substance of the letter, the timing could hardly have looked worse. Not only was Blainey himself not in a position to respond, as he was on a long-planned tour of major archaeological sites in Europe when the letter was published, it also followed the death of his father. Robertson wrote to Blainey expressing his condolences and recognised how unfortunate it was that his father's passing 'should have happened at a time when you are undoubtedly under strain on other fronts, and that strain may be aggravated by an initiative of members of this Department including myself'.[76]

Blainey first heard about the Department's letter via a phone call while he was in London. On his return to Melbourne, he described his reaction to learning of it as one of 'intense disappointment'.[77] He agreed to attend a 'Special Friday Afternoon Discussion' in the Margaret Kiddle Room in the History Department on 1 June. One thing that he said caused 'great surprise in the History department' was that, in expressing views on immigration, he was 'speaking very much as a historian', arguing that their surprise was a product of the fact that 'many of them know no Australian history'.[78] Of course, it was not the first time that Blainey had combined history and contemporary debates but, unlike the immigration issue, none of his colleagues had objected when he had compared providing literary grants in the 1970s with providing free education in the 1870s; or when he had defended Concorde by referring to steamships and steam trains.

The issue of whether Blainey had any special authority on the immigration issue because of his expertise as a historian was keenly debated. One interstate colleague, Geoffrey Bolton argued that Blainey's views had no more authority than those of 'the man in the street', prompting Blainey to ask in reply what else he had to do to become qualified. The exchange left Bolton 'depressed and intensely agitated' and feeling, as he had with the controversy over *The*

---

75   Letter to Blainey, 21 May 1984, Blainey Papers, MS 9225/2/10 Box 1, NLA.
76   Ian Robertson to Blainey, 21 May 1984, Blainey Papers, MS 9225/2/17 Box 3, NLA.
77   Tate, 'Blainey defends Asian views'.
78   Duncan, 'Blainey sees a threat emerge to free speech', 26.

Tyranny of Distance, at a disadvantage in public debate with Blainey who was 'sure in his judgements and unyielding in controversy'.[79]

Relations between Blainey and his own Department were further strained when Blainey was the subject of a rowdy demonstration on campus on Monday 18 June and one of the organisers claimed on radio that they had the support of the History Department.[80] This was largely untrue. Many of Blainey's colleagues reacted like Chips Sowerwine, who sent a note saying that he was 'appalled that your right to teach – which I regard as sacred – should so be challenged'.[81] Another colleague, Donna Merwick, explained 'how distressed I was for you yesterday and worried indeed for your safety'.[82]

While the majority of Blainey's academic critics attempted to retain some degree of decorum in their statements, a couple of his Melbourne History Department colleagues were gratuitously offensive. David Phillips not only suggested in *Farrago* that Blainey's work did not measure up to first year standard and that he should be awarded a 'Goebbels prize', but he also alleged that Blainey was only prepared to speak to 'passively receptive audiences of Warrnambool Rotarians, Brisbane engineers and readers of the Melbourne *Herald*'.[83] Phillips seemed to believe that only professional historians were likely to be able to challenge Blainey's arguments.

Another colleague, John Lack, suggested that Blainey should be docked all his university pay for the time he had been participating in the immigration debate.[84] There is no evidence that Lack had expressed a similar opinion when Blainey was spending the same amount of time on matters related to government committees. Department Head Robertson wrote to Blainey saying that he was 'very shocked and upset' to read Lack's comments and stating that 'those of us who are involved with working with you as Dean know that, despite your public involvement in debate about immigration policy, you have continued to fulfil your responsibilities as Dean with energy, imagination and fairness'.[85]

---

79   Macintyre, 'Geoffrey Bolton: A Lifetime of History'.
80   Blainey to David Phillips, 25 June 1984, History Department Papers, Acc. No. 100/59, UMA.
81   Chips Sowerwine to Blainey, 18 June 1984, Blainey Papers, MS 9225/2/23 Box 4, NLA.
82   Donna Merwick to Blainey, 19 June 1984, Blainey Papers, MS 9225/2/23, NLA.
83   David Phillips, 'Anyone for Blainey', *Farrago*, vol. 62 no. 15, 22 October 1984, 20; and Phillips, 'Blainey Critic Replies'.
84   Louise Carbines, 'Return four months pay to uni: colleague', *The Age*, 13 July 1984, 3.
85   Ian Robertson to Blainey, 17 July 1984, Blainey Papers, Acc. No. 89/145, Box 7, UMA.

Others in the History Department tried to adopt a more conciliatory tone than Phillips and Lack. When in March 1985, the *National Times* suggested that there was opposition in the Department to Blainey ever returning, Professor Greg Dening wrote to assure Blainey that this was a 'complete fabrication' and that 'all of us deplore such an unprofessional notion'. Dening went further, proposing some practical action towards reconciliation:

> I honestly do not know how deep wounds are healed or divisions made up and pessimistically feel that they are only made worse by mutual isolation. Is there any way that you could see your way to coming to lunch with some of us, or could we meet for lunch somewhere? Just to talk, not to argue a case.[86]

A week later, Blainey replied saying that it was 'kind of you to write' and that he was 'very happy to take up your suggestion', but it appears that nothing came of this.[87]

The demonstration also saw Blainey receive notes of support from senior members of the academy, such as Keith Hancock and Manning Clark. The former wrote that Australia's immigration policies owed a lot to Calwell and successive Liberal Governments but 'we owe nothing at all to the orators of the Newest Left', while the latter hoped Blainey was not upset by 'the activities of the 'Rent a Mob' people'.[88] In the same week as the Melbourne University demonstration Blainey also spoke at an extremely rowdy meeting in Sydney's Kings Cross, which saw further clashes between police and demonstrators, while a fortnight later at the University of Queensland protesters attempted to disrupt a lecture he was delivering.[89] Blainey argued that he had to continue making his case because, if he stopped, he would be 'giving in to bullies'.[90] He expressed a similar sentiment a few months later when his daughter Anna was seriously assaulted when walking home in North Fitzroy. His assumption was that the attack was random but, if it was not, he would not be deterred. Another by-product of the uproar was

---

86   Greg Dening to Blainey, 29 March 1985, History Department Papers, Acc. No. 100/59, UMA.

87   Blainey to Greg Dening, 7 April 1985, History Department Papers, Acc. No. 100/59, UMA.

88   Keith Hancock to Blainey, 19 June 1984, and Manning Clark to Blainey, 18 June 1984, Blainey Papers, MS 9225/2/21 Box 3, NLA.

89   Bailey and Norrington, 1; and 'Blainey dodges uni protesters', *Courier-Mail*, 6 July 1984, 1.

90   Bowers, 'Blainey stirs, rather than mixes, the pot'.

that he felt he could no longer watch football matches on his own in the outer as had previously been his custom.

Although Blainey did not stop pursuing the issue, he was forced to stop making public appearances, as he explained when writing to cancel a scheduled appearance at a College of Advanced Education in Wagga:

> I have decided, after listening to advice, to cancel virtually all engagements to speak in public during July and August. Three times now, in different cities, a small group who do subscribe to violence ... have placed pickets at meetings, twice engaging in activities leading to arrests and disrupting seriously parts of each meeting. On two of these occasions I was not speaking on a controversial topic ... public meetings at present make me – and those who attend them – vulnerable. It is rather absurd that one should have to withdraw from speaking engagements in a democracy; but there it is.[91]

Most of the organisations whose events Blainey could not attend accepted the reason. One which was harder to convince was the Australian Historical Association (AHA), the professional historians' association, whose annual conference was scheduled for Melbourne University in late August. Despite several representations from Andrew Markus, Graeme Davison and others, Blainey declined to attend as the University administration made it clear that the security issues were too great. Security issues also meant that a forum proposed by some members of the SRC did not take place, although the SRC President, Melissa Daly, was actually pleased it was called off as, in her view, 'just to allow him to speak is to give him a platform where he can put forward his frankly racist views'.[92]

The police and University administration believed there was a serious physical threat to Blainey in this period. He was provided with a 24-hour police security number and the University acquired an anti-explosive machine to sort all the mail. The University was reluctant to spend more money on the sort of security which would be needed if Blainey conducted further speaking engagements on campus. The fact that he did not led some of Blainey's colleagues, such as Phillips, to claim he lacked the courage to participate in a debate with them, a debate that was precluded by the degree of vitriol which they bore some responsibility for inflaming. Blainey argued that, if a major accusation against him was that he might encourage the 'ratbag fringe', he was

---

91   Blainey letter, 10 July 1984, Blainey Papers, MS 9225/2/26 Box 4, NLA.
92   Kathy Constan, 'Blainey backs down', *Farrago*. 62, no. 12, 17 September 1984, 3.

perfectly entitled to claim that his academic opponents had done the same.⁹³ And their participation in the debate required less courage, as nobody was picketing their public appearances.

Blainey's correspondents certainly believed that he was exhibiting 'courage', or taking a 'courageous stance', along with lots of mentions of the writers being part of the 'silent majority'. Many commented that it was the first time they had written to a public figure and several said the letter was on behalf of 'my husband and I' or 'my wife and I'. By the end of 1984, Blainey had replied to 1,455 letters, often with a standard response typed by his secretary, Liz Carey. The letters also revealed that Blainey received some benefit from previously banked goodwill, as demonstrated by a letter he received from a typist from the outer eastern Melbourne suburb of Croydon:

> Some years ago I typed all or part of a draft of *The Rush That Never Ended* and you wrote a gracious letter of thanks. In doing so you unwittingly became the only person to take the trouble to put pen to paper and say thank you to me for a job apparently well done. That is a historical fact.⁹⁴

Other correspondents were less sympathetic. The Nobel Prize-winning novelist Patrick White wrote to Blainey asking him to quietly resign from the committee which helped White judge the Patrick White Award, designed to support a writer who had not received the recognition he or she deserved. White explained to Blainey that 'the presence of so-called ethnics' was what made Australia 'bearable' and that Blainey remaining on the committee would be against both their principles.⁹⁵

The immigration debate prompted numerous calls for Blainey to contest the next Federal Election as an independent. In a 1986 press interview, Blainey observed that opinion polls in 1984 had shown that he could have won a Senate seat in any state if he had chosen to stand, but he did not see value in being elected to Parliament on a single issue.⁹⁶

After the election was held, the immigration issue began to quieten down. However, it was rekindled in March by the publication of a book of essays, *Surrender Australia?*, designed to challenge both Blainey's arguments on immigration and his status as a historian. The contributors were mainly

---

93 Blainey to David Phillips, 4 July 1984, Blainey Papers, MS 9225/3/29 Box 12, NLA.
94 Letter to Blainey, 2 April 1985, Blainey Papers, MS 9225/2/42 Box 6, NLA.
95 Rodney, Wetherell, 'Kindness of a best-selling monster – for those remaindered', *Sydney Morning Herald*, 8 November 2002 (accessed online).
96 Charles De Lisle, 'The Blainey View: on the New Right, Liberty and Australia's Day of Reckoning', *The Australian* (Supplement), 11-12 October 1986, 3, 20.

historians, with the editors and almost half the eleven writers coming from Monash University. The editors, Andrew Markus and Merle Ricklefs, were explicit in the Introduction that 'the essays here are critical of Blainey both as a historian and as immigration polemicist' and 'while recognising the breadth and value of his contributions to Australian history', the contributions criticised his work for 'misconceptions, misunderstandings and faulty judgments'.[97] There were no essays sympathetic to Blainey.

The sense that Blainey's critics were ganging up on him may have been reduced if the book had been the work of a single author, but eleven critiquing one was always going to make Blainey appear something of a martyr. Any hope of avoiding this impression faded further when Henry Reynolds was quoted as saying that 'a whole team got together with the jackhammers' to compile it, after Blainey 'had lost the respect of practically the whole profession' through his intervention in the immigration debate.[98] Reynolds wrote to Blainey to explain that the journalist, Helen Trinca, had 'seriously distorted what I had said'. Reynolds could not even recall using the word 'jackhammer' but, if he had, it was specifically targeted at Blainey's views on immigration but not 'to the great bulk of your work - or your overall reputation', a comment which seemingly contradicted the editors stated intention.[99]

While most of the authors were well known within the academy, the point was made in the media that, with one possible exception, 'the public would be hard pressed to name a book by any of the authors'.[100] Blainey was surprised by some of the names and clearly felt a sense of betrayal that individuals whom he had considered to be friends had contributed, pointing out that 'several, at vital stages of their career, had required my help and reputation in order to further their career, and here they were trying to demolish that reputation'.[101] At least one of the contributors anonymously tried to soften the blow by telling the press that 'Blainey is a nice bloke and it took some pressure from the editors for us to move against him'.[102]

---

97 Markus and Ricklefs, 'Introduction'.
98 Helen Trinca, 'Historians to take the legend of Blainey "head on" in new book', *The Weekend Australian*, 16-17 February 1985, 3.
99 Henry Reynolds to Blainey, 29 March 1985, Blainey Papers, MS 9225/2/7, NLA.
100 Anne Levinson, 'Academic firing squad takes aim at Blainey', *Sydney Morning Herald*, 29 March 1985, 1. The suggested exception was Tom Stannage's *The People of Perth*.
101 Geoffrey Blainey, 'Have they come to bury me?', (Melbourne) *Herald*, 28 March 1985, 5.
102 Williamson, 'Geoffrey Blainey's Year of Living Dangerously', 4.

Some of the chapters reflected criticisms that some writers, such as Reynolds and Tom Stannage, had made in earlier reviews of Blainey books. Other chapters contained novel criticisms. For instance, Frank Broeze's chapter on *The Tyranny of Distance* was, in many ways, no more critical of Blainey's most famous book than John Hirst had been in *Historical Studies* in 1975. Yet context was everything. Contributing a chapter to a book designed to diminish Blainey's standing meant Broeze's views, which in another context would have appeared to be worthwhile commentary, here looked like part of a hatchet job.

Sir John Bunting, former head of the Prime Minister's Department, with whom Blainey had served on the Australia Council, was a source of advice to Blainey, and he recommended that the best tactic for negating the impact of the book would be to write one comprehensive response but not to go on television or radio, thus avoiding potentially sales-boosting ongoing controversy.[103] So when extracts from *Surrender Australia* appeared in weekend newspapers, they were accompanied by a vigorous response from Blainey saying that he could not 'remember in recent years any other book which omits or alters so much crucial evidence in order to reach its conclusion'.[104]

Blainey was able to point to some obvious flaws. John Rickard based his whole chapter on the premise that Blainey had used the system of note-taking devised by Beatrice Webb, which Blainey had described in his 1954 journal article 'Scissors and Paste in Local History'. Unfortunately for Rickard, while Blainey had tried the Webb system at that time, he found it did not suit him and had never used it in the composition of a book. He also upbraided Rickard for arguing that Blainey had become more critical of 1850s Chinese immigrants in successive books and yet ignoring what he had said about the Chinese in *The Blainey View*, because it would not fit into the paradigm. Similarly, Blainey wrote of Reynolds that 'only by ignoring the evidence can he conclude that I gave a "bloodless account of pioneering"' and gave examples to prove his point.

The social scientist and immigration expert James Jupp explained in a review in *Australian Book Review* that contributors had needed to make a choice between 'denouncing Blainey's views on immigration, or attacking his standing as a historian'.[105] Jupp thought the former would be easy as *All for Australia* was 'a very bad book', but most had plumped for the much

---

103 Devine, 'A Conversation with Geoffrey Blainey', 50.
104 Geoffrey Blainey, 'The Blainey Reply', *The Age* (Saturday Extra section), 30 March 1985, 8; also published as 'The accused shoots back', *Sydney Morning Herald*, 30 March 1985, 43.
105 Jupp, 'Blainey, fashionable old-fashioned historian', 12.

harder task of doing the latter. He argued that they largely failed to fully prosecute their case, in part because the chapters were too short and just as arguments were becoming interesting 'the page is turned to reveal its termination'.[106]

ANU historian Paul Bourke made a similar point in his review which appeared in *Historical Studies* some three years later.[107] Bourke made a clear distinction between the four authors who dealt with the immigration issues Blainey had raised and the seven who assessed his historical practice. Six of the latter seven contributed only 36 pages between them and Bourke argued that these chapters were 'not scholarly efforts', as the link between Blainey as commentator and historian was 'simply asserted and announced rather than explored', resulting in pieces that are little more than 'crude reductionism'.[108] He was particularly critical of Reynolds for suggesting that Blainey had 'laid an intellectual foundation for others to use racism', writing that 'I cannot believe Reynolds intends what this seems to say'. Bourke asked rhetorically whether Reynolds actually meant that 'Blainey should have suppressed his historical judgements because they might give aid and comfort to the right?'[109]

By the mid-1980s, it was generally recognised that the interests of historians had changed radically. Some, such as Jupp, saw that one benefit of *Surrender Australia* was that it would at least expedite the process of shaking Australian history out of a narrow nationalism, and that this is what 'the younger and more critical generation' of Australian historians was committed to doing.[110] In an attempt to make sense of the shift, Tim Jordan in an article in *Arena* described two schools – the dominant national school of history and the social history one which had emerged in the past decade to challenge it.[111] To make sense of the immigration debate he placed Blainey in the former category, but even the editors of *Arena* were unconvinced, pointing out in an introductory comment that those who accepted the dichotomy might still argue that Blainey was 'wrongly posted in the national box when his writings might qualify him rather well as an early starter in the social history stakes'.[112]

---

106 Ibid.
107 Paul Bourke, 'Making Professional History', *Australian Historical Studies* 23, no. 91 (October 1988): 193–201.
108 Ibid., 194.
109 Ibid., 195.
110 Jupp, 'Blainey, fashionable old-fashioned historian', 14.
111 Tim Jordan, 'Migration: History and Politics', *Arena*, no. 73 (1985), 81–94.
112 'The Blainey Debate: Editorial Comment', *Arena*, no. 73 (1985), 80–81.

Ultimately, it is debateable whether the manner of the academy's intervention had helped or hindered the case for a higher rate of Asian immigration to Australia. Blainey argued that it was not his statements which had stirred up immigration as an issue, but rather he had merely drawn attention to an existing and legitimate major public concern.[113] There is another explanation for why the issue became so prominent, which is that the strength of the reaction to Blainey's remarks stirred the issue up far more than either Blainey's comments, or pre-existing community views, could ever have done.

The La Trobe University sociologist Claudio Veliz felt that some explanation was needed to explain why Blainey was treated more as a heretic than just wrong and why his views on immigration necessitated 'detailed researches into all his published works in order to uncover the genesis of evil and uproot it at the source'.[114] Veliz made it clear that he disagreed with Blainey's views on immigration, believing that Australia had a moral obligation to accept those with whom it fought in the Vietnam War, that suggestions of the Asianisation of Australia were exaggerated and that immigrants would be more of an asset than a burden in tough economic times. It was a common reaction: disagreement with Blainey's views, but outrage at his treatment. The fact that many of Blainey's fellow historians, particularly younger historians, were in the vanguard of the reaction to his comments did not escape the notice of some senior members of the academy. Perhaps the most striking assessment of their role came from Manning Clark:

> I have never heard of anything like this happening in other parts of the world, except in the Soviet Union, where a historian who has reigned for a while is suddenly found to be a hyena and roundly condemned. If you disagree with anyone the way to show it is to get on with your own work, not knock someone else's down. I don't agree with what Blainey said about immigration. But young people today are so self-righteous.[115]

Blainey had himself been contemplating why ideas and attitudes move in and out of favour. For a decade, he had been periodically working on a book which would seek to show how intellectual mood swings had profound effects on public attitudes. This was published as *The Great Seesaw* in 1988.[116] Some

---

113   Blainey, 'The Blainey Reply'.
114   Claudio Veliz, 'Professor Blainey's Heresy: An Ocker Inquisition?' *Quadrant* 29, no. 5 (May 1985): 10–13.
115   Williamson, 'Geoffrey Blainey's Year of Living Dangerousl', 4.
116   Geoffrey Blainey, *The Great Seesaw: A New View of the Western World*, (Melbourne: Macmillan, 1988). The work is considered in greater detail in Chapter 11.

historians, when discussing Blainey's career, have interpreted *Seesaw* through a political prism and related it to the public policy debates in which Blainey was engaged when writing the book. Tom Griffiths has argued that Blainey was 'trying to use history to alleviate future social and political crisis ... a stance that is both idealistic and conservative', while Davison opined that the theories Blainey was espousing 'probably have an inherent appeal to business people and economic liberals'.[117]

But which was Blainey – conservative or liberal? In his review of *Surrender Australia*, Jupp wrote that Blainey seemed 'poised uncertainly between conservative pessimism and liberal optimism'.[118] Blainey had been closer to the latter position when he joined the academy in the early 1960s and had shifted to a more conservative pessimistic outlook. This change contributed to a major fracture in his career progression.

---

117 Tom Griffiths, 'Light Green, Dark Green', in *The Fuss That Never Ended: The Life and Work of Geoffrey Blainey*, eds Deborah Gare et al. (Melbourne, Melbourne University Press, 2003), 60; and Graeme Davison, *The Use and Abuse of Australian History* (Sydney: Allen & Unwin, 2000), 234.

118 Jupp, 'Blainey, fashionable old-fashioned historian', 13.

Chapter 8

FREELANCE AGAIN

From mid-1985 immigration was a less prominent public issue, but the events of 1984-85 were the catalyst for the fact that, before the decade was out, Blainey had resigned his academic post and was back where his career had begun, working as a freelance historian.

The trigger for Blainey's departure was his return to the History Department in 1988, after his term as Dean of the Faculty of Arts had been completed. His relationship with his departmental colleagues had been less crucial while he was Dean but, having been re-elected unopposed to the position at the height of the initial immigration controversy in 1984, Blainey narrowly lost an election in 1987 when he sought a third three-year term.

Blainey's defeat in that ballot generated significant press coverage and speculation that his colleagues had punished him for his political views. Others saw the result coming more as a positive vote for the victor, Marion Adams partly based on a desire to have a female Dean for the first time. Blainey's own measured stance, when asked at the time, was to observe that 'some say a lot of the voting was definitely on political lines and others say that it wasn't'.[1] Some high-profile outsiders offered assistance. One was businessman Ron Walker, who wrote that 'if there is anything I can do personally to help your situation at the University, I will certainly get together an impressive bunch of people and talk to the Board'.[2]

And there were plenty of others who, while strongly disagreeing with Blainey's views, lamented the degree of invective that came his way. The novelist Tom Keneally wrote to Blainey shortly after he lost the position of Dean and prior to them both going as travelling speakers on a cruise ship in the upcoming summer:

---

1 Standard response to letters of support, 2 September 1987, Blainey Papers, Acc. No. 89/145 Box 49, UMA.
2 Ron Walker to Blainey, 10 September 1987, Blainey Papers, Acc. No. 89/145 Box 49, UMA.

> I regret very much the impulse of some people to attempt to discredit your history in the simple-minded and intellectually fascist belief that this would somehow undermine your social and political arguments. I don't care whether you accept this or not, but you are for me one of the very finest Australian writers and historians. As for the rest, our disagreements are a matter of record.[3]

Blainey decided to delay his full-time return to the Department by taking special leave for the whole of the 1988 academic year. However, his absence did not postpone conflict. Correspondence between Blainey and the Chairman of the Department, Greg Dening, as the two attempted to negotiate an appropriate teaching load for Blainey in 1989, reveals a worsening relationship. After Blainey lost the ballot for Dean, Dening wrote, in similar friendly tones as he had in 1985, saying 'how much I personally and as chairman am looking forward to your return to the Department' and assuring Blainey of a 'warm welcome from the Department in general'.[4] Yet, when the two men began discussing specifics, real differences arose. Blainey indicated that he would like his main focus to be Australian history, but Dening argued that this would undermine the work done by the incumbents in that field – Lloyd Robson, Noel McLachlan and Stuart Macintyre. Trying to conclude matters before going on leave, Dening wrote to Blainey in April 1988:

> Your expression 'I wish to take charge formally of the undergraduate "Australian History", either alone or jointly with Lloyd' rides roughshod over Noel and Stuart, as well as Lloyd, who have put ten years in good times and bad in developing the subject. The present arrangements for the subject will remain ... Please take my advice that I have now proffered three times, and go to them of your own accord and talk with them of your engagement in the subject. I will be glad to be free of the tedium of these matters, but will leave disappointed that I have been unable to persuade you to take even one positive step in filling what I believe to be your professional responsibilities *in* [Dening's emphasis] the department.[5]

---

3   Tom Keneally to Blainey, 12 October 1987, Blainey Papers, Acc. No. 89/145 Box 49, UMA. Blainey responded on 23 October, writing that 'we can disagree amicably'.

4   Greg Dening to Blainey, 13 October 1987, History Department Papers, Acc. No. 100/59, UMA.

5   Greg Dening to Blainey, 22 April 1988, History Department Papers, Acc. No. 100/59, UMA.

A few weeks later matters had obviously been elevated to higher authorities within the university, leading an even more exasperated Dening to write again to Blainey, reversing his earlier decision:

> The Vice-Chancellor has informed me that you put great store by being the coordinator of the subject 'Australian History'. Remarkable though this seems to me, I am intent on seeing that there are no obstacles at all to your return to the department. Therefore, please let me change my letter of April 22 to read that your responsibilities in 1989 include being coordinator in 'Australian History'. Noel, Lloyd and Stuart will have responsibilities elsewhere. This one is yours.[6]

Complicating an already messy situation, a family illness prompted Blainey to cancel the trip overseas he had planned for the second half of 1988 and return to work on 1 July. David Phillips, acting chair in Dening's absence, claimed that the first he knew about the change of plans was when Blainey appeared in the staff room for morning tea on that day. Some hasty re-arranging of staff responsibilities saw Phillips put together a package of duties for Blainey that included some lecturing in the subject 'European Hegemony 1400-1800', two tutorials per week in 'Australians at War' and thesis supervision. Blainey wrote back that he was 'very happy to help in the areas you indicate'.[7] However, tensions remained. Phillips wrote an acerbic letter to the Dean of the Arts Faculty complaining that 'the History Department has been the subject of a great deal of ill-informed, even malicious, rumour in recent months, some of which seems to be given credence in some higher levels of the University'.[8] He also forwarded a copy of the correspondence to the Vice-Chancellor who wrote back expressing surprise at the tone of the letter and pointing out that the responsibilities of professors was a matter of legitimate concern for a Vice-Chancellor. He stated that, given Blainey's heavy media schedule, he 'wanted to be sure that we were not subject to criticism now that the University is employing him as an academic but not requiring him to take a normal teaching load thus leaving him free to be heavily engaged in his outside lecturing and journalistic activities'.[9]

---

6 Greg Dening to Blainey, 8 June 1988, History Department Papers, Acc. No. 100/59, UMA

7 Blainey to David Phillips, 12 July 1988, History Department Papers, Acc. No. 100/59, UMA.

8 David Phillips to Marion Adams, 14 July 1988, History Department Papers, Acc. No. 100/59, UMA.

9 David Penington to David Phillips, 22 July 1988, History Department Papers, Acc. No. 100/59, UMA.

The events from 1984 onwards had clearly changed how Blainey felt in the university environment. Macintyre recognised that Blainey had gone from being someone 'who had such easy relations with people' and had always enjoyed 'the goodwill of his audience', to appearing 'extraordinarily on edge', as he found himself no longer assured of a positive reaction from colleagues or students.[10] Blainey himself was quite sanguine about the changed attitudes:

> There are certain groups who once were sympathetic to me who are no longer, and those groups are probably fairly strong in universities. My view is there is nothing I can do about it. If I believe something is right then it should be said. If people react in a certain way then so be it. If I believe something is in the long-term interest of the nation, I'll say it, even if it is not in my own short-term interest.[11]

Some years later, in a 1996 interview, journalist Doug Aiton asked Blainey whether those who had spurned him initially had made an effort to re-establish cordial relations. Blainey responded:

> All except one have never raised the immigration matter again. Several did obliquely. But I knew what they meant. Several have said they are embarrassed. But a good number have stuck to their views.[12]

Just six months back in the Department was enough to convince Blainey that it was better for him to leave. He did not explain his reasons in any detail at the time. Gerard Henderson interviewed him on the day he was packing up his office and related that 'Professor Blainey consciously chose not to discuss with me the reasons for his premature departure … I had a feeling that he may have felt let down by his colleagues … but he did not say so'.[13] In 2000, Blainey was reported as confirming that he could have stayed on, and that it was his decision to resign. Blainey recalled that 'I thought I've only got one life and I better start afresh … It was a sensible decision'.[14] Nonetheless, as he commented a few years later, 'it was a great disappointment having to leave'.[15]

---

10 Gordon, 'Geoffrey Blainey comes in from the cold'.
11 Peter White, 'Dumped but defiant', *Sydney Morning Herald*, 29 August 1987, 43.
12 Aiton, 'Tomorrow the world'.
13 Henderson, *Australian Answers*, 61.
14 Gordon, 'Geoffrey Blainey comes in from the cold'.
15 Devine, 'A Conversation with Geoffrey Blainey', 50.

There has been considerable debate about who should wear the responsibility for the parting of the ways between Blainey and the Melbourne University History Department. The most often cited culprit by Blainey's supporters is Stuart Macintyre, who was actually on leave at the time. According to Macintyre, John Howard once accused him of being one of those who had 'forced out' Blainey. However, as Macintyre related the story, he had the opportunity to put his side of the case and, having listened to the explanation, Howard 'acknowledged he was mistaken'.[16]

Not all of Macintyre's critics have been so easily convinced. Blainey's friend Peter Ryan argued in *Quadrant* that a 'squalid academic assassination had been perpetrated by lesser historians', an assassination he tried to personalise largely on the basis that Macintyre subsequently became the Ernest Scott Professor, an argument that Keith Windschuttle repeated in the same journal eight years later.[17] Another critic of the role of other historians in the departure of Blainey from the university was China specialist Ross Terrill, who described it as 'the unfaced Dreyfus case of recent Australian history' and asserted that 'ninety-nine per cent of intellectuals have drawn a curtain of silence over the outrage'.[18] Melbourne University historians seem keen to avoid any culpability for his departure. For instance, in 2006, the acting Department Head Joy Damousi wrote to *The Age*:

> Your senior arts writer says Geoffrey Blainey lost his post at the University of Melbourne in the late 1980s for criticising Asian immigration and Aboriginal land rights. In fact, he resigned in 1988 after he had completed two terms as dean of arts and four years after the immigration debate. Many of his colleagues disagreed with his views on that issue; many of us regretted the loss of such an outstanding writer and teacher.[19]

The letter is somewhat misleading for, although it is true that his resignation was four years after the initial immigration debate, 1988 was a year when immigration was a major political issue in Australia and Blainey, with a weekly column in a major newspaper, was a participant in that debate, to

---

16 Stuart Macintyre and Anna Clark, *The History Wars* (Melbourne: Melbourne University Press, 2003), 92.
17 Peter Ryan, 'Apologies', *Quadrant* 44, no. 3 (March 2000): 88; and Keith Windschuttle, 'Stuart Macintyre and the Blainey Affair', *Quadrant* 52, no. 10 (October 2008): 35.
18 Ross Terrill, *The Australians: The Way We Live Now* (Sydney: Doubleday, 2000), 273.
19 Joy Damousi, Letter to the editor, *The Age* (Insight section), 2 September 2006, 8.

the extent that in March one of his columns precipitated a debate in Federal Parliament. More than that, his views on other issues, in articles where he was described as 'Professor of History, University of Melbourne', would only have tended to aggravate those colleagues who were already annoyed by his desire to determine his own teaching responsibilities. Very little that happened between 1984 and 1988 would have given Blainey much confidence that he could have returned to the congenial working environment he had enjoyed at the university in earlier years, and any hopes of such an outcome were further reduced by the resentment felt in the Department after the intervention of the Vice-Chancellor.

Blainey had remained silent on the immigration issue for a significant time after the initial controversy faded. He explained to one correspondent in August 1985 that 'in recent months I have made no comment publicly on the immigration issue, largely because the Government is quietly modifying its programme'. He reiterated to another letter-writer in June 1986 that 'I'm not at present speaking on the immigration issue'.[20] Many continued to urge him to run for Parliament, but he explained that 'I would prefer not to stand for parliament, though the day may come when reluctantly I change my mind'.[21]

After losing the ballot for Dean, Blainey conducted several press interviews. Asked whether he still maintained the same position on immigration, he confirmed that he did. One recent development which Blainey believed helped his argument was the May 1987 coup in Fiji, which meant that his critics could no longer laud that country as an example of multi-racial harmony, given its obvious ethnic tensions.[22] Adding to Blainey's prominence, his monthly column in *The Weekend Australian* became a weekly one in August 1987. The newspaper launched a new opinion page and Blainey shared it with John Hyde, Greg Sheridan, Norman Podhoretz and Gary Punch. Blainey covered diverse topics including Aboriginal affairs, football, the painter Hugh Ramsay and American attitudes to Australia. During 1988 he devoted several columns to the referendum questions that were being put in September that year. In particular, he opposed the proposed four-year terms which he said 'will actually take away the people's right to remove an incompetent government with

---

20 Blainey correspondence, 26 August 1985, Blainey Papers, MS 9225/2/46 Box 7, NLA; and Blainey correspondence, 4 June 1986, Blainey Papers, Acc. No. 89/145, Box 35, UMA.

21 Blainey correspondence, 12 September 1986, Blainey Papers, Acc. No. 89/145 Box 42, UMA.

22 White, 'Dumped but defiant'.

that speed hitherto available'.[23] However, his staple topics were immigration and multiculturalism.

Immigration was always going to be a big issue in 1988, as the Hawke Government had commissioned Blainey's former deputy at the Australia-China Council, Stephen FitzGerald, to write a report on the topic. However, immigration was in the headlines well before the report was released following provocative comments, first by John Stone and then by leading Aboriginal figure, Charles Perkins. Blainey leapt to the defence of both men in his weekly column. Stone had called for immigration policy to favour English-speaking migrants, a view Blainey endorsed as he believed that sharing a common language was an important factor in a well-functioning democracy.[24] A month later, Blainey argued that the reaction to Perkins' opposition to the level of Asian immigration had shown that many politicians held the inherently racist view that 'a spokesman for Aborigines must automatically side with other coloured people' and, by breaking down this stereotype, Perkins had 'courageously defied this cult of double talk'.[25]

The Fitzgerald Report was released in June. It was certainly no whitewash of the Government which had commissioned it. Fitzgerald found serious flaws in how the immigration policy was being run and noted how over-zealous multiculturalism had actually undermined support for non-discriminatory immigration. Blainey praised the Inquiry for having 'the perception to see that in some ways immigration was a divisive issue and summoned the courage to state the truth'.[26] Yet, while Blainey and FitzGerald diagnosed similar problems with current policies, their solutions were quite different. Blainey claimed that the report's seventy-three recommendations were a 'potential disaster'. Paul Kelly summed up the divide:

> The Blainey-Stone line was rooted in a diagnosis of community concerns similar to Fitzgerald's – but they offered conflicting solutions. The Blainey-Stone line sought a concession from the non-discriminatory policy to ease community concerns. Fitzgerald sought an aggressive

---

23 Geoffrey Blainey, 'Limiting the power of voters – in the name of democracy', *The Weekend Australian*, 28–29 May 1988, 24

24 Geoffrey Blainey, 'Reaction to Stone a clue to illness in our society', *The Weekend Australian*, 5–6 December 1987, 26

25 Geoffrey Blainey, 'Perkins a brave man for showing up "racist humbug"', *The Weekend Australian*, 16–17 January 1988, 20.

26 'Holding gives report a very cool reception', *The Weekend Australian*, 4–5 June 1988, 1; and Geoffrey Blainey, 'Immigration debate will not go away', *The Weekend Australian*, 11–12 June 1988, 20.

defence of non-discrimination through restoring national confidence and purpose in immigration overall.[27]

As the debate proceeded after the release of the Fitzgerald report, Blainey was finally superseded as the *bête noire* of the committed multiculturalists. Opposition Leader, John Howard, who until this point had endorsed the generally bipartisan immigration consensus, now suggested that some slowing in the rate of Asian immigration might be justified. The reaction to his remarks was similar to that which had met Blainey in 1984. Blainey argued that what Howard was saying was 'less dramatic and less illuminating than the strong reactions to his words'.[28] In Blainey's eyes, the attacks on Howard's stance highlighted the fact that 'too many commentators were moulded by the immigration crusade of the 1960s and by the Vietnam War and the counter-culture and they feel strongly on racial and ethnic issues'.[29] When listening to them, Blainey just heard 'pious affirmations of the moral superiority of the commentator's own viewpoint' and contempt for the Australian people who commentators seemed to regard as 'puppets, ready to jump if a politician pulls the string'.[30] Blainey continued to try to argue his case, but now the attention was on Howard, whether he would persist, or back down, and how his stance would affect his tenuous hold on the Liberal Party leadership.

Howard's new position was not universally held by his own side of politics, and his critics were not just at the 'small l liberal' end of the spectrum. Just as in 1984-85, the immigration issue in 1987-88 did not exhibit a simple Left versus Right divide. On the broader Right, figures as diverse as the socially conservative B.A. Santamaria and the economically liberal John Hyde both disagreed with the 'Blainey-Stone line'. Santamaria queried to what extent existing Australians were 'morally entitled to monopolise resources that they will never develop and for which genuinely poor people, albeit of a different culture, have desperate need?'[31] Hyde, writing in his column on the same opinion page as Blainey, lamented the way critics attacked Blainey and others who raised the immigration issue, but was unconcerned about the level of Asian immigration:

---

27 Kelly, *The End of Certainty*, 422.
28 Geoffrey Blainey, 'Dubious reaction to Howard', *The Weekend Australian*, 13–14 August 1988, 24.
29 Geoffrey Blainey, 'Media bullies the blind puppeteers on immigration', *The Weekend Australian*, 3–4 September 1988, 26.
30 Ibid.
31 B.A. Santamaria, 'Right out: The freedom of a liberal university', *The Australian*, 1 September 1987, 9.

Now as Prof Blainey has pointed out, 48 per cent of net migration comes from Asia. Here I part company with the professor, Senator Stone, Mr Sinclair and indeed most Australians. I am not worried by this figure because I see no sign of serious racial tension involving Asian immigrants.[32]

Although clearly not the view of all, there were certainly a great many people in the broader community who continued to see Blainey as their champion. A correspondent from Warracknabeal in country Victoria assured him that 'there are many Australians in the "silent majority" who value and appreciate your comments'.[33] While many of the letters he received came from country towns and working-class suburbs, a survey of 'attitudes to public figures' among the middle-aged upper middle-class alumni of private schools in Melbourne's eastern suburbs showed Blainey was also widely admired there. The survey, undertaken by Janet McCalman and Mark Peel in September 1990 and included as an appendix in the former's book, *Journeyings*, reported that amongst alumni of Scotch College, Blainey had a 55/3 admire/deplore ratio, only bettered by long-retired political figures Robert Menzies and Henry Bolte and equalled by John Curtin. He rated way ahead of any contemporary political or business figures.[34]

By the late 1980s, Blainey undoubtedly felt greater empathy with what he saw as the 'silent majority' than he did with his university colleagues. In 1984, he felt the need to advise a young academic, who sympathised with his view on immigration, to stay silent as expressing such a view would clearly be harmful to his career prospects.[35] In October 1988, Blainey provided an insight into how he viewed contemporary universities in a period when university staff members were complaining loudly about the Dawkins reforms to higher education.[36] Blainey did not approve of the degree of centralisation the reforms entailed, but felt that Dawkins was right to challenge the universities, as students 'do not receive as wide-ranging and as stimulating an education as

---

32 John Hyde, 'Self-appointed elites showing their true colours', *The Weekend Australian*, 20–21 August 1988, 30.
33 Letter to Blainey, 15 June 1988, Blainey Papers, Acc. No. 89/145 Box 49, UMA.
34 Janet McCalman, *Journeyings: The Biography of a Middle-Class Generation 1920–1990* (Melbourne: Melbourne University Press, 1993), 329–330.
35 Blainey correspondence 10 May 1984, 11 June 1984 and 19 June 1984, Blainey Papers MS 9225/2/17 and MS 9225/2/20 Box 3, NLA.
36 Geoffrey Blainey, 'Australian Universities: Some Fashions and Faults', *Conversazione*, 7–9 October 1988. See also Geoffrey Blainey, 'Dawkins cooking up a storm with his radical recipe', *The Weekend Australian*, 17–18 September 1988, 20.

they should receive from a staff which is now much larger and a library which is far larger'. He did not see that it was a problem for the user to pay a proportion of the cost of his or her university education, as users paid a proportion of the cost of many public services, such as public transport, public housing and public health, and had done in earlier generations for tertiary education.

In an opinion piece the following month, Blainey made the point that one of the reasons why governments needed to rein in expenditure was the problem of overseas debt. He argued that universities were 'one of the indirect causes of our poor economic performance' because it had become 'almost an axiom in many departments of history, sociology, anthropology and political science in the 1970s that somehow we did not need to export in Australia ... the main export industries were seen as villains'.[37]

It is important to remember that in his early days as an academic Blainey had been sufficiently in step with his colleagues to be selected as one of the authors of the 'Red Book'.[38] He had changed; his colleagues had changed. When he moved to the History Department in 1977, he did not know how much it had changed; but he had learnt to his cost. Academic historians' treatment of him and their interpretation of the events of the 1980s has clearly remained a highly sensitive issue for Blainey. While generally not commenting on these matters in the subsequent three decades, more recently he took exception to the depiction of his role in the immigration debate in historian Frank Bongiorno's 2015 work, *The Eighties: The Decade That Transformed Australia*. Blainey was sufficiently upset to have his lawyer write to Bongiorno's publisher demanding changes.[39]

As Blainey departed academic life in 1989, Australia was only a year or two away from 'the recession we had to have', a far more serious economic downturn than the 1961 credit squeeze which had prompted Blainey to embrace the financial security of the academy. Now he was heading back into the marketplace to once again try to earn an income from writing commissioned histories.

Blainey produced six commissioned histories in the 1990s. These covered topics including football, mining and manufacturing. They were bookended by works on two institutions which reflected the self-help ethos of much of

---

37   Geoffrey Blainey, 'Fear spreads as market forces invade campus', *The Weekend Australian*, 5–6 November 1988, 42.
38   See Chapter 3.
39   Richard Guillliatt, 'He's Got History', *The Weekend Australian*, Magazine, 29–30 October 2016, 12–16; and Frank Bongiorno letter, *The Weekend Australian*, Magazine, 12–13 November 2016, 8.

the second half of the nineteenth century, covering a friendly society, *Odd Fellows: A History of IOOF Australia* (1991), and an insurance company, *A History of the AMP 1848-1998* (1999).[40]

Writing the history of a friendly society was 'new terrain' for Blainey, but he instantly warmed to it. He discovered that it revealed 'much about the daily life and attitudes of a typical Australian breadwinner, especially those on the lower rungs of the income ladder'. Writing about it gave him the opportunity to redress what he perceived as a historical anomaly that had produced 'a score of research projects on the history of unions for every one on the history of friendly societies', despite the fact that in the nineteenth century the friendly societies were more influential.[41] Blainey liked the self-help ethos of friendly societies, where members had to make a contribution in normal times to ensure they were covered if they then hit hard times. Friendly societies flourished in this period when it was accepted, even by early trade unions, that 'in a land as favoured as Australia it was possible for the average hard working family to provide its own social security by joining one of the friendly societies'.[42]

The increasing demands for government intervention in the provision of welfare in the late nineteenth century, and the consequent tax increases, were 'about to challenge that concept of self-help' on which friendly societies and life offices were founded.[43] The heyday of self-help ended when both Victoria and New South Wales introduced an old age pension in 1901. At the time, no one envisaged that providing some basic government benefits would undermine the whole notion of self-help. In Blainey's view, it would be unfair to have expected contemporaries to foresee this outcome for while 'in theory the friendly societies should have defended themselves from this assault on their underlying principles and their long-term future', this was only clear with hindsight.[44]

In his history of AMP, Blainey argued that the unusual bedfellows, the welfare state and commercialisation, each contributed to changing societal attitudes to self-help in the twentieth century. The former meant that people had less fear of destitution if they did not provide for themselves, while

---

40   Geoffrey Blainey, *Odd Fellows: a history of IOOF Australia* (Sydney: Allen & Unwin, 1991); and Geoffrey Blainey, *A History of the AMP 1848-1998* (Sydney: Allen & Unwin, 1999).
41   Blainey, *Odd Fellows*, 151. This is a similar point to the one Blainey made about Jews and Methodists (see chapter 1).
42   Blainey, *Odd Fellows*, 81.
43   Blainey, *A History of the AMP*, 139.
44   Blainey, *Odd Fellows*, 113.

the latter encouraged spending on the latest heavily advertised product. Throw in the Keynesian argument that in economically troubled times the salvation was spending, and one can see why Blainey argued that 'one of the profound changes in the thinking and morality of the Western world was underway'.[45]

Blainey's only book specifically about sport, *A Game of Our Own: The Origins of Australian Football* (1990) was commissioned by the National Australian Football Council (NAFC).[46] It followed an earlier approach to write a history for the Victorian Football League, which did not proceed.[47] The NAFC particularly wanted Blainey's assessment of whether the Australian game was a child of Gaelic football. His answer was an emphatic 'no'. In a chapter titled 'The Gaelic Myth', Blainey asserted that 'not even one piece of positive evidence for a Gaelic origin of Australian football has been found', while there was considerable circumstantial evidence, such as an over-representation of Protestants as players and administrators in the game's early years, which argued that it had more English origins.[48]

Blainey also considered whether the game had Aboriginal origins, noting that there had been suggestions that a ball game played by Aboriginals 'provided the special ingredients of Australian football'.[49] With the possible exception of high marking, he dismissed the idea because 'generally the new settlers from the British Isles learned almost nothing from Aboriginal rituals and customs, even when learning could be to their advantage', so it was highly unlikely that they would have copied an Aboriginal version of football.[50] Between the first edition in 1990 and a new edition in 2003, some writers had continued to push the Aboriginal origins theory. Blainey pointed out that by comparing an Aboriginal game to modern Australian football, these writers were ignoring the fact that, in its early decades, the latter had few of the features, such as the high mark, which we now associate with it. And while proponents of the Aboriginal theory pushed the fact that a key early figure in the game, Tom Wills, had close ties with Aborigines, Blainey argued that, given how much evidence there was of Wills' promotion of Aboriginal cricket, the fact that

---

45   Blainey, *A History of the AMP*, 267.
46   Geoffrey Blainey, *A Game of Our Own, The Origins of Australian Football* (Melbourne: Information Australia, 1990).
47   Paula Kempton (VFL Media Liaison Officer) to Blainey, 2 April 1985, Blainey Papers, MS 9225/3/16 Box 10, NLA.
48   Blainey, *A Game of Our Own*, 89.
49   Ibid., 95.
50   Ibid., 96.

there is no evidence of his promoting Aboriginal football undermined the theory.[51] In a further edition in 2010, Blainey explained that recent work in the field by Gillian Hibbins and Wills' biographer Greg De Moore had further undermined the Aboriginal influence theory.[52]

In assessing why football became popular in 1858, Blainey identified previously unrecognised factors such as the arrival in Melbourne in the summer of 1857–58 of the book *Tom Brown's Schooldays*, which extolled the virtues of Rugby football, and the fact that 1858 was an unusually dry winter. Hence, he theorised that the harder than usual grounds in the winter of 1858 meant that there was a strong danger of serious injury if unmodified Rugby rules were adopted in Melbourne.[53] Sydney, with significantly higher average winter rainfall than Melbourne, could afford to play Rugby. Another important discovery Blainey made was that Victorian football was played on rectangular fields before its unique oval became standard in the 1870s. The rapid development of Australia's own football code provided fertile ground for Blainey to find instances of Australian, or more specifically Victorian, exceptionalism, citing the well-travelled writer R.E.N. Twopeny, who believed that a football match in Melbourne was one of 'the sights of the world'.[54]

Blainey's respect for Australian achievement was visible in his Kalgoorlie mining history *The Golden Mile* (1993), commissioned by the Chamber of Mines and Energy in Western Australia.[55] He nailed his colours to the mast as early as the preface when he described Kalgoorlie as 'the most productive goldfield in one of the world's great gold nations'.[56] Blainey acknowledged that early Kalgoorlie was 'an eyesore'; yet this tough ugly town was able to rise to great human heights.[57] In a caption to the photograph of a funeral procession, Blainey commented that 'Kalgoorlie and Boulder came to treat death with all the dignity and even grandeur they could muster'.[58] And while individuals may pass away, the mining field remained a source of optimism, 'its poppet head standing on the low hill was brilliantly lit at

---

51   Geoffrey Blainey, *A Game of Our Own, The Origins of Australian Football* (Melbourne: Black Inc., 2003 edition), 204.
52   Geoffrey Blainey, *A Game of Our Own, The Origins of Australian Football*, (Melbourne: Black Inc., 2010 edition), viii.
53   Blainey, *A Game of Our Own*, 31.
54   Ibid., 76, 84. The 2003 edition added more detail on the longer histories of many of Melbourne's clubs compared to the overseas clubs of other football codes.
55   Geoffrey Blainey, *The Golden Mile*, (Sydney: Allen & Unwin, 1993).
56   Blainey, *The Golden Mile*, vii.
57   Ibid., 25.
58   Ibid., 39.

night – one of the finest industrial sites in Australia and the beacon of the revived goldfield'.[59]

The building of a water pipe from Perth to the Goldfields provided scope for Blainey to pursue two of his recurring historical themes. First, Australia was a world-leader, as the project was 'one of the most remarkable public works the world had seen' and, second, things done in the past were often more significant than things done more recently as the goldfields water scheme was bolder and more ambitious than was the Snowy Mountains scheme.[60]

Blainey considered the causes of the January 1934 ethnic riot, the most dramatic event in the city's history and, as he had with Eureka and the Jameson Raid three decades earlier, found material factors influenced it. One was geographic, the long time it took sufficient police numbers to reach an isolated community. The second was that grievances about foreigners taking jobs are always much higher in a one-industry town. He argued that 'it was hardly surprising if local residents felt especially aggrieved at losing their only opportunity of work', a reality he stated was 'somewhat overlooked by policy-makers of the day', and 'ignored by moralisers of later days'.[61]

Of all Blainey's commissioned works, the one which perhaps most required exceptional writing skills was the story of how a small Melbourne tyre company became the diversified industrial conglomerate Pacific Dunlop, published as *Jumping Over the Wheel* (1993).[62] In many of Blainey's mining histories, there was no conflict between describing a range of small companies on a field, if ultimately they are all to be subsumed in the larger dominant company that is officially the subject of the work. The challenge was far greater when dealing with a geographically and product-diverse industrial company, which evolved through mergers and takeovers. Blainey adopted a pattern of including the pre-history of the acquired company at the point in the narrative when it joined, even in cases when its previous role as a competitor had seen it receive some treatment earlier in the narrative. This approach worked very well, ensuring that the major focus remained upon how the modern company was created, whilst smoothly incorporating relevant and interesting background material on the acquisitions.

Reviewing the book in *The Age*, director of the National Centre for Australian Studies at Monash University Peter Spearritt thought it a 'superb account' of

---

59   Ibid., 161.
60   Ibid., 55, 65.
61   Ibid., 141.
62   Geoffrey Blainey, *Jumping Over the Wheel*, (Sydney: Allen & Unwin, 1993).

much of the firm's history, with 'brilliantly sketched' character descriptions, but found the work not as strong when dealing with the modern impersonal multinational.[63] There were periods when the company had not prospered. To make them more evocative Blainey created imaginary scenarios to illustrate his point, such as writing that, after a period without dividends, 'angry gentlemen must have been seen jumping from the cable tram in Flinders Street and entering the head office to speak their mind'.[64] Another literary device Blainey continued to deploy was the list, as in the following account of the menu at a 1972 Alcoa dinner related in *White Gold: The Story of Alcoa of Australia* (1997):

> At the Parmelia Hotel that evening 55 guests dined their way through what is now a museum-piece menu of the era: one dozen Sydney rock oysters, fillets of sole caprice, roast duckling with orange sauce, tartufo ice cream, cheese and coffee along with Australian wines, port and cigars.[65]

White Gold is also notable for containing praise of a politician. The former Western Australian premier Charles Court 'played the crucial political role in the development of the alumina industry in Western Australia' and did 'more for mining in Australia than probably any other politician of the post-war years'.[66] The role that politicians played in Australia was something upon which Blainey reflected a lot in the 1990s. For unlike in the 1950s, Blainey in this second freelance period had another potential source of income beyond writing books. He was now one of the most sought-after contributors of opinion pieces to the Australian media.

---

63 Peter Spearritt, 'Black Tyres and the Blue Pacific', *The Age* (Extra section), 19 March 1994, 8.
64 Blainey, *Jumping Over the Wheel*, 50.
65 Geoffrey Blainey, *White Gold: The Story of Alcoa of Australia* (Sydney: Allen & Unwin, 1997), 132.
66 Ibid., 68.

Chapter 9

THE CONTROVERSIALIST

From 1984 onwards, Blainey became one of the most prominent commentators on public affairs in the nation. Blainey had regular columns with *The Herald* in Melbourne and then with *The Australian*. He covered a broad range of public policy issues and matters of human interest such as the travails of moving house, which the Blaineys did in 1986 when they departed Ivanhoe after 28 years to move to East Melbourne. Blainey lost his weekly column in *The Australian* around the same time he left Melbourne University, but over the next few years he found roles with *Business Review Weekly* and *The Age*.

One issue which had arisen in the period between the immigration controversies of 1984-85 and 1988 was a proposed Bill of Rights, something which Blainey regarded as potentially the most significant change to the conduct of Australian politics since the introduction of democratic government. Blainey was a trenchant critic of the Federal Government's Bill, arguing that it was 'quietly removing vital rights, amid a fanfare of humbug'.[1] He argued that there were several areas in the Bill where rights were in conflict and that in the case of conflict the Human Rights Commission would arbitrate, thus producing a significant transfer in power from elected politicians to unelected bureaucrats and judges. He also pointed out that the Bill did not include a right to private property, and thus would make it easier for a government to nationalise industries or to close private schools. Such arguments had an effect. The Bill was dropped late in 1986.

An even bigger issue in 1986 was industrial relations, as a number of high-profile industrial disputes led to demands for reform. Blainey got drawn into the issue when he agreed to launch the newly formed H.R. Nicholls Society's collection of essays, *Arbitration in Contempt*. Some saw the formation of the H.R. Nicholls Society as part of the rise of the 'New Right' in Australia. Asked if he was part of the New Right, Blainey demurred, saying 'I would rather remain unlabelled: a lot of my views would be seen as right-wing but

---

1   Geoffrey Blainey, 'But who will guard our basic liberties?', *Courier-Mail*, 3 March 1986, 5.

a lot aren't'.² And one only needs to look at the economic debate in the 1980s and early 1990s to see the truth of this statement.

Today, many commentators and politicians from both sides of politics look back on the 1980s as something of a golden age of economic reform. Those with this perspective tend to accept the thesis Paul Kelly outlined in his landmark book, *The End of Certainty: The Story of the 1980s* (1992), that the 1980s was the decade that brought an end to the Australian Settlement. As Kelly defined it, the Settlement, which had been reached in the decade after Federation, could be summarised by five headings: White Australia, Industry Protection, Wage Arbitration, State Paternalism and Imperial Benevolence. Some of these had begun to be unwound before the 1980s, but Kelly argued that the decade witnessed a decisive shift, so much so that, by its end the key battle of ideas was no longer between Labor and Liberal, but between 'international rationalists and the sentimentalist traditionalists; it is between those who know the Australian Settlement is unsustainable and those who fight to retain it'.³

Blainey did not read the 1980s that way at the time and, to a large degree, still does not. He reviewed Kelly's 2009 sequel, *The March of Patriots*, for Kelly's own newspaper, *The Australian*, and expressed his scepticism about Kelly's overall thesis:

> The book argues that Australia's strong financial position in these past 15 months of fears and shudders owes much to the way in which Bob Hawke and Keating, and Howard and Costello, reshaped and managed Australia's economy during a quarter of a century. This is a bold conclusion.⁴

According to Kelly, one of the crucial decisions in the quarter century of reform between 1983 and 2007 was an act of political bravery by Paul Keating:

> Keating's main economic achievement as prime minister is largely unremarked: he refused to buckle on market based reforms despite the recession and thunderous demands from special interests, the Labor Party, the welfare lobby and much of the trade unions. Confronting an unemployment rate of more than 10 per cent, Keating defied a century of politics and kept the tariff cuts in place. 'You have a choice', he said. 'You can either duck for cover or [be] prepared to take the risk'.

---

2   De Lisle, 'The Blainey View'.
3   Kelly, *The End of Certainty*, 2.
4   Geoffrey Blainey, 'The romantic and the pragmatist', *The Weekend Australian* (Review section), 26–27 September 2009, 22–23.

Holding the line on free trade was the fundamental step for Australia's prosperity cycle.[5]

Kelly could have added Blainey to the list of those who opposed the tariff cuts that were announced in March 1991 and implemented over subsequent years. Earlier in his career, Blainey been an opponent of protection, often pointing out how the export-oriented mining sector had suffered compared to the protected industries and his history of ICIANZ was not published due to his criticism of its reliance on protection. In the early 1990s, Blainey still acknowledged that protection had often led to inefficiency in Australian industry but argued that, while cutting tariffs might make sense in prosperous times, it should not be done in the middle of a recession when the country had large overseas debt.[6] He painted a sorry picture of the harm the policy would cause:

> Lower tariffs will initially bring in more imports than we can pay for. The crisis in our balance of payments will be aggravated. In 1995 the federal government, whether Liberal or Labor, will probably have to restore or increase some of the import duties. By then hundreds of factories will be closed and their machines, shipped away, will be working 24 hours a day in south-east Asia. Other nations will have the factories: we will have the unemployed.[7]

When writing works of history in the 1990s, Blainey still accepted that protection had been a problem in Australia; for example, the broadening of it to cover almost the whole economy by the 1920s showed an unhealthy reliance on politics to solve economic problems:

> Henceforth nearly every major industry – except wool and silver-lead-zinc and frozen meat – relied on political lobbying as much as its own efficiency. So was accentuated the tendency to see politics as the prime solution to those problems which might for the most part have better been solved by economic vigour.[8]

---

5   Paul Kelly, 'Mr Rudd, you have to share the credit', *The Weekend Australian*, 12–13 September 2009, 11.

6   Geoffrey Blainey, 'Blainey Slams Decade of Decadence', *Australian Business Monthly*, January 1992, 41–42.

7   Geoffrey Blainey, 'Reflections on the Current State of the Nation' (paper presented as the 1991 Sir Robert Menzies Lecture, Monash University Liberal Club, Melbourne, 28 November 1991).

8   Geoffrey Blainey, *A Shorter History of Australia*, (Sydney: Random House Vintage, 1994), 177.

Likewise in the 1950s, the Menzies Government's 'heavy restrictions placed on imports injected a cosy inefficiency into many factories, thus handing a problem to Australians of later decades'.⁹ However, Menzies was at least imposing this protection for what Blainey argued had been a legitimate reason as 'a decade of large-scale immigration and big national projects, the 1950s sometimes put heavy strain on the balance of payments' and Menzies understood that this was a strain which had to be eased, unlike contemporary politicians who seemed oblivious to the problem.¹⁰

In his corporate histories in the 1990s, Blainey endorsed the protection his subjects had received, arguing that an early Alcoa smelter would have been 'uneconomic without a ban against excessive imports of aluminium ingot and fabricated products' and that 'this initial Commonwealth protection proved crucial'.¹¹ Protection was even more crucial for many decades in the operations of Pacific Dunlop. Whilst acknowledging in places that protection masked inefficient practices, Blainey generally noted its presence without negative commentary. Sometimes he even implied that Governments should have done more to protect Dunlop's activities, such as in the 1920s, when an approach to the Tariff Board to complain about cars being imported from the US with tyres already fitted was met with 'a shrug of the official shoulders'.¹² Following the tariff reductions of the 1970s and 1980s, Pacific Dunlop sensibly adopted a policy of avoiding industries that were protected by tariffs (although in tyres it still had to rely on protection), but Blainey could not resist some commentary on contemporary economic policy:

> If in Canberra the federal ministers and advisers were wondering why Australia was facing a crisis in the balance of payments, and why in essence it was so busy as an importer and so sluggish as an exporter, a visit to the deserted factory at Richmond would have illuminated their thinking. Here was one of the most successful factories in Australian history, moving its machinery to Asia and locking its doors, largely because governments did not understand what made a factory profitable.¹³

---

9   Geoffrey Blainey, '50 Years Back, 20 Years On', *IPA Review* 46, no. 3, 1993, 41.
10   Ibid.
11   Blainey, *White Gold*, 92.
12   Blainey, *Jumping Over the Wheel*, 106.
13   Ibid., 295.

In the 1980s, Blainey believed that contemporary politicians were finding too much fault in the past. He argued that it was not legitimate to attribute any of Australia's economic difficulties, which culminated in the recession of the early 1990s, to the closed economy of earlier decades, observing that 'while Mr Hawke and Mr Keating say they are now repairing the disgraceful inefficiency inherited from the 1950s and 1960s, they are really blaming the past as an excuse for their own neglect'.[14] He drew a stark contrast between the eras of Menzies and Hawke:

> It was Menzies' gift to preside over increasing prosperity for all Australians. It was Hawke's gift to give the impression that he was presiding over increasing prosperity for all Australians, when in fact he was not.[15]

Although conceding that there was a little too much protection under Menzies, Blainey nonetheless painted a generally happy picture of a post-war economic consensus which had supported increasing the population, strengthening the manufacturing base, achieving a higher standard of living and attaining a reasonable level of fairness. He argued that 'the great majority of Australians shared all those goals, their only disagreement being how far the government should intervene and regulate and nationalize'.[16]

Blainey had made the point in a 1985 essay for the American journal *Daedalus*, that in Australia 'neither right-wing nor left-wing governments had a strong objection to heavy government interference in industry and commerce'.[17] However, soon after he wrote the *Daedalus* paper, Blainey began to focus on the nation's balance of payments, which was to be his overriding economic concern for much of the 1980s and early 1990s. In February 1985, a dive in the value of the recently floated Australian dollar led him to colourfully write that 'we went to pay our bills overseas and were politely informed by the officials who scrutinised our money: "We're sorry Australia, but that's not real money"'.[18] In January the following year, he worried about the 'fragile'

---

14   Geoffrey Blainey, 'Manufacturing a recovery', *Australian Business Monthly*, March 1992, 48.
15   Blainey, 'Reflections on the Current State of the Nation'.
16   Blainey, '50 Years Back, 20 Years On', 42.
17   Geoffrey Blainey, 'Australia: A Bird's Eye View', *Daedalus* 114, no. 1 (Winter 1985): 20–21. He argued that compared to the rest of the world, this feature had been strongest from 1895 to 1920, increasing at a slower rate than many other Western Countries after the Second World War.
18   Geoffrey Blainey, 'Sorry Australia, that's not real money', *The Herald (Melbourne)*, 28 February 1985, 4.

balance of payments and the nation's 'vulnerable' standard of living, also observing that 'our economic situation, compared to other western countries, has deteriorated strongly in the last ten years'.[19] He did not believe that the policies implemented by Hawke and Keating would reverse that decline. Perhaps he also harboured some doubts about whether the John Howard led Opposition had the answers. In early 1987, when Queensland Premier Joh Bjelke Petersen launched his quixotic 'Joh-for-Canberra' campaign (which did significant damage to Howard's electoral prospects at that year's Federal Election) Blainey wrote sympathetically of Bjelke Petersen, describing him as 'one of the quiet giants of Australian history' for his role in developing Queensland.[20]

The Menzies Lecture that Blainey delivered on 28 November 1991 provided probably his most comprehensive critique of the state of the contemporary Australian economy.[21] He argued that Australia was in its third-worst predicament since 1850 and that the recession should be called a depression. To make matters worse, it was largely self-inflicted; Blainey lamented that it was 'tragic to see a once-prosperous nation, economically mutilating itself'.[22] Having underperformed the rest of the world in the 1980s, the nation had thus started from a worse base when the world economy deteriorated at the end of the decade. Further, Blainey's 'reading of history' told him that the conflict between Hawke and Keating, which was shortly to reach its conclusion, was 'one of the gravest leadership crises in Australia since the Commonwealth was founded' and was 'economically ... more dislocating than the constitutional crisis of 1975'.[23]

Always striving for some degree of fairness, Blainey acknowledged that 'the Hawke-Keating government made some constructive and courageous changes'. However, financial deregulation, the entry of too many foreign banks, and taxation laws (which encouraged borrowing) all contributed to the growth of Australia's foreign debt. He was clear that bank deregulation

---

19   Geoffrey Blainey, 'This country is too good to ruin' (address to Australia Day Luncheon, Melbourne, 24 January 1986).
20   Geoffrey Blainey, 'Why the constant sniping at Sir Joh?', *The Australian*, 20 March 1987, 11.
21   Blainey, 'Reflections on the Current State of the Nation'. The lecture was put on annually by the Monash University Liberal Club and Blainey delivered it a decade after he had given the equivalent Melbourne University Liberal Club lecture, the Alfred Deakin Lecture. The contrast in tone between the two lectures is striking, the later one being vastly more polemical.
22   Ibid.
23   Ibid.

had gone 'too far'.[24] Local asset values climbed as restrictions on foreign ownership of real estate were relaxed and high levels of immigration increased demand. Unlike the Australian economy of the 1950s and 1960s, with its strong manufacturing base, Blainey now believed 'our standard of living was propped up by this borrowed money'. His argument always came back to the balance of payments and he observed that 'Mr Hawke rarely gave priority to Australia's overseas debt'.[25] The issue had been prominent when Keating gave his 'banana republic' speech in 1986, but Blainey saw no ongoing action to fix the problem.

The issue of overseas debt played a role in the 1990 Federal Election campaign. The Business Council of Australia organised a Debt Summit early in the campaign at which Blainey was the keynote speaker.[26] Blainey pointed out that Australia had crossed the debt danger zone, when one dollar in every four of exports was being sent straight back overseas to service the debt. This situation had only occurred twice before, in the 1890s and 1920s, in both cases presaging depression. Later in the year, in another speech at the same venue, Melbourne's Regent Hotel, he observed that 'the mountain of debt ... is a reflection of the capacity of Australia's cities to be more energetic in criticising others than in producing the wealth they so eagerly consume'.[27] The Hawke Government could at this time point to the fact that it had paid down Commonwealth debt, but Blainey argued that when the world looked at Australia it 'lumps our debts together'.[28] Political journalist, George Megalogenis, who has a similar position on Australia's modern political and economic narrative as his former *Australian* colleague Paul Kelly, has delivered a verdict that 'Blainey was wrong; the world did not foreclose on the Australian economy'.[29] However, one could also argue that contributions such as Keating's 'banana republic' comments in 1986, or Blainey's repeated efforts particularly in 1990, kept enough focus on the issue to prevent it becoming an even greater problem.

---

24 Blainey, *A Shorter History of Australia*, 228–229. Interestingly, the lack of coverage of the Hawke-Keating economic reforms in the original version of the curriculum produced after the Howard Government's History Summit in 2006 was cited as one of the reasons which necessitated a further revision by a panel headed by Blainey.

25 Blainey, 'Reflections on the Current State of the Nation'.

26 Geoffrey Blainey, 'Sounding an Alarm Bell for Australia's Foreign Debt' (address to the Debt Summit, Melbourne, 1 March 1990).

27 Geoffrey Blainey, 'The Quality of Life in Australia' (paper presented as the inaugural Jennings Group Lecture, Melbourne, 24 October 1990 and included in Blainey, *Eye on Australia*, 270).

28 Blainey, 'Sounding an Alarm Bell for Australia's Foreign Debt'.

29 George Megalogenis, *The Longest Decade* (Melbourne: Scribe, 2006), 255.

In his Menzies Lecture, Blainey argued that there were several other forces, aside from foreign debt, that were conspiring to impede economic growth. These included 'dark green' environmentalism, multiculturalism and Aboriginal opposition to many developments, and they led him to conclude that 'never before in Australian history have the enemies of prosperity been so powerful'. By the time he spoke in 1993, on the occasion of the fiftieth anniversary of the Institute of Public Affairs, the Mabo judgement had added another reason for economic pessimism.

In the period between these two speeches, the Federal Government had moved closer to Blainey's position in at least one policy area. In May 1992, newly installed Prime Minister Keating slashed the annual immigration intake from 111,000 to 80,000. Debate about this decision highlighted the fact that Blainey was out-of-step on this topic with the views of many others perceived to be on the political Right. *Australian Business Monthly* juxtaposed Blainey's views against those of pro-immigration business leaders.[30] Many associated Blainey with Western Mining boss Hugh Morgan on the issue of Aboriginal land rights issues, but the two disagreed on immigration. While Blainey supported the cut in numbers, Morgan wanted a dramatic increase, arguing that Australia should accept half a million migrants annually. Blainey has maintained his stance that the concerns about immigration he expressed in the 1980s and early 1990s were justified, arguing in 2003 that 'it is fair to say that Australia's post-1975 refugees, so far, have not been as successful as the post-1945 refugees'.[31]

In 1996, the year when the Hawke-Keating Governments' thirteen years in power came to an end, Blainey was still in a pessimistic mood. He noted that the developed world had moved beyond the era of quick growth, but that Australia was even worse off than most others, with 'additional reasons for its lacklustre performance, including national complacency born of success in the 1950s and 1960s and erratic leadership which in the 1980s led to unduly high inflation and persistent deficits in the balance of payments'.[32] In 1998, he interpreted the rise of the xenophobic One Nation as the start of a move against economic rationalism and predicted that the next 15 years

---

30   Bruce Jacques, 'The Immigration Debate: Blainey vs Business', *Australian Business Monthly*, July 1992, 28–34.
31   Geoffrey Blainey, 'Laughing Jackass or Kookaburra', in *The Multicultural Experiment* ed. Leonie Kramer, (Sydney: Macleay Press, 2003), 20.
32   Geoffrey Blainey, 'The End of Prosperity', *The Independent Monthly*, May 1996, 30–35.

would see the rise of a 'strong, articulate leftist movement', which could lead to re-nationalisations of industries.[33]

However, from the mid-1990s onwards, Blainey commented much less on economic matters. One reason was the arrival of more balance in the reform process as industrial relations was no longer a notable absentee. Initially under Labor, and then under the Coalition, industrial relations reform began to catch up with industry reform. Blainey worried about how successful the Howard Government would be in its plans to reform the tax system and introduce a GST when 'people don't know what you are reforming', but there is no doubt he believed that the 1996 election and subsequent re-election of the Howard Government had brought an end to the earlier 'erratic leadership'.[34] Moreover, the ongoing solid performance of the Australian economy removed the sense of crisis that had been a periodic feature since the 1970s.

One other result of the economy's continued solid performance from the early 1990s onwards was that it was better able to integrate new migrants than a weak one would have been. Thus, one can reasonably contend that Blainey's overly pessimistic take on the Australian economy also contributed to his being too pessimistic about the effects of high levels of immigration. If he had known how resilient the Australian economy would prove to be, he might not have been as worried about the nation's capacity to absorb new migrants.

There are many parallels between Blainey's attitude to economic policy and immigration policy. His position was that in the 1950s the nation was too wedded to the White Australia policy and protection, but by the 1990s, we were too wedded to multiculturalism and free trade. He opposed both White Australia and protection when they were entrenched policy and, when others moved to what he saw as the other extreme, he opposed that too. Thus, with the economic debate, as with the immigration one, he could see his position as being close to the centre of the political pendulum.

However, Blainey's view that Australia should proceed with caution on economic reform brought none of the attacks that his view that Australia should proceed with caution on immigration induced. Indeed, many of his immigration critics shared his scepticism about the rapid opening up of the Australian economy, which perhaps shows a much greater consistency on his part than on that of many of his critics.

---

33   Paul Sheehan, 'Blainey predicts economic backlash', *Sydney Morning Herald*, 8 August 1998, 14.

34   Clinton Porteous, 'GST a threat, says Blainey', *Herald Sun*, 10 July 1999, 11.

Although Blainey would undoubtedly disagree with the author of one study of Paul Keating's career, David Love, who described the floating of the dollar as Australia's 'greatest historical development', academic historians were generally engaged with topics other than the economy.[35] Thus they did not pay much attention to Blainey's strongly held economic views in the 1980s and early 1990s. When they did comment on economic matters, historians and other public intellectuals often lumped supporters of radical free market reform and their opponents, such as Blainey, together under the one 'conservative' label. One historian even glibly asserted that Blainey was 'increasingly influenced by doctrines of economic rationalism', without acknowledging that in key aspects he was quite sceptical about the application of those policies.[36] Yet when Blainey talked about issues of race or national identity, contemporary historians closely scrutinised every word.

Just as the Warrnambool speech kicked off the immigration debate, so the Latham Lecture Blainey delivered on Wednesday, 28 April 1993 had a major impact on Australia's cultural discourse for the next decade and beyond.[37] By using the term 'black armband' to describe the new pessimistic interpretation of Australian history that had challenged the previously prevailing more optimistic versions, Blainey provided the nomenclature for the history wars. As Stuart Macintyre commented, 'Blainey had once again coined a phrase that gained universal currency'.[38] Blainey recalls that while having had some initial impact, the phrase became firmly entrenched when used by newly elected Prime Minister, John Howard, in 1996:

> The speech aroused interest but, so far as I can remember, no strong criticism or praise. About three years later Mr Howard as prime minister used the phrase in an address at Monash University. Suddenly it took off like a rocket, and became one of the common phrases of public and academic discourse.[39]

---

35   David Love, 'The Aussie float – a love story', *The Age* (Business section), 17 February 2011, 8.
36   Charlie Fox, 'My Lord the Workingman?', in *The Fuss That Never Ended: The Life and Work of Geoffrey Blainey*, eds Deborah Gare et al. (Melbourne: Melbourne University Press, 2003), 139.
37   Geoffrey Blainey, 'Drawing up a balance sheet of our history', (Latham Lecture, 28 April 1993) and reproduced in *Quadrant* 37, no. 7–8 (July-August 1993): 10–15. It was also included as 'The Black Armband View of History', in Blainey, *In Our Times*, 3–14.
38   Macintyre and Clark, *History Wars*, 131.
39   Blainey, *In Our Times*, vi.

As Paul Kelly subsequently argued:

> Blainey had written the text for Howard's prime ministership. Coming a year after Keating's Redfern speech and the High Court's Mabo decision with its condemnation of Australia's past, its brilliance was to throw the progressive intellectuals onto the defensive.[40]

Kelly's point is underscored by how the very use of the term 'black armband' became a subject of debate between Blainey and the 'progressive intellectuals', who found the term at least inappropriate, if not offensive.

The Latham Lecture is accepted as being the first occasion when Blainey used the term 'black armband' in this context, but he had in fact done so on at least one previous occasion. In his weekly newspaper column on the weekend after the Bicentennial celebration of Australia Day 1988, Blainey noted that Bob Hawke had a couple of years earlier shifted the balance of the day from an overwhelmingly negative sentiment to a more positive mood and argued that this change had 'paved the way for a day of celebration to replace the black armband he had originally sanctioned'.[41] In the same year, John Hirst used similar language, without specifically mentioning the armband, to describe the shift towards pessimistic history, referring to a 'Black School' of Australian historians in an article titled 'The Blackening of Our Past'.[42]

Some have doubted Blainey's explanation that the use of the 'black armband' metaphor related purely to the practice of footballers wearing a black armband to acknowledge the passing of someone associated with their club. Macintyre says this was 'surely strained' as in the football case it was worn with respect, whereas Aboriginal groups had been wearing them since the 150th anniversary of British Settlement in 1938 as a symbol of protest and thus many saw Blainey's appropriation of the term in this context as 'insensitive'. Another historian, Bain Attwood, has written that the failure to recognise the fact that 'black armbands had become a symbol of mourning and protest among Aboriginal people and their sympathisers' meant that 'the attack on black armband history reflected an inability or at least an unwillingness to mourn this history'.[43]

---

40 Paul Kelly, *The March of Patriots: The Struggle for Modern Australia* (Melbourne: Melbourne University Press, 2009), 335.

41 Geoffrey Blainey, 'Triumph of the quiet majority', *The Weekend Australian*, 30–31 January 1988, 20.

42 John Hirst, 'The Blackening of Our Past', *IPA Review*, vol. 42 no. 3, December 1988–February 1989, 49–54.

43 Bain Attwood, *Telling the Truth About Aboriginal History* (Sydney: Allen & Unwin, 2005), 33.

Blainey became concerned about this interpretation of the phrase when he read Mark McKenna's entry on 'black-armband history' in *The Oxford Companion to Australian History*. Blainey asserted, both in a letter to McKenna and publicly, that 'the phrase was neither borrowed from the Aborigines nor was it, in the way I used it, anti-Aboriginal'.[44] Blainey argued that black armbands were a product of white, not black, Australia and said that the metaphor came to him early in the 1993 football season. In Blainey's eyes it had been deliberately 'converted into an anti-Aboriginal phrase by historians, politicians and commentators who then complained in public that it was anti-Aboriginal'. This was a microcosm of the broader schism between Blainey and academic historians. One saw a black armband and thought about football; the other saw a black armband and thought about Aboriginal protest from 1938 onwards. Both struggled to accept that the other's position was genuinely held.

In his Latham Lecture, Blainey juxtaposed the new 'black armband' type of history against an earlier 'three cheers' one, which was both patriotic and optimistic. Importantly, the 'three cheers' straddled the ideological divide as, when Blainey was young, 'the left wing and the right wing were alike in their congratulations, though they rarely congratulated the same events'. The fact that one of the previous common optimistic interpretations of Australian history had come from some left-wing historians was a point that seemed to become obscured in many of the debates of the 1990s and 2000s.

The optimistic historiographical brand of the earlier decades of the twentieth century, the 'Whig interpretation of Australian history' had been discussed by historians Allan Martin and Michael Roe. In 1977, Roe had identified some of the elements which made Australian history a success story for the Old Left.[45] The Old Left historians had taken pride in the fact that 'Australians had outpaced Britons in gaining many of the radical boons defined most emphatically by the Chartists', precipitated by developments including the Eureka Stockade, the spread of pastoralism and, most of all the rapid rise of the Labor Party before the First World War.[46] Roe pointed out that 'Australian Whiggery has had a strong Marxist tincture', evidenced he argued by historians such as Brian Fitzpatrick, Russel Ward and R.A. Gollan, all of whom 'were confident that Australia was peculiarly the product and property of the

---

44   Geoffrey Blainey, 'A Black Arm-Band for Australia's 20th Century?' (paper presented at the Twelfth Conference of the Samuel Griffith Society, Sydney, 10–12 November 2000).
45   Roe, 'Recent Historical Writing', 2–13.
46   Ibid., 2.

working man'.⁴⁷ This was a working man who read *The Bulletin*, loved the poems of Henry Lawson, idealised mateship, voted Labor and to whom no policy mattered more than White Australia. Historian John Thompson has described what happened to this version of history in more recent decades:

> The radical national or Old Left tradition of Australian history has long since passed from favour. Indeed, its conspicuous masculinist values and its perceived limitations, evasions or omissions concerning subjects such as race and cultural diversity have been powerfully challenged and progressively revised from the time of the first assault in the late 1960s to the present.⁴⁸

Many date the 'first assault' to 1968, when New Left historian, Humphrey McQueen, launched an attack on Ward and his most famous work, *The Australian Legend*. One of Ward's main arguments, in his response to McQueen's critique, was that McQueen was not following the normal forms of historical disagreement and he hoped that 'some sense of group solidarity with one's fellow historians should help us disagree without rancour and to debate without sneering'.⁴⁹

Another intriguing aspect of McQueen's attack on Ward was identified in Pascoe's 1979 study of Australian historiography. Pascoe drew attention to the fact that many of McQueen's criticisms of the Old Left were similar to those made by conservative writer Peter Coleman in 1962.⁵⁰ As noted in Chapter 2, Coleman had assigned to Manning Clark the role of the counter-revolution against the Old Left.⁵¹ While in the early 1960s Clark's pessimistic take on Australian history could be seen as a conservative critique of the Old Left, by the time Blainey gave his Latham Lecture in 1993 it had become an obvious example of the now more pessimistic Left view which Blainey sought to criticise. Blainey said that Clark 'had done much to spread the gloomy view', although he noted also that he had spread 'the compassionate view'.⁵² Clark's most recent biographer Mark McKenna has observed that 'Blainey was gracious in his criticism' of Clark's pessimism, which was not something which could be said of several other subsequent critics of Clark

---

47   Ibid., 3.
48   Thompson, *The Patrician and the Bloke*, 13.
49   Russel Ward, 'Britannia Australis', *Overland* no. 47 (Autumn 1971): 47–49.
50   Pascoe, *Manufacture*, 142.
51   Coleman, 'Introduction: The New Australia', 7.
52   Blainey, 'Drawing up a balance sheet of our history'.

and his work.[53] Oddly the 'black armband' debate seemed to force Blainey into the situation where he became the personification of optimism. For instance, commentator Michael Duffy wrote:

> There are two broad schools of Australian history – Triumphalism and Failure Studies. Their headmasters are Blainey and Clark. Blainey is an optimist and has few pupils. Clark was a pessimist and many historians appear to be in accord with the mood, if not always the scholarship, of his work.[54]

There are dangers in seeing the two most prominent Australian historians of the later twentieth century as opposites. In many ways, their position vis-a-vis the modern academy is similar. They both believed that writing style was important, and that history should be a public exercise, not something conducted solely within the walls of the universities. Blainey himself commented that while their interpretations were often 'poles apart', their views on historical method were 'much closer'.[55] Further, as Beverley Kingston observed:

> Clark's position never was a simple story of left or right. Nor was Blainey, who has also been demonised, the archetypal representative of the right. The truth is that in their very different ways both Clark and Blainey have written about Australian history so as to capture an enviable popular readership, and no lists of suitable or approved topics or prescriptions for making history attractive again can compete with old-fashioned drama, moral tales and inspired word-spinning.[56]

In the Latham Lecture, Blainey identified four areas where, in his lifetime, the interpretation of Australian history had been affected by 'the swing of the pendulum from a position that had been too favourable, too self-congratulatory, to an opposite extreme that is even more unreal and decidedly jaundiced'.

To illustrate the change in attitude to the environment in histories of Australia, Blainey provided 'A Scoreboard of Ecology'. This catalogued many of the ways in which 'the colonising of Australia since 1788 has done great damage to the environment' but made the point that 'the Aboriginal

---

53   McKenna, *An Eye for Eternity*, 686.
54   Michael Duffy, 'Past Masters', *The Independent Monthly*, October 1993, 49-51.
55   Blainey, 'The Manning Clark School of History', 63.
56   Beverley Kingston, review of *Suspect History: Manning Clark and the Future of Australia's Past* by Humphrey McQueen, *Australian Journal of Politics and History* 43, no. 3, (1997): 449.

record of damage was also high'. Under the heading 'Economic Success or Failure' Blainey painted his familiar tale of Australia being 'one of the great economic success stories' until, from the 1970s onwards, a combination of poor political decision making and adverse cultural factors had triggered an economic decline.

His third heading of 'Democracy' had a similar trajectory. Our early and thorough adoption of democracy was 'one of the major credits on the national balance sheet' but this success had been undermined by our becoming a 'rights-mad society in the 1970s and 1980s', a trend made worse, he argued, by the High Court becoming more political. In Blainey's view, 'a firm right granted to one person or group is often the loss of a right to another person or group' and the move towards a more legalistic, rights-based society meant that 'it would be unwise, indeed complacent, to see democracy as a permanent victory for Australia'.

The last of the four areas Blainey assessed in his Latham Lecture was 'The Aborigines', the section devoted to this topic being almost as long as the previous three combined. He began by noting how many more Australians now saw 'the treatment of Aborigines, since 1788, as the blot on Australian history' and asked whether 'deep shame or wide regret' was 'the more appropriate response'. Noting that 'the meeting of the incoming British with the Aborigines, at a thousand different parts of Australia spread over more than a century, was possibly a unique confrontation in recorded history', Blainey reiterated that, although the semi-nomadic Aboriginal society was economically successful, it was still bound to be overthrown. This was far from a unique occurrence. It had happened to other such societies around the world during the Neolithic revolution, a point Blainey expanded on in an opinion piece in *The Age* three months later:

> What happened to the Aborigines after 1788 had probably happened a few thousand years earlier to all our ancestors, whether they lived on the northern plains of Europe, the coasts of east Asia or an island in the Mediterranean. All over the world the relatively simple way of life of hunters and gatherers was wrecked by the coming of people who domesticated plants and animals. A new economy arose, a new way of holding and working land arose and, everywhere, groups of people lost their vast sweeps of land and became the possessors – if they owned anything – of tiny areas of land.[57]

---

57   Geoffrey Blainey, 'Mabo – What Aboriginals Lost', *The Age* (Saturday Extra section), 31 July 1993, 2.

Blainey's perception of the inevitability of the Neolithic and Industrial Revolutions arriving in one hit on the Australian continent did not mean he excused the often 'lamentable' treatment of Aborigines by settlers, treatment which manifested itself in 'frequent contempt' for their culture, loss of freedom, and the breaking of the link with their tribal lands. He also pointed out that, by the 1850s, the scientific consensus was that the Aborigines were doomed to extinction, a view which did not help their prospects. However, Blainey argued that while settlers were way too critical of Aborigines in the nineteenth century, 'present day moralists, scholars, journalists and filmmakers' were guilty of being way too critical of the settlers. Such people were exaggerating the number of Aborigines killed by Europeans, ignoring violence within Aboriginal society and incorrectly claiming that Aborigines did not have the vote until 1967. Blainey was particularly critical of the use of the word 'racist' to describe those who did not subscribe to the 'black armband' view, arguing that 'racist' had become 'the favourite word of the prejudiced, the ignorant and often the intellectually unscrupulous' and that 'nothing does less to promote thoughtful discussion'.[58]

The views Blainey expressed about Aboriginal history in the Latham Lecture were ones which he deployed in the debate about arguably the biggest cultural issue in Australia in the 1990s: the High Court's *Mabo* decision of June 1992 and the Keating Government's response to it in late 1993. In this landmark decision, the High Court found that the notion of *terra nullius* did not apply where there had been previous Indigenous occupants of the land, thus opening the way for Indigenous Australians to pursue native title claims on land, provided that title had not been extinguished by crown grants.

While historical interpretation had played a significant role in Blainey's earlier battle over immigration and multiculturalism, it was central to *Mabo*. For most of the period of the *Mabo* debate Blainey had a weekly column in *The Age*, contributed to *Australian Business Monthly* and delivered around one hundred speeches per year, so he had plenty of opportunities to mount his arguments. Indeed, he claimed a particular expertise in the area 'as one of the few historians who have tried to study the economic history of traditional Aboriginal as well as European Australia'.[59] As such, he read the 150 pages of the High Court's reasoning with 'intense interest' and found that the Justices of the High Court had delivered perhaps 'the most revolutionary' judgement

---

58   Geoffrey Blainey, 'Drawing up a balance sheet of our history'.
59   Geoffrey Blainey, 'Sitting in Judgment on History', *Australian Business Monthly*, August 1993, 44.

in its history.⁶⁰ Blainey argued that to extrapolate from a case related to the Murray Islands whose inhabitants 'kept gardens and had a more European style of land tenure' and moreover 'were not Aborigines' was an attempt by the High Court to appeal to what it felt were 'the contemporary values of the Australian people'. In doing so, it became a maker, rather than an interpreter, of the law. He further observed that the majority of justices had based their decision on a highly debatable version of Australian history with 'at least two justices making rash statements about Australian history, and specifically giving an erroneous explanation of why Aborigines were wiped out or almost obliterated in many Australian regions'. This made him ponder 'where they learned their history, because the High Court on Mabo is as much a reinterpretation of history as a reinterpretation of the common law'.⁶¹

In a speech, Blainey even called for the resignation of the Chief Justice, which earned him a rebuke from conservative commentator, Gerard Henderson, who commented that in his speeches Blainey was giving 'the impression of being dogmatic and at times strident'.⁶² Henderson continued:

> The problem with the lecture circuit is that it does not provide opportunities for reflective and considered responses to public events. The more Geoffrey Blainey has been in the public eye, the less convincing his work has been.⁶³

Given Henderson's critique, it is worth noting that before launching into his discussion of Aboriginal issues in the Latham Lecture, Blainey explained that he had now held his own position on these matters 'for some 20 years, have often reconsidered it, and will hold onto it until contrary evidence arrives'. Certainly, back in 1982, Blainey had worried that 'the granting of land rights may well create problems, animosities and contradictions which we do not at present foresee' and also pointed out that the land rights movement was 'running against one of the strongest currents of recent history' which was to reduce hereditary rights. Yet in 1982 he also commented that there were 'good arguments in favour of giving land to Aborigines' and that it was 'essential that Aborigines should once again feel at home in their own land'.⁶⁴

---

60 Ibid.
61 Ibid.
62 Gerard Henderson, 'Time for Blainey to step off his soapbox', *The Age*, 23 November 1993, 13. Also published as 'Tyranny of Distance Twixt Scholar and Pedagogue' in *Sydney Morning Herald*, 23 November 1993, 11.
63 Ibid.
64 Duggan, 'Land Rights and Future Wrongs'.

By the end of 1993, the legislative response to the *Mabo* judgement had been enacted and, although expressing some admiration for Keating's political skill, Blainey was left lamenting how little opportunity there was for citizens to even obtain a copy of the *Mabo* judgement, let alone make a meaningful contribution to the debate.[65] Certainly, the academic historians wanted to debate Blainey's views, their most detailed response being produced by Bain Attwood.[66] Attwood criticised Blainey, and other critics of the *Mabo* decision, for failure to accept responsibility for the actions of their forebears, writing that 'in doing so, Blainey, like the other conservatives, is not only denying the determinative role of the Aboriginal colonial past (and simultaneously erasing one of the most salient markers and sources of Aborigines' difference), but also its explanatory power with reference to the Aboriginal present'.[67] Attwood went as far as to compare 'this denial of the past ... to those Germans who desperately seek to "revise" their nation's Nazi past'.[68]

Attwood recognised that Blainey was the 'principal exponent' of a position 'conceded and even articulated by some conservatives', which wrote favourably of pre-colonial Aboriginal history. However, in Attwood's eyes, this positive depiction contradicted the conservative position on the post-colonial period and was thus a source of 'puzzlement'. The explanation Attwood suggested was that it was a form of compartmentalisation which enabled Blainey 'to valorise the Aboriginal past as long as it does not occupy the same time as the Australian past of his traditional narrative'.[69] Hence, praising it could be done safely, without having any impact on contemporary conceptions of the Australian state. Blainey addressed this alleged contradiction as follows:

> Pride in the achievements of Aborigines before 1788 is not in itself inconsistent with pride in what the Europeans have largely achieved since then. It is possible to be proud of both. But in practice most Australians barrack either for one or the other, as if they are opposing teams.[70]

---

65 Geoffrey Blainey, 'Mabo in black and white', *Australian Business Monthly*, January 1994, 92–95.

66 Bain Attwood, 'Mabo, Australia and the end of history', in *In The Age of Mabo: History Aborigines and Australia*, ed. Bain Attwood (Sydney: Allen & Unwin, 1996), 100–116.

67 Ibid., 107.

68 Ibid., 108.

69 Ibid., 109.

70 Geoffrey Blainey, *This land is all horizons: Australian fears and visions* (Sydney: ABC Books, 2001), 56.

Attwood's analysis categorised all opponents of the new history as 'conservatives' and ascribed to them the view that 'history has an evolutionary trajectory', and was 'inevitably the story of progress', which is surely a liberal, rather than a conservative, concept.[71] Similarly, the historian and Keating speech-writer Don Watson said that those opposing the black armband view were trying to pretend that the dark side of human nature does not exist.[72] Blainey took umbrage, pointing out that he had done just that in his Latham Lecture, when he stated that 'the treatment of Aborigines was often lamentable'.[73] More fundamentally, it is unusual for conservatives to be accused of not placing enough emphasis on the dark side of human nature, when normally that is seen as an integral feature of conservatism, often contrasted with liberalism's optimism about the perfectibility of humanity.

Another critic of Blainey's approach was the philosopher and writer, Raimond Gaita, who argued that the act of balancing the harm done to Indigenous Australians, against the positive aspects of the nation's history, inherently made light of that harm. In his view, those who insist on some sort of summing up 'should not be surprised when Aborigines are insulted by the implication that the evil done to them should be treated as lightly as it is by those who sneer at "black armbands"'.[74]

In the wake of the High Court's December 1996 *Wik* decision, which found that native title could co-exist with pastoral leases, Blainey made some of his strongest comments yet on Aboriginal land rights. In an April 1997 *Bulletin* article, he slammed Justices Deane and Gaudron for having got their history wrong in the *Mabo* judgement.[75] He accused them of not knowing that disease was the main killer of Aborigines, and in their ignorance deciding 'to pin the blame on the British and to look for ways of compensating Aborigines for what they called "a national legacy of unutterable shame"'.[76] Blainey saw that the one-sided, pro-Aboriginal view posed a real risk of a return to a one-sided, anti-Aboriginal view. Such a development would undo the good work which had led to a new 'willingness to examine the long years of traditional

---

71   Attwood, 'Mabo, Australia and the end of history', 109.

72   Don Watson, 'Back to the Past - Australian history is in crisis, polarised, demonised, misused and misunderstood, and barely breathing in our schools', *The Australian's Review of Books*, 1997, 6–7, 10.

73   Geoffrey Blainey, 'Black Future', *The Bulletin*, 8 April 1997, 22–23.

74   Raimond Gaita, *A Common Humanity: Thinking About Love & Truth & Justice* (Melbourne: Text Publishing, 1999), 104.

75   Blainey, *Black Future*.

76   Ibid.

Aboriginal history with sympathy and understanding'. By insisting 'that the treatment of Aborigines was so disgraceful that no reparations might be adequate', there was a risk that there might be a reversion to a less respectful view of the Aboriginal past.[77]

While the support for Pauline Hanson in the late 1990s, in part due to her views on Aboriginal issues, was a portent that Blainey's fear might be realised, fortunately, over the next decade, the debate on Aboriginal issues became more nuanced, with the growing prominence of figures such as Noel Pearson, who seemed to provide a bridge between previously polarised positions. And the *Mabo* and *Wik* judgments failed to have the negative impact on Australian prosperity that Blainey had feared.

In the same period when Blainey was provoking many academic historians by commenting extensively on Aboriginal land rights, the Right were also taking aim at the recently deceased Manning Clark. In 1993, Clark's former publisher Peter Ryan launched a scathing attack on the quality of his work. In 1996, the *Courier-Mail* published allegations that Clark was a Soviet spy, in the wake of which John Howard commented that he had 'always had a less than rapturous view of the Manning Clark view of Australian history'.[78] One result of the attacks on Clark was a book by McQueen, *Suspect History*, which included, in its defence of Clark, a chapter on Blainey whom, McQueen claimed, 'has not been subjected to the same scrutiny', but had 'comparable faults' to Clark.[79]

A different angle of attack on Blainey came from Gerard Henderson, another burst of 'friendly fire' after his criticism of him for his comments about the Chief Justice a few years earlier. Henderson's thesis was that the intellectuals had been much more alienated from Australia in the period from the late 1960s to the early 1980s when, despite being 'Australia's best equipped conservative-inclined historian … [Blainey] said all but nothing against alienated (or black armband) history', but was now speaking out when 'if anything, matters have improved'.[80] Yet, despite Henderson's call for all sides 'to drop the slogans', the battle lines for the next decade of the history wars were drawn.

---

77 Ibid.
78 McQueen, *Suspect History*, 3.
79 Ibid., 187.
80 Gerard Henderson, 'Our History Need Mourn No More', *Sydney Morning Herald*, 8 April 1997, 17; and also published as 'Black Armbands Have Since Faded To Grey', *The Age*, 8 April 1997, 15.

Crucially, the replacement of the Old Left historical paradigm, first by the New Left and then by the influence of identity politics meant that, whereas in the past ordinary working-class Australians were idealised by some historians of the Left, they had now come to be regarded with a growing suspicion. Instead of Australians being praised for their belief in democracy, progress and material prosperity, such concepts became problematic. This view became more entrenched amongst intellectuals when Australians used their democratic rights to protect their material prosperity by voting Liberal in December 1975. Within a couple of decades, the unthinkable had happened - concepts such as mateship were being used more by John Howard, than by the Left, and his ability to attract support from a section of the working class, dubbed 'Howard's battlers' was considered an important element of his electoral success.

When controversy erupted around the use of the term mateship in the proposed preamble to the Constitution, which Howard announced in March 1999, Blainey pointed out that 'mateship had belonged to the left wing tradition in Australian ideology'.[81] The reference to 'mateship' did not survive the revision of the draft, which was completed by Howard in August, working closely with Aboriginal Democrats Senator, Aden Ridgeway. Howard had shown the March draft, which he had composed with the assistance of the poet Les Murray, to Blainey a fortnight before its public release but then, according to Blainey, he had rejected almost all the suggestions Blainey had made. Blainey thought that Howard had made 'a strong effort to occupy the middle ground and even put a toehold to the left of that middle ground'.[82] Evidence of this leftward slant was mentioning immigrants in two of the eight paragraphs but not recognising the non-Aboriginal native born; not referring to British laws and institutions such as the monarchy; and stating that Aboriginals had been here since 'time immemorial', which suggested they had always been here when, in fact, they were immigrants.[83]

The issue of the preamble was part of the republic debate, which culminated in the Referendum held on 6 November 1999. As with the Aboriginal land rights, the debate about whether Australia should become a republic was a significant issue through the 1990s and raised many similar issues

---

81 Geoffrey Blainey, 'The Preamble's Not So Bad, Mate', *The Age*, 25 March 1999, 17; and also published as 'Howard's Grand Gesture', *Sydney Morning Herald*, 25 March 1999, 21.

82 Ibid.

83 Ibid.

about how the nation's history should be seen and how its national identity should be portrayed. Yet, in one sense, monarchists faced less risk than opponents of the land-rights agenda: monarchists tended only to be branded as monarchists, whereas opponents of the *Mabo* judgement risked being branded racists.

The tone of Blainey's comments on the republic was much milder than those he espoused in the *Mabo* debate, becoming more polemical only when he alleged that Keating had distorted the historical record. For instance, he claimed that Keating's 1993 Anzac Day address 'belittled the nation and the men whose memory he intended to honour'.[84] Unsurprisingly, Keating did not choose Blainey to be a member of the Malcolm Turnbull-chaired Republic Advisory Committee established in 1993. Under the committee's unusual model, the states collectively were given two representatives, one for NSW and Victoria combined, and one for all the others. The states could either agree on a choice or submit their individual selections for Prime Ministerial arbitration. Victoria's Kennett Government got in first, nominating Blainey, but the Fahey Government in NSW had its own candidate, a 31-year old Sydney republican, Namoi Dougall, who despite being a Liberal Party member, was always likely to be preferred by Keating.[85] Given the fact that Blainey himself was 'not surprised he was overlooked', one could see why *The Age* editorialised that Victorian Premier Jeff Kennett's decision to nominate him had been 'a piece of political mischief'.[86]

At this time, Blainey used the republican proposal as a hook to return to other themes. He argued that 'ballooning debt and a shrinking defence force' were greater threats to Australian independence than the remaining ceremonial ties to Britain.[87] Later, after the change of government in 1996 made him more content with the overall direction of the nation, and with the approach for determining whether the nation would become a republic, he became a picture of moderate conservatism:

> I support the present mode of government in Australia, including the symbolic role of the monarchy, but I am willing to change my mind – if a superior method is put forward. No system of government is perfect,

---

84 Geoffrey Blainey, 'The Real Enemies of Independence', *The Age* (Extra section), 8 May 1993, 2.
85 M. Coultan, 'PM's Dilemma: Namoi or the Prof', *Sydney Morning Herald*, 18 May 1993, 1; and Innes Willox, 'Blainey rejected for republican forum', *The Age*, 26 May 1993, 3.
86 Editorial, 'Right Man, Wrong Job', *The Age*, 27 May 1993, 17.
87 Willox, 'Blainey Rejected for Republican Forum'.

but I am wary of supporting changes until such time as the changes, and what they will mean in practice, are carefully spelled out.[88]

However, he did create a minor controversy as a delegate at the February 1998 Constitutional Convention when he referred to the Governor-General, Sir William Deane, as the 'shadow minister for social welfare' and pointed out that while many delegates may enjoy Deane being a 'persistent advocate' for causes they supported, they would be 'indignant if the next Governor-General or president turned out also to be a crusader, but crusading on the other side of politics'.[89] The former NSW Premier Neville Wran intervened in the proceedings to disassociate himself from the 'shameful attack' on the Governor General.[90] In contrast, the next speaker, former Brisbane Lord Mayor Sallyanne Atkinson, said that no contribution to the Convention had been better than Blainey's.[91]

Blainey's critique of Deane's behaviour was one of several astute observations in his speech. He began by noting the constant calls by republican delegates for 'gender balance' in a republic, calls made without any acknowledgement on their part that 'in the history of Australia since self-government the monarchy was for long the only official position where women had a chance … for 100 of the last 150 years, a woman has been the monarch'.[92] Also, in an echo of his 'Godzone' article from thirty years earlier, Blainey expressed sympathy for citizens-initiated referenda as a better way to enhance democracy than electing a president.[93] In the days after his speech, Blainey continued to be an active participant in proceedings making a number of procedural and policy contributions.

Between the Constitutional Convention and the November 1999 referendum, Blainey was one of a group who drafted a brochure for the public information campaign for the referendum, along with the likes of John Hirst, Colin Howard and Cheryl Saunders. According to Malcolm Turnbull's account, 'the whole process was a disaster' as the monarchists Blainey and

---

88   Geoffrey Blainey, 'Uneasy lies a nation that has no crown', *The Australian*, 21 January 1998, 13. Blainey had made the point in *Daedalus* (1985) that Australia is 'in practice a republic' and 'behind the colonial-like façade of dependence is an independence that came more quickly to Australia than to the United States' (14–15).

89   Constitutional Convention Transcript of Proceedings, 4 February 1998.

90   Ibid.

91   Ibid.

92   Ibid.

93   Ibid.

Colin Howard wielded too much influence.[94] Blainey was critical of the tactics of the Australian Republican Movement, citing their inflexibility and comparing this unfavourably with the Federalists in the 1890s, a group who had made sufficient compromises to deliver their desired outcome.[95] Blainey also defended John Howard against attacks he had rigged the process. He argued that Howard had shown 'fairness rarely seen in Australian politics' by holding the Convention, accepting its 'unpalatable verdict' and putting the issue to a vote.[96]

Although the Kennett Government had been unable to secure Blainey's place on Turnbull's 1993 republic committee, it did appoint him to other roles solely within its own remit. He became foundation Chancellor of the new university at Ballarat, a position he held until 1998, with his contribution being recognised by having an auditorium named after him and the awarding of a Doctor of Letters. The university's library was also the recipient of a significant donation of works from Blainey's extensive book collection.

The Kennett Government also appointed Blainey as chair of the Historic Contents sub-committee for the Eureka Interpretation Centre (subsequently called the Eureka Stockade Centre). This sub-committee became controversial as critics noted that academic historians who had written about Eureka, such as Weston Bate and John Molony, were excluded, while local amateur historians, including the former State Liberal MP, Tom Evans, who disagreed with some of the academics' views, were appointed.[97] The absence of a contemporary academic contribution led to claims from one academic that the history provided by the sub-committee 'did not try to extend experiences beyond the personal and familial' and by its emphasis on 'the need for facts, it ignored imaginative representation and the possibility of exploring and challenging myths and legends'.[98]

---

94 Malcolm Turnbull, *Fighting For The Republic* (Melbourne: Hardie Grant Books, 1999), 159.
95 Jacob Ramsay, 'Why Republic Failed: Blainey', *Australian Financial Review*, 27 October 2000, 19.
96 Geoffrey Blainey, 'Why the Republic had to lose', *The Sunday Age*, 7 November 1999, 12.
97 Anne Beggs-Sunter, 'Contested Memories of Eureka: Museum Interpretations of the Eureka Stockade', *Labour History*, no. 85 (November 2003), 34. In 2001, Blainey and Beggs-Sunter debated Eureka on the *Lateline* program on the ABC. Of course, Blainey had attacked the academics' approach to Eureka as early as 1963.
98 Beggs-Sunter, 'Contested Memories of Eureka: Museum Interpretations of the Eureka Stockade'.

Whether it was *Mabo*, the republic, or Eureka, Blainey's take on history was very different from that of the historians who remained in the academy. This fact was underscored by an article by young Western Australian historian, Deborah Gare, who clearly recognised that the failure to seriously consider Blainey's work was a problem:

> For those of my generation, who passed through the university system after the major Blainey controversies ... the opportunity to 'objectively' review Blainey's historiography has been limited. Today's students are either influenced by the feelings of their lecturers towards Blainey as a historian, or are only sparingly introduced to his work on reading lists at all.[99]

Gare also made the point that 'heated debate can be quickly incited by merely mentioning his name amongst my young colleagues (particularly those of a non-British ethnic background)'.[100] To her credit, Gare was clearly trying to understand Blainey's position and the fact that she chose to publish her article in the conservative journal *Quadrant* was a sign of an attempt to break down the ideological divide. In her article, she defended Blainey where she could, for instance, against 'unwarranted and unfair' attacks by Humphrey McQueen over Blainey's treatment of workers in *The Peaks of Lyell*. Yet, despite her attempts at sympathy, she could not accept the fact that any historian could legitimately oppose Australia becoming a Republic. For Gare, opposing the Republic was a 'refusal to come to terms with Australian independence from Britain', and thus she claimed that Blainey had not 'personally come to terms with the fact that Australia is now living in the ashes of empire'.[101]

Blainey had already described the trap into which Gare had fallen in a paper he gave at a symposium to celebrate the twentieth anniversary of the establishment of the Chair of Australian Studies at Harvard. Blainey outlined six types of Australian nationalism, one of which he called 'Red, White and Blue Nationalism'.[102] He said that the 'serious media' now just regarded this as British nationalism but, until recent times, this kind of nationalism assumed that Australia 'had built a new and superior edifice on British foundations'. A couple of years later, after the defeat of the Republican referendum, Blainey

---

99 Gare, 'White Ghost of Empire?', 38.
100 Ibid.
101 Ibid., 42.
102 Geoffrey Blainey, 'Not As the Song of Other Lands' in *Approaching Australia: Papers from the Harvard Australian Studies Symposium*, eds Harold Bolitho and Chris Wallace-Crabb (Cambridge Mass: Harvard University Press, 1997), 129–137.

observed that it was those with less formal education and those in rural Australia who voted against the Republic and yet 'this part of Australia, interestingly, tends to be more proud of the nation and its independence'.[103] In contrast, what Blainey categorised as 'Black nationalism' condemned much of what had happened since 1788 and promoted a belief that 'Aboriginal life before 1788 was not too far from utopia'.[104] This brand of nationalism had risen dramatically in prominence in recent decades and had delivered 'an astonishing rewriting of large slices of Australian history', becoming ubiquitous in 'history books, films, parliamentary debates and the high court'.[105]

One of the key architects of that change in how Australian history was perceived and written, Henry Reynolds, has been refreshingly honest in expressing the view that 'the purpose of intellectual endeavour is not just to understand the world but to change it'.[106] In his professional career he has wanted 'to contribute to some cause greater than the dissemination of knowledge'.[107] The change Reynolds and others have precipitated has been so profound that it has meant that, while Blainey often presents himself as being in a centrist position, he is nonetheless well outside the mainstream of academic history, as Graeme Davison commented:

> Blainey's homely metaphors – the pendulum, the balance sheet, the loaded dice – are as telling as his arguments: they place him in the middle ground when, in fact, there is hardly a historian of any substance to the right of him. That he can credibly do so is a measure, not only of his own rhetorical skill, but of the distance which has now opened up between the intellectual milieu of academic history and the lay audience of professional and business people that Blainey now addresses.[108]

Blainey had argued as far back as 1966 that 'when a historian lacks the orthodox assumptions of his times, the complaint is loud that he is biased or that his methods are odd; this merely means that so many writers share a common bias that they have ceased to realize that it is a bias'.[109] In 1999,

---

103 Blainey, *This land is all horizons*, 45.
104 Blainey, 'Not As the Song of Other Lands', 135.
105 Ibid.
106 Mark McKenna, 'Silence shattered with a whisper to the heart', *The Australian* (Literary Review), 4 March 2009, 16.
107 Ibid.
108 Davison, *The Use and Abuse of Australian History*, 17.
109 Geoffrey Blainey, 'Brian Fitzpatrick (1906-1965) and his works', *Business Archives and History* 6, no. 1 (February 1966): 77–78.

Blainey commented that he was 'seen to have Liberal Party connections' which was 'unusual in Australian social science and humanities circles, [and] that's why I'm called ultra-right'.[110] It raises the interesting question as to how much of a free market liberal or a conservative an individual can be and still remain within the bounds of academic history. One historian who arguably fitted the latter category was John Hirst, a historian with an eclectic mix of positions with a reasonable degree of overlap with Blainey, but who prospered within the ranks of academic historians. Another more explicitly conservative historian, in this case an older contemporary of Blainey, who had a successful academic career was John Manning Ward at Sydney University. Ward 'approached history ... from a broadly liberal-conservative outlook' and emphasised the influence of conservative values in the development of Australia. A foreword to one of works observed that 'his analysis was rather different from scholars in either an older nationalist, or more contemporary, progressivist approach – let alone a broadly radical view'.[111]

For Gare, and others brought up within the new orthodoxy, the key marker of Blainey's own historical writing was his treatment of the meeting of Aboriginal Australians and settler Australians on the frontier in the nineteenth century. Gare wrote that Blainey performed a 'juggling act of different interests', but to express empathy for both groups, as Blainey did, was clearly unacceptable:

> While Blainey's respect for empire and Australian nationalism can usually co-exist quite happily, in the story of Aboriginal history they are completely incompatible and are, in fact, fatal enemies. And in this case, his respect for empire probably won out.[112]

In a response to Gare, the Newcastle-based academic economist, John Fisher, argued that she was making the mistake of viewing 'history as *judgement*' (his emphasis), an approach he dubbed 'the Manning Clark version of historical method'.[113] While acknowledging that Blainey's 'values and beliefs undoubtedly influence his choice and treatment of historical subjects

---

110   Terrill, *The Australians*, 273.
111   Deryck M. Schreuder and Brian H. Fletcher, 'Foreword' to John Manning Ward, *The State and the People: Australian Federation and Nation-Making 1870–1901* (Sydney: The Federation Press, 2001). Ward spent the last decade of his academic career in the 1980s in administration, being Vice-Chancellor of Sydney University from 1981 until his retirement early in 1990. He died in a train disaster later the same year.
112   Gare, 'White Ghost of Empire?', 40.
113   John Fisher, 'History Master', *Quadrant* 44, no 4 (April 2000): 59.

and topics', Fisher could not accept that 'any combination of nationalist pride and respect for empire is the key to understanding his research and writing'.[114] What actually drove Blainey was 'intellectual curiosity, by a desire to understand why things happened and, ultimately perhaps, why we are as we are now'.[115]

Blainey had always accepted that historical writing could not be 'unbiased', as he had written in 1966:

> It seems to me that one of the real dangers of interpreting the past is to treat so-called facts ... as capable of selecting themselves, as capable of expressing themselves, and, above all, of interpreting themselves. Rather than being articulated, they are often very dumb, and rather than being free of bias, they are often very biased.[116]

When Reynolds conceded in 1985 that the history profession was 'obviously left of centre', he was reflecting something which had been the case for decades.[117] The difference was that as issues such as race and gender took over from the material condition of the working class as the main preoccupation of the Left, it came to matter more. In Blainey's eyes, many historians had failed to acknowledge that intellectual fashions change:

> As human beings we sometimes move from one extreme to another. A task of the historian, a difficult task, is to audit those extreme swings of opinion. In my view those historians, politicians and commentators – and even those High Court Justices – who now wear the black armbands, tend to offer an unfair assessment of that earlier Australia. Criticisms, often strong criticisms, can fairly be made of Australia since or before 1900. But on the balance, the nation's story is more a success than a failure, unless by chance the failures on certain fronts are exaggerated.[118]

Blainey made these comments in a reassessment of his 'black armband' speech in 2000. Whether it was the gradual improvement in the Australian economy as the 1990s progressed, or the change of Federal Government in 1996, Blainey seemed to have become more bullish about the nation in the intervening seven

---

114   Ibid.
115   Ibid.
116   Blainey, 'Problems of Interpretation (II)', 125.
117   Trinca, 'Historians to take the legend of Blainey "head on" in new book'.
118   Blainey, 'A Black Arm-Band for Australia's 20th Century?'.

years. Even when considering the twentieth century on its own, he considered 'the nation's successes ... outweigh its failures by a large margin'.[119]

Blainey delivered this speech to a friendly audience at the Samuel Griffith Society conference on the second weekend of November 2000. The following weekend he was to attend another conference with a more critical audience, as a collection of academic historians gathered to consider his work. However, the very fact that the conference was being held was a sign that a degree of conciliation was in the wind.

Things had begun quietening down by the mid-1990s. Blainey no longer had a weekly newspaper column and the election of the Howard Government meant there were fewer decisions being made with which he strongly disagreed. He seemed to have decided to comment less on public controversies, while there also seemed to be a sense amongst some of those who had fought against him in those controversies that it was time for a truce, if not reconciliation.

Gradually the historian again began to dominate the controversialist.

---

[119] Ibid.

Chapter 10

AUSTRALIAN HISTORIAN

The publication of Blainey's *A Shorter History of Australia* (1994) reinforced a striking feature of Australia's historiography, namely that so many of the country's most prominent historians have written single-volume national histories. In addition to Blainey, the list includes Hancock, Scott, Crawford, Shaw, Ward, Clark and Macintyre.

However, it needs to be noted that telling the national story in abbreviated form has rarely been a primary goal of these historians' careers. W.K. Hancock reflected that his *Australia* 'was off the main highroad that I was trying to follow in my teaching and thinking and was not in any strict sense a work of research', while Manning Clark explained that his short history 'was written for money', as he was offered a sum equal to the cost of a car, something which would particularly benefit the large Clark family.[1] Similarly, for Blainey, producing *A Shorter History of Australia* was almost a consolation for not having yet finished 'a very long and many-sided book' on which he has been spasmodically working for many years.[2]

The fact that *A Shorter History of Australia* was published after Blainey had been a prominent public commentator for several years meant that it was likely to be read to see how much it reflected his controversial public views. Blainey attempted to pre-empt criticism by writing in the Preface that 'my own attitudes and preferences of course are present but on some important topics I have tried to give space to alternative viewpoints though I don't necessarily accept them'.[3] Critics divided over the extent to which he had succeeded.

Historian Michael Cathcart observed that, 'unlike Blainey's newspaper columns', *A Shorter History of Australia* was 'rarely overtly polemical … the prose

---

1   W.K. Hancock, *Country and Calling*, (London: Faber & Faber, 1954), 109; and Manning Clark, 'Manning Clark' in Crawford, Clark and Blainey, *Making History*, 55.
2   Blainey, *A Shorter History of Australia*, vii. He was still reported to be working on such a work in 2006 (Devine, 'A Conversation with Geoffrey Blainey', 52).
3   Blainey, *A Shorter History of Australia*, viii.

is constantly searching for balance, moderation and reasonableness'.[4] Cathcart disagreed with much of the work, but thought it would 'give the levellers amongst us a workout which can only do us good'.[5] Other historians, such as Charlie Fox, failed to notice the characteristics Cathcart identified, instead seeing the work as confirming Blainey's move from the 'even-handedness that had characterised some of his 1960s and 1970s writings' to a new role 'as the right's favourite historian'.[6] One example Fox gave was that 'attacks on union power and the arbitration system now come with evangelical force'.[7]

It is true that industrial relations and attitudes to work were key themes of *A Shorter History of Australia*. Blainey's thesis was that a decisive turning point in Australian history had come in the 1890s, a decade which ushered in changed cultural attitudes that had begun a decline that had culminated in the economic and social problems the nation had experienced since the 1970s. Australians who lived in the period from the gold rushes to 1890 have clearly been ones with whom Blainey felt a particular affinity. Australians of that period compared well, not just with their modern counterparts but with their contemporaries back in England. As Blainey pointed out, the Australian poet Adam Lindsay Gordon was 'a man of action, a far cry from Browning and Tennyson and the sit-about poets of England'.[8]

Blainey skilfully linked his argument about the significance of the 1890s to Tom Roberts' famous 1890 painting, 'Shearing the Rams', a picture Blainey believed 'managed to capture that special time in Australian history when so many people found pleasure in hard work'. He continued:

> 'Shearing The Rams' shows energy and contentment, with smiling boys lending a hand, the shearers busy, and an old boss smoking his short pipe – a mixture of individualism and teamwork. The painting remains a celebration of work and the part played by the everyday person … Tom Roberts painted his energetic picture just before some of the energy and competitiveness was subsiding in many workplaces. There

---

4   Michael Cathcart, 'A brisk tour through Australian history', *Australian Book Review*, no. 167 (December 1994-January 1995): 23.
5   Ibid., 24. Cathcart echoed Blainey's own comments in a foreword to a short history of Australia written by French historian, Robert Lacour-Gayet in the 1970s. Blainey observed that 'every decade or so there appears a history of Australia which quietly opens the eyes of readers even if they disagree'. (Geoffrey Blainey 'Foreword' in Robert Lacour-Gayet, *A Concise History of Australia* (Melbourne: Penguin, 1976), x.)
6   Fox, 'My Lord the Workingman?', 144.
7   Ibid., 145.
8   Blainey, *A Shorter History of Australia*, 106, 111.

was to be more and more regulating of the pace of work and the hours of work. Australia's two cultures, sport and work, were beginning to go their separate ways, and increasingly the competitiveness was to be seen more often on the sporting field than in workplaces.[9]

The 1890s had been where Blainey left off the national story in *A Land Half Won*. In that work, he had implicitly criticised late nineteenth-century Australians for their failure to appreciate the nature of the land. A decade and a half of national economic difficulty and bruising public debate later, Blainey focused more on the economic behaviour, than the attitudes to the land, of this generation.

The Australia which evolved in the twentieth century had several less appealing features for Blainey. He combined three of them in a sentence about the problems that disrupted the country's war efforts in the early days of the Second World War, observing that 'more could have been done but for the strikes in the New South Wales coalfields, the reluctance of public opinion to accept sacrifices, and a political deadlock in Canberra'.[10] Contrast that with the halcyon days when 'Australia's progress seemed easy' as, in the period from 1850 to 1890, 'the combination of hard work and natural wealth, bright technical ideas and sober English capital worked wonders'.[11]

Of course, there can be a risk in writing the history of one country to over-emphasise national characteristics as explanations for events. While Australia was at the forefront of countries who legislated to regulate the pace and hours of work, it was not unique. However, Blainey had, for a number of years, made the point that Australia had declined economically relative to other countries and, while recognising that some of the causes of that decline were purely economic, he argued that 'several major causes of our economic decline are cultural', and reflected a cultural aversion to taking work seriously.[12]

The very fact that a key theme of Blainey's work in Australian history was the nation's economic performance put him in a minority among other Australian historians. Others were much more inclined to focus on issues of identity, particularly of race and gender.

Labour historian Frank Bongiorno has described 'a rapid transformation of Australian historiography' between 1970 and 1985, which saw social history

---

9   Ibid., 118.
10   Ibid., 182.
11   Ibid., 99.
12   Geoffrey Blainey, 'Be A Sport and Get A Job', *Australian Business Monthly*, November 1993, 112–113.

shift from being 'history with the politics left out' to 'a resolutely political "history from below"' propagated by a generation of 'activist-scholars of the New Left'.[13] Down below were Aborigines, women, gays and immigrants, all of whom the New Left historians claimed had been victimised by Blainey's favourites, the self-sufficient settler Australians of the nineteenth century.

In the 1980s and 1990s, 'history from below', or microhistory as this historiographical movement became known internationally, meant that historians, as Canadian historian Mark Salber Phillips has described, were able to 'pursue closer emotional and ideological identification with the experiences of women, peasants, religious non-conformists and others whose lives seemed to have been erased from larger-scale narratives'.[14] Phillips further explained the creed:

> By 'rescuing' lives ... from the 'enormous condescension of posterity', many historians hoped to give their work a sense of moral witness that transcended mere professionalism. History became – though we didn't yet have the phrase – the scholarship of truth and reconciliation, offering the dignity of narrative as compensation for lifetimes of oppression and exclusion.[15]

When Blainey looked at the past he did not see 'lifetimes of oppression and exclusion'. Indeed, as Blainey made clear in an introduction to a collection of Henry Lawson's works, admirable historical characters are those who battle against whatever adversity they may have encountered. Unlike Banjo Paterson's swagman, who took the easy way out, 'nearly all of Lawson's swagmen, selectors and goldminers labour away, often fighting against high odds', the epitome of the Australians who began to disappear from the 1890s onwards.[16]

While Blainey's high regard for Lawson was shared by many in the Old Left, there was a significant divide between his outlook and theirs. As Beverley Kingston commented, 'Blainey is far from sympathetic to the old Whiggish tale of the growth of an Australian version of democracy shaped by the initiatives of the labour movement and the resistance of capital'.[17]

---

13 Frank Bongiorno, 'Australian Labour History: Contexts, Trends and Influences', *Labour History*, no. 100, (May 2011), 8.

14 Mark Salber Phillips, 'Distance and Historical Representation', *History Workshop Journal*, no. 57 (Spring 2004): 128.

15 Mark Salber Phillips, 'On the Advantage and Disadvantage of Sentimental History for Life', *History Workshop Journal*, no. 65, (Spring 2008): 55.

16 Geoffrey Blainey, 'A Genius to the Fingertips', in *Henry Lawson*, ed. Geoffrey Blainey (Melbourne: Text Publishing, 2002), xxxi.

17 Beverley Kingston, review of *A Shorter History of Australia*, *Australian Historical Studies* 28, no. 108 (April 1997), 196.

Although not a follower of the old Whig version of the nation's past, Blainey was even further removed from the new history. As John Hirst put it, Blainey challenged 'a view of Australian history which has become common currency during the past 20 years and was unimaginable before then'. Hirst explained that Blainey was 'interested in particular people', but 'has little time for people organised in groups'.[18] Like other historians, Blainey considered the treatment of groups including Aboriginals, immigrants, convicts, Catholics and women; but, where they saw much to condemn, he took a more benign view.

Pre-1788 Aboriginal history had largely been absent from short histories in earlier generations. Unsurprisingly, the author of *Triumph of the Nomads* included it, devoting a similar amount of space to pre-1788 Australia in *A Shorter History of Australia* as do other modern short history writers, and he continued to refer to Aboriginal issues through the post-1788 narrative. Blainey gave even more space, 15 of 24 chapters, to pre-colonial Aboriginal society in the first of his two volumes of Australian history published in 2015, prompting historian Alan Atkinson to comment that 'probably no general history of Australia has given so much space to the original inhabitants'.[19] However, while the space Blainey devoted to Aboriginal history may have been similar to other contemporary historians, some of his commentary was quite different.

Blainey sought to correct the recent historical record in relation to the treatment of Aborigines by settler Australians, writing that it was 'a modern myth that early in the nineteenth century the Aborigines were universally despised, not least by government officials' and the belief 'that no Aborigines had the right to vote until the 1960s is another myth'.[20] Rather than apportioning blame for the clashes which took place between Indigenous Australians and settlers, Blainey saw them as inevitable as 'even with goodwill on both sides' the two groups were 'incompatible' and thus clashes were 'difficult to avoid'.[21] What Blainey did not like was modern government policy towards the Indigenous population. He noted that when, in the 1960s, the Arbitration Commission granted equal pay to Aboriginal pastoral workers it 'increased the pride but diminished the well being of Aboriginal stockmen', as the numbers employed

---

18 John Hirst, 'History's Rum Gos', *The Age* (Extra section), 26 November 1994, 8.
19 Alan Atkinson, 'The Triumph of Unity', *The Weekend Australian* (Review section), 18–19 April 2015, 18–19.
20 Blainey, *A Shorter History of Australia*, 44, 45.
21 Ibid., 22, 41.

quickly fell.[22] When it came to Native Title, Blainey argued that it 'had little practical relevance' to the modern urban-based Aboriginal majority.[23]

As well as the treatment of the Aboriginal population from 1788 onwards, the other controversial aspect of Australia's racial history was the White Australia Policy. In *A Shorter History of Australia*, Blainey described it as 'inevitable', making the point that 'the White Australia Policy was far from unique', listing a range of other countries with similar policies, and argued that 'Australia was more willing than most other nations or tribes to admit people who seemed different'.[24] As with the modern writing of Aboriginal history, Blainey identified errors in the presentation of immigration history, observing that 'in recent years some critics have claimed that the White Australia Policy actually excluded Mediterranean people, but in the twelve years to 1914 a total of 4,775 Greeks arrived in Australian ports, and only one was excluded, and he had been in gaol'.[25]

For Blainey, the major cost of the White Australia Policy was the failure to develop tropical northern Australia once cheap Pacific Islander labour had been excluded. He cited this as an example of a phenomenon where 'in politics nearly every solution to a problem begins to germinate a new problem'.[26] Looking back on the policy, Blainey argued that 'it had been essential for Australia's survival as a young democracy in that era when the gulf, in religion, culture, language and skills, between a Chinese peasant and an Australian worker was unimaginably wide'.[27] And he defended the generation of Australians who produced it:

> Australians of that generation are sometimes depicted as isolationist, turning their backs on any culture except the British ... In 1890 almost every people in the world, and probably the Chinese even more than the Australians, shunned alien cultures to some degree.[28]

Blainey argued that the cultural gap narrowed after the Second World War, helped by factors such as Asian students studying in Australia under the Colombo Plan. Blainey noted that the Colombo Plan was started by Percy Spender in 1950, that the dictation test was abolished in 1958, and the policy

---

22 Ibid., 219.
23 Ibid., 237.
24 Ibid., 135–136.
25 Ibid., 137.
26 Ibid.
27 Ibid., 217.
28 Ibid., 106.

itself was 'virtually abandoned' in 1966. Blainey does not explicitly say it, but he was clearly making the point that all this progress occurred under a Liberal government.[29]

In Blainey's opinion, the pioneers who had built the nation were, by the final decades of the twentieth century, getting a raw deal from many historians. He was keen to salvage the settlers' reputation. For instance, regarding the treatment of convicts, he wrote that 'probably in our eyes convictism, and especially the floggings, seems a harsh punishment; but the treatment of convicts conformed to the standard of an era when Europe's soldiers, sailors and schoolboys were treated to floggings often similar to those endured by convicts in Australia'.[30] Likewise, he pointed out that the Protestant majority had not been unusually tough on the Catholic minority as 'perhaps in no other Protestant part of the world had Catholics enjoyed such political success, and in few if any Catholic parts of the world had Protestants enjoyed comparable success'.[31]

As well as wanting to correct several negative interpretations of Australian history, Blainey also felt that several positive aspects of the national story were not receiving due recognition. A standard feature of Blainey's writing has always been to highlight areas where Australia was the first, best, or biggest and occasionally even the worst. Sometimes this provided an avenue to incorporate worldwide trends, with a local flavour, such as writing that 'Australians were taking to the car and truck with an enthusiasm shown by few other nations' or 'the Liverpool pop stars, The Beatles, received a welcome which they thought was unparalleled in the world'.[32]

A key Blainey argument was that Australians, and their historians, have undervalued the importance of technology and other material factors, and overvalued politics. In *A Shorter History of Australia* Blainey highlighted examples where technology had been a driver of politics. He wrote of the 1840s that 'the latest technology was as important as increasing liberty in enabling Australians to shape part of their future', while in the quarter century after the Second World War 'technology more than politics was remoulding Australia'.[33]

Politics did not feature strongly in *A Shorter History of Australia*. The most dramatic event in federal political history, the Dismissal of the Whitlam Government, merited only half a paragraph, Blainey commenting that each

---

29   Ibid., 218.
30   Ibid., 58.
31   Ibid., 176.
32   Ibid., 168, 207.
33   Ibid., 56, 209.

side had a 'valid case'.³⁴ Curtin and Menzies were among the few politicians to merit biographical sketches. Blainey did not appreciate the contemporary tendency to sneer at the latter for, while Menzies was now depicted as too subservient to Britain, he was 'to most people of his own generation, a nationalist, building up the nation like nobody before him'.³⁵

John Hirst, reviewing *A Shorter History of Australia* in *The Age*, cited several important political struggles that did not make it into the narrative, and argued that 'politics in Blainey's hands is severely handicapped'.³⁶ Hirst had made a similar observation a decade earlier, when reviewing *Our Side of the Country*, Blainey's history of Victoria. He argued then that the failure to consider in detail the great Victorian constitutional crisis of 1877-81 was like writing 'nineteenth-century British history without the Reform Bill'.³⁷ As significant a figure as reforming Premier Graham Berry, described by one political historian as an 'undisputed colossus of Victorian public life', did not rate a mention in Blainey's book.³⁸

When a new edition of *Our Side of the Country* was released in 2006 with a new title, *A History of Victoria*, Blainey wrote the history of the more recent past in a different way to how he dealt with more distant events. While in its coverage of the nineteenth century and early twentieth century the book had a strong weighting towards social history and against political history, one of Blainey's new chapters was titled 'Whirlwind In Spring Street', thus emphasising the significance of politics and of the Kennett Government in particular.³⁹ The absence of contemporary social history and the increased political content in his works creates something of a paradox, as Blainey's interest in politics appears to have grown in an inverse relationship with that of the community.

---

34 Ibid., 222. In 2005, Blainey wrote a lengthy article on the 30th anniversary of the Dismissal for *The Age*.

35 Blainey, *A Shorter History of Australia*, 188–189, 198–201.

36 Hirst, 'History's Rum Gos'.

37 J.B. Hirst, review of *Our Side of the Country* in *Royal Australian Historical Society Journal* 71, no. 3 (1985): 229.

38 Paul Strangio, 'Broken heads and flaming houses: Graham Berry, the wild colonial' in *The Victorian Premiers 1856–2006*, eds Paul Strangio and Brian Costar, (Sydney: The Federation Press, 2006), 51.

39 Blainey, *A History of Victoria*, 241. In a generally positive summation of Kennett's role, Blainey commented that 'the most impressive measure of his success was that finally he halted and then reversed the long-term exodus from Victoria to the other states'. The modern social history gap was illustrated by Blainey's treatment of music. While he was able to write five pages on the successful female singers Victoria produced between the 1880s and 1930s, other than one passing reference to Kylie Minogue, no modern popular music artists, female or male, were mentioned.

As he himself noted, newspapers in colonial times, which had far higher per capita circulation than their modern equivalents, had none of the light material of today and 'politics was their daily bread'.[40] Politics had now become Blainey's historical daily bread when covering more recent events.[41]

One aspect of social history in which Blainey has retained a clear interest is sport. However, even with that topic he has tended to give more detailed treatment to the nineteenth century. In *A Shorter History of Australia*, Blainey devoted a chapter to 'The rise of the sporting hero' in which he detailed the country's growing love of sport in the late nineteenth century; however, he only touched on sport in the twentieth century. Hence, rower, Henry Searle, and jockey, Tommy Corrigan, merit whole paragraphs; on the other hand, Don Bradman only gets mentioned in the single sentence devoted to the Bodyline test series.

The rationale was undoubtedly that the nineteenth century was when Australia was unique, as the first country in the world to give a strong emphasis to spectator sport. For instance, in 1886, it produced the largest football crowd in the world to that time and featured the fastest runners in the world on its professional foot-running circuit.[42] It also had a higher proportion of female spectators than other countries did.[43] Yet, even with its comparatively sparse coverage of twentieth century sport, Blainey's overall treatment of the topic presented a striking contrast with previous short history writers. In Manning Clark's earlier work, for instance, there is no mention of Bradman, the Melbourne Cup, the native code of football or the 1956 Olympics, hardly due to lack of personal interest as Clark played first-class cricket for Oxford University and was a keen Carlton supporter.

While sport was in, other items were out. Blainey's former History Department colleague Noel McLachlan, reviewing the book in *The Australian*, criticised the scant attention Blainey had paid to Eureka Stockade leader Peter Lalor, Ned Kelly, the Boer War, poet Charles Harpur, convict 'Frank the poet' and *The Bulletin*, absences he explained on the basis that 'quirks have always been Blainey's delight'.[44] One could also add items such as Bligh and the Rum Rebellion, Phar Lap and rock and roll to McLachlan's list.

---

40   Blainey, *Our Side of the Country*, 90.
41   A further new edition of his Victorian history, published in 2013, had some more social history in its concluding chapters than the 2006 edition had contained.
42   Blainey, *A Shorter History of Australia*, 109–116.
43   Ibid.
44   Noel McLachlan, 'Provoking look at past', *The Australian* (Review section), 17 December 1994, 5.

Overall, McLachlan rated Blainey's short history as 'every bit as readable' as Manning Clark's 1963 effort, 'even if a breath more breathless'.[45] He also recognised his own 'debt' to Blainey, as an example of how 'often one can be deeply influenced by people one does not agree with'.[46]

Hirst identified that the continuing characteristics of Blainey's work were 'the puzzles, oddities and off-beat comparisons of his restless, quirky intelligence, constantly astonished and endlessly engaging'.[47] However, Kingston worried that Blainey's 'uncanny eye for contradictions, paradoxes [and] inconsistencies' may make the book difficult for readers with limited background in Australian history, for some of the patterns were 'deep in the soil, almost archaeological, needing an experienced reader to bring them to light'.[48]

Revealingly, Kingston's review appeared last of the forty-six reviews published in the April 1997 issue of *Historical Studies*. To the review editors of the pre-eminent journal of the history academy in Australia, Blainey was now apparently less worthy of prominence than he had been when he wrote for *Historical Studies* as an undergraduate almost fifty years earlier. Similarly, when a follow-up to the 1979 work, *Historical Disciplines and Cultures in Australasia: An Assessment*, appeared in 1995, the editor John Moses noted that many of the original contributors 'had died, or retired, or simply given up reflecting'.[49] Blainey had not died and was as prolific as ever, but he was notable by his absence, not just as an author but in the limited references to him in other essays.

Blainey's next book about Australian history was a further departure from the type of work being produced by contemporary academic historians, as it was very much the older type of social history, history with the politics left out. The genesis of *Black Kettle and Full Moon: Daily Life in a Vanished Australia* (2003) lay back in 1974 when Blainey gave a talk in honour of fellow Melbourne University historian Norman Harper at Swan Hill and chose the topic of everyday life in the second half of the nineteenth century.[50] For many subsequent years, Blainey would deliver speeches on aspects of the topic, adding new material as it came to light. The speeches provided a base for the

---

45   Ibid.
46   Ibid.
47   Hirst, 'History's Rum Gos'.
48   Kingston, review of *A Shorter History of Australia*, 196.
49   *Australian Journal of Politics and History* 41, Special Issue, Historical Disciplines in Australasia: Themes Problems and Debates, ed. John A. Moses (1995), vii.
50   Geoffrey Blainey, *Black Kettle and Full Moon: Daily Life in a Vanished Australia* (Melbourne: Penguin Viking, 2003).

book, but he also added significant fresh material. Blainey argued that the book was about 'average Australians', excluding both the rich and very poor, the latter category including Aborigines. As he put it in a radio interview after the book's launch, while work had been done 'on various facets of social history', he thought 'most historians' were 'not interested in everyday life'.[51] The book's emphasis on the minutiae of daily life fitted snugly into the key Blainey theme that material developments were more important than political ones:

> Some history books suggest that visitors a century ago were surprised the most by Australia's radical politics, particularly the secret ballot and the vote for most men. Visitors were surprised less by the vote than by the meat. That every man could vote was interesting. That nearly every man and woman could eat meat at nearly every meal was astonishing.[52]

The people whose everyday life Blainey described were living in something of a golden age, 'a period of plenty and contentment'.[53] Blainey had already highlighted in *Our Side of the Country* that the late nineteenth century was when Australians began realising how idyllic their lives were. He described the experience of Western District farmer, Thomas Shaw, who returned to Europe after an absence of forty years, a trip which made him realise that, in western Victoria, he was actually living in the 'biblical land of Goshen'.[54] As Manning Clark wrote in his review of that book, some may complain that Blainey did not outline a vision for Victoria, but he was not required to do so. According to Clark, Blainey's attitude to Victoria's past was akin to the one 'God is reported to have taken to his own creation: he found it good'.[55] Clark argued that Blainey's interpretation was 'not very fashionable at the moment when the voice of the compulsory improvers of humanity is again becoming shrill ... but Blainey has come not to praise or blame but to see it all with eyes of still laughter'.[56] For Blainey, contemporary historians' interest in identifying with the excluded was part of a broader malaise, as society moved away from the self-help ethos that produced friendly societies in the late nineteenth century:

---

51 Geoffrey Blainey, interview with Annie Warburton, ABC Radio, 9 October 2003.
52 Blainey, *Black Kettle and Full Moon*, 197.
53 Ibid., 428.
54 Blainey, *Our Side of the Country*, 130.
55 Manning Clark, 'Blainey's book: The touch of the master', *Sun Herald*, 20 May 1984, 112.
56 Ibid.

> In what was once Australia's best known verse, Adam Lindsay Gordon proclaimed that two things stood like stone – 'kindness in another's trouble, courage in your own'. He would be slightly puzzled if he could see the present tendency to blame someone else when trouble crops up.[57]

The period Blainey described in *Black Kettle* was one of rapid social change. For example, there was the rapid uptake of cigarettes:

> The craving for cigarettes ... was to sweep swiftly through Australia. Ned Kelly, hanged in 1880, presumably had never smoked a cigarette, for it was a novelty and also despised as sissy. But little more than a generation later, maybe half of the soldiers who sailed away to Gallipoli smoked nothing else.[58]

And, while he even-handedly treated the merits and downsides of the great Australian drinking institution – the shout – Blainey was more of a partisan when it came to the traditions around the use of tobacco, noting that 'to refuse to lend a knife (to cut tobacco) was almost a declaration of war in an equalitarian society'.[59] Blainey, himself for many years a devotee of the practice, lamented the decline of roll-your-own cigarettes:

> Sadly, that simple, hand-shaped commodity has almost vanished from public life ... There was something gregarious and generous about this custom. 'Could you lend me the makings?' or 'Could you pass me the makings?' asked tens of thousands of Australians of their friends or colleagues each day.[60]

Blainey, a life-long tea-drinker, also related how tea drinking tastes changed rapidly from favouring Chinese tea, to a preference for the product from India and Ceylon. When change was driven by fashion rather than innovation, Blainey wrote with wry amusement that 'in the 1880s during the summer months it became fashionable for the wives of richer men to escape the mainland heat by holidaying for a few weeks in Hobart ... A century later, climatic preferences have turned a somersault, their great-granddaughters fly to Surfers Paradise and lie in the hot sun'.[61]

---

57 Blainey, *This land is all horizons*, 74.
58 Blainey, *Black Kettle and Full Moon*, 326.
59 Ibid., 350–352, 314.
60 Ibid., 326–327.
61 Ibid., 24.

The second half of *Black Kettle*, 'The Black Kettle Sings', can be readily summarised as a description of every aspect of food-related life. The first half, 'Ocean and Moon', is harder to categorise as it covered topics including lighting (household and public), transport, communications, cosmetics, watches, clocks and currency. Across the various topics, the book had three clear messages for its readers. First, there was as much change, and hence historical interest, in periods of the past as in recent years; second, there were good reasons for doing things the way they were done in the past and hence our predecessors' actions should not be subject to ridicule; and, finally, we should not assume that what we perceive as a tradition is in fact a long-standing practice.

Blainey's clear love of the period and this old-style social history makes the comment of historian Robyn Annear in her *Age* review that Blainey was 'struggling to maintain his interest' when writing on some of the topics somewhat bemusing.[62] In contrast, Hirst thought that the book was 'a testament to the bond Blainey has with the people whose lives he has celebrated', a fact also reflected in the lively interaction Blainey had with audience members when he delivered his numerous speeches on these themes.[63] And although there was always a risk that such a work would end up a bit like a country museum where much has been collected, but nothing interpreted, historian George Parsons observed that while every page was 'graced by facts', it was these very facts which gave 'a convincing, sympathetic picture of a lost world, a reconstruction free from anachronism and antiquarianism'.[64]

Blainey emphasised that social historians had to deal with the fact that 'the simple things in daily life are often undocumented' and while 'what was said from the political platform or pulpit was reported every day in the press ... the social rules for each section of society did not have to be reported: nearly everyone knew them'.[65] Blainey cited other historians' work more often than in many of his other works, for instance referring to Graeme Davison's 'masterly study of time', Peter Yule's history of Melbourne's children's hospital, and Beverley Kingston's 'pioneering study of women and domestic work'.[66]

---

62   Robyn Annear, 'A brief history of the commonplace', *The* Age (Review section), 11 October 2003, 5.

63   John Hirst, 'A Headful of Details', *Australian Book Review*, no. 256 (November 2003): 13.

64   George Parsons, review of *Black Kettle*, *Australian Quarterly* 76, no. 4 (July-August 2004), 36.

65   Blainey, *Black Kettle and Full Moon*, 149, 264.

66   Ibid., 167, 228.

A work where Blainey relied less on the work of other recent historians was *Sea of Dangers: Captain Cook and His Rivals* (2008).[67] The idea for this book lay in the early 2000s when Blainey was traveling through Torres Strait on a cruise ship on which he was a guest lecturer. He reflected on what the same experience must have been like for Captain Cook more than two centuries earlier and, on returning home, began reading the journals of both Cook and Joseph Banks. As 'new insights' emerged, Blainey began to see the potential for a book.[68]

This focus on the individual, Cook, meant that *Sea of Dangers* was to be the closest book to a biography since Blainey's work on Essington Lewis was published in the early 1970s. While researching Cook, Blainey found out about a French explorer named Jean de Surville and perceived that the Frenchman could be used as a point of comparison with Cook. Critics were divided on whether the introduction of de Surville into the standard Cook story worked. John Gascoigne suggested that 'bringing the English and French together is a telling way of drawing out the European motives for exploring the South Pacific and their responses to what they saw', but David Day queried Blainey's positioning Cook and de Surville as 'rivals', as 'each was oblivious of the other and their intentions were dissimilar'.[69]

As well as using a contemporary comparator, Blainey also deployed J.C. Beaglehole, whose landmark biography of Cook was published in 1974, as a historiographical foil.[70] Although noting that Beaglehole's work was 'full of careful detail and insights', Blainey commented that 'like many biographers he [Beaglehole] became so close to his subject in spirit and sympathy that he was almost a disciple, and sometimes very reluctant to criticise him'.[71] Blainey created an impression that Beaglehole's work had remained largely unchallenged in the intervening period, whereas there had been numerous works on the topic, many quite critical of Cook. Thus, Gascoigne commented:

> It is largely written in an historiographical vacuum and does not engage with (or even mention) such highly pertinent works as the recent major anthropologically informed biography of Cook by Anne Salmond. The

---

67   Geoffrey Blainey, *Sea of Dangers: Captain Cook and His Rivals* (Melbourne: Penguin Viking, 2008).
68   Ibid., x.
69   John Gascoigne, review of *Sea of Dangers*, *Journal of the Royal Australian Historical Society* 95, no. 2 (November 2009), 215; and David Day, 'Cook's mixed endeavours', *The Age* (A2 section), 8 November 2008, 21.
70   J.C. Beaglehole, *The life of Captain James Cook* (London: A. and C. Black, 1974).
71   Blainey, *Sea of Dangers*, 383.

work is largely pitched at a general audience but would have gained further resonance with greater acknowledgement of the way in which others have attempted to understand Cook.[72]

The blurb on the dust jacket of *Sea of Dangers* referred to Blainey 'challenging accepted views' and there are several places in the text where he explicitly criticised omissions in other narratives. In his description of the day when the crew of the *Endeavour* first began examining the practices of Aboriginal Australians, Blainey observed that 'this Sunday was one of the more eventful days in the history of the world's exploration, though it is not yet regarded as such in the mainstream accounts written on the history of Australia'.[73]

One significant correction to the work of others was to argue that Cook was more culpable than previously recognised for the *Endeavour* almost being shipwrecked on the Great Barrier Reef. Blainey wrote that Cook's 'loyal defenders do not realise that on two previous occasions he had sailed into trouble on moonlit nights' and, failing to learn his lesson, almost irretrievably wrecked his ship.[74] Another aspect of the Cook legend Blainey reconsidered was the degree of credit he deserved for preventing his crew suffering from scurvy. He acknowledged that Cook was much more successful than his contemporaries, but 'he could not yet explain *why* he was successful'.[75]

A major focus of Blainey's account of Cook's voyage up the east coast from Point Hicks to Cape York was the impressions that the Europeans formed of the Indigenous population, and speculation about what the Aborigines may have thought of the Europeans. In trying to capture how the Indigenous population may have felt about this extraordinary visitation upon their traditional lands, Blainey used the skilful device of writing a paragraph made up almost entirely of questions. The reader only had to think about the speculative answers to realise that 'the local inhabitants were entitled to be wary'.[76] Blainey summed up the attempts to establish relations with the words that 'the Aborigines could not enter the mind of the newcomers nor could the newcomers enter the mind of the Aborigines'.[77]

The encounters with the Australian Aborigines were not the only encounters with indigenous populations described in *Sea of Dangers*. In Tahiti, there

---

72 Gascoigne, review of *Sea of Dangers*.
73 Blainey, *Sea of Dangers*, 179–180.
74 Ibid., x.
75 Ibid., 327.
76 Ibid., 192.
77 Ibid., 194.

had been initial difficulties between Cook's men and the locals as 'there was little agreement on trading rules and on punishments for disobeying rules'.[78] Problems of this type were magnified when the crew of the *Endeavour* interacted with Maori, who had no previous experience of the European worldview:

> These tattooed Maori were intent on stealing captivating items. This was not surprising: the Englishmen were intent on stealing fresh water and greens and firewood without making the kind of payment that Banks would have demanded if a party of Dutchmen had crossed the North Sea and landed, uninvited, on his Lincolnshire estate with their axes and water buckets and vegetable baskets.[79]

This analogy was quoted by historian of the Pacific, Claire Brennan, in her review of the book, in which she writes that it provided 'a good introduction to the views of indigenous peoples as recorded by 18th century observers'.[80]

As the 2000s progressed, the history, or culture, wars continued unabated. Mark McKenna has argued that the debate in the 2000s was 'not as personal as the attack on Blainey in the 80s or on Clark in the 90s' had been, instead being 'much more a sustained media offensive on the history profession as a whole'.[81] Of course, the history profession also continued to vigorously respond to its critics. Blainey's name was still invoked but was now more often in the background chapters of the books which were written on the topic, rather than in the frontline.

One sign of a more tolerant, or perhaps resigned, attitude towards Blainey was that when he was chosen as the ABC's annual Boyer Lecturer in 2001, there was little adverse comment from the Left about the choice and certainly none of the controversy and complaints from the Right that had greeted the selection of Manning Clark for the role a quarter of a century earlier.[82]

Blainey chose as his title 'This land is all horizons'. This was an adaptation of a line from the poet Mary Gilmore who had written that 'Europe has its peaks piercing the sky but we have the horizon'.[83] Blainey commented that

---

78   Ibid., 37.
79   Ibid., 94.
80   Claire Brennan, review of *Sea of Dangers*, *Journal of Pacific History* 45, no. 3 (December 2010): 376.
81   McKenna, 'Silence shattered with a whisper to the heart', 15.
82   McKenna, *Eye for Eternity*, 586–587. It should also be noted that by the time Blainey delivered the Lectures in 2001, they had probably lost some of the 'privileged position' which McKenna described them as having in 1976.
83   Blainey, *This land is all horizons*, 15.

'rarely has one sentence said so much about Australia', because the vast open spaces of this nation had, for most of its history since British Settlement, seemed like a major opportunity. However, in recent times, factors such as the lack of jobs created by new mining and agricultural developments, and the absence of perceived defence threats to Australia, had reduced pro-development sentiment. Blainey argued that this made it 'probably the first relatively prosperous period in approximately 150 years in which the majority of Australians do not call for a fast-expanding population'.[84]

Blainey used the lectures to argue that Australia had been a success, particularly because of the basis laid in the nineteenth century. His list of reasons was long – equality of religion, democratic innovation, relaxed social mores, trust, educational opportunity and the enjoyment by the average Australian of close to the highest standard of living in the world. He disputed the common complaint that Australia was 'the land of the philistines', pointing out that this was 'patently untrue of living painters of landscape ... in perhaps no nation of Europe are they so honoured'.[85] Blainey examined a number of paradoxes, such as economic nationalism being stronger in Australia in the heyday of the British Empire than in modern times and that Aboriginal land rights and environmental movements were making Australia more like Europe and less independent by opposing mining developments. Further, if Australia became a republic, any sense of independence thus gained 'will be tiny compared to the autonomy that the Australian government has lost through international agreements it has signed in the last thirty years'.[86]

Taking Blainey's place as the new *bête noire* of the history academy was Keith Windschuttle whose book *The Fabrication of Australian History* generated significant controversy when it was published in 2002. Blainey was asked to review Windschuttle's work in an American journal and, while reading it, 'felt an initial sympathy towards the Australian and overseas historians who were under such intense scrutiny'.[87] However, he found after doing some checking of his own that 'many of their errors, made on crucial matters, beggared belief'. He argued that Windschuttle's book 'offers so many examples of the misuse of the original records that it would require many pages for a reviewer even to summarize the case laid out against the various historians involved'.[88]

---

84   Ibid., 11–12.
85   Ibid., 51.
86   Ibid., 61.
87   Geoffrey Blainey, 'Native fiction', *The New Criterion* 21 (April 2003): 79.
88   Ibid.

Blainey noted that he diverged from Windschuttle's depiction of the indigenous Tasmanians, writing that his view was that 'the original Tasmanians were not as backward, mentally and culturally, as Windschuttle sometimes depicts them ... they were often ingenious as fighters and raiders on their home terrain'. However, he believed that Windschuttle's book 'will ultimately be recognized as one of the most important and devastating written on Australian history in recent decades'. This was a rare occasion when a historical debate in Australia received international attention. A work by a Canadian Professor of History called *A Global History of History* cited Windschuttle's refusal to give weight to Aboriginal oral tradition compared to white documents as an example of how 'history wars' were playing out in many countries.[89]

The Australian front even got its own book on the wars, *The History Wars*, by Stuart Macintyre and Anna Clark. The book tried to straddle twin roles, being both a history of the wars and a defence of one of the competing sides. According to the book's narrative, academic historians were only forced to join in once the wars had 'opened with a series of pre-emptive strikes launched from conservative think tanks and their house journals'.[90] Blainey was clearly the most prominent figure in the book, his index entry being longer than other prominent players such as Manning Clark, John Howard, Robert Manne, Henry Reynolds and Keith Windschuttle.

Macintyre and Clark generally maintained a civil attitude towards Blainey, even while criticising him, something Macintyre attributed to the example of Blainey's friend, Dinny O'Hearn, who would argue with Macintyre, while assuming 'that I would not allow my disagreement to spill over into personal antagonism for such a fine and decent scholar'.[91] Given the authors were attempting to portray the academic historians as the civilised bunch fighting off the attack dogs of the Right, it was perhaps a curious decision to invite Paul Keating to launch *The History Wars*. Keating was in vintage form, targeting his attack on Howard and Blainey:

> I've never understood why the Howards and the Blaineys are so defensive, are so resistant to novelty and to progress. You know, they're more than

---

89   Daniel Woolf, *A Global History of History* (Cambridge: Cambridge University Press, 2011), 501. He mentioned Blainey and the phrase 'Black Armband History'.
90   Macintyre and Clark, *History Wars* (Melbourne: Melbourne University Press, 2003), 11.
91   Ibid., 90.

conservatives, they're reactionaries. At the heart of their wrong-headed campaign is an attempt to contain and censor the human spirit.[92]

When Phillip Adams raised Keating's hyperbolic comments with Blainey on his *Late Night Live* show on ABC Radio, Blainey laughed and commented that it did not worry him in the slightest. He was more interested in establishing whether Keating had described him and Howard as 'piccaninnies' or 'flibberdygibbets'.[93]

In the same year, a book of essays about Blainey, *The Fuss That Never Ended*, was published. This book was the product of a conference held at the State Library of Victoria in November 2000 to discuss Blainey's work. The fact that Blainey agreed to attend and speak at the conference prompted a headline in *The Age* of 'Blainey comes in from the cold'.[94] Yet Blainey clearly remained suspicious about how he might be treated in the book and chose not to provide his conference remarks as a chapter. One critic, Andrew Markus, who was not part of the conference line-up, instead delivered a paper about Blainey to a separate gathering at the University of Melbourne, and this was included as a chapter in the book.

Six of the fourteen chapters assessed Blainey's work through the prism of key interests of the contemporary academy: Aboriginal issues, the environment, gender, British imperialism, labour history, and race. Although a number of these essays made worthwhile points, and some of their criticism was tacitly acknowledged as philosophical difference, the overwhelming impression was that Blainey's was being criticised for his failure to appreciate the centrality of each writer's historical specialty to the telling of the Australian story.

The other eight essays in the book were more nuanced. The three senior historians, Stuart Macintyre, Graeme Davison and Geoffrey Bolton all identified numerous praiseworthy aspects of Blainey's work; Morag Fraser presented a balanced chapter on his career as a controversialist; and, while critical of aspects of his work in the field, Ian Hodges' piece on Blainey's war studies was also a well-rounded contribution. Tom Stannage praised Blainey for always remembering to include sport in his writing of Australian history and also provided a nice little character study of Blainey with two anecdotes,

---

92 'Howard altered nation's moral compass: Keating', *Sydney Morning Herald*, 4 September 2003, 2.
93 Geoffrey Blainey, interview with Phillip Adams, *Late Night Live*, ABC Radio National, 8 October 2003.
94 Gordon, 'Geoffrey Blainey comes in from the cold'.

one of which showed Blainey's lack of pretension and the other his generosity towards those with whom he had professional disagreements.

The twin publications of 2003, *The Fuss That Never Ended* and *The History Wars*, reinforced Blainey's status as Australia's most discussed living historian. As well as his production of new books on Australian topics, Blainey remained in the public eye in other ways. He had a monthly column in the *Herald Sun* for a few years in the 2000s, which he often used to mark historically significant events in the Australian calendar, such as Australia Day or Anzac Day, or to comment on happenings with historical significance such as the discovery of the wreck of the HMAS *Sydney*. He also wrote articles arguing that the drought that Australia was experiencing in the 2000s was not as bad as the Federation drought of a century earlier. In a wrap of the year for the Fairfax broadsheets at the end of 2011 he argued that the current mining boom had not been generated by luck:

> Many observers in the eastern states say it is simply luck, but WA in the last half century also possessed - among other assets - a few political and business leaders who devised policies that boosted the finding and developing of new mineral fields. One odd hallmark of Australia today is widespread ignorance about why mining is currently its most successful industry. A booming China is only one ingredient in the explanation.[95]

Blainey's sustained interest in topics such as mining and other export industries distinguished him from many academic historians. It also meant that he had opportunities to engage with significant business figures, something which academic historians were probably not offered or indeed desired. As one 2012 article about fund managers explained, they 'seek out the opinions of the best business brains to construct portfolios', including getting 'perspectives from people such as Professor Geoffrey Blainey, who speaks of the similarities and differences of the current climate with the Great Depression of his youth'.[96]

Blainey saw many historians writing books and journal articles to reinforce their recognition within the academy as an expert in a particular field. By contrast, his own perception of his broader interaction with the community

---

95 Geoffrey Blainey, 'Turbulent times but journeys to remember', *The Age*, 30–31 December 2011, 16–17 and also published as 'Debt crisis, natural disasters and against the odds, success', *Sydney Morning Herald*, 30 December 2011, 11.

96 Stewart Oldfield, 'DIY investors still need a hand from experts', *The West Australian*, 9 May 2012.

gave him both a different audience for his work, and crucially, a different authority from which to write. This point was made by two academics in 1996, when comparing Blainey to his friend John Mulvaney, saying that while 'Blainey has often sought to give authority to his public statements by claiming to speak for "ordinary Australians", Mulvaney's authority is explicitly disciplinary, institutional and specialized'.[97] Blainey admired the professionalised scholarship of a Mulvaney, but he argued that having a broader perspective could also deliver benefits. Reviewing a new volume of the *Australian Dictionary of Biography* in 2008, he claimed that 'some of the most readable or incisive articles come from contributors who are not historians'.[98]

As he approached the age of eighty, Blainey wrote more book reviews than he had at any time since the 1960s, contributing to Australian newspapers, *Australian Book Review* and *English Historical Review (EHR)*. One book Blainey reviewed for *EHR* was Ged Martin's history of the role of New Zealand in the Federation process, in the process realising that a key determinant in colonies' support for Federation was how prosperous they were: 'the more optimistic Australian economies were wary of federating and the more struggling economies were eager to federate'.[99]

Another book he reviewed for *EHR* was the edited collection on *Australia's History: Themes and Debates*, a book whose best chapters were 'worth reading more than once'.[100] On the other hand, some of the other chapters failed to measure up, partly because they were written by 'the wave of historians who, since the 1970s, have become absorbed in issues such as Aborigines and their plight, immigration and multiculturalism, racism, relations with Asia, national memorials and symbols, or urbanisation – themes about which they tend to think alike'.[101]

One of Blainey's most lively newspaper book reviews was of another work by academic historians, *What's Wrong with Anzac: The Militarisation of Australian*

---

97   Tim Bonyhady and Tom Griffiths, 'The Making of a Public Intellectual' in *Prehistory to Politics: John Mulvaney, the Humanities and the Public Intellectual*, ed. Tim Bonyhady and Tom Griffiths (Melbourne: Melbourne University Press, 1996), 5.

98   Geoffrey Blainey, 'Pick a letter', review of *Australian Dictionary of Biography vol. 17, 1981–1990 A–K*, ed. Diane Langmore, *Australian Book Review*, no. 298, (February 2008): 14.

99   Geoffrey Blainey, review of *Australia, New Zealand and Federation, 1883–1901* by Ged Martin, *English Historical Review* 117, no. 473 (September 2002): 1017.

100   Geoffrey Blainey, review of *Australia's History: Themes and Debates* ed. by Martyn Lyons and Penny Russell, *English Historical Review* 122, no. 496 (April 2007): 576.

101   Ibid., 575.

History.[102] Blainey identified numerous examples where the authors had slanted their writing. One of the most telling was that they almost completely ignored the Second World War, presumably on the basis that it was much harder to argue against Australian participation in it. Having ridiculed those concerned about a potential Japanese threat to Australia between 1904 and 1914, they fell silent when that threat became real in 1942:

> You could read this book and not learn that Japan invaded New Guinea and bombed Darwin. Japan's record in World War II is not really mentioned. Do the authors support Australia's participation in World War II? ... It is unusual to see the RSL being singled out as an enemy of national values, while wartime Japan and Nazi Germany are essentially exempt from criticism.[103]

Blainey argued that the authors simplified Australia's participation in wars, a typical example being Henry Reynolds' assertion that the reason the six colonies fought in the Boer War was because we were 'wreathed in royalist sentimentality'.[104] Blainey cited Craig Wilcox's 2002 study of the Boer War to show that motives were more complex and considered it hard to argue that the war was irrelevant to Australians when so many of them were working in the Transvaal mines that Australian football was being played there. Reynolds claimed similar motives for the First World War but, as Blainey pointed out, Germany was a significant Pacific power and a clear potential threat to Australia.

The authors' main target was the Howard Government, which they argued spent large sums on Anzac-related themes to divert attention from Aboriginal dispossession and frontier massacres. Blainey found this assertion ridiculous, as the amount spent on promoting Anzac was 'far exceeded by expenditure on building, running and publicising the National Museum in Canberra [and] as that is infinitely more a home of Aboriginal history than of military history ... would a government that really wished people to forget Aboriginal history give massive subsidies to a museum so vigorously promoting that same history?'[105]

---

102 Geoffrey Blainey, 'We weren't that dumb', review of *What's Wrong with Anzac? The Militarisation of Australian History* by Marilyn Lake and Henry Reynolds (with Mark McKenna and Joy Damousi), *The Australian* (Literary Review), 7 April 2010, 3–4.
103 Ibid.
104 Ibid.
105 Ibid.

More than a defence of Howard, Blainey's review, like so much of his writing on Australian history, was a defence of previous generations of Australians. He asked rhetorically 'were the Australian people really so dumb in 1914 and in 1939 that they blindly supported their leaders at home and their Empire's leaders abroad, and even at the expense of their own perceived interests?'[106]

Whether Australian children should learn more, or less, about Anzac or Aboriginal dispossession had certainly been an issue for Blainey in the later Howard years. He was chosen by the Howard Government as one of the delegates to the History Summit, which was held in Canberra in August 2006. The History Summit had arisen from Prime Minister Howard's concern that history, particularly Australian history, was not being well-taught in Australian schools and he hoped that a summit might endorse a curriculum more to his liking.

Reading the transcript of the proceedings it is striking that Blainey's main entry into the debate was a practical, rather than policy, one, and it clearly showed the benefit of his committee work from the 1960s to 1980s. He pointed out that something needed to be sorted out by 5pm and proposed the idea of a steering committee to do more work.[107] He was the first to foreshadow a motion:

> This summit affirms the importance of the study of Australian history in schools. Australia's human history is longer than that of most European countries and is in many ways unique. Australia is one of the world's oldest continuous democracies and, moreover, it compels people to vote. A knowledge of our history is therefore vital. Nearly all of the public and parliamentary debates embody an appeal to history. We are convinced that a nationwide revival in the teaching of Australian history is urgently needed and that steps be taken to enlist all states or all relevant authorities in the task.[108]

The idea of a committee was adopted, and the final communiqué incorporated the majority of Blainey's initial draft as the third of twelve dot points. It excluded the words 'human' and 'parliamentary', and deleted the reference

---

106 Ibid.
107 The Australian History Summit: Transcript of Proceedings, 17 August 2006 (Department of Education, Science and Training). Blainey had made one contribution to the morning session, arguing that the study of history in primary school be confined to social history.
108 Ibid.

to compulsory voting, while adding that Australian history should be taught in 'its global, environmental and social contexts'.

However, when the first draft curriculum did not satisfy Howard, he asked Blainey to be a member of a new committee, which became known as the 'Blainey Panel', to review it and develop a further draft for years 9 and 10.[109] This was released in October 2007, but never implemented because of the Howard Government's defeat at the polls the following month. One interesting view Blainey expressed about the efficacy of school education was that one of the biggest changes over the past fifty years had been an improvement in young people's pronunciation and grammar, but he argued that this was caused by the influence of television and films, not schools.[110]

Another role Blainey was given by the Howard Government was as a judge for the Prime Minister's Prize for Australian History. This became the subject of a minor controversy, once again placed by the media in the context of the History Wars, when Howard reportedly insisted on Les Carlyon being added as a joint winner with the judges' choice of Peter Cochrane. Gideon Haigh commented that the final decision to award the prize jointly 'smacked of a PM over-eager to distribute the spoils of victory in the culture wars'.[111] Unusually, this time Blainey was portrayed as being on the side of the professional historian rather than the populist Howard.

Blainey evidently did not hold a grudge as just ten days later, in the wake of Howard's defeat at the polls, he wrote a complimentary political eulogy, praising Howard for promoting the virtues of democracy, giving praise to his opponents, creating jobs, controlling inflation, reforming the tax system, responding to the threat of terrorism and being one of the outstanding debaters in the nation's history.[112] He panned those who criticised Howard for his stands on global warming and Aborigines, describing them as 'moral mountains on which many of his critics like to stand and do nothing'.[113]

---

109 Justine Ferrari, 'History students may skip Gallipoli', *The Australian*, 27 June 2007, 1; Anna Patty, 'PM's lesson: cash for history', *Sydney Morning Herald*, 11 October 2007, 1 and 6; Jewel Topsfield, 'Rudd to scrap Howard's history', *The Age*, 10 January 2008, 1; and Tony Taylor, 'Howard's way fails school test', *The Age*, 14 January 2008, 13.

110 John Masanauskas, 'Thank TV for top talkers', *Herald Sun*, 15 September 2009, 7. The story related to a book launch Blainey did at the Institute of Public Affairs. He had made the point about the standardisation of punctuation and grammar in Blainey, 'A Methodist Childhood', 112.

111 John Lyons, 'Blainey ire over PM's history prize', *The Weekend Australian*, 17–18 November 2007, 1.

112 Geoffrey Blainey, 'From triumph to a tragic', *Herald Sun*, 27 November 2007, 20–21.

113 Ibid.

And while, in the aftermath of losses, defeated leaders look like a 'headless chook', Howard 'will be seen by vast numbers of Australians as one of the great prime ministers'.[114]

The demise of the Howard Government also marked a turning point in the 'History Wars'. While some members of the history academy, such as Bain Attwood, thought the 'History Wars' had already ended in the 'mid 2000s', one of the many big statements of Kevin Rudd's first Prime Ministership was a declaration ending them in 2009.[115] When asked by the media Blainey said he thought most of what Rudd had said comprised 'sensible comments' and that the speech was 'a balanced summary of our past'.[116] Asked if he had been a partisan in the wars Blainey replied:

> I don't comment on the so-called history wars, but I'm said to be a major player. I think the phrase history wars is exaggerated but there's widespread disagreement about the interpretation of Australia's past and we're more likely to reach agreement if we have some of the balance that I think I can see in Mr Rudd's speech. If people who belong to one side are willing to look at the other point of view and even if they disagree with it, listen carefully and likewise the same goes for the other side. It's a matter of listening as much as talking.[117]

Debates about the nation's history continued into the following decade and Blainey continued to contribute to them. In 2017, in the wake of the decisions by some local councillors to no longer recognise Australia Day, and some comments by Indigenous journalist Stan Grant, Blainey wrote an opinion piece for *The Weekend Australian* in which he argued Grant 'had soared into fantasy', in part led astray by 'dubious comments in textbooks and some university lectures'.[118] Blainey acknowledged that he had himself used the

---

114 Ibid.
115 Bain Attwood, 'Historical Controversy and the History Wars in Australia', in *Frontier Skirmishes: Literary and Cultural Debates in Australia after 1992*, eds Russell West-Pavlov and Jennifer Wawrzinek, (Heidelberg: Universitätsverlag Winter, 2010), 37. While acknowledging that it might be too soon to judge the outcome, Attwood was strongly tempted to claim victory in the History Wars. He argued that the impact of the wars had been 'both temporary and superficial' and that 'the new Australian history' continued to dominate films and museums.
116 Geoffrey Blainey, interview on *PM* program, ABC Radio, 27 August 2009.
117 Ibid.
118 Geoffrey Blainey, 'Let's reclaim history rather than distorting it', *The Weekend Australian*, 26–27 August 2017, 15, 19.

term 'invasion' to describe British Settlement, but believed that there was now misunderstanding of the nature of the invasion.

When the memoir of the first forty years of his life, *Before I Forget*, was published in 2019, the 89-year old Blainey did a series of media interviews to promote the work. In these, he was not afraid to discuss controversies in contemporary Australia, such as climate change and free speech. He described the debate around the former as 'the most difficult and interesting intellectual argument of the last 100 years', while disputing that current changes in climate were unique in human history.[119] On the latter topic, he argued that seeing schools, universities and parts of the broader community 'forbidding debate or frowning on debate … is a great deteroration in public life'.[120] He was also keen to stress that he did not see himself as a conservative, asserting that 'I am a radical, I am pro-change'.[121] At the same time, he was also involved in a controversial debate about the treatment of the history of Australian Football, lending his support to a proposal by Geelong Football Club President, Collin Carter, to recognise premierships prior to the formation of the current league in 1897.[122] Most other football historians disagreed with the Carter proposal.

In his seventies and eighties, Blainey also continued to update earlier works of Australian history. A revised edition of *A Shorter History of Australia* included a new final chapter, which summarised his position on his country's story after writing about it for six decades. He began the chapter by asking:

> What makes the history of Australia so distinctive? Two factors or influences – distance and climate – strongly shaped it during the last two centuries and even shaped the earlier Aboriginal history.[123]

And, materialist to the end, he concluded it with the observation:

> If the outback constituted a separate nation, it might well rank as the most deserted of all the world's nations. That simple statistic is a measure of how much the duo of distance and drought still shape the continent.[124]

---

119 Tony Wright, 'Lunch with Geoffrey Blainey', *The Age* (Spectrum section), 6 July 2019, 4–5.
120 Troy Bramston, '"Radical" Blainey adds his life to the story of our past', *The Australian*, 2 July 2019, 12.
121 Wright, 'Lunch with Geoffrey Blainey'.
122 Geoffrey Blainey, 'It's time to fly the flag for football's pioneers', *Herald Sun*, 5 June 2019, 26–27.
123 Geoffrey Blainey, *A Shorter History of Australia* (Sydney: Random House Vintage, revised edn 2009), 295.
124 Ibid., 304.

As with the earlier edition, it failed to gain much recognition from academic historians, for instance, not featuring in a list of 'General histories' recommended for further reading at the end of *The Cambridge History of Australia* (2013).

Blainey continued to refine his positions on various aspects of Australian history, producing a new two-volume work, *The Story of Australia's People*. The first volume, *The Rise and Fall of Ancient Australia*, published in 2015, was an amalgam of much of *Triumph of the Nomads* and *A Land Half Won*, with revisions and some new material added, followed in 2016 by a second volume, *The Rise and Rise of A New Australia*. Its reception showed that the fault lines remained clear. On the one hand it was joint winner of the Prime Minister's Literary Award for Australian History, on the other it was slammed in a critical review by La Trobe University historian Clare Wright for 'a stubborn refusal to engage in the past four decades of scholarship and scientific research'.[125]

However, Blainey's interpretation of Australian history had long ceased to be the only string on his historian's bow. By the time the twenty-first century dawned, Blainey had become a historian of the world.

---

125 Clare Wright, 'A Voice form the past', *The Age* (Spectrum section), 7 January 2017, 20–21.

Chapter 11

WORLD HISTORIAN

A major part of Blainey's historical writing since leaving the academy has been on a global scale, producing histories of the world, the twentieth century and Christianity. However, they were preceded by another global work, which very much had its origins in Blainey's time as an academic and sought to explain why the intellectual environment had changed so much in his 27 years at the University of Melbourne.

As a young academic, Blainey's opinions had often generated lively debate, but they were always accorded a respectable place at the table. By the mid-1980s, his views on some issues had come to be regarded as unacceptable by large swathes of the Australian intelligentsia. The changed attitude to Asian immigration between the eras of Calwell and Hawke was just one example of a broader shift in political, social and intellectual attitudes. Blainey may have been out of step with other intellectuals when he chose Mt Lyell, ahead of Oxford, as his preferred destination in 1951, but this new divide was far more significant.

The first signs of the developing chasm had appeared when Blainey felt 'puzzled by the extent of the opposition' to the Vietnam War.[1] He had attempted to make at least some sense of that puzzlement by writing *The Causes of War*. Yet even after the war ended, the new intellectual environment continued. Not only did students look different, with their long hair and frayed jeans; their views bemused Blainey, who commented that 'the counter-culture became prominent and Nature was spoken of with a veneration I hadn't heard – certainly in my youth...I felt mystified about so many events in the world ... I could not place the opinions'.[2] An example which particularly struck Blainey was hearing students in a tutorial argue that snakes were benign.[3]

---

1 Rodney Cavalier, 'Modern History as Nature v Technology – the Blainey Seesaw', *Australian Financial Review* Magazine, 4 November 1988, 5.

2 Ibid.

3 Diana Bagnall, 'Geoffrey Blainey: Lunch with Diana Bagnall', *The Bulletin*, 18 October 2005, 46.

Blainey felt a need to understand what was happening around him and to put these unusual views into some sort of historical context. Historicising what happened in the late 1960s was not a quick process for Blainey. He explained that it took him 'a long while to pick up the extremes' and to recognise that 'there was a kind of pattern' to how interests and attitudes came in and out of fashion.[4] It was not until two decades after the highpoint of the counter-culture, and after more than a decade of research and thought, that Blainey's explanation of the changed intellectual mood, *The Great Seesaw: A New View of the Western World 1750-2000* (1988) was published.[5]

An important early development in Blainey's thinking on the topic came through writing *Triumph of the Nomads*, which made him consider western attitudes to indigenous populations. In writing this work he was himself part of a shift in attitudes to focusing on the positive aspects of an indigenous population. And Blainey saw this as a positive, for 'if Australian Aboriginals and other simple societies gained from this latest exaggerated tilt of the seesaw, it was a belated justice, because their ancestors a century ago had suffered through the tilting of the seesaw in the opposite direction'.[6] The strength of the tilt was readily apparent in Melbourne academia in the 1970s and 1980s, as historians such as Greg Dening, Donna Merwick, Inga Clendinnen and Rhys Isaac became known as 'the Melbourne School' for their work in trying to tell the stories of groups of Polynesians, African-American slaves and Aztecs, whose history was not recorded in any written account.[7]

Although Blainey had occasionally put this work on hold, it had still taken a lengthy period of research or, as he put it in the opening chapter, an 'absurd' amount of time.[8] He lectured on the topic in both Economic History and History, gradually firming up his thesis, and did significant work on it while at Harvard in 1982. His research had led him to the conclusion that, far from being unique, the intellectual mood swing away from technology and towards nature that he had witnessed in the late 1960s fitted an historical pattern of such shifts, dating back at least two centuries. Similarly, the seesaw sometimes tilted strongly the other way, producing periods of optimism and a widespread belief that the modern world could successfully develop technology to solve problems.

---

4   Cavalier, 'Modern History as Nature v Technology – the Blainey Seesaw'.
5   Geoffrey Blainey, *The Great Seesaw: A New View of the Western World, 1750–2000* (Melbourne: Macmillan, 1988).
6   Ibid., 72.
7   Alison Durant, 'Historian made his own history', *The Age*, 9 November 2010, 19.
8   Cavalier, 'Modern History as Nature v Technology – the Blainey Seesaw', Blainey referred to working on it as early as 1977, see Nicklin, 'Blainey is the new chairman'.

The dramatic changes of the late 1960s, when 'cultural and intellectual life temporarily seemed to lose its sense of direction', were perhaps not as threatening when one realised that they bore a strong resemblance to the romantic movement, which dominated European culture around 1800, or to many of the intellectual trends that strengthened in the 1890s.[9]

Developing his theory and the 'seesaw' metaphor not only helped Blainey make sense of the change in intellectual mood that had taken place in the late 1960s but was also was a culmination of his quest to make the historian as useful a predictor of future events as were the economists and other social scientists. He argued that 'if in the late 1960s the economic forecasters had paid attention to the new cultural mood and to the swing of the seesaw as a whole, they might have predicted the serious economic downturn of the following decade'.[10]

Just as Russian economist Nikolai Kondratieff had identified economic cycles, Blainey saw himself as a pioneer of the study of intellectual and cultural cycles. However, historian George Seddon believed Blainey did himself a 'disservice' with his claims to both 'originality' and 'potency'.[11] On the former, Seddon pointed out that the patterns he described had 'been part of cultural history for many years', including 'in the idea of Classical and Romantic phases; in Nietzsche's "Apollonian" and "Dionysian" in *The Birth of Tragedy*; in Rattray Taylor's Freudian fluctuations in *Sex in History* under the label "patrist" and "metrist"'. Seddon was also unimpressed with the metaphor of the seesaw as a new way of expressing a similar concept to Kondratieff's long waves in economic activity. He argued that by taking a metaphor from a children's playground, instead of using 'the usual wave or pendulum', Blainey had given 'an infantile character to these great swings of mood'.[12]

Whatever metaphor he chose, Blainey had a harder task than Kondratieff, because the concepts which hung off it were less tangible and more subjective. Blainey described his seesaw with 'love of Technology' at one end and 'love of Nature' at the other and, as the seesaw went up and down, each movement was 'in a sense a swing between optimism and pessimism'.[13] Blainey saw himself as occupying a position towards the optimistic, pro-technology end of the seesaw, a point he noted in 'A Final Word on Bias'. However, to

---

9   Blainey, *The Great Seesaw*, 1.
10 Ibid., 3.
11 George Seddon, review of *The Great Seasaw*, *Australian Historical Studies* 24, no. 94 (April 1990): 142.
12 Ibid.
13 Blainey, *The Great Seesaw*, 1–3.

show that his bias was not too pronounced he also added that he saw 'many virtues as well as defects in the so-called savage, backward, primitive or simple societies'.[14] In one interview around the time the book was published, he actually placed himself in the middle of his seesaw, justifying this by saying, 'Well, why not, I made it'.[15]

Earlier in his career, such as in his *Godzone* article in 1967, Blainey was the optimist assailing the pessimists. In 1988, he appeared to still consider himself to be one, even in a period when his public commentary generally was pessimistic, predicting gloomy outcomes for Australia, due to the immigration and economic policies of the Hawke Government.

There were certainly aspects of progress that did not meet with Blainey's approval, for instance, modern architecture which 'for all its merits, expressed much that was hollow and misguided … what was sick as well as what was noble in the age of the machine'.[16] Blainey also recognised the risks that extreme optimism, or over-confidence, posed when the seesaw tilted too far in that way, observing that 'it is a sobering lesson of modern history that some of the most optimistic periods, in their very confidence, sow the seeds of some of the most depressing episodes'.[17] Likewise, Blainey was critical of the 1860s optimism of political economist William Hearn, especially his belief that there would be fertile lands in central Australia, using him to illustrate his argument that 'the tendency to float from fact towards fantasy is common at the extreme angles of the seesaw'.[18]

Even with caveats, Blainey's linking of love of technology with optimism and love of nature with pessimism was never likely to meet with universal agreement. In one of the most revealing passages in the book, Blainey discussed why pessimism was visible in Germany in the late nineteenth century prior to its reaching England. He described how Germany was the home of poetry, philosophy, criticism and theology and thus 'these German fields of excellence, encompassing the spiritual and mental rather than the material conditions of mankind, were more like to harbour pessimism than were engineering, natural history and those rather empirical fields in which Britain led the world'.[19] Yet at least one other historian, the 'agnostic English liberal' Lawrence Stone, had a quite different position, writing that 'at bottom it

---

14   Ibid., 315.
15   Cavalier, "Modern History as Nature v Technology – the Blainey Seesaw".
16   Blainey, *The Great Seesaw*, 44.
17   Ibid., 52.
18   Ibid., 51.
19   Ibid., 101.

seems to come down to whether he takes an optimistic or pessimistic view of human society: optimists stress ideals, pessimists material interests'.[20]

Given the potential for confusion it is not surprising that at the time of the book's publication, even Blainey himself was unsure if he had done the right thing in using optimism and pessimism as key words. Asked about it in an interview, he responded by saying that he thought about using different words and 'if that question is continually raised, it will turn out that my decision has been wrong'.[21] It remains debatable whether the decision was correct, because in some aspects the terms worked well; in others less so.

The link between regard for technology and optimism was clear enough when dealing with issues such as the extent to which resources are finite and the degree to which humans would be able to innovate their way out of problems. Blainey marshalled a strong case that fears of global over-population, famine and mineral shortages have come to the fore in pessimistic periods. The fact that two decades of growth in food production exceeding population growth was the precursor to the dire warnings of the Club of Rome was strong evidence of Blainey's thesis that intellectual mood was more important than new facts. As Blainey observed, 'one is forced to conclude that the pessimists – and the massive audiences which listened to them – were influenced more by the mood of the time than by the evidence from farms and grain silos'.[22] One of these pessimists was Swedish agriculture expert Georg Borgstrom, who in 1969 argued that, due to the excess number of people in the world, there would be worldwide famine by 1984. Blainey noted that 'Professor Borgstrom held that view which tends to become the first commandment whenever the seesaw dips towards pessimism – the idea that the world's main period of inventiveness is over, and that new inventions cannot be expected'.[23]

The sections of the book relating to the economics of, and attitudes towards, mineral discovery were, as one would expect given Blainey's background, argued with authority. Blainey provided an economic history of coal as the lead-in to his chapter on the 1970s oil crisis, relevant because one significant reason why the crisis had such a big impact in the United States was that restrictions had been imposed on the ability to use more coal in lieu of oil.

---

20   Joel Berlatsky, 'Lawrence Stone: Social Science and History' in ed. Walter L. Arnstein, *Recent Historians of Great Britain* (Ames: Iowa State University Press, 1990), 86; and Lawrence Stone, *The Causes of the English Revolution 1529–1642*, (London: Routledge & Kegan Paul, 1972), 40.

21   Cavalier, "Modern History as Nature v Technology – the Blainey Seesaw".

22   Blainey, *The Great Seesaw*, 233.

23   Ibid.

He argued that 'in the early 1970s it was in America's strategic interest to subsidise the mining of more of its own coal but instead, in the interests of the environment, it imposed obstacles against the opening of new coal projects'.[24] Thus, 'the so-called energy crisis, which is usually seen as an economic crisis, was just as much a political crisis', with the political decisions having, in turn, been precipitated by the mood shift away from technology and towards nature.[25] Seddon described the section on the oil shock as 'beautifully balanced analysis', and commented that 'the best of the book and its most original contribution is this ability to put recent economic events in their cultural context'.[26]

While it worked well in areas such as global resources, the two-dimensional nature of Blainey's seesaw metaphor created a danger when applied more broadly. As *Sydney Morning Herald* reviewer and former *Bulletin* editor, Peter Hastings, commented, this 'sort of dichotomy is a useful shorthand guide but, beyond that, is too neat by half … I have known too many espousing some of the values of both classifications'.[27]

In trying to explain intellectual mood swings, Blainey ran the risk of trying to bring too many characteristics together and creating some unlikely bedfellows. Making this more readily apparent was the checklist of fourteen characteristic contrasts between optimists and pessimists provided in the first chapter of the book. Most of these items fitted comfortably into the model he was developing. Hence, optimists liked industrial civilization, new technology, reason, change and competition, and believed that 'the golden age lies in the present and future and not in the past'; on the other hand, pessimists liked nature, simplicity, imagination and stability, and believed that 'the golden age lies in the past and maybe in a far-away, utopian future'.[28]

Some of the categorisation made sense only if one accepted the original dichotomy. For instance, in considering the French Revolution Blainey gave significant weight to the fact that it was inspired by the ideas of Rousseau and supported by those who 'were willing to believe that the overthrow of the present civilisation might restore a lost and innocent world'. Thus, it was pessimistic.[29] Others writing on the topic have taken exactly the opposite

---

24 Ibid., 249.
25 Ibid.
26 Seddon, review of *The Great Seesaw*, 142.
27 Peter Hastings, 'Optimism Blowing Hot and Cold', *Sydney Morning Herald* (Spectrum section), 29 October 1988, 89.
28 Blainey, *The Great Seesaw*, 6.
29 Ibid., 29.

view. Roger Scruton, a conservative British philosopher, categorises Rousseau as an optimist because, by his definition, optimists are those with a utopian view of an alternative society, whereas pessimists accept that the world is imperfect and make the best of it.[30]

Less obvious was the decision to ascribe the work ethic and specialisation to the optimists, while leisure and the all-rounder were put in the pessimists' column.[31] Even more problematic was Blainey's categorization of attitudes to issues such as fashion, sex and climate. Blainey claimed that 'the heyday of progress had been marked by diligence in publicly concealing the female body, so that prudery and progress walked hand in hand'.[32] Yet, while he described slightly more revealing fashions in the pessimistic 1890s, he did not consider many contradictory actions of the era such as increasing restrictions on the use of barmaids.[33]

Blainey's thesis on fashion also struggled when applied to the 1960s, as the revealing mini skirt surely represented the optimistic mood of the early and middle parts of the decade, while long peasant dresses become more fashionable when, later in the decade, the mood changed to nature-loving pessimism. It may also have surprised many to learn that discussion of sex is a sign of pessimism, with Blainey arguing that 'Freud helped to lift that taboo – so strong in the heyday of progress – against the discussing of sex'.[34]

A favourite Blainey topic, climate, featured in a couple of ways. One was a warning to the agricultural optimists who in the 1960s had underplayed 'the erratic role of climate', a trait which was 'the Achilles' heel of the optimists'.[35] Then, there were personal attitudes to climate where 'the growing preference for a warm climate is one of the fascinating changes of recent decades, and also one of the least explained'.[36] Blainey is unusually equivocal about whether this change is tied to the seesaw, or not.[37] Certainly he notes that 'primitive' societies tended to live in warm places. Thus, someone planning a future on a tropical island utopia may have seen themselves as an optimist, but the desire

---

30   Roger Scruton, *The Uses of Pessimism and the dangers of false hope* (London: Atlantic Books 2010).
31   Blainey, *The Great Seesaw*, 262, 294–295. In these references he attacks economists and the education system for too much specialisation.
32   Blainey, *The Great Seesaw*, 109.
33   Ibid.
34   Ibid., 99.
35   Ibid., 231.
36   Ibid., 224.
37   Ibid., 225.

to leave behind the technologically advanced West meant that, according to Blainey, it was an ambition driven by pessimism.

Ultimately, these topics showed what Blainey himself at some points acknowledged, namely that the seesaw was not all-encompassing and 'the dominant school of thought is never held unanimously'.[38] There could be examples such as the Boy Scouts who 'occupied an unusual position, with a foot at both ends of the seesaw, but their concern for nature was an attitude that a mass movement could not have held a generation earlier'.[39] The nature of the seesaw also meant that, despite their radically different economic prescriptions, Adam Smith and Karl Marx shared the same optimistic end of the seesaw. Blainey recognised that this might surprise some readers, explaining that while 'curiously Marx is depicted so often as the historian of misery and the prophet of calamity … his ultimate optimism is easily overlooked'.[40]

As recently as the late 1990s, Blainey wrote that applied science was the 'lode star' of Western Civilisation, continuing the distinction he had made in *The Great Seesaw* where science was placed firmly on the side of civilisation and the optimists, and opposed to the Nature-loving pessimists. He maintained the theme that the increased focus on the environment and Aboriginal issues had seen 'Nature and those believed to be living close to Nature rise in esteem' while, conversely, 'our science-based civilization' had tended to lose some lustre.[41]

Having written supportively of science for much of his career, Blainey now thinks the pendulum has swung too far in its favour. This view came out in an interview he undertook in 2011, when he commented that 'maybe we've reached an unusual stage in the flow of ideas where the science is too much on top'.[42] It was a fascinating change in outlook. When he was younger, Blainey defended the failures of science and technology from what he called 'the great fool theory'; now he felt those failures were too readily forgotten. And while some may see scientists making dire predictions about the potential consequences of global warming as being pessimistic, Blainey suggests that scientists saying that the problem can be solved if action is taken, places them on the optimistic end of the seesaw.

---

38   Ibid., 59.
39   Ibid., 106.
40   Ibid., 41.
41   Blainey, 'Not As the Song of Other Lands', 136.
42   Nick Cater, 'Gadfly Blainey comes to praise Christianity, not to bury it', *The Weekend Australian*, 29–30 October 2011, 18.

In *Seesaw*, Blainey's ability to stimulate the reader with unusual ideas was matched by his acuteness as a social observer. This skill was captured in a paragraph when he discussed how 'democratic, capitalist nations have another in-built mechanism which promotes changes of outlook' including delivery of 'high rewards for novelty'. However, he did not just confine this observation to technology, gadgets and even fashion as others might, but extended it to recognise that 'even in a bookshop, one of the most conservative of institutions, the newest books occupy the window and the front shelves'.[43]

The sheer complexity of the task Blainey had embarked upon could well have seen lesser writers lose the thread entirely, but Blainey marshalled his observations and arguments in a very readable manner. Former NSW Labor Minister, Rodney Cavalier, described how Blainey moved 'effortlessly through the major themes … encountering and explaining the writings of such diverse talents as Marx, Freud, Nietzsche, the French encyclopaedists, Joseph Banks, Malthus, Keynes, Rachel Carson and Jack London to name just a few'.[44]

Blainey made big claims for his thesis, writing that 'if my description of the seesaw of ideas is accepted, then scholars will have to scrutinise again the way in which they explain the rise and fall of many of the attitudes and ideas which, to my mind, move with the seesaw'.[45] In terms of criteria such as securing overseas reviews and sales, *Seesaw* was a failure but if, as Cavalier wrote, its purpose was 'to provoke thought' rather than to secure 'a ready acceptance of his views', it undoubtedly succeeded with those who did read it closely.[46] It also said something very interesting about how Blainey saw the state of historical knowledge by 1988:

> We cannot understand the rise of these unusual moods, whether of pessimism or confidence, without realising that they are linked to an interpretation of history. We feel a need to know the past: if we don't know it we unintentionally make it up. One hallmark of the radical movements of the late 1960s was their weak knowledge of history. Likewise some of the conservative movements of the 1980s shunned history and thought in the booming share market of 1987 that a repetition of the Wall Street Crash of 1929 was virtually impossible.[47]

---

43 Blainey, *The Great Seesaw*, 299.
44 Cavalier, 'Modern History as Nature v Technology – the Blainey Seesaw'.
45 Blainey, *The Great Seesaw*, 7.
46 Cavalier, 'Modern History as Nature v Technology – the Blainey Seesaw'.
47 Blainey, *The Great Seesaw*, 304.

Blainey continued to write history on a global scale, forming the intention early in the 1990s to write a world history. However, it was only later in the decade, when he was more financially secure, that he felt able to devote time to a project driven by his own interest, without a guaranteed monetary return. As things turned out, the decision to write world history proved to be not only intellectually satisfying, but also profitable, as *A Short History of the World* (2000) and *A Short History of the 20th Century* (2005) both sold well.[48] These two works were followed by another book with a global scope, *A Short History of Christianity* (2011).[49]

Blainey's own global outlook had continued to be broadened by his extensive overseas travel. Of course, it is not essential to travel to a country to write about it, as Blainey showed with his article on the Jameson Raid for *The Economic History Review*, but travel was an important factor in nurturing his global vision. For instance, it was Zanzibar which played a part in steering him towards writing *A Short History of Christianity*. Visiting the Anglican cathedral there, Blainey noticed an old organ. He asked if someone could play it and an organist was found who managed, despite the poorly tuned instrument, to do a rendition of 'Onward Christian Soldiers'. Blainey was deeply moved and, as he told a 2011 dinner, the idea of writing a history of Christianity was planted.[50] As his interest in world history grew, Blainey tailored his travel to satisfy his desire to visualise places about which he might wish to write.

Unknowingly, and somewhat ironically, Blainey was following something of a trend of the history academy by pursuing world history in the 1990s. A recent historiographical study observed that 'one marked change since the end of the Cold War has been the increased attention given to world history and global history'.[51] The initial professionalisation of history in Germany in the early nineteenth century had been committed to universal history. However, the methods and procedures that evolved there, particularly under the influence of Leopold von Ranke, led to an increased dependence on archival sources and a tendency to regard any 'attempts at broader transnational or even

---

48 Geoffrey Blainey, *A Short History of the World*, (Melbourne: Viking Penguin, 2000); Geoffrey Blainey, *A Very Short History of the World*, (Melbourne: Viking Penguin, 2004); and Geoffrey Blainey, *A Short History of the 20th Century* (Melbourne: Viking Penguin, 2005).

49 Geoffrey Blainey, *A Short History of Christianity* (Melbourne: Viking Penguin, 2011).

50 Peter Coleman, 'Australian Notes', *The Spectator Australia*, 17–24 December 2011, vi.

51 Georg G. Iggers and Q. Edward Wang with contributions from Supriya Mukherjee, *A Global History of Modern Historiography*, (London: Pearson Education, 2008), 387.

trans-cultural history' as likely 'to violate criteria of rigorous scholarship'.[52] In the 1990s and 2000s, world history became academically acceptable again.

A Short History of the World provided a summary of the factors which Blainey, after fifty years as a historian, considered to be fundamentally important in shaping the past and present. The event to which Blainey gave the greatest weight in his world history was something that happened to humans rather than being done by them. Describing the rising of the seas between 15,000 BC and 8,000 BC, he wrote that 'this was the most extraordinary event in human history during the last 100,000 years – far more influential than the invention of the steam engine, the discovery of bacteria, the landing on the moon and indeed all the combined events of the 20th century'.[53]

The rising of the seas, of course, had particular significance in Blainey's native land, isolating the Aboriginal population from the rest of humanity for millennia, and the prominence he accorded it in his world history provided continuity with Blainey's previous best-sellers, *The Tyranny of Distance* and *Triumph of the Nomads*. Blainey emphasised events which separated, or brought together, different parts of the world. Just as the rising of the seas separated peoples, the European explorers of the fifteenth century brought them back together and thus the voyages of Christopher Columbus and Vasco da Gama 'were amongst the most important events in the history of the world'.[54]

The crucial role of geography in Blainey's account was reflected in his chapter devoted to the 'Amazing Sea', describing the influence of the Mediterranean on the cultures that developed around its shores. He pursued a similar theme in the following chapter when he explored how the geography of the Yellow and Ganges Rivers provided 'the secret of their capacity to support such large populations'.[55] In more modern times Blainey observed that the availability of coal was one of the key factors in determining that the industrial revolution began in north-western Europe rather than elsewhere.[56] More recently, geography, along with technology, determined that the Middle East 'became important again'.[57] Blainey made counter-factual points to emphasise how geography influenced outcomes, including several in a section on sub-Saharan Africa's development, or lack of it, pointing out that 'the history of Europe would have been different if the Danube, Rhine, Rhone and Elbe had also

---

52   Ibid.
53   Blainey, *A Short History of the World*, 31.
54   Ibid., 304.
55   Ibid., 139.
56   Ibid., 535.
57   Ibid., 478.

been interrupted by waterfalls [like the Zambezi, or the rapids on the Zaire and the Congo]'.[58]

Another topic to which Blainey explicitly decided to pay 'special attention' was technology and skills, on the basis that 'they have done so much to shape the world'.[59] This task was made harder by the fact that 'the excitement of these new inventions can hardly be conveyed to present generations whose sense of wonder has been almost saturated by wave after wave of innovations'.[60] Blainey reeled off a long list of significant changes to the human condition that technological advances have delivered; however, he also acknowledged that 'so many of the triumphs of science and technology were skin-deep', observing that 'none of these profound changes altered the human will, human restlessness, the human desire either for freedom or conformity'.[61]

These aspects of the human condition have clearly been influenced by religion, a topic of sufficient importance for Blainey to devote four consecutive chapters in *A Short History of the World* to the rise of 'the three crusading universal religions': Christianity, Islam and Buddhism. Until this point in his career, Blainey had treated religion sparingly. One writer with a religious background, Tom Frame, argued that Blainey's coverage of the role of churches and religion in Australian history had been 'minimal'.[62] Frame praised Blainey greatly for a range of other attributes as a historian, including a 'breathtaking' understanding of politics, economics and technology but lamented that, on the subject of religion, he displayed 'neither a good grounding in theology nor wide reading in the field of Australian church history' making his treatment of the topic 'uncharacteristically superficial'.[63] In this critique, Frame displayed a similar tendency to the specialist labour and feminist historians in *The Fuss That Never Ended*, underling the fact that the generalist can never meet the expectation of a specialist in a particular field that it deserves prominence.

Blainey regarded the fact that all three universal religions arose in a period of little more than a thousand years as significant, describing this period as 'a special phase in human history', confirmed by the fact that no new universal religion has arisen since. Their success 'reflected a transition from the belief that God was predominantly a symbol of fear to a conviction that love was

---

58   Ibid., 459.
59   Ibid., Preface.
60   Ibid., 483.
61   Ibid., 605.
62   Tom Frame, 'Geoffrey Blainey, Religion and the Churches in Australian History', *Lucas: An Evangelical History Review*, nos. 23–24 (December 1997-June 1998): 94
63   Ibid., 99.

divine' and this 'heightened sense of humanity' was a clear driver of their expansion. He also devoted a chapter to the Reformation, with Martin Luther getting one of the most detailed character sketches in the book.[64] It was no coincidence that the Reformation happened when it did. Linking the voyages of discovery, new technology (such as the printing press) and religion, with a touch of the arts thrown in, Blainey argued that 'what happened in the western half of Europe just before 1500 was one of the most remarkable convergences of influential events in the known history of the world to that time'.[65]

Blainey's focus on factors such as geography, climate, technology and religion has led to suggestions that Blainey is a follower of the *Annales* School of history and its concept of the 'longue duree'. World history has a natural appeal to anyone with sympathy towards the *Annales* position and historiographer John Burrow has made the point that its most prominent exponent, Fernand Braudel was 'the most famous later-twentieth-century historian to be drawn towards world history'.[66] One who considered this link was Don Watson who commented that in Blainey's '"materialist conception" there were hints of masters like Fernand Braudel and even Marx, but there was more of a businessman's or a Methodist's regard for utility and commonsense'.[67]

This 'regard for utility' was reflected in his view that some wars have been overemphasised in other histories.[68] After all, many famous wars failed to have much impact on the daily lives of the majority of citizens. For example, the wars of independence in Latin America produced a radical political rearrangement, but 'the languages and religion and many of the social and political institutions of the conquerors largely remained in place'.[69] Consistent with his view of what made explorers important, Blainey emphasised the role of military leaders who achieved trans-continental victories, such as Genghis Khan and Hernan Cortes.[70] Similarly, the Vikings colonising Greenland and reaching Newfoundland was mentioned, but their invasion of Britain was not.

Fellow historian, Gregory Melleuish, criticised *A Short History of the World* for being written in such a way that 'warfare and the state hardly figure in the story'. Melleuish attributed this to Blainey's 'own distaste for militarism'

---

64 Blainey, *A Short History of the World*, 334–338.
65 Ibid., 293.
66 John Burrow, *A History of Histories: Epics, Chronicles, Romances and Inquiries from Herodotus and Thucydides to the Twentieth Century* (London: Allen Lane, 2007), 508.
67 Watson, 'The untamed tyrant'.
68 Blainey, *A Short History of the World*, 537.
69 Ibid., 446.
70 Ibid., 254, 312.

which, for instance, meant 'an inability to understand the militaristic nature of Roman society'.[71] Yet, five years later, when *A Short History of the 20th Century* was published, one American reviewer of the book commented that Blainey addressed 'some major themes with a focus on war and peace'.[72] However, while focusing more on war, Blainey was still keen to show that it was not as unique an event as many others claim:

> When we visit the war cemeteries ... and see the headstones ... we lament the death of so many, most of whom were young. But if we visit a thousand civilian cemeteries and are shown the scattered graves of the young who died in the same period of simple diseases that are now curable, we might equally be shocked. In the course of the 40 years after the outbreak of the First World War those who died of infectious diseases are likely to have far exceeded those who died violently on the battlefields.[73]

Another great twentieth-century killer was the application of communism to agriculture. While Blainey noted that in the Soviet Union in the 1930s 'as many as 10 million people died', and that under Mao's Great Leap Forward, 'in the famine of 1959-61 close to 30 million people are said to have died', it could be argued that he does not provide the detailed analysis that these cataclysmic events demand.[74] Mao's millions of victims are one of a list of tragedies that prompted *Bulletin* book reviewer, Barry Oakley, to dispute Blainey's claim that the second half of the twentieth century was one of most favourable periods in human history.[75]

The absence of war in *A Short History of the World* was replicated by an absence of politics. Blainey was clearly aware that this might be a potential source of criticism, acknowledging in the Preface that 'such influential leaders as Garibaldi, Roosevelt, Churchill and Nasser surely deserve a mention' and putting their absence down to the dilemma of 'how much space to allot to the last 150 years'. One could also add names such as Chiang Kai-Shek, Deng Xiaoping, Ronald Reagan, Mikhail Gorbachev, Nelson Mandela and several others to the list of major twentieth-century absentees. Absentees from

---

71 Gregory Melleuish, 'Blainey, Europe and the World', *Quadrant* 44, no. 12 (December 2000), 30.
72 Grace J Chae, review of *A Short History of the 20th Century*, *Journal of World History* 20, no. 3 (September 2009), 475.
73 Blainey, *A Short History of the 20th Century*, 392.
74 Ibid., 120, 454–455.
75 Barry Oakley, 'Books', *The Bulletin*, 15 November 2005, 69.

earlier millennia include Julius Caesar (mentioned in passing much later in the narrative in relation to the calendar) and Charlemagne.

What made the exclusions of many well-known names more striking was the inclusion of several more obscure ones such as Grijalva, Francisco Pizarro, Hans Lippershey, Anton van Leeuwenhoek, Robert Hooke, Carolus Linnaeus, Thomas Savery, Thomas Newcomen, Alfred Wegener, Albert Schweitzer and Father Damien. Blainey included many of these individuals as part of the 'slow bowling', which he explicitly deployed to temper the pace of his dash through world history. One reviewer observed that 'for some readers, this frequent change in narrative velocity may prove annoying … for others, it may save the day'.[76] The American social historian Raymond Grew was in the latter category, believing that 'well-chosen anecdotes mix with some handsomely written passages to convey a sense of how people lived'.[77] In her *Age* review of *A Short History of the 20th Century*, Morag Fraser described Blainey's 'characteristic technique' of using 'both a panoramic camera and a telephoto lens, so the reader can keep her bearings and miss none of the nitty-gritty'. She continued:

> He gives the historical co-ordinates and then proceeds by idiosyncratic vignette, providing specific and tantalising detail … There is nothing random, for all their variety, about the vignettes. They are all adduced in a pattern that is coherent and cumulative.[78]

Another feature of Blainey's writing was his personal intrusion into the narrative. In *A Short History of the 20th Century*, Blainey continued to make references to his own travels, some stretching back to his 1966 trip which produced the book *Across a Red World*, observing that 'to travel by train across China in summertime in the mid-1960s was to revisit scenes that belonged to the economic life of the Old Testament'.[79] Making a point about the Jewish presence in Singapore, Blainey described a synagogue 'whose lofty pillars, balconies and whirring fans can still be seen in Waterloo Street', noting in the Selected Sources 'Singapore synagogue: visited by author in 1988'.[80]

---

76   W. Warren Wagar, review of, *The A Short History of the World*, *International History Review* 25, no. 1 (March 2003): 119–120.

77   Raymond Grew, 'Expanding Worlds of World History', *Journal of Modern History* 78, no. 4, (December, 2006): 895.

78   Morag Fraser, 'Traversing 100 years of tempest', *The Age* (A2 section), 5 November 2005, 25.

79   Blainey, *A Short History of the 20th Century*, 455.

80   Ibid., 203, 520.

Across these works, he also drew many analogies with contemporary events. In *A Short History of Christianity*, he compared the shock of hearing of the fall of Constantinople in 1453 with the attack on the twin towers in New York in 2001; the arrival of printing with that of the internet; and the conversion of John Henry Newman to Catholicism in 1845 as akin to 'the foremost intellectual in atheism becoming an eloquent pastor of the Assemblies of God'.[81] He even saw similarities between John Bunyan's chief pilgrim and Harry Potter.[82]

The dominant role of war and politics in *A Short History of the 20th Century* made Chapter 25 ('Cities, Sports and Tongues') stand out as one of the few places in the book where Blainey discussed major worldwide themes such as global population growth, mortality rates and movement of peoples from country to cities. He concluded by saying that 'the rise of the huge city, the growing mania for spectator sport, the spread of foreign travel, the dissemination of English as the global language, the shipping of food to famine-stricken lands, and even the status of a pair of jeans in the universal language of dress, all were chapters in the shrinking of the world'.[83] One aspect of this modern homogenised world of which he clearly disapproved was popular music:

> At the same time a few of the new singers were beginning to shun the lessons in taste, morality, diction and grammar that compulsory schooling had once emphasised. The ubiquitous schoolroom, expected in the 19th century to be the saviour of civilisation, was being confronted by a persuasive and sometimes ignorant opponent.[84]

Fraser cited this as an example of how Blainey's outlook is often 'odd and oddly revealing' as he did not explain whether 'new singers' meant rock, jazz or blues, but tolerantly Fraser commented that 'one doesn't go to Blainey for a social history of popular music'.[85] Yet, in *The Great Seesaw*, Blainey had recognised that popular music was significant, writing that 'it is fair to say that in the late 1960s, on the eve of the main turning point in post-war economic

---

81   Blainey, *A Short History of Christianity*, 231, 278, 411.
82   Ibid., 356.
83   Blainey, *A Short History of the 20th Century*, 485.
84   Ibid., 146.
85   Fraser, 'Traversing 100 years of tempest'. Interestingly, in 2016, Blainey made an attempt to include rock music in a historical narrative by listing some well-known bands, along with one very obscure one, in his new book on Australian history (Blainey, *The Story of Australia's People: The Rise and Rise of A New Australia*, 348).

life, the portents of change were more visible in the music charts of the Top Forty than in the latest securities chart from Wall Street'.[86]

Another interesting difference in emphasis between *The Great Seesaw* and *20th Century* was Blainey's treatment of Keynes. In the earlier book, Blainey wrote that 'by playing down the dangers of inflation, Keynes helped give confidence to economic activity but, as the Austrian and Chicago schools of economists warned, inflation would remain a danger'.[87] In the latter, Blainey wrote Depression history as a Keynesian, describing Keynes as 'the Cambridge genius who eventually did so much to strengthen and repackage capitalism' and chided classical economic theory for being 'suspicious of perhaps the wisest solution: for governments to pour money intelligently into the sick economy'.[88] While this book covered Keynes thoroughly, there was no mention of the views of any prominent anti-Keynesian economists, such as Friedrich Hayek or Milton Friedman, or the economic agendas of Ronald Reagan or Margaret Thatcher, as the world moved away from Keynesianism in the 1970s and 1980s.

One odd feature of *The Great Seesaw* was the fact that, although published in 1988, it was given a sub-title which extended its range through to 2000. *A Short History of the 20th Century* had a chapter titled 'The Seesaw Moves' which provided some insights into Blainey's views on what ended up happening in this period. He observed that, in the 1990s, the collapse of communism produced 'a floodlight of optimism'. Comparing it to the end of the First World War, Blainey said that, while the optimism of 1918 was geographically limited and short-lived, 'the ending of the Cold War was almost world-embracing in its optimism'.[89] He noted wryly that it was thought that the world had changed forever with democracy triumphant, the collapse of trade barriers imminent and future wars unlikely. The fact that the internet appeared at the same time added to the optimistic spirit of the age. Blainey thought that this heady mood was just another swing of the seesaw, and that any 'end of history' type conclusion was 'surprising because no triumph in history is likely to be permanent', and events subsequently proved that 'the optimism was premature'.[90]

While *The Great Seesaw* was explicitly about the Western World, an area of dispute between reviewers of *A Short History of the World* was whether Blainey

---

86 Blainey, *The Great Seesaw*, 174.
87 Ibid., 164.
88 Blainey, *A Short History of the 20th Century*, 184–185.
89 Ibid., 459–460.
90 Ibid.

had written a Eurocentric work. World historian, David Christian, then based at Macquarie University, found Blainey's work 'often strikingly Eurocentric'; Stuart Macintyre disagreed, suggesting that in trying to avoid Eurocentrism, Blainey might have gone too far in the other direction. He cited the fact that 'in Blainey's history Western Europe remains a backward extremity of the Euro-Asian landmass until we are one-third of the way into the book ... [which] probably underplays the potency of the expansionist Frankist kingdoms that existed in the early part of the second millennium'.[91] Perhaps the different views can be partly explained by whether being Eurocentric relates to the amount of European content, or whether it means looking at history through Western eyes. If the former, then Blainey has managed to balance European with non-European content; if the latter, there are certainly numerous occasions where Blainey relates events in other regions to their Western equivalents.[92]

In *A Short History of the World*, Blainey defended certain peoples against allegations of backwardness compared to the West. He defended Native Americans from allegations of backwardness for not inventing the wheel, using similar arguments to the ones in *Triumph of the Nomads* where he had tried to provide an antidote to Western triumphalism about the economic standard of living of pre-colonisation Aboriginal Australians. In the case of the Native Americans he pointed out that since they had neither horses nor bullocks, there would have been no point in inventing a wheeled cart, and the fact that llamas could carry significant weights compensated for the absence of the wheel in the Andes.[93]

In *A Short History of Christianity*, Blainey accused European scholars of missing the fact that at the same time religious observance had declined in Europe the Pentecostal movement had gained adherents rapidly in Latin America and Africa.[94] Indeed, the Christian church became so strong in the Third World that by the end of the twentieth century 'the typical Anglican worshipper would be a 24-year-old African woman living south of the Sahara'.[95] In contrast, *A Short History of the 20th Century* has a greater focus

---

91 David Christian, 'It's a Small World', *Sydney Morning Herald* (Spectrum section), 4 November 2000, 5; and Stuart Macintyre, 'Of Train Tracks and the Rise and Fall of Empires', *The Age* (Extra section), 7 October 2000, 11.

92 For instance, he compared the scale of the Taiping Rebellion to the American Civil War, the 8th century smallpox epidemic in Japan to the Black Death and says that the empire of the Incas made the empires of Spain and Portugal seem small.

93 Blainey, *A Short History of the World*, 87, 310, 320.

94 Blainey, *A Short History of Christianity*, 525.

95 Ibid., 537–538.

on the West, with regions such as Latin America barely being mentioned. Perhaps the clearest manifestation of Eurocentricity in the work came when the narrative reached the Communist takeover of China in 1949. To that stage, China had scarcely been discussed, so Blainey had to provide a crash course in the history of China in the first half of the century to explain how this situation had eventuated.

More problematic in Blainey's world histories is the number of references to Australia. Some matters, such as the isolation of the Aboriginal population from the rest of humanity and the early rise of the sporting spectator, are clearly of world significance. However, the overall degree of attention to Australia becomes particularly notable in the *Very Short History of the World* edition, where most of the Australian references are retained, while other countries lose some of theirs.[96] Thus, Australia took up one column of the index, the same as the United States and Britain and only exceeded by China.

Given the author's profile in Australia, compared to overseas, the book's initial market was always going to be Australia, so targeting Australian readers at least made commercial sense. The publisher, Penguin, also sought to encourage sales amongst as wide an element of the book-buying public as possible by including the word 'Short' in the title, not a term one would normally associate with a 160,000-word book.

Gradually, the work was taken up by overseas publishers. This was helped by the production of the shorter version, slightly more than half the length of the original, which was cheaper to translate. This strategy worked, and the book has been translated into a variety of other languages, including Spanish, Italian and Turkish. The Portuguese language version proved to be a hit in Brazil after its 2007 release, ending up spending 140 weeks on the Brazilian non-fiction best seller list.[97]

While writing a more detailed history of the twentieth century was a logical sequel to Blainey's world history, his history of Christianity was a less obvious choice of topic. Zanzibar had sown the seed, but the attacks on New York and Washington by Islamic extremists in September 2001, and the debates about religion and civilisation which followed, stimulated Blainey's curiosity. As he explained on ABC radio, 'I did it out of curiosity; a large proportion of what I write is to satisfy me first because I am curious and I want to know'.[98]

---

96   Geoffrey Blainey, *A Very Short History of the World*, (Melbourne: Viking Penguin, 2004).
97   Cater, 'Gadfly Blainey comes to praise Christianity, not to bury it'.
98   Geoffrey Blainey interview on *Sunday Night with John Cleary*, ABC Local Radio, 11 December 2011.

The al-Qaeda attacks made him question whether Western Civilisation was worth defending and, if so, why. Believing that Christianity was the single most important element in that civilisation Blainey decided to become more educated in its history and, being Blainey, to write a book about it.[99]

Given Blainey's parsonage upbringing, it might seem strange that Blainey felt the need to become better educated about Christianity. Yet Blainey's Methodist childhood seemed to have less direct influence on his work as a historian than did the upbringing in vicarages of other Australian historians, most notably Manning Clark. It is striking how little Blainey has commented on his own religious beliefs or how rarely, in stark contrast to Clark, he made religious allusions in his writing. However, Blainey did not doubt the importance of knowledge of the topic, having made the point at the History Summit in 2006 that knowledge of religion needed to be resurrected as it explained much about society.[100]

One thing which struck Blainey, as he tried to educate himself on the topic, was how inaccessible existing histories of Christianity were for the general reader. Looking at the general histories of Christianity in libraries, he discovered that most such works were written for specialists. So Blainey saw a gap in the market and became determined to fill it with a work that could be read without a glossary of religious terms.[101] He was keen to ensure that his work considered on-the-ground social practice as much as theological ideas, writing that it should 'not simply encompass the lives of those who became known for preaching new doctrines' but rather focus on 'the everyday life of the people who practised – or neglected – their religion'.[102]

His focus on everyday life meant he was wary of commentators who asserted that modern Catholics' blatant disregard for papal decrees on birth control was unprecedented, arguing that 'we know far too little about the daily life and beliefs of ordinary Christians during the last 2,000 years' to make such claims.[103] An example of what Blainey was attempting was his discussion of Gothic cathedrals, in which he noted that one practical result of building

---

99   Coleman, 'Australian Notes'.
100 The Australian History Summit: Transcript of Proceedings, 17 August 2006.
101 Blainey, *Sunday Night with John Cleary*. Other histories of Christianity were being published around the same time, including Robert Bruce Mullin's *A Short World History of Christianity* (2008) and Diarmaid MacCulloch's *Christianity: The First Three Thousand Years* (2009), the latter in particular being regarded as both scholarly and accessible to a broad readership.
102 Blainey, *A Short History of Christianity*, 423.
103 Ibid., 512–513.

such grand cathedrals in medieval times was that 'the standard of living of many families had to be sacrificed' before, in typical Blainey fashion, he also provided a detailed description of the development of new methods of making the stained glass which adorned them.[104] He came into his own when discussing nineteenth-century social history, explaining how the Seventh Day Adventists created the modern western breakfast, when December replaced May as the busiest shopping month, and why the fact that the majority of people worked long hours in generally physical jobs reinforced the religious rationale for a day of complete rest on the Sabbath.[105]

Turning the idea of a history of Christianity into the reality of a book proved far harder than Blainey expected. He worked on it, as his main task, for two and a half years, at one stage thinking he would conclude at 1800, until receiving advice from a cricket-writing friend that he should continue to the current day, as 'you've got to know the score'.[106] As in a number of other recent works, Blainey gave particular credit in the Acknowledgements to 'John Day (of Wangaratta)' who he commented 'has an eye for sentences and arguments that don't stand up to inspection'.[107] This was also a work for which his wife Ann had been of significant assistance, as the possessor of 'a detailed knowledge of theology'.[108]

Blainey's histories of the world and Christianity both attracted criticism for similar reasons from members of the academy in Australia. David Christian alleged that in *A Short History of the World*, Blainey had 'not engaged seriously enough with recent writing on world history' and claimed that he seemed 'uninterested in many of the historiographical issues that concern contemporary world history'.[109] In relation to *A Short History of Christianity* Monash University's Constant Mews wrote that Blainey was 'not concerned to trouble the reader with recent historiographical discussions about how the history of Christianity has been and can be framed'.[110]

In contrast, literary critic Peter Craven enjoyed reading a work that was 'so unencumbered by cant and fashion and all the tangled nets of methodology

---

104 Ibid., 171.
105 Ibid., 413–423.
106 Geoffrey Blainey, talk at Melbourne Writers' Festival, Federation Sqaure, 31 August 2012.
107 Blainey, *A Short History of Christianity*, 555.
108 Ibid., 556.
109 Christian, 'It's a small world'.
110 Constant Mews, 'A historian rises again', *The Age* (Life & Style section), 26 November 2011, 27.

that beset the professional historian of religion'.[111] While Mews detected that Blainey's work was 'Methodist in sympathy', Craven was struck by 'how much Blainey's Christianity breathes the spirit of ecumenism', a position endorsed by Roy Williams who commented that 'perhaps the book's best feature is its ecumenism'.[112] Liberal Catholic Frank Brennan 'was surprised at how uplifting' he found it and 'took delight in the variety of expressions of Christian faith'.[113]

As well as accusing Blainey of applying 'a familiar mediaeval trope' to Muhammad, which was 'not only wrong but morally irresponsible, as they will be used to perpetuate naive stereotypes by those who seek authority for their prejudice', Mews argued that Blainey displayed 'a neo-Enlightenment lack of sympathy for the monastic vision'.[114] Christian claimed that Blainey was 'evolutionist' and 'diffusionist', terms which no doubt had many *Sydney Morning Herald* readers scurrying off to reference books to try to find out what the problem was. To many, the term evolutionist was the counterpoint to creationist and hence a progressive concept; clearly to some in the academy it now had conservative overtones, and in Christian's case, there was a sense of surprise, even shock, that an educated person such as Blainey used 'metaphors of social evolution, apparently quite unselfconsciously'. Christian continued:

> Its models of historical processes ... are surprisingly old-fashioned. This does not mean they are wrong of course. But the historian who adopts models and assumptions abandoned by many other historians is surely obliged to alert readers to what is going on and to justify such an eccentric approach.[115]

The fact that Mews could use 'neo-enlightenment' and Christian use 'social evolution' as critical terms illustrated just how far some academic historians had moved from earlier ways of thinking about history. The fact that the historical method of Australia's highest profile historian could be described as 'eccentric' by a fellow historian indicated just how great the divide between Blainey and the academy had become.

---

111   Peter Craven, 'True believer', *The Weekend Australian* (Review section), 3 December 2011, 26–27.
112   Roy Williams, 'What hath God wrought?', *The Spectator Australia*, 17 December 2011, xii–xiii.
113   Frank Brennan, 'John XXIII's half century challenge', *Eureka Street*, 26 March 2012.
114   Mews, 'A historian rises again'.
115   Christian, 'It's a Small World'.

The concept of 'big history', which Christian and others were promoting, should have appealed to Blainey, but the difficulty was that the academic historians saw it as another specialty. And, according to Blainey, specialisation was ruining history:

> In many countries (the United States possibly offers more exceptions) most historians continue to teach, year after year, their own narrowish specialities. It is usually left to the puzzled undergraduate to fit together the dozen pieces of the jigsaw presented during the three or four years of lectures and seminars, and to fill in the huge historical gaps not touched, or barely hinted at. Physics, chemistry and geology would not dream of teaching their own fields of knowledge in this totally fragmented way, and History some day will take notice.[116]

It was a neat summation of why Blainey felt that his approach to acquiring and disseminating knowledge did not belong within the history academy. While most professional historians might be focused tightly on their specialist areas, Blainey in his seventh decade as a historian, was still as keen as ever to learn about the world around him and to make sense of it by writing its history.[117]

---

[116] Geoffrey Blainey, review of *A Brief History of the Human Race* by Michael Cook, *English Historical Review* 120, no. 488 (September 2005): 1068.

[117] At the age of 88 he read Yuval Noah Harari's *Sapiens: A Brief History of Humankind* and found the author 'wary – perhaps unduly so – about the world's future'. Quoted in Stephen Romei 'Books of the Year', *The Weekend Australian* (Review section), 22–23 December 2018, 14–16.

CONCLUSION

In the years since 1984, Geoffrey Blainey's contribution as one of the most significant public figures in post-war Australia has continued to be recognised with numerous appointments and awards, including the Australian Government's highest honour, an AC, and selection as a Living National Treasure. The University of Melbourne, which many saw as rejecting him in the late 1980s, awarded him an honorary Doctor of Laws in 2007 and its Tucker Medal for 'outstanding academic achievement' in the Arts Faculty in 2013. Internationally too, he has been feted with honours, such as an *Encyclopaedia Britannica* gold medal for excellence in the dissemination of knowledge.

However, despite this recognition of the contribution Blainey has made, both before and after 1984, there is no doubt that the Asian immigration controversy of that year both altered Blainey's attitudes to many of his fellow historians, and fundamentally changed perceptions of Blainey. The events of 1984 entrenched him as a 'conservative historian' and ensured that in the following decades his writing has largely been seen through that prism by friend and foe alike.

In one sense, the controversy was as much an illumination of changes which had already occurred as it was the trigger for further change. By 1984, Blainey was no longer the optimistic liberal who in 1967 had criticised the more pessimistic 'Godzone' contributors in *Meanjin*. As many aspects of the cultural revolution of the late 1960s left him bemused and his worries about the decline in Australia's economic fortunes in the 1970s grew, Blainey had become more pessimistic about the ability of Australians to adapt to radical alterations in the demography and economy of the nation. This pessimism, combined with the desire generated by his time in the Commerce faculty to use history to make predictions, meant that Blainey was more likely to predict future gloom from government immigration policies than he would have been earlier in his career.

Alongside the alteration in Blainey's outlook, there had been even more significant developments in the history profession and the broader intellectual and cultural environment between the late 1960s and the 1980s. This was highlighted by the fact that whereas Blainey's writing on pre-colonial Aboriginal society in *Triumph of the Nomads* was generally seen in 1975 as progressive, a decade later it was more commonly regarded as regressive.

The history academy had not necessarily become more left-wing than it had been early in Blainey's career, but whereas he was able to co-habit with many older and contemporary members of the Left, he struggled to do so with the younger generations of historians. A key reason was that the former tended to be more interested in economics than the latter, demonstrated by the fact that younger historians closely examined every word Blainey spoke on immigration, Aboriginal affairs or national identity, but rarely commented on anything he said about the nation's economy, a topic on which his opinions were just as provocative.

By overlooking Blainey's economic views, most historians seemed to miss the fact that he was often a conservative critic of the evolving bipartisan liberal consensus in Australia. As the academic historians did not prioritise placing these changes in their historical context, the best-known historical interpretations of Australia's economic development in the quarter century from 1983 to 2007 have been written by journalists such as Paul Kelly and George Megalogenis.

The fact that Blainey has again been successful as a freelance historian since he left the university has meant that he has felt little need to engage with academic historians. Consequently, his view of the academy has at times appeared to be stuck in 1989, unaware of the variety of historiographical turns which have taken place in his absence. If that is considered a weakness in Blainey's work, it has been balanced by having in his second freelance period, a broad range of interactions with many people across diverse parts of the community, including many parts of the business community, just as he had gained that broader perspective when he chose the path of heading to Queenstown as a twenty-one-year old in 1951.

This enjoyment of the company of practical types is one of many examples of continuity in Blainey's career. Another is his constant and prolific output of work across the past six decades. He has given thousands of lectures and talks, written hundreds of articles and reviews, penned dozens of forewords, served on numerous committees and written forty books, which have collectively sold over one million copies, a significantly higher number than other famous Australian historians such as Hancock, Clark or Reynolds. The fact that Blainey has on average written one book every eighteen months for over sixty years, while doing so many other things, is a testament to his industry. Somewhat like the miners and engineers whose company he has kept, he has got on with the job, rather than spending too much time reflecting on the inner lives of historical figures or himself.

Another constant has been Blainey's quality as a wordsmith, in particular his ability to create evocative phrases, best illustrated by his coining the phrase 'the tyranny of distance'. Reviewers who have been critical of Blainey's historical method and conclusions have almost invariably praised the quality of his writing.

Even more striking than the quantity and eloquence of Blainey's output is the range of topics he has covered: mining, local, business, economic, social, sporting, national and world history. Indeed, citizens of Camberwell in eastern Melbourne are surely in the unique situation of having had the same historian write their local, provincial, national and world history, with the histories of their favourite sport and dominant religion thrown in for good measure. Blainey was an early writer of social history, describing how the average citizen actually lived and worked, recognising the importance of sport, and placing a significantly reduced emphasis on political history in comparison to many of his contemporaries.

If Blainey's home ground was the social and technological history of Australian mining fields, he certainly had no fear about playing away games, being prepared to tackle almost any topic that took his interest, and indeed to attack other historians who only stuck to their specialties. In his most ambitious ventures, *The Causes of War* and *The Great Seesaw*, he was able to produce well-researched and thought-provoking books, even if both works contained arguments which did not persuade all readers.

The key message in *The Great Seesaw* was that those pushing ideas were often just slaves to fashion. In Blainey's perspective, ideas ebb and flow but factors like geography, climate and technological change are the real drivers of history. This reflects a common aspect of Blainey's work, across a variety of genres, that economic and material interests are paramount. In pre-colonisation Aboriginal history what was important was not the Dreamtime but the practical issue of how Aboriginals fed themselves in a seemingly harsh environment. In the history of Christianity, his interest was as much about how Christians lived their daily lives as the intricacies of theology. Similarly, Blainey thought the growth of democratic features in Australian society was important in the latter nineteenth century, but noted that what observers found truly remarkable was that everyone in that society ate meat. Material factors, not political ideology, were the major contributors to Eureka and the Jameson Raid.

This focus on material conditions is something that, in historiographical terms, might place Blainey nearer to Marxism, or at least the *Annales* school, than to what most consider to be conservative historiography. Yet, partly because of the focus of most contemporary academic historians on identity rather than the economy, and partly because of his own political views, Blainey has been accorded the 'conservative historian' label. As noted in the Introduction, there is no school of 'conservative historians' and, even if there were, it is hard to imagine that Blainey could be part of it, or any other school for that matter. His range of interests, historical method and writing style are all highly distinctive. His approach to history has not been imitated by any particular historian, nor has it produced any disciples.

Throughout his career, Blainey's approach to writing history has been clear, constant, and driven by a strong self-belief. He has retained the insatiable curiosity he exhibited as a teenager reading old newspapers in the State Library. And reflecting his practical outlook on life, he has for more than six decades been able to earn a living by sharing what he has learnt with as wide an audience as possible.

SELECT BIBLIOGRAPHY

Archives

Geoffrey Blainey Papers, National Library of Australia, MS 9225.
Geoffrey Blainey Papers, University of Melbourne Archives, Acc Nos. 75/38, 77/3, 80/17, 80/66, 81/9 and 89/145.
S.C. Blainey Papers, State Library of Victoria, MS 9889.
Max Crawford Papers, University of Melbourne Archives, Acc No. 1991.0113.
History Department Papers, University of Melbourne Archives, Acc No. 100/59.

Newspapers and magazines

Adelaide Advertiser, 1955
The Age, 1955-2019
The Argus, 1947
The Australian, 1973-2019
Australian Business Monthly, 1992-1994
Australian Financial Review, 1969-2000
The Bulletin, 1963-2005
Business Review Weekly, 1990
Burnie Advocate, 1953
Canberra Times, 1972-2012
Christian Science Monitor, 1983
Courier-Mail, 1984-1986
The Economist, 1976
Farrago, 1949-1984
The Guardian, 1975
The Herald (Melbourne), 1975-1985
Herald Sun, 1999-2019
Hobart Mercury, 1953
Independent Monthly, 1993-1996
IPA Review, 1988-1994
Lion: The Wesley College Community Magazine, 2010
Look & Listen, 1984
National Times, 1973-1985
Nation Review, 1974-1975
The Spectator Australia, 2011
Sun Herald, 1984
The Sunday Age, 1991-1996
The Sun News Pictorial, 1984
Sydney Morning Herald, 1955-2011
Times Literary Supplement, 1968-1969
Tribune, 1976
The Standard (Warrnambool), 1984-2008

The Weekend Australian, 1984-2017
University of Melbourne Gazette, 1955
West Australian, 1955-2012
Women's Weekly, 1975

Works by Geoffrey Blainey

(In order of publication.)

Books

The Peaks of Lyell (Melbourne: Melbourne University Press, 1954).
The University of Melbourne: A Centenary Portrait (Melbourne: Melbourne University Press, 1956). Arranged and illustrated by Norman H Oliver, narrative by Geoffrey Blainey.
Johns and Waygood Limited: one hundred years, 1856-1956 (Melbourne: Johns and Waygood, 1956).
Centenary History of University of Melbourne (Melbourne: Melbourne University Press, 1957).
Gold and Paper: A history of the National Bank of Australasia Limited (Melbourne: Georgian House, 1958).
Mines in the Spinifex: The Story of Mt Isa Mines (Sydney: Angus and Robertson, 1960).
The Rush That Never Ended: A History of Australian Mining (Melbourne: Melbourne University Press, 1963).
A History of Camberwell (Brisbane: Jacaranda Press, 1964).
The Tyranny of Distance: How Distance Shaped Australia's History (Melbourne: Sun Books, 1966 and Sydney: Pan Macmillan, 2001).
[with S.E.K. Hulme & James Morrissey], *Wesley College: The First Hundred Years* (Melbourne: Wesley College in association with Robertson & Mullens, 1967).
The Rise of Broken Hill (Melbourne: Macmillan, 1968).
Across a Red World (Melbourne: Macmillan, 1968).
The Steel Master: A Life of Essington Lewis (Melbourne: Macmillan, 1971).
The Causes of War (London: Macmillan, 1973).
Triumph of the Nomads: A History of Ancient Australia (South Melbourne, Macmillan, 1975).
A Land Half Won (Melbourne: Sun Books, 1980).
The Blainey View (Sydney: Australian Broadcasting Corporation and Melbourne: Macmillan, 1982).
Our Side of the Country: The Story of Victoria (Sydney: Methuen Haynes, 1984).
A History of Victoria (Melbourne: Cambridge University Press, 2006 and 2013).
All for Australia (Sydney: Methuen Haynes, 1984).
The Great Seesaw: A New View of the Western World, (Melbourne: Macmillan, 1988).
A Game of Our Own: The Origins of Australian Football (Melbourne: Information Australia, 1990 and Melbourne: Black Inc., 2003 and 2010).
Odd Fellows: a history of IOOF Australia (Sydney: Allen & Unwin, 1991).
Eye on Australia: Speeches and essays of Geoffrey Blainey, (Melbourne: Schwartz Books, 1991).
The Golden Mile, (Sydney: Allen & Unwin, 1993).
Jumping Over the Wheel, (Sydney: Allen & Unwin, 1993).
A Shorter History of Australia, (Sydney: Random House Vintage, 1994 and 2009).

White Gold: The Story of Alcoa of Australia (Sydney: Allen & Unwin, 1997).
A History of the AMP 1848-1998 (Sydney: Allen & Unwin, 1999).
In Our Time: The Issues and the People of Our Century (Melbourne: Information Australia, 1999).
A Short History of the World, (Melbourne: Viking Penguin, 2000).
A Very Short History of the World, (Melbourne: Viking Penguin, 2004).
This land is all horizons: Australian fears and visions (Sydney: ABC Books, 2001).
Black Kettle and Full Moon: Daily Life in a Vanished Australia (Melbourne: Penguin Viking, 2003).
A Short History of the 20th Century (Melbourne: Viking Penguin, 2005).
Sea of Dangers: Captain Cook and His Rivals (Melbourne: Penguin Viking, 2008).
A Short History of Christianity (Melbourne: Penguin Viking, 2011).
The Story of Australia's People: The Rise and Fall of Ancient Australia (Melbourne, Penguin Viking 2015).
The Story of Australia's People: The Rise and Rise of a New Australia (Melbourne, Penguiin Viking, 2016).
Geoffrey Blainey, *Before I Forget: An Early Memoir* (Melbourne: Hamish Hamilton, 2019).

Chapters in books, journal articles and reviews, and papers

'The Role of Economic Interests in Australian Federation: A Reply to Professor R.S. Parker', *Historical Studies Australia and New Zealand*, vol. 4 no. 15 (November 1950): 224–237.
'History of Victoria', in *Introducing Victoria*, ed. G.W. Leeper (Melbourne: Australian and New Zealand Association for the Advancement of Science and Melbourne University Press, 1955), 1–18.
'Biographical Study', in Sir Samuel Wadham, *Selected Addresses* (Melbourne: Melbourne University Press, 1956), 1–16.
'Gold and Governors', *Historical Studies Australia and New Zealand* 9, no. 36 (May 1961): 337–350.
'Abe Lincoln and Ben Chifley', *Australian Book Review* 1, no. 1 (November 1961): 8.
'Wanted: Publisher's Reader', *Australian Book Review* 1, no. 7 (June 1962): 98.
Review of *Australia and New Zealand Bank: The Bank of Australasia and the Union Bank of Australia Limited 1828–1951* by S.J. Butlin, *The Business History Review* 37, no. 3 (Autumn 1963): 300–302.
Review of *Visions and Profits: Studies in the Business Career of Thomas Sutcliffe Mort* by Alan Barnard, *The Australian Journal of Politics and History* 9, no. 2 (November 1963): 271–272.
'Lost Causes of the Jameson Raid', *The Economic History Review* 18, no. 2 (August 1965): 350–366.
'Problems of Interpretation (II)', *The Victorian Historical Magazine* 37, nos. 2 and 3 (May and August, 1966): 123–132.
'Brian Fitzpatrick (1906–1965) and His Works', *Business Archives and History* 6, no. 1 (February 1966): 77–81.
'Godzone: 7. The New Australia: A Legend of the Lake', *Meanjin Quarterly* 26, no. 4 (December 1967): 364–380.
'A Reply: I Came, I Shaw ...', *Historical Studies: Australia and New Zealand* 13, no. 50 (April 1968): 204–206.
'Mining – and Undermining', *Economic Record* 44 (December 1968): 470–479.
'Government Patronage and Literature', *Overland* no. 57 (Summer 1973–1974): 37–43.

'Foreword', in Robert Lacour-Gayet, *A Concise History of Australia* (Melbourne: Penguin, 1976), ix–x.
'The Politics of Big Business: A History' (paper presented at the annual lecture of the Academy of the Social Sciences in Australia, Canberra, 2 November 1976).
'Antidotes for History', in *Historical Disciplines and Culture in Australasia*, ed. John A Moses (Brisbane: University of Queensland Press, 1979), 82–100.
'Interstate Rivalries – a Historian's View' (paper delivered as the 1981 Alfred Deakin Lecture, Melbourne University Liberal Club, 23 September 1981).
'Towards Today', *Hemisphere* 27, no. 2 (September–October 1982): 98–99.
'Foreword', in *Memories of Melbourne University: Undergraduate Life in the Years Since 1917*, ed. Hume Dow (Melbourne: Hutchinson, 1983), vii–ix.
'Our Relations With China: A Backward and Forward Glance', *The Australian Journal of Chinese Affairs*, no. 11 (January 1984): 99–104.
'Geoffrey Blainey', in R.M. Crawford, Manning Clark and Geoffrey Blainey, *Making History* (Melbourne: McPhee Gribble; Fitzroy: Penguin, 1985), 69–81.
'Australia: A Bird's Eye View', *Daedalus* 114, no. 1 (Winter 1985): 1–27.
'This Country Is Too Good to Ruin' (address to Australia Day Luncheon, Melbourne, 24 January 1986).
'Australian Universities: Some Fashions and Faults', *Conversazione*, 7–9 October 1988.
'Sounding an Alarm Bell for Australia's Foreign Debt' (address to the Debt Summit, Melbourne, 1 March 1990).
'The Manning Clark School of History', *Scripsi* 6, no. 2 (August 1990): 61–65.
'The Quality of Life in Australia' (paper presented as the inaugural Jennings Group Lecture, Melbourne, 24 October 1990 and included in Blainey, *Eye on Australia*, 270).
'Reflections on the Current State of the Nation' (paper presented as the 1991 Sir Robert Menzies Lecture, Monash University Liberal Club, Melbourne, 28 November 1991).
'Drawing up a Balance Sheet of Our History' (Latham Lecture, 28 April 1993 and reproduced in *Quadrant* 37, no. 7–8 (July–August 1993), 10–15 and was also included as 'The Black Armband View of History', in *In Our Times*, 3–14).
'Not As the Song of Other Lands', in *Approaching Australia: Papers from the Harvard Australian Studies Symposium*, eds Harold Bolitho and Chris Wallace-Crabb (Cambridge Mass: Harvard University Press, 1997), 129–137.
'A Methodist Childhood', *Proceedings of the Uniting Church Historical Society Synod* 6, no. 2 (December 1999): 110–118.
'Some Thoughts on 200 Years: The Jews in Australia', in *The Australian Jewish Experience: A Colloquium. Papers presented on 26 August 1997 to honour Rabbi Dr John S. Levi*, ed. Malcolm J. Turnbull (Melbourne, 1998).
'A Black Arm-Band for Australia's 20th Century?' (paper presented at the 12th Conference of the Samuel Griffith Society, Sydney, 10–12 November 2000).
'A Genius to the Fingertips', in *Henry Lawson*, ed. Geoffrey Blainey (Melbourne: Text Publishing, 2002), vii–xxxii.
Review of *Australia, New Zealand and Federation, 1883–1901* by Ged Martin, *English Historical Review* 117, no. 473 (September 2002): 1016–1017.
'Native Fiction', *The New Criterion* 21 (April 2003): 79.
'Laughing Jackass or Kookaburra', in *The Multicultural Experiment*, ed. Leonie Kramer (Sydney: Macleay Press, 2003), 9–24.
Review of *A Brief History of the Human Race* by Michael Cook, *English Historical Review* 120, no. 488 (September 2005): 1068–1069.

Review of *Australia's History: Themes and Debates* by Martyn Lyons and Penny Russell, *English Historical Review* 122, no. 496 (April 2007): 575–576.

'A Key to Australia's Economic Distance Dilemma', *CEDA Growth* no. 58 (July 2007): 6–9.

'"Tasmania, Tasmania!" The Birth of a Book', *Tasmanian Historical Studies* vol. 13, 2008: 3–13. (Based on a paper delivered at the Centre of Tasmanian Historical Studies conference entitled 'Enterprise and Livelihood in the Tasmanian Past', October 2007.)

'Pick a Letter', review of *Australian Dictionary of Biography Vol. 17, 1981–1990 A–K*, ed. Diane Langmore, *Australian Book Review* no. 298 (February 2008), 14.

'Diminishing Returns', review of *Castles, Battles & Bombs: How Economics Explains Military History* by Jurgen Brauer and Herbert van Tuyll, *Australian Book Review* no. 303 (July–August 2008): 35–36.

'Writing Australian History: A Few Reflections' (paper presented as Stephen Murray Smith Lecture, State Library of Victoria, 5 November 2008).

Works by others

Books

Alexander, Fred, *Moving Frontiers: An American Theme and its Application to Australian History* (Melbourne: Melbourne University Press, 1947).

Atkinson, Alan, *The Europeans in Australia 1: The Beginnings* (Melbourne: Oxford University Press, 1997).

Attwood, Bain, *Telling the Truth About Aboriginal History* (Sydney: Allen & Unwin, 2005).

Beaglehole, J.C., *The Life of Captain James Cook* (London: A. and C. Black, 1974).

Blainey, Hilda, *Hilda Blainey's Story* (compiled by Judy Parker, unpublished, 2006).

Blainey, S.C., *A Pastor Recalls* (unpublished, 1975).

Bolton, Geoffrey, *The Oxford History of Australia Volume 5, The Middle Way 1942–1995* (Melbourne: Oxford University Press, 2nd edn 1996).

Burrow, John, *A History of Histories: Epics, Chronicles, Romances and Inquiries from Herodotus and Thucydides to the Twentieth Century* (London: Allen Lane, 2007).

Calwell, Arthur, *Be Just and Fear Not* (Melbourne: Lloyd O'Neil, 1972).

Cashman, Greg and Leonard C. Robinson, *An Introduction to the Causes of War: Patterns of Interstate Conflict from World War One to Iraq* (Washington: Rowman & Littlefield, 2007).

Davenport, Rodney and Christopher Saunders, *South Africa: A Modern History* (Basingstoke: Macmillan, 5th edn, 2000).

Davies, Susan, ed., *Dear Kathleen, Dear Manning: The Correspondence of Manning Clark and Kathleen Fitzpatrick 1949–1990* (Melbourne: Melbourne University Press, 1996).

Davison, Graeme, *The Use and Abuse of Australian History* (Sydney: Allen & Unwin, 2000).

Davison, Graeme, John Hirst and Stuart Macintyre, eds, with the assistance of H. Doyle and K. Torney, *The Oxford Companion to Australian History* (Melbourne: Oxford University Press, 1998, 2001).

Day, David, *Claiming a Continent: A New History of Australia* (Sydney: Harper Perennial, 1996).

Denoon, Donald with Balam Nyeko and the advice of J.B. Webster, *Southern Africa since 1800* (London: Longman, 1972, 1984).

Gare, Deborah, Geoffrey Bolton, Stuart Macintyre and Tom Stannage, eds, *The Fuss That Never Ended: The Life and Work of Geoffrey Blainey* (Melbourne: Melbourne University Press, 2003).
Eastwood, J.J. and F.B. Smith, eds, *Historical Studies: Selected Articles* (Melbourne: Melbourne University Press, 1964).
Fitzpatrick, Sheila, *My Father's Daughter: Memories of an Australian Childhood* (Melbourne: Melbourne University Press, 2010).
Frost, Alan, *Botany Bay: The Real Story* (Melbourne: Black Inc., 2011).
Frost, Alan, *The First Fleet: The Real Story* (Melbourne: Black Inc., 2011).
Gaita, Raimond, *A Common Humanity: Thinking About Love & Truth & Justice* (Melbourne: Text Publishing, 1999).
Hancock, W.K., *Country and Calling* (London: Faber & Faber, 1954).
Henderson, Gerard, *Australian Answers* (Sydney: Random House Australia, 1990).
Howson, Peter, *The Howson Diaries: The Life of Politics* (Melbourne: Viking Press, 1984).
Hughes, Robert, *The Fatal Shore: A History of the Transportation of Convicts to Australia 1787–1868* (London: Collins Harvill, 1987).
Humphreys, R.A. and R.S. Ward, *Religious Bodies in Australia: A Comprehensive Guide* (Melbourne: New Melbourne Press, 1995).
Iggers, Georg G. and Q. Edward Wang with contributions from Supriya Mukherjee, *A Global History of Modern Historiography* (London: Pearson Education, 2008).
Kelly, Paul, *The End of Certainty: The Story of the 1980s* (Sydney: Allen & Unwin, 1992).
Kerr, Colin, *Archie: The Biography of Sir Archibald Grenfell Price* (Melbourne: Macmillan, 1983).
London, H.I., *Non-White Immigration and the 'White Australia' Policy* (Sydney: Sydney University Press, 1970).
Macaulay, Anne, *Geoffrey Blainey: A Bibliography* (Melbourne: Monash University Library, 1985).
Macintyre, Stuart and Anna Clark, *The History Wars* (Melbourne: Melbourne University Press, 2003).
Stuart Macintyre and Sheila Fitzpatrick, eds, *Against the Grain: Brian Fitzpatrick and Manning Clark in Australian History and Politics* (Melbourne: Melbourne University Press 2007).
Markus, Andrew and M.C. Ricklefs, eds, *Surrender Australia? Essays in the Study and Uses of History: Geoffrey Blainey and Asian Immigration* (Sydney: Allen & Unwin, 1985).
McCalman, Janet, *Journeyings: The Biography of a Middle-Class Generation 1920–1990* (Melbourne: Melbourne University Press, 1993).
McKenna, Mark, *An Eye for Eternity: The Life of Manning Clark* (Melbourne: Miegunyah Press, Melbourne University Publishing, 2011).
McQueen, Humphrey, *Suspect History* (Adelaide: Wakefield Press, 1997).
Martin, Ged, ed., *The Founding of Australia: The Argument about Australia's Origins* (Sydney: Hale & Iremonger, 1978).
Megalogenis, George, *The Longest Decade* (Melbourne: Scribe, 2006).
Moore, Robert, *Faces of the Eighties: Interviews by Robert Moore* (Sydney: Australian Broadcasting Commission, 1980).
Moses, John, ed., *Historical Disciplines and Culture in Australasia* (Brisbane: University of Queensland Press 1979).
Moses, John, ed., *Historical Disciplines in Australasia: Themes Problems and Debates*, Australian Journal of Politics and History 41, Special Issue (1995).
Mulvaney, John, *Digging up a Past* (Sydney: UNSW Press, 2011).

Nelson, Keith L. and Spencer C. Olin, *Why War? Ideology, Theory and History* (Berkeley: University of California Press, 1979).
Parnaby, Owen, *Queen's College, University of Melbourne: A Centenary History* (Melbourne: Melbourne University Press, 1990).
Pascoe, Rob, *The Manufacture of Australian History* (Melbourne: Oxford University Press, 1979).
Popkin, Jeremy D., *History, Historians & Autobiography* (Chicago: University of Chicago Press, 2005).
Poynter, John and Carolyn Rasmussen, *A Place Apart: The University of Melbourne: Decades of Change* (Melbourne: Melbourne University Press, 1996).
Russell, Roslyn, ed., *Ever Manning: Selected Letters of Manning Clark 1938–1991* (Sydney: Allen & Unwin, 2008).
Scott, Ernest, *A History of the University of Melbourne* (Melbourne: Melbourne University Press, 1936).
Scruton, Roger, *The Uses of Pessimism and the Dangers of False Hope* (London: Atlantic Books 2010).
Selleck, R.J.W., *The Shop: The University of Melbourne 1850–1939* (Melbourne: Melbourne University Press, 2003).
Shapcott, Thomas, *The Literature Board: A Brief History* (Brisbane: University of Queensland Press, 1988).
Stone, Lawrence, *The Causes of the English Revolution 1529–1642* (London: Routledge & Kegan Paul, 1972).
Terrill, Ross, *The Australians: The Way We Live Now* (Sydney: Doubleday, 2000).
Thompson, John, *The Patrician and the Bloke: Geoffrey Serle and the Making of Australian History* (Canberra: Pandanus Books, 2006).
Thompson, Lindsay, *I Remember* (Melbourne: Hyland House, 1989).
Turnbull, Malcolm, *Fighting For the Republic* (Melbourne: Hardie Grant Books, 1999).
Whitlam, Gough, *The Whitlam Government 1972–1975* (Melbourne: Viking Penguin, 1985).
Winks, Robin W., ed., *The Historiography of the British Empire-Commonwealth: Trends, Interpretations and Resources* (Durham: Duke University Press, 1966).
Woolf, Daniel, *A Global History of History* (Cambridge: Cambridge University Press, 2011).

Chapters in books, journal articles and reviews, and papers

Attwood, Bain, 'Mabo, Australia and the End of History', in *In the Age of Mabo: History, Aborigines and Australia*, ed. Bain Attwood (Sydney: Allen & Unwin, 1996), 100–116.
Attwood, Bain, 'Historical Controversy and the History Wars in Australia', in *Frontier Skirmishes: Literary and Cultural Debates in Australia after 1992*, eds Russell West-Pavlov and Jennifer Wawrzinek (Heidelberg: Universitätsverlag Winter, 2010), 33–44.
Aveling, Marian, 'The History Debate: A False Dichotomy', *Arena* no. 75 (1986): 150–157.
Barnard, Alan, review of *The Rush That Never Ended*, *Business Archives and History* 4, no. 1 (February 1964): 85–87.
Bastin, John, 'Federation and Western Australia: A Contribution to the Parker-Blainey Discussion', *Historical Studies Australia and New Zealand* 5, no. 17 (November 1951): 47–58.
Bateson, Charles, 'Wrecked – and Far from Home', *Australian Book Review* 6, no. 2 (December 1966–January 1967): 22.

Beddie, Brian, 'The Cause of War', *Quadrant* 17, no. 5–6 (September–December 1973): 61–65.

Beggs-Sunter, Anne, 'Contested Memories of Eureka: Museum Interpretations of the Eureka Stockade', *Labour History* no. 85 (November 2003), 29–45.

Berlatsky, Joel, 'Lawrence Stone: Social Science and History', in ed. Walter L. Arnstein, *Recent Historians of Great Britain* (Ames: Iowa State University Press, 1990), 75–100.

Berndt, Ronald M., review of *Triumph of the Nomads*, *Historical Studies* 17, no. 69 (October 1977): 530–533.

Bolton, G.C., review of *The Rush That Never Ended*, *Historical Studies Australia and New Zealand* 11, no. 42 (April 1964): 279–281.

Bolton, G.C., 'The Hollow Conqueror: Flax and the Foundation of Australia', *Australian Economic History Review* 8, no. 1 (March 1968): 3–16.

Bolton, Geoffrey, 'Geoffrey Blainey', in *Encyclopaedia of Historians and Historical Writing*, vol. 1, ed. Kelly Boyd (Chicago: Fitzroy Dearborn, 1999): 93–94.

Bolton, Geoffrey, 'The Tyranny of Distance Revisited', in *The Fuss That Never Ended: The Life and Work of Geoffrey Blainey*, eds Deborah Gare et al. (Melbourne: Melbourne University Press, 2003): 28–38.

Bolton, Geoffrey, 'The Problem of History' (paper presented as the inaugural Kenneth Binns Lecture, National Library of Australia, Canberra, 29 April – 1 May 2005).

Bongiorno, Frank, 'Australian Labour History: Contexts, Trends and Influences', *Labour History* no. 100 (May 2011): 1–18.

Bonyhady, Tim and Tom Griffiths, 'The Making of a Public Intellectual', in *Prehistory to Politics: John Mulvaney, the Humanities and the Public Intellectual*, eds Tim Bonyhady and Tom Griffiths (Melbourne: Melbourne University Press, 1996), 1–19.

Bourke, Paul, 'Making Professional History', *Australian Historical Studies* 23, no. 91 (October 1988): 193–201.

Brennan, Claire, review of *Sea of Dangers*, *The Journal of Pacific History* 45, no. 3 (December 2010): 376.

Brown, Philip L., 'Victoria's Golden Decade', *Meanjin Quarterly* 22, no. 4 (December 1963): 429–433.

Buckley, Vincent, 'Intellectuals', in *Australian Civilization*, ed. Peter Coleman (Melbourne: Cheshire, 1962), 89–104.

Burley, K.H., review of *The Rush That Never Ended*, *The Economic History Review* (2nd series) 17, no. 1 (August 1964): 184–185.

Cathcart, Michael, 'A Brisk Tour through Australian History', *Australian Book Review* no. 167 (December 1994–January 1995): 23–24.

Chae, Grace J., review of *A Short History of the 20th Century*, *Journal of World History* 20, no. 3 (September 2009): 475–478.

Coleman, Peter, 'Introduction: The New Australia', in *Australian Civilization*, ed. Peter Coleman (Melbourne: Cheshire, 1962), 1–11.

Corris, Peter, review of *Triumph of the Nomads*, *Historical Studies* 17, no. 69 (October 1977): 533–535.

Costigan, Michael, 'My Decade at the Literature Board', *Southerly* 56, no. 2 (Winter 1996): 148–156.

Dallas, K.M., review of *The Peaks of Lyell*, *Historical Studies* 7 no. 25 (November 1955): 101–102.

Davison, Graeme, 'Unemployment, Race and Public Opinion: Reflections on the Asian Immigration Controversy of 1888', in *Surrender Australia? Essays in the Study and Uses of History: Geoffrey Blainey and Asian Immigration*, eds Andrew Markus and Merle Ricklefs (Sydney: George Allen & Unwin, 1985), 101–111.

Davison, Graeme, 'Blainey, Geoffrey Norman (1930–)', in *The Oxford Companion to Australian History*, eds Graeme Davison, John. Hirst and Stuart Macintyre with the assistance of H. Doyle and K. Torney (Melbourne: Oxford University Press, 1998, 2001), 74–76.

Davison, Graeme, 'Half a Determinist', in *The Fuss That Never Ended: The Life and Work of Geoffrey Blainey*, eds Deborah Gare et al. (Melbourne: Melbourne University Press, 2003), 15–27.

Denoon, D.J.N., '"Capitalist Influence" and the Transvaal Government during the Crown Colony Period, 1900–1906', *The Historical Journal* 11, no. 2 (1968): 301–331.

Devine, Frank, 'A Conversation with Geoffrey Blainey', *Quadrant* 50, no. 10 (October 2006): 48–52.

Editorial, 'The Blainey Debate: Editorial Comment', *Arena* no. 73 (1985): 80–81.

Fisher, John, 'History Master', *Quadrant* 44, no. 4 (April 2000): 58–60.

Fitzhardinge, L.F., 'Writings on Australian History, 1955', *Historical Studies Australia and New Zealand* vol. 7, no. 26 (May 1956): 222.

Fox, Charlie, 'My Lord the Workingman?', in *The Fuss That Never Ended: The Life and Work of Geoffrey Blainey*, eds Deborah Gare et al. (Melbourne: Melbourne University Press, 2003), 136–147.

Frame, Tom, 'Geoffrey Blainey, Religion and the Churches in Australian History', *Lucas: An Evangelical History Review* nos. 23–24 (December 1997–June 1998): 83–109.

Gare, Deborah, 'White Ghost of Empire?', *Quadrant* 43, no. 12 (December 1999): 38–42.

Gascoigne, John, review of *Sea of Dangers*, *Journal of the Royal Australian Historical Society* 95, no. 2 (November 2009): 215.

Ginswick, J., review of *The Peaks of Lyell*, *Bulletin of the Business Archives Council of Australia* 1, no. 1 (May 1956): 30–33.

Goodman, David, '"There is no-one to whom I can talk" – Norman Harper and American History in Australia', *Australasian Journal of American Studies* 23 (2004): 5–20.

Grew, Raymond, 'Expanding Worlds of World History', *Journal of Modern History* 78, no. 4 (December, 2006): 878–898.

Griffiths, Tom, 'Light Green, Dark Green', in *The Fuss That Never Ended: The Life and Work of Geoffrey Blainey*, eds Deborah Gare et al. (Melbourne, Melbourne University Press, 2003), 53–66.

Hiatt, L. R., 'Dreamtime Archaeology', *Quadrant* 20, no. 3 (March 1976): 53–55.

Hirst, J.B., review of *Our Side of the Country* in *Royal Australian Historical Society Journal* 71, no. 3 (1985): 229.

Hirst, John, 'Distance in Australia – Was It a Tyrant?', *Historical Studies* 16, no. 64 (April 1975): 435–447.

Hirst, John, 'A Headful of Details', *Australian Book Review* no. 256 (November 2003): 13.

Hodges, Ian, 'From the Frontier to the Gulf', in *The Fuss That Never Ended: The Life and Work of Geoffrey Blainey*, eds Deborah Gare et al. (Melbourne: Melbourne University Press, 2003), 114–124.

Inglis, Ken, 'The Melbourne School of History: Memories and Reflections', in *The Fuss That Never Ended: The Life and Work of Geoffrey Blainey*, eds Deborah Gare et al. (Melbourne: Melbourne University Press, 2003), 157–172.

Jordan, Tim, 'Migration: History and Politics', *Arena* no. 73 (1985): 81–94.

Jupp, James, 'Blainey, Fashionable Old-Fashioned Historian', *Australian Book Review* no. 70 (May 1985): 12–14.

Katz, Elaine N., 'Outcrop and Deep Level Mining in South Africa before the Anglo–Boer War: Re-examining the Blainey Thesis', *The Economic History Review* (2nd series) 48, no. 2 (May 1995): 304–328.

Kennedy, D.E., 'Review Articles: The Causes of War', *Historical Studies* 16, no. 62 (April 1974): 109–111.

Kerley, William, review of *Triumph of the Nomads*, *Journal of Australian Studies* no. 1 (June 1977): 93–94.

Kingston, Beverley, review of *Suspect History: Manning Clark and the Future of Australia's Past* by Humphrey McQueen, *Australian Journal of Politics and History* 43, no. 3 (1997): 449.

Kingston, Beverley, review of *A Shorter History of Australia*, *Australian Historical Studies* 28, no. 108 (April 1997): 196–197.

La Nauze, J.A., 'The Study of Australian History', *Historical Studies Australia and New Zealand* 9, no. 33 (November 1959): 1–11.

Macintyre, Stuart, 'The Making of a School', in *Making History*, eds R.M. Crawford, Manning Clark and Geoffrey Blainey (Melbourne: Penguin, 1985), 3–33.

Macintyre, Stuart, 'Settlement', in *Oxford Companion to Australian History*, eds Graeme Davison, John Hirst and Stuart Macintyre (Melbourne: Oxford University Press, 1998, 2001), 586.

Macintyre, Stuart, 'Blainey and the Australian Historical Profession', in *The Fuss That Never Ended: The Life and Work of Geoffrey Blainey*, eds Gare et al. (Melbourne: Melbourne University Press, 2003), 1–14.

Macintyre, Stuart, 'Geoffrey Bolton: A Lifetime in History', in *A Historian for All Seasons: Essays for Geoffrey Bolton*, eds Stuart Macintyre, Lenore Layman and Jenny Gregory (Clayton: Monash University Publishing, 2017), 1–39.

Macintyre, Stuart, 'Going down from Melbourne: Oxford, Scholarship and Journalism', paper delivered at 'Ken Inglis in History: A Laconic Collloquium', at Monash University, 24–25 November 2016.

Macintyre, Stuart and Fay Anderson, 'History in the Headlines', in *The Life of the Past: The Discipline of History at the University of Melbourne, 1855–2005*, eds Fay Anderson and Stuart Macintyre (Melbourne: RMIT Publishing, 2006), 355–376.

Markus, Andrew and M.C. Ricklefs, 'Introduction', in *Surrender Australia? Essays in the Study and Uses of History: Geoffrey Blainey and Asian Immigration*, eds Andrew Markus and M.C. Ricklefs (Sydney: George Allen & Unwin, 1985).

McAllister, Ian, 'Immigration, Bipartisanship and Public Opinion', in *The Politics of Australian Immigration*, eds James Jupp and Marie Kabala (Canberra: Australian Government Publishing Service, 1993), 161–180.

McCalman, Janet, 'Community Spirit', review of *A History of Camberwell*, *Australian Book Review* 29 (April 1981): 16–17.

McCarty, J.W., 'Prospectors and Planters', *Overland* 29 (April 1964): 56–57.

McCulloch, Samuel Clyde, review of *Tyranny of Distance*, *American Historical Review* 5, no. 74 (June 1969): 1692–1693.

Manne, Robert, 'The Blainey Affair: All for Australia?', *Quadrant* 29, no. 3 (March 1985): 18–21.

Melleuish, Gregory, 'Blainey, Europe and the World', *Quadrant* 44, no. 12 (December 2000): 28–32.

Mendelsohn, Richard, 'Blainey and the Jameson Raid: The Debate Renewed', *Journal of Southern African Studies* 6, no. 2 (April 1980): 157–170.

Merritt, John, review of *A Land Half Won* in *Victorian Historical Journal* 52, no. 3 (August 1981): 199–201.

Mol, Hans, 'Nonconformists', in *The Australian People: An Encyclopedia of the Nation, Its People and Their Origins*, ed. James Jupp (Cambridge: Cambridge University Press, 2001), 325–328.

Morris, Barry, 'Making Histories/Living Histories' *Social Analysis* no. 27 (April 1990): 83–92.
Mulvaney, John, 'The Melbourne School of History: Memories and Reflections', in *The Fuss That Never Ended: The Life and Work of Geoffrey Blainey*, eds Deborah Gare et al. (Melbourne: Melbourne University Press, 2003), 157–172.
Murray-Smith, Stephen, 'Paydirt in Plenty', review of *The Rush That Never Ended*, *Australian Book Review* 2, no. 12 (October 1963): 194.
Murray-Smith, Stephen, 'Swag', *Overland* no. 58 (Winter 1974): 36–38.
Parker, R.S., 'Some Comments on the Role of the Economic Interests in Australian Federation', *Historical Studies Australia and New Zealand* 4, no. 15 (November 1950): 238–240.
Parsons, George, review of *Black Kettle*, *Australian Quarterly* 76, no. 4 (July–August 2004): 36.
Phillips, Mark Salber, 'Distance and Historical Representation', *History Workshop Journal* no. 57 (Spring 2004): 123–141.
Phillips, Mark Salber, 'On the Advantage and Disadvantage of Sentimental History for Life', *History Workshop Journal* no. 65 (Spring 2008): 49–64.
Porter, Kenneth Wiggins, review of *The Peaks of Lyell*, *Business History Review* (December 1955): 371.
Poynter, John, 'The Melbourne School of History: Memories and Reflections', in *The Fuss That Never Ended: The Life and Work of Geoffrey Blainey*, eds Deborah Gare et al. (Melbourne: Melbourne University Press, 2003), 157–172.
Poynter, John, 'Wot Larks To Be Aboard: The History Department 1937–1971', in *The Life of the Past: The Discipline of History at the University of Melbourne 1855–2005*, eds Fay Anderson and Stuart Macintyre (Melbourne: RMIT Publishing and Department of History, University of Melbourne, 2006), 39–91.
Reynolds, Henry, 'Blainey and Aboriginal History', in *Surrender Australia? Essays in the Study and Uses of History: Geoffrey Blainey and Asian Immigration*, eds Andrew Markus and M.C. Ricklefs (Sydney: George Allen & Unwin, 1985), 82–89.
Rickard, John, 'In Dialogue with the Environment', *Australian Book Review*, no. 28 (March 1981): 44.
Rimmer, Gordon, review of *The Tyranny of Distance*, *Australian Economic History Review* 7, no. 2 (September 1967): 194–196.
Roe, Michael, 'Challenges to Australian Identity and Esteem in Recent Historical Writing', (paper delivered as 1977 Eldershaw Memorial Lecture), published in *Tasmanian Historical Research Association Papers and Proceedings* 25, no. 1 (March 1978): 2–13.
Rowse, Tim, 'Triumph of the Colonists', in *The Fuss That Never Ended: The Life and Work of Geoffrey Blainey*, eds Deborah Gare et al. (Melbourne: Melbourne University Press, 2003), 39–52.
Ryan, Peter, 'Apologies', *Quadrant* 44, no. 3 (March 2000): 87–88.
Salmond, John, 'Adapting to Change: The History Department, 1970–2004', in *The Life of the Past: The Discipline of History at the University of Melbourne, 1855–2005*, eds Fay Anderson and Stuart Macintyre (Melbourne: RMIT Publishing, 2006), 93–126.
Sayers, Stuart, 'Australian Historiography: A Layman's View', *Victorian Historical Journal* 48 (1977): 281–294.
Schedvin, C.B., review of *Mines in the Spinifex*, *Business Archives and History* 2, no. 1 (February 1962): 81–86.
Schedvin, C.B., 'Midas and the Merino: A Perspective on Australian Economic Historiography', *The Economic History* Review 32 no. 4 (November 1979): 542–556.

Schultze, Peter, 'North Mount Lyell Disaster – a Miscarriage of Justice', *Journal of Australasian Mining History* 9 (September 2011): 94–116.
Seddon, George, review of *The Great Seasaw*, *Australian Historical Studies* 24, no. 94 (April 1990): 142.
Shaw, A.G.L., 'New Explanations in Australian History', *Meanjin Quarterly* 26, no. 2 (June 1967): 216–221.
Shaw, A.G.L., 'The Hollow Conqueror and the Tyranny of Distance', *Historical Studies: Australia and New Zealand* 13, no. 50 (April 1968): 195–203.
Sinclair, W.A., review of *Gold and Paper*, *Bulletin of the Business Archives Council of Australia* 1, no. 6: 64–65.
Sinclair, W.A., review of *A Land Half Won*, *Australian Economic History Review* 22, no. 1 (March 1982), 79–80.
Stannage, Tom, review of *A Land Half Won*, *Historical Studies* 20, no. 78 (April 1982): 114–116.
Strangio, Paul, 'Broken Heads and Flaming Houses: Graham Berry, the Wild Colonial', in *The Victorian Premiers 1856–2006*, eds Paul Strangio and Brian Costar (Sydney: The Federation Press, 2006), 51–73.
Stretton, Hugh, 'Review Articles: The Causes of War', *Historical Studies* 16, no. 62 (April 1974): 104–106.
Tauman, Merab, 'A Critical Comment of Australian Business Histories' (paper presented at the University of Melbourne, 6 February 1960) and published in *Bulletin of the Business Archives Council of Australia* 1, no. 9 (August 1961).
Turner, L.C.F., 'Review Articles: The Causes of War', *Historical Studies* 16, no. 62 (April 1974): 106–109.
Veliz, Claudio, 'Professor Blainey's Heresy: An Ocker Inquisition?', *Quadrant* 29, no. 5 (May 1985): 10–13.
Wagar, W. Warren, review of *A Short History of the World*, *The International History Review* 25, no. 1 (March 2003): 119–120.
Walsh, Maximillian, 'The Politics of It All', in *How Many Australians? Immigration and Growth*, ed. John Wilkes (Sydney: Angus and Robertson, 1971), 168–182.
Warne, Colston E., review of *The Peaks of Lyell*, *The Journal of Economic History* 16, no. 2 (June 1956): 250–251.
Wills, Neville, review of *The Steel Master*, *The Australian Quarterly* 46 (December 1974): 103–108.
Windschuttle, Keith, 'Stuart Macintyre and the Blainey Affair', *Quadrant* 52, no. 10 (October 2008): 30–35.

Websites, online media, television and radio

Blainey, Geoffrey, interview with Phillip Adams, *Late Night Live*, ABC Radio National, 8 October 2003.
Blainey, Geoffrey, interview with Annie Warburton, ABC Radio Hobart, 9 October 2003.
Blainey, Geoffrey, interview on *PM* program, ABC Radio, 27 August 2009.
Blainey, Geoffrey, interview on *Sunday Night with John Cleary*, ABC Local Radio, 11 December 2011.
Blainey, Geoffrey, *The Blainey View*, television series, ABC television, 1982.
Encyclopaedia Britannica Online, entry on 'Strategy – Bibliography', accessed 6 February 2013.
Giannini, Grace, *Bibliography: Geoffrey Blainey* (2001), http://arrow.monash.edu.au/hdl/1959.1/699354, accessed 2006–2014.

Jakubowicz, Andrew, '"I Love Pho": Tough Love Democracy and the Vietnamese Journey', *The Conversation*, 15 January 2012, accessed 8 August 2012.
Museum Victoria, http://museumvictoria.com.au/collections/themes/1257/blainey-house-ivanhoe-1957, accessed 11 January 2010.
Scouts Australia website, accessed 23 November 2011.
Stonier, Brian, speech at the launch of an exhibition on Sun Books, Monash University library, 31 May 2005. http://monash.edu/library/collections/exhibitions/sunbooks/opening-address.html, accessed 12 August 2009.
Yule, Valerie, 'University Memories', The History of the University Unit on www.huu.unimelb.edu.au/memories/stories, accessed 23 March 2010.

Other

Constitutional Convention Transcript of Proceedings, 4 February 1998.
The Australian History Summit: Transcript of Proceedings, 17 August 2006 (Department of Education, Science and Training).

INDEX

A

ABC
  Background Briefing, 145
  Boyer Lectures 1968, 94
  Boyer Lectures 2001, 226–7
  Faces of the Eighties, xi, 134, 140
  Four Corners, 145
  portrayal of Blainey, 145
  Pressure Point, 149
ABC Radio, 256
  Late Night Live program, 229
ABC Rural Division, Big Country series, 134
Aboriginal Australians, 92–104
  black armband as sign of protest, 192
  botanic knowledge and expertise, 108
  changing societal attitudes towards, 239, 261
  culture of violence in, 97–8, 108
  depiction of Tasmanian, 228
  equal pay for pastoral workers, 215–16
  exclusion from mainstream history, 214
  football, 178–9
  growing awareness of, 94–5, 196–7
  inclusion in *A Land Half Won*, 107, 114–15
  inclusion in *A Shorter History of Australia*, 215–16
  settler interactions with, 92–3, 108–9
  sources of environmental change, 95–6
  See also Triumph of the Nomads (1975)
Aboriginal land rights, 197–201
  Blainey's criticism of High Court ruling, 200–1
  See also Mabo decision; *Wik* decision
academic historians
  Blainey's difference from, 231
  career path, 19
  History department disassociates from Blainey, 155–6
  schism between Blainey and, xi, 176, 193, 259–60, 262
  take issue with criticism by Blainey, 56
Across a Red World (1968), 78–82, 252
  comparisons between *Meeting the Soviet Man* and, 81
  reviews, 78–9
activism
  Blainey's views on anti-war, 147
  peace, 86
  student, 82
Adams, Marion, 167

Adams, Phillip, 229
Adelaide Advertiser reviews
  The Peaks of Lyell, 26
Advisory Board of the Commonwealth Literary Fund (CLF), 119–22
  abolishment of, 122
  Blainey as Chair, 122
  change in membership, 121–2
  See also Literature Board
The Age, 107, 142, 144, 171, 203, 229
  Blainey's article in Education section, 100
  Blainey's commentary column, 182, 196, 197
  Book of the Year award 1974, 128
The Age reviews, 143
  Black Kettle and Full Moon, 223
  The Blainey View, 134
  Jumping Over the Wheel, 180–1
  The Peaks of Lyell, 26
  A Short History of the 20th Century, 252
  A Shorter History of Australia, 218
  Triumph of the Nomads, 100
  The Tyranny of Distance: How Distance Shaped Australia's History, 61
AHA, 160
AHC, 128–30
Aiton, Doug, 170
Alexander, Fred, 54
All for Australia (1984), 144, 146, 148, 150
ALP Club, 15
al-Qaeda, 257
American Historical Review, 60
AMP, 177–8
Anderson, John, 12
Annales school, 68, 250, 263–4
Annear, Robyn, 223
Annual Lecture of the Academy of the Social Sciences (1976), 133
ANZAAS, 29, 43
Arbitration Commission, 215
Arbitration in Contempt (1986), 182–3
Arena, 147, 153, 164
articles
  The Age Education section, 100
  'The Blackening of Our Past' (Hirst, 1988), 192
  Bulletin (1997), 200
  'The Cargo Cult in Mineral Policy' (1968), 71
  Daedalus (1985), 186
  first non-Australian topic, 74–7

'Godzone', 71–3, 241
Historical Studies, 38–9
'Lost Causes of the Jameson Raid' (1965), 75–7
'Origins of the Pacific War' (1976), 132
'Scissors and Paste in Local History' (1954), 163
'Slaves of the ten-fingered hand?' (unpublished), 137–8
use of distance in, 55
Ashbolt, Allan, 71, 149–50
Asian immigration, 261
  Blainey claims moderate approach to, 145–7
  debates in 1987/88, 173–5
  economic argument against, 151
  National Press Club, 141
  Rotary Conference Warrnambool, ix, 140
Atkinson, Alan, 106, 215
Atkinson, Sallyanne, 204
Attwood, Bain, 192, 199, 200, 235
Australasian Institute of Mining and Metallurgy, 35, 68
Australia Council, 129
Australia–China Council, 130–1, 141
Australia–Japan Bilateral Conference of Editors and Publishers (1978), 133
The Australian, 128, 133, 182
Australian and New Zealand Association for the Advancement of Science (ANZAAS), 29, 43
Australian Book Review, 231
  Blainey reviews for, 51–2
  The Rush That Never Ended: A History of Australian Mining, 36–7
  Surrender Australia? Essays in the Study and Uses of History: Geoffrey Blainey and Asian Immigration, 163–4
Australian Business History conference 1958, 34
Australian Business Monthly, 189, 197
Australian Council for the Arts, 122
Australian Economic History Review, 27
  The Tyranny of Distance: How Distance Shaped Australia's History, 57
Australian economy
  commentary on contemporary, 185
  critique of Hawke–Keating handling, 186–8
  factors impeding, 189–90
  under Howard Government, 190
  overseas debt, 187–8
  parallels between immigration policy and, 190
  See also protectionism
Australian Heritage Commission (AHC), 128–30
Australian Historical Association (AHA), 160

Australian history
  'black armband' view, 191
  interpretation of, 237
  key themes, 213
  optimism in, 193
  reinterpretation of, 207
  in schools, 233–4
  schools of, 164–5, 195
  Whig interpretations, 43, 101, 193–4
The Australian Journal of Politics and History, 39
Australian Left, shifting views, 146–8 *See also* New Left movement; Old Left movement
The Australian Legend (Ward, 1958), 194
Australian National University, 48
The Australian opinion column, 131–2, 182
Australian Republican Movement, 205
The Australian reviews, 107
  The Causes of War, 89
  The March of Patriots, 183–4
  A Shorter History of Australia, 219
  What's Wrong with Anzac? 231–3
Australian Right movement
  views on immigration, 174
  views on unemployment and unions, 151
Australia's History: Themes and Debates (Lyons & Russell, 2005), 231
awards and honours
  Companion of the Order of Australia (AC), 261
  Doctor of Laws, 261
  Doctor of Letters, 205
  Ernest Scott prize, 29

B

Baillieu Library HSC Lectures, 118
Ball, William Macmahon, 51, 135
Ballarat, 6–7 *See also* Eureka Stockade
Ballarat High School, 8
bank nationalisation proposal, 9–10
Baracchi, Guido, 154
Barassi, Ron, 117
Barker, Herbert, 56
Barnard, Alan, 39, 41, 42
Barnard, Marjorie, 51–2
Basin, John, 18
Bassett, Marnie, 21
Bassett, Sir Walter, 21
Bate, Weston, 33, 52, 205
Battersby, Jean, 122, 125, 129
Beaglehole, J.C., 224
Beddie, Brian, 84
Before I Forget: An Early Memoir (2019), xiv, 236
Belshaw, Dick, 9
Berndt, Ronald, 97–8, 100–1
Berry, Graham, 218

Index

BHP commissions biography of Lewis, 65–7
bias
   in historical writing, 207, 208–9
   limiting bias in argument, 240–1
   in museum exhibits, 94
Bill of Rights, 182
biography, Blainey's attitude towards, 67–8
'black armband', 191–3, 195, 197
   as Aboriginal sign of protest, 192
   reassessment, 209–10
Black Kettle and Full Moon: Daily Life in a Vanished Australia (2003), 220–1, 222–3
   reviews, 223
Blainey, Ann (wife), 46, 25
Blainey, Anna (daughter), 46, 159
Blainey, Clifford (father), 1, 6
   death, 157
   as Methodist minister, 2, 5
   record-keeping, 4
Blainey, Geoffrey, xiv
   appreciation for Australian landscape, 104
   approach to counter-culture, 238–9
   archaeological expedition with Mulvaney, 93
   attacks by colleagues, 155–6, 157, 158
   attitude towards biography, 67–8
   attitude towards fiction, 16–17, 67
   awards and honours, 29, 205, 261
   birth of daughter Anna, 46
   Boyer Lecture (2001), 226–7
   calls for Chief Justice to resign, 198
   compared to Clark, 195
   compared to Mulvaney, 231
   criticises Hawke Government's migration policies, 141
   delight in roll-your-own cigarettes, 23
   difference from other academic historians, 230–1
   discussions about Asian immigration, 140–1, 189
   engagement with communist countries, 125, 131
   features of work, 217–18
   as foundation Chancellor University of Ballarat, 205
   high regards for Lawson's works, 214
   ideological influences on work, 263–4
   as judge for Prime Minister's Prize for Australian History, 234
   on limitations of specialist historians, 260
   marriage to Ann Heriot, 46
   national prominence contributing factors, xi, 117, 119, 133, 172
   personal intrusion into narrative of books, 252
   professional output and success of books, 52, 262, 263
   on providing reference to source materials, 63
   reasons for backing immigration comments, 143–6
   response to History department letter, 157
   response to media coverage of speech, 142–3
   response to *Surrender Australia*, 163
   schism between academic historians and, xi, 176, 193, 259–60, 262
   storytelling abilities, 67, 263
   storytelling devices, 80–1, 181
   support from colleagues, 158, 159
   travelogue skills, 78–9
   on tyranny phrase and misuse, 62
   varied viewer responses to immigration debate, 149–50
   withdrawal from public engagements, 160–1
   work load of Australia–China Council Chairmanship, 131
   work load of Literature Board Chair, 122–3
Blainey, Geoffrey (academic historian)
   book reviewing for *Australian Book Review*, 51–2
   breadth of commissioned projects, 64–73
   change in approach to history, 55–6, 87
   converts Aboriginal history course material into book, 94
   as Dean of Faculty of Arts, 136
   difficulty writing biography of Lewis, 65–7
   fills in for Inglis at University of Adelaide, 47, 48
   first article on non-Australian topic, 74–7
   first overseas research trip, 74, 77–81
   'Godzone' article, 71–3
   points out contributions of forgotten inventors, 60
   popularity with undergraduates, 118–19
   professional output, 52
   as Ernest Scott Professor of Economic History, 74, 117
   as Professor of History, 117–19
   promotion to Readership, 47–8
   public policy articles, 71
   reaction to overseas response to *The Causes of War*, 90
   reasons for becoming, 46–7
   resigns from History department, 170–1, 176
   tribute to Fitzpatrick, 50
   as Visiting Professor at Harvard, 135–6
   See also University of Melbourne Economic History department; University of Melbourne History department
Blainey, Geoffrey (early childhood), 3–4
   attachment to Geelong Football Club, 5–6

Ballarat as inspiration for interest in history, 6–7
birth, 1
health problems in early infancy, 1–2
jobs as youth, 6
love of reading, 7–8
recollections of childhood, 5
Blainey, Geoffrey (education)
influential teachers, 9
primary and secondary, 8–9
Blainey, Geoffrey (freelance historian 1950s–60s)
awarded MA, 29
critical commentary of historians' works, 31, 32
Mount Lyell project, 21–4
review of Barnard's book, 39
skill of writing evocative characters, 24–5, 32–3
success of, 262
time at Queenstown, 22–3
University of Melbourne, 30–1
view on gold mining, 39–40
wins Ernest Scott Prize, 29
Blainey, Geoffrey (freelance historian 1990s)
A Game of Our Own: The Origins of Australian Football, 178–9
The Golden Mile, 179–80
A History of AMP 1848–1998, 177–178
Jumping Over the Wheel, 180–1
Odd Fellows: A History of IOOF Australia, 177
White Gold: The Story of Alcoa of Australia, 181
Blainey, Geoffrey (university years), 10–20
Clark's reflection on attitude of, 13–14
editorship at *Farrago*, 15–16
experience of History School, 13–14
holiday jobs, 14
residence at Queen's College, 15
response to Parker's Federation article, 17–19, 58
Blainey, Hilda (mother), 1, 2, 3, 4
Blainey, John (brother), 1, 2
Blainey–Stone line 173–4
The Blainey View (tv series), 5, 8, 51, 134, 163
controversial episode, 135
Bloch, Marc, 68
Bolte, Henry, 175
Bolton, Geoffrey
on affordability and accessibility of *Tyranny of Distance*, 61
on Blainey's authority on immigration issues, 157–8
career path, 19
critique of *The Rush That Never Ended*, 35–6, 40–1
critique of *The Tyranny of Distance*, 57, 58, 105

The Fuss That Never Ended chapter, 229
on History School, 12
on timing of Blainey's mining books, 42
Bongiorno, Frank, 176, 213–14
books not published, 33–4, 53–4, 65, 184
books written about Blainey's works, xiii *See also Surrender Australia? Essays in the Study and Uses of History: Geoffrey Blainey and Asian Immigration* (1985); *The Fuss That Never Ended: The Life and Work of Geoffrey Blainey* (2003)
Borgstrom, Georg, 242
Bourke, Paul, 164
Bowers, Peter, x
Boyer Lectures 1968, 94
Boyer Lectures 2001, 226–7
Bradman, Don, 219
Braudel, Fernand, 68, 250
Brennan, Claire, 226
Brennan, Frank, 259
Bright, John, 85
Britannica Online, 90–1
British settlement in New South Wales
Blainey's argument about, 56–8
importance of climate, 110
as invasion, 108, 235–6
renewed debates, 105–7
Broeze, Frank, 163
Broken Hill, 68–70
Brown, Philip, 40
Buckley, Vincent, 12
Buckley, William, 97–8
The Bulletin, 94, 200
Bulletin of the Business Archives Council of Australia, 27–8, 32 *See also Business Archives and History*
Bunting, Sir John, 163
Burley, K.H., 41
Burns, Arthur, 13, 53
Burrow, John, 250
Business Archives and History, 27, 50 *See also Australian Economic History Review*
Business Council of Australia, Debt Summit 1990, 188
business history
Blainey's reputation for, 46–7
timing and boom of popularity, 42–3
The Business History Review, 28, 74
Business Review Weekly, 182
Butlin, Noel, 48
Butlin, Sydney, 74
Butterfield, Herbert, 43

C

Cairncross, Frances, 62
Calwell, Arthur, 125, 146

Index

The Cambridge History of Australia (Bashford & Macintyre, 2013), 237
Cambridge History of the British Empire (Holland et al., 1960), 43
Cambridge University Press, 28
Cameron, John, 129
Campbell, Ross, 94
Canberra University College, 44
Carey, Liz, 161
Carlyon, Les, 90, 234
   on Blainey as lecturer, 49
Carter, Collin, 236
Cathcart, Michael, 211–12
The Causes of War (1973), 82–91, 147, 238, 263
   book launch, 88
   common critiques, 82–4
   identifying ideological argument in, 84–5
   new chapter in Australian-only edition, 132
   reviews and praise, 88–9
   trends identified in, 87–8
Cavalier, Rodney, 246
A Centenary History of University of Melbourne (1957), 30, 31
Chamber of Mines and Energy (WA), 179
Chamberlain, Joseph, 75
Channel 7, 134
Chifley, Ben, 9–10, 51
Childe, V.G., 43, 44
China, Blainey's travelogue of, 78–9
Chisholm, A.R., 120
Christian, David, 255, 258, 259, 260
Clark, Anna, 228
Clark, Manning, xii, 2, 122, 159, 220
   The Age Book of the Year award 1974, 128
   attacks on, 201
   Canberra University College inaugural lecture, 44
   career path, 19
   encourages Blainey to apply at ANU, 117
   as figure of controversy, 139
   friendship with Blainey, 30
   historical narrative style, 17
   influence on Blainey, 16
   omits sports from short history, 219
   pessimist view of Australian history, 194
   reasons for writing single-volume national history, 211
   reflection on Blainey's undergraduate attitude, 13–14
   religious allusions in writing, 257
   review of *Our Side of the Country*, 221
   on treatment of Blainey by other historians, 165
   on tutorship offer to Blainey, 19–20
   as Visiting Professor at Harvard, 135
Clark, Sir George, 86–7
Clarke, Jim, 142
Clendinnen, Inga, 239
climate, 244–5
   as feature in British settlement, 110
   as theme in works, 250
climate change, 236
Cobden, Richard, 85
Cochrane, Peter, 234
Coleman, Peter, 43–4, 194
Colombo Plan, 216
commissioned projects
   AMP, 177–8
   Australasian Institute of Mining and Metallurgy, 68–70
   Camberwell local history, 33
   Chamber of Mines and Energy (WA), 179
   general history of mining, 34–45
   IOOF, 177
   Jaques Limited, 65
   Johns & Waygood, 29, 30
   mining industry, xiii, 21–4, 32–3, 65–7, 68–70, 179–80
   Mount Lyell Mining Company, xiii, 21–4
   Mt Isa Mines, 32–3
   National Australian Football Council (NAFC), 178–9
   University of Melbourne, 30–1, 154
   unpublished, 33–4, 53–4, 65
   variety of topics covered (1990s), 176–81
   Wesley College history, 64–5
committee appointments (1967–84)
   The Age Book of the Year award panel, 128
   Australia Council chairmanship, 129
   Australia–China Council chairmanship, 130–1
   Australian Heritage Commission (AHC), 128–30
   Committee of Inquiry into the Development and Co-ordination of Museums and Collections, 127–8
   Commonwealth Literary Fund (CLF), 119–22
   Eureka Interpretation Centre, 205
   Fellowship of Australian Writers, 30
   Industries Assistance Commission, 130
   Literature Board, 122–5, 127, 131
   MUP Board of Directors committee, 50–1
   Public Records Advisory Committee, 128
   workload, 122–3, 131
Commonwealth Literary Fund (CLF) *See* Advisory Board of the Commonwealth Literary Fund (CLF)
communism
   applied to agriculture, 251
   Blainey's neutrality in writing about, 79–80
Communist Party of Australia (CPA), 127
Concorde jet, support for, 132–3

conferences
  ANZAAS (1962), 43
  Australia–Japan Bilateral Conference of Editors and Publishers (1978), 133
  Australian Business History (1958), 34
  Debt Summit (1990), 188
  Rotary Conference Warrnambool (1984), ix, 140
  Samuel Griffith Society conference (2000), 210
Connell, R.W., 52
conservative historian label, xii, 84, 191, 208, 261
  limitations of, 264
Constitution preamble, 202–3
Constitutional Convention 1998, 204
controversies
  Asian immigration speech, 140–3, 261
  Blainey View episode, 135
  National Times column, 132, 135
  political, 45
  Windschuttle's book, 227–8
  See also British settlement in New South Wales
Cook, Captain James, 224–6 *See also Sea of Dangers: Captain Cook and His Rivals* (2008)
Coombs. H.C. 'Nugget', 122, 125
Corrigan, Tommy, 219
Corris, Peter, 100
Costigan, Michael, 122
counter-culture, 238–9, 240, 261
Courier-Mail, 201
Court, Charles, 181
Craven, Peter, 49, 258–9
Crawford, Max, 11, 12
  career path, 19
  offers Blainey tutorship, 20
  recommends Blainey for Mount Lyell, 21
  reference for Blainey, 47–8
  secures commissions for Blainey, 30
credit squeeze (1960/61), 47
Crisp, L.F., 51
Cross, Robert, 82
Crotty, James, 24–5
cultural cringe, television programming, 134
culture wars, 153, 226, 234 *See also* history wars
Curtin, John, 175, 218

D

Daedalus, 186
Dallas, Ken, 56–7
  reviews *The Peaks of Lyell*, 27, 28
Daly, Fred, 146
Daly, Melissa, 160
Damousi, Joy, 171

Davison, Graeme, xii–xiii, 160, 223
  on *Across the Red World*, 81
  on Blainey's approach to Eureka Stockade, 37–8
  critique of *The Causes of War*, 83, 84, 85, 86
  The Fuss That Never Ended chapter, 229
  on *The Great Seesaw*, 166
  on growing pessimism in Blainey's works, 111
  on intellectual environment of Commerce faculty, 53
  on schism between academia and Blainey, 207
Dawkins reforms to higher education, 175–6
Day, David, 224
De Moore, Greg, 179
de Surville, Jean, 224
Deane, Sir William, 204
The Death of Distance (Cairncross, 1997), 62
Debt Summit 1990, 188
Deeming, Alfred, 40
democracy
  Blainey's pessimism about, 72–3, 196
  secret ballots, 111–12, 143–4
Dening, Greg, 159, 168, 169, 239
Dennis, C.J., 68
Denoon, Donald, 76
Derham, David, 117
dial-a-book and poem services, 124
distance concept, 62–3
  critiques about use of, 60–1
  as theme in works, 54, 55
Dougall, Namoi, 203
drought and pessimism, 110
Duffy, Michael, 195
Duggan, Tom, 136–7
Dutton, Geoffrey, 56, 122

E

economic history, 48–9, 87, 115–16
  growth in status, 116
  interpretations of, 262
  reform of 1980s and 1990s, 183–4, 191
The Economic History Review, 41, 75, 247
Economic Record, 71
The Economist, 98–9
Ehrlich, Paul, 83
The Eighties: The Decade That Transformed Australia (Bongiorno, 2015), 176
Ellicott, Bob, 129
Elliott, Jimmy, 23
Encyclopaedia Brittanica, 85
The End of Certainty: The Story of the 1980s (Kelly, 1992), 183
English Historical Review (EHR), 231
environment, changing attitudes in Australian history, 195–6

Index

Ernest Scott Prize, 29
Ernest Scott Professor of History, 117, 171
ethnic riots in Kalgoorlie (1934), 180
Eureka Interpretation Centre, 205
Eureka Stockade, 37–8, 193
  evolving judgements about, 109
Eureka Stockade Centre, 205
Eurocentrism debates, 254–6
Evans, Huw, 149
Evans, Tom, 205
Evatt, H. V., 43, 44

F

The Fabrication of Australian History (Windschuttle, 2002), 227–8
Faces of the Eighties (ABC), xi, 134, 140
Fahey Government (NSW), 203
Fairbairn, David, 71, 144
Farmer, Richard, 128
Farrago, 158
  Blainey's editorship at, 15–16
The Fatal Shore (Hughes, 1987), 106
Federal Election campaign (1990), 188
Federal Election senate seat speculation (1986), 161
Federation, 109–10, 111
  Blainey–Parker discussion/debate, 17–19
Fellowship of Australian Writers, 30
Fevre, Lucien, 68
fiction, Blainey's attitude towards, 16–17, 67
Financial Review, 71
Fisher, George, 34–5
Fisher, John, 208–9
FitzGerald, Stephen, 131, 173
FitzGerald Report (1988), 173
Fitzhardinge, L.F., 27
Fitzpatrick, Brian, 43, 44, 49–50, 193
Fitzpatrick, Kathleen, 63
Fitzpatrick, Sheila, 50
flax and pine theory *See* British settlement in New South Wales
floating of Australian dollar, 186–7, 191
football
  controversial debate about treatment of history, 236
  popularity in nineteenth century, 219
footnotes
  Blainey's views on, 63
  reviewers' complaints about lack of, 28–9, 41, 56
Forrest, Alexander, 114
Forrest, John, 114
The Founding of Australia: The Argument about Australia's Origins (Martin, 1978), 106
Fox, Charlie, 212
Frame, Tom, 249

Fraser, Morag, 229, 252, 253
Fraser Government
  Australia–China Council, 130–1
  Australian Heritage Commission (AHC), 128–30
  funding, 129–30
free trade, 190
freedom of speech, 153–5, 236
friendships
  with Clark, 30
  with Ryan, 34
  with Waten, 127
Frost, Alan, 105, 107
Fulton, Don Hendry, 46
funding
  Blainey advocates for arts, 130
  under Fraser Government, 129–30
  increase in CLF writing grants, 122
  increase in literary, 123–4
  universities in 1940s, 11
  university research, 47, 119
  under Whitlam Government, 123–4
  writing grants, 119–20, 122
The Fuss That Never Ended: The Life and Work of Geoffrey Blainey (2003), xiii, 37, 90, 108, 229–30
  critiques, 249
  'Triumph of the Colonists', 103

G

Gaita, Raymond, 200
A Game of Our Own: The Origins of Australian Football (1990), 178
Gare, Deborah, 7, 206, 208
Gascoigne, John, 224–5
Geelong Football Club, 5–6
generalist historians, 115, 249
geography
  as theme in works, 54, 248–9, 250
  use in travelogue, 80–1
George, Henry, 112
Gilmore, Mary, 226
Ginswick, Jules, 27–8
A Global History of History (Woolf, 2011), 228
'Godzone' series *See under Meanjin*
Gold and Paper: A History of the National Bank of Australasia Limited (1958), 31
  Blainey declines offer to update, 137
  dominant themes, 54
  journal reviews, 32
gold mining, 39–40
The Golden Mile (1993), 179–80
goldfield riots, 37–8 *See also* Eureka Stockade
Gollan, R.A., 193
Goodwin, Richard, 141–2

Gordon, Adam Lindsay, 212, 222
Gordon, Michael, 153
Gorton, John, 121
Gorton Government, 71
government funding *See* funding
Grant, Stan, 235
'The Great Australian Silence', 94
'great fool theory', 59, 245
The Great Seesaw: A New View of the Western World 1750–2000 (1988), 165–6, 239–46
   astute observation skills, 246
   key themes in, 241–2, 244–5, 263
   reason for subtitle, 254
   reviews, 243
   successful chapters, 242–3
   treatment of Keynes in, 254
Grew, Raymond, 252
Griffiths, Tom, 166
Groves, Murray, 15
Guardian, 99–100
Gwillim, Arthur E., 9

H

Haigh, Gideon, 234
Haley, Ken, 142
Hamer, Dick, 156
Hamer Government (Vic), 128
Hancock, Keith, xii, 2, 42, 159, 211
Hanson, Pauline, 201
Hardy, Frank, 121
Hargrave, Lawrence, 60
Harold, Tony, 15
Harper, Norman, 156, 220
Harrison, James, 60
Harvard University, 206
   Visiting Professors of Australian Studies, 135–6
Hastings, Peter, 243
Hawke, Bob, 192
Hawke Government, 141, 143
   Bill of Rights, 182
   commissions immigration report, 173–4
   compared to Menzies Government, 186
   critique of handling of economy, 187–8
   migration policies, 146
Hearn, William, 241
Heidelberg School, 104
Hemisphere, 138
Henderson, Gerard, 143, 170
   criticises Blainey's land rights arguments, 198, 201
The Herald, 182
Herald Sun, 230
Heriot, Ann *see* Blainey, Ann
Hiatt, L.R., 94
Hibbins, Gillian, 179

Hirst, John, 163, 204, 208, 215, 220
   'The Blackening of Our Past' (1988), 192
   critique of *The Tyranny of Distance*, 60–1
   review of *A Shorter History of Australia*, 218
   review of *Black Kettle and Full Moon*, 223
   review of *Our Side of the Country*, 218
historians
   point of difference between Blainey and, 213–14
   single-volume national histories, 211
   types of, 52–3, 54, 249
   See also academic historians; generalist historians; specialist historians
historical determinism, 38, 52–3
Historical Disciplines and Cultures in Australasia: An Assessment (Moses, 1995), 220
Historical Journal, 76
Historical Studies
   Blainey's article, 38–9
   Blainey's response to Parker's article, 17–19
   Eureka Stockade supplement, 37–8
Historical Studies reviews
   The Causes of War, 89–90
   The Peaks of Lyell, 26–7
   The Rush That Never Ended: A History of Australian Mining, 35–6, 40–1
   A Shorter History of Australia, 220
   Surrender Australia? Essays in the Study and Uses of History: Geoffrey Blainey and Asian Immigration, 164
   Triumph of the Nomads, 100–1
   The Tyranny of Distance: How Distance Shaped Australia's History, 57, 163
history
   'blackarm band' view, 191–3
   historiographical movements, 213–14
   state of historical knowledge, 246
   'three cheers' view, 193
   See also Australian history; business history; economic history
history academy
   schism between Blainey and, xi, 176, 193, 259–60, 262
   world history trends in, 246–7
   See also academic historians
'history from below' movement, 213–14
A History of Australia (Barnard, 1963), 51–2
History of Australia vol 3 (Clark, 1974), 128
History of Australia vol 5 (Clark, 1982), 138, 139
A History of the AMP 1848–1998 (1999), 177
A History of Victoria (2006), 218
History Summit 2006, 233–4, 257
history wars, 109, 226, 234
   book about, 228–9, 23
   turning point, 235

The History Wars (Macintyre & Clark, 2003), 228–9, , 230
Hodges, Ian, 90, 229
Hodgman, Michael, 145
Hollow, Monty, 15
Holt, Harold, 50, 120
Holt, Stephen, 42
Hoover, Herbert, 69
Hope, A.D., 122
Horne, Donald, 63
Howard, Colin, 204, 205
Howard, John, 171, 187, 191, 201, 205
   position on Asian immigration, 174
   use of term 'mateship', 202
Howard Government, 190
   Blainey praise for, 234–5
   defeat of, 234–5
   History Summit 2006, 233–4, 257
   Prime Minister's Prize for Australian History, 234
   republic debate 1999, 202–4
   roles for Blainey, 233–4
   spending on Anzac, 232
Howson, Peter, 121
H.R. Nicholls Society, 182–3
Hughes, Harry, 64
Hughes, Robert, 106
Hulme, S.E.K., 9, 64
Hyde, John, 172, 174–5

I

identity politics, 202
ideological turning points in Australia, 152–3
If I Remember Rightly: The Memoirs of W.S. Robinson (Robinson, 1967), 77
immigration, 171–3
   Blainey's shifting views on, 147–9
   Keating reduces intake, 189
   parallels between economic policy and, 190
   post-war migrant public opinion polls 1950s, 150–1
   See also Asian immigration
Imperial Chemical Industries Australia & New Zealand (ICIANZ), 33–4, 184
Indigenous Australians *See* Aboriginal Australians
industrial relations, 182–3, 212
Industrial Workers of the World, 25, 69
Industries Assistance Commission, 130 *See also* Productivity Commission
Inglis, Ken, 12, 16, 52, 117, 131
   Blainey fills in for (University of Adelaide), 47
   career path, 19
   as Visiting Professor at Harvard, 135

Institute of Public Affairs, 189
intellectual mood, 261
   evolving cycles, 238–40, 243
international reviews *See* overseas journal reviews
interviews
   Aiton (1996), 170
   about gap in writing (1975–80), 131
   Gare (1997), 7
   Henderson, 170
   Late Night Live program (2003), 229
   Pascoe (1979), 87
   press (1987), 172
   Pressure Point program, 149
   promotion for memoir (2019), 236
   Rintoul (1988), 16–17
   on science and technology (2011), 245
Introducing Victoria (1955), 29–30
IOOF, 177
Ireland, David, 128
Isaac, Rhys, 239

J

Jameson, Leander Starr, 75
Jameson Raid, 74, 247
Japan and Pacific War, 132
Jaques Limited, 65
Johns & Waygood, 29, 30
Jonson, Peter, 138
Jordan, Tim, 164
Journal of Australian Studies, 101
The Journal of Economic History, 28
journal reviews
   Blainey's contribution to, 71
   Gold and Paper: A History of the National Bank of Australasia Limited), 32
   Triumph of the Nomads, 100–1
   See also literary journal reviews; overseas journal reviews
Journeyings (McCalman, 1993), 175
Joyce, Alan, 62
Jumping Over the Wheel (1993), 180–1
Jupp, James, 163

K

Kalgoorlie mining history, 179–80
Karmel, Peter, 129
Katz, Elaine N., 76
Keating, Paul, 183–4, 189
   Anzac Day address (1993), 203
   banana republic speech (1986), 188
   launches *The History Wars*, 228–9
Keating Government, 143, 189
   Republic Advisory Committee, 203
Keesing, Nancy, 122

Kelly, Paul, 151, 173–4, 188, 192, 262
   The End of Certainty, 183
   The March of Patriots, 183
Keneally, Tom, 167–8
Kennedy, Don (D.E.), 19, 84, 89
Kennett Government (Vic), 203, 218
   roles for Blainey, 205
Kerley, William, 101
Keynes, John Maynard, 254
Kiddle, Margaret, 44
Kings Cross Community and Information Centre, x, 159
Kingston, Beverley, 195, 214, 220, 223
Knopfelmacher, Frank, 152
Kondratieff, Nikolai, 240
Kramer, Leonie, 134, 135, 136

L

La Nauze, John, 43, 54, 63
   as Ernest Scott Professor of History, 117
   as Visiting Professor at Harvard, 135
Labor Club, 12, 15
Labor Party, 193
   bank nationalisation proposal, 9–10
   early colonial, 112
   support for White Australia Policy, xii, 146
Lack, John, 158
laissez-faire liberalism, 85–6 *See also* Manchester School
A Land Half Won (1980), 104–16, 145, 150, 213
   absence of women in, 114–15
   continuation of themes from *Triumph of the Nomads*, 107, 108
   criticisms of, 114–15
   economic historical focus in, 115–16
   reviews, 112–13
   signs of pessimism in, 110–11
Lane, William, 113
Lanyon, Henry Maynard, 7
Lanyon, Hilda *See* Blainey, Hilda
Latham Lecture 1993, 191, 192, 193, 194, 195–7
Launceston Examiner, 25
Lawson, Henry, 214
lectures/speeches
   as base for writing *Black Kettle*, 220–1
   Boyer Lectures (1968), 94
   Boyer Lectures (2001), 226–7
   Latham Lecture (1993), 191, 192, 193, 194, 195–7
   Menzies Lecture (1991), 187, 189
   'A Methodist Childhood' (1999), 3
   National Press Club (1983), 141
   'The Politics of Big Business: A History' (1976), 133
   Tokyo (1982), 133

Leehy, Valda, 120
Lewis, Essington, 65–7, 68, 80
literary journal reviews, 40
Literature Board
   Blainey as Chair, 122–5, 127, 131
   Blainey's departure from, 131, 144
   increased funding, 123–4
   influence of bureaucracy in, 125–6
local history, Blainey as advocate for, 33
Long Strike 1919–20, 69
Love, David, 191
luck, reference in works, 114
Lucock, Philip, 121

M

Mabo decision, 199, 201
   Blainey's views on, 197–201
   critique of Blainey's views on, 198–200
Macfie, Alec Lawrence, 86, 87
Macintyre, Stuart, 29, 68, 168
   on 'black armband' term, 191
   on Blainey in History department, 118, 170
   blamed for Blainey's resignation, 171
   on British settlement debate, 106
   on Eurocentrism debate, 255
   The Fuss That Never Ended chapter, 229
   on History department letter, 156
   The History Wars, 228, 230
Mackellar, Dorothea, 104
Macmillan
   publishes *A Land Half Won* (1980), 104
   publishes *The Causes of War* (1973), 82, 89
   releases deluxe package of books, 104
Main, Jim, 19
Manchester School, 85–6
Manne, Robert, 147, 152
The Manufacture of Australian History (Pascoe, 1979), 44–5
The March of Patriots (Kelly, 2009), 183
Markus, Andrew, 160, 162, 229
Marshall-Hall, G.W.L., 154
Martin, Allan (A.W.), 43, 52, 193
Martin, Ged, 106, 231
Maurice, John Frederick, 89
Mawby, Maurie, 77
McCalman, Janet, 33, 175
McCarthy, Phillip, 129
McCarty, John, 36, 40, 48
McCaughan, K., 26
McCulloch, Samuel Clyde, 60
McEwen, John, 121
McKenna, Mark, 193, 194–5, 226
McLachlan, Noel, 59, 71, 168, 219–20
McLean, Ian W., 61

Index

McQueen, Humphrey, 52, 66
  on *Across the Red World*, 81
  criticises Old Left, 194
  on *The Peaks of Lyell*, 206
  on *The Rise of Broken Hill*, 69
  Suspect History, 201
Meanjin, 40
  'Godzone' series of articles, 71–3, 204, 241
media
  Blainey's response to coverage of speech, 142–3
  coverage of Blainey's Warrnambool speech, 141–2
  coverage of demonstrations against Blainey, ix, x
  criticism of history profession, 226
  portrayal of Blainey, 136–7, 145
Medley, John, 154
Meeting Soviet Man (Clark, 1960), 81, 127
Megalogenis, George, 188, 262
'The Melbourne School', 239
Melbourne University Press (MUP)
  Board of Directors committee, 50–1
  marketing *The Rush That Never Ended*, 42
  publishes *Introducing Victoria* (1955), 29–30
  publishes *Peaks of Lyell* (1954), 25–6
Melleuish, Gregory, 250
Mendelsohn, Richard, 76
Menzies, Robert, 120, 218
Menzies Government, 47
  compared to Hawke Government, 186
  protectionism under, 185, 186
Menzies Lecture 1991, 187, 189
Merritt, John, 112–13, 115
Merwick, Donna, 158, 239
Methodism
  lack of historians' interest in, 2–3
  rise in popularity, 4–5
Mews, Constance, 258, 259
Michell, A.G.M., 60
microhistory, 214
Miles, John Campbell, 32–3, 68
Miller, J.D.B., 71
Mines in the Spinifex: The Story of Mt Isa Mines (1960), criticisms, 32–3
Molony, John, 107, 205
Monash University, 82, 162
Moore, Bob, 134
Moore, Tom Inglis, 120, 122
moral war, 84
Morgan, Hugh, 102, 189
Morris, Barry, 103
Morrissey, James, 64
Mort, Thomas, 39
Moses, John, 59, 220

Mount Lyell Mining and Railway Company, 21–4
multiculturalism
  Blainey's views on, 151–2, 190
  FitzGerald Report (1988), 173–4
Mulvaney, John (D.J.), 18, 19, 99–100, 127, 135
  compared to Blainey, 231
  influence on *Triumph of the Nomads*, 93, 94
Murdoch, Rupert, 50
Murray, Les, 202
Murray-Smith, Stephen, 30, 36–7, 40
  on Blainey's departure from Literature Board, 125–6
  on impact of culture wars, 153
museums
  bias in, 94
  Whitlam Government's inquiry, 94, 127–8

N

narrative historians, 13
Nation Review, 100, 126
National Australian Football Council (NAFC), 178–9
National Estate, 129
National Press Club, 141
The National Times, 103–4, 159
  Blainey's articles and book reviews, 132
  Pacific War article (1976), 132, 135
nationalism, types of, 206–7
native title claims, 197, 200, 216
nature
  intellectual swing towards, 238–9
  pessimism, 241, 245
Nelson, Keith L., 84
New Left movement, 147, 153, 194
  historians, 52
  rise of, 202, 213–14
New Right movement, 182–3
New South Wales Government, Indecency Law, 124
newspaper columns by Blainey
  The Age, 182, 196, 197
  The Australian, 131–2, 182
  Australian Business Monthly, 189, 197
  Business Review Weekly, 182
  The Herald, 182
  Herald Sun, 230
  influence of writing, 171–2, 182
  The Weekend Australian, 172
newspaper reviews, 98, 99 *See also individual newspapers*
1967 Referendum, 94
Norris, Dr Kingsley, 1
North American history frontier thesis, 54
North Lyell Mining Company, 23

O

Oakley, Barry, 251
Odd Fellows: A History of IOOF Australia (1991), 177
O'Donnell, Joan, 125
O'Hearn, Dinny, 157, 228
Old Left movement, 147, 153, 193, 194, 214
Old Tote Theatre, 129
Olin, Spencer C., 84
One Nation, 189
optimism, 36
    1940s and 1950s, 150
    checklist, 243, 244
    counter-arguments to, 88
    dangers of excessive, 241
    in 'Godzone' article, 72–3, 241
    as key theme in *The Great Seesaw*, 242, 245
    in technology, 239, 240, 241, 242
    See also 'three cheers' approach to history
oral history, 23
Our Side of the Country: The Story of Victoria (1984), 137, 218
    reviews, 218, 221–2
    revised edition (2006), 218
    See also A History of Victoria (2006)
'outcrop/deep level theory' (South Africa), 75, 76
Overland, 40
overseas journal reviews
    The Peaks of Lyell, 28–9
    The Rush That Never Ended: A History of Australian Mining, 41
    The Tyranny of Distance: How Distance Shaped Australia's History, 60
The Oxford Companion to Australian History (1998, 2001), xii–xiii, 48, 106, 193

P

Pacific Dunlop, 180, 185
The Pacific Historical Review, 28
Parker, R.S., 17–19
Parkes, Henry, 111
Parnaby, Owen, 15
Parsons, George, 223
Pascoe, Rob, 44–5, 137, 194
    on Blainey's use of distance, 55
    on *The Causes of War*, 87
    classification of historians, 52–3
Patrick, Alison, 156
Patrick White Award, 161
peace activism, 86
The Peaks of Lyell (1954), xi, 21, 43
    controversial aspects, 25
    dominant themes, 54
    evocative characters, 24–5
    journal reviews, 26–7
    MUP publishes, 25–6
    newspaper reviews, 26
    overseas journal reviews, 28–9
    overseas rights, 28
Pearson, Noel, 201
Peel, Mark, 175
Penguin Books
    commissions *Tyranny of Distance*, 53
    rejects *Tyranny of Distance* manuscript, 55–6
    Very Short History of the World (2004), 256
Pepper, Stephen C., 52
Perkins, Charles, 173
pessimism
    about democracy, 72–3
    about direction of western society, 81–2
    about level of immigration, 152, 241
    checklist, 243, 244
    conservative, 166
    as growing feature in works, 110–11, 138–9
    as key theme in *The Great Seesaw*, 242, 245
    associated with nature, 241, 245
    reasons for economic, 189–90
    shift towards, 192, 261
    See also 'black armband'
Petersen, Joh Bjelke, 187
Petersen, Nicolas, 100
Phillips, A.A., 9, 30
Phillips, David, 155–6, 158, 160, 169
Phillips, Mark Salber, 213–14
Phillips, W.A.P., 44
Pigott, Peter, 127, 128
Podhoretz, Norman, 172
politics
    absence in *A Short History of the World*, 251–2
    absence in *A Shorter History of Australia*, 217–18
    increased content in *A History of Victoria*, 218
    in *A Short History of the 20th Century*, 253
polls
    Blainey and potential senate seat, 161
    public opinion on post-war migration, 150–1
    responses to Blainey's immigration comments, 149
    support for Blainey, 175
Popkin, Jeremy, 16
popular music, Blainey's views on, 253–4
Porter, Kenneth Wiggins, 28–9
Poynter, John, 11, 19, 117
Price, Archie Grenfell, 120, 121
Prime Minister's Literary Award for Australian History 2017, 237
Prime Minister's Prize for Australian History 2007, 234

Index

Pringle, John Douglas, 98
Productivity Commission, 130
protectionism
   exceptions for corporations, 185
   under Menzies, 185, 186
   opposition to, 35, 184–5, 190
Pryor, Dennis, 134
Public Lending Right, 124
public policy articles, 143, 182
Public Records Office, 128
Punch, Gary, 172

Q

Quadrant, 40, 84, 121, 171, 206
Queen's College, 15
Queenstown (Tas), 22–3, 24

R

racism
   moral crusade against, 149
   as the new form McCarthyism, 153–66
Rasp, Charles, 70
Red Book of academic grievances, 50, 119, 176
religion as theme, 249–50, 256–8
Republic Advisory Committee, 203
Republic Referendum 1999, 202–4
   defeat of, 206–7
   public information campaign, 204–5
   See also Constitution preamble
reviews by Blainey
   for *Australian Book Review*, 231
   Blainey's return to book reviewing, 231
   changed attitude to writing reviews, 137, 138
   contributions, 74
   for *English Historical Review*, 231
   History of Australia vol 5, 138, 139
   The March of Patriots, 183
   for *The National Times*, 132
   The Fabrication of Australian History, 227–8
   What's Wrong with Anzac? 231–3
Reynolds, Henry, 162, 164, 207, 209
   review of *Triumph of the Nomads*, 102
   What's Wrong with Anzac? 231–3
Rhodes, Cecil, 75
Rickard, John, 115, 163
Ricklefs, Merle, 162
Ridgeway, Aden, 202
Rimmer, Gordon, 56
The Rise of Broken Hill (1968), 65, 68–70
Roberts, Tom, 212–13
Robertson, Ian, 156, 157, 158
Robinson, Harry, 134–5
Robinson, W.S., 77–9
Robson, Lloyd, 168

Roe, Michael, 101–2, 193
romantic movement, 240
Rotary Conference Warrnambool (1984), ix, 140
Rothwell, Nicholas, 28
Rowse, Tim, 103, 108
Rudd, Kevin, 235
The Rush That Never Ended: A History of Australian Mining (1963), xi, 34–45
   critical reviews, 35–6, 40–1
   international reviews, 41
   literary journal reviews, 40
   newspaper reviews, 41–2
   reprints and updates, 42
   second edition (1969), 44–5
   use of distance in, 55
Rushmer, Jane, 5
Russia, Blainey's views on, 80
Ryan, Peter, 90, 171, 201
   appointment at MUP, 51
   friendship with Blainey, 34

S

Salmond, Anne, 224
Samuel Griffith Society conference 2000, 210
Santamaria, B.A., 174
Saunders, Cheryl, 204
SBS Television, 145
Schedvin, Boris, 32, 115
Scotch College, 8–9
Scott, Ernest, 31
Scruton, Roger, 244
Sea of Dangers: Captain Cook and His Rivals (2008), 67, 224–6
   reviews, 226
Searle, Henry, 219
secret ballots, 111–12, 143–4
Seddon, George, 240, 243
Selleck, Richard, 31
Serle, Geoffrey, 19, 31, 71, 72
settlers, interaction with Aboriginal Australians, 92–3, 108–9
Shann, Edward, 31
Shaw, A.G.L., 32, 56
   critique of *The Tyranny of Distance*, 57, 105
Shaw, Thomas, 221
Sheridan, Greg, 172
A Short History of Christianity (2011), 247, 253, 255
   reasons behind writing, 256–7
   reviews, 258–9
A Short History of the 20th Century (2005), 247
   dominant themes, 253
   Eurocentrism in, 255–6
   reviews, 251, 252
   treatment of Keynes in, 254

A Short History of the World (2000), 247, 248
  absence of politics in, 251–2
  absence of war in, 251
  critiques, 249, 250–1, 258
  debates about Eurocentrism of, 254–6
  discussion of religion in, 249–50
  reviews, 252
A Shorter History of Australia (1994), 104–5, 211–13
  absence of politics in, 217–18
  inclusion of Aboriginal history pre-and-post 1788, 215–16
  key themes, 212
  reviews, 218, 219–20
  revised edition (2009), 236–7
  treatment of sports in, 219
  White Australia Policy commentary, 216–17
Simon, Julian L., 83
Sinclair, W.A., 32, 113, 115
single-volume national histories, 211
Six Months In A Leaky Boat (Split Enz, 1982), 62
Slessor, Kenneth, 120, 122
Snedden, Billy, 120, 129
social history
  Black Kettle and Full Moon, 222–3
  Blainey as advocate for everyday people, 220–1, 263
  The Blainey View, 135
  of Christianity, 257–8
  importance of recording, 223
  lack of commentary in *A History of Victoria*, 218
Socialist Party of Australia (SPA), 127
societal attitudes
  changing, 103–4, 238–9, 261
  towards Aboriginal Australians, 239, 261
sociological historians, 52
Sodeman, Arthur, 5
Soulsby, Ian, 140
South Africa, Blainey's contribution to historiography of, 74–7
Southern Africa since 1800 (Denoon & Nyeko, 1972, 1984), 76
Sowerwine, Chips, 158
Spearritt, Peter, 180–1
specialist historians, 115, 249
  Blainey on downsides to, 260
speeches *See* lectures/speeches
Spender, Percy, 216
Split Enz, 62
sport
  Blainey's interest in, 219
  commissioned book, 178–9
  See also football
Stafford, John, 9

Staley, Tony, 129
The Standard, 141–2
Stannage, Tom, 107, 163
  The Fuss That Never Ended chapter, 229–30
Stanner, Bill, 94
The Steel Master: A Life of Essington Lewis (1971), 65–7
Stewart, Douglas, 120
Sticht, Robert, 24
stock responses, rejection of, 59–60
Stone, John, 173
Stone, Lawrence, 241–2
Stonier, Brian, 55–6, 61
The Story of Australia's People: The Rise and Fall of Ancient Australia (2015), 98, 237
The Story of Australia's People: The Rise and Rise of New Australia (2016), 237
Stretton, Hugh, 19, 52
  critique of *The Causes of War*, 83, 84
  praise for *The Causes of War*, 89
student activism, rise in university campuses, 82
Student Christian Movement (SCM), 12
Suich, Max, 132
The Sun, ix
Sun Books, 55–6, 61 *See also* Dutton, Geoffrey; Stonier, Brian
Surrender Australia? Essays in the Study and Uses of History: Geoffrey Blainey and Asian Immigration (Markus & Ricklefs, 1985), xiii, 141, 161–4, 166
  Blainey's reponse to, 163
  reviews, 163–4
Suspect History (McQueen, 1997), 201
Sydney Morning Herald, x, 143, 144
Sydney Morning Herald reviews
  The Blainey View, 134–5
  The Great Seesaw, 243
  A Land Half Won, 107
  The Peaks of Lyell, 26
  Triumph of the Nomads, xii, 98
  The Tyranny of Distance, 61

T

tariff reductions in 1970s and 1980s, 185
Tauman, Merab, 42–3
Taylor, A.J.P., 84
technology
  intellectual swing away from, 239, 240
  links to optimism, 239, 240, 241, 242
  as theme in works, 249, 250
television documentaries
  'Fall of Eagles' (Channel 7), 134
Temple, Peter, 75–6, 137
Tennant, Kylie, 120
terra nullius concept, 197

Index

Terrill, Ross, 171
Theodore, Ted, 68
Thompson, John, 19, 194
Thompson, Lindsay, 15
3XY phone-in poll, 149–50
'three cheers' approach to history, 193
Times Literary Supplement, 28, 78–9
Tom Brown's Schooldays (1857), 179
Trinca, Helen, 162
Triumph of the Nomads (1975), 255, 261
   controversial aspects, 97–8
   critiques, 97–8, 99, 100, 101
   dominant themes, 96–7
   important influences in, 93–5, 239
   influence in changing societal attitudes, 103–4
   response from anthropology community, 97–8, 100
   reviews, xii, 98–103
   success of, 92, 103–4, 117
Tuchman, Barbara, 88
Tucker Medal (2013), 261
Turnbull, Malcolm, 203, 204–5
Turner, Frederick Jackson, 54
Turner, Ian, 71
Turner, L.C.F., 84, 88, 89–90
Twopenny, R.E.N., 179
The Tyranny of Distance: How Distance Shaped Australia's History (1966), xi
   accessibility and affordability, 54, 61
   controversial topics, 56–9
   criticisms of, 56
   critiques of, 60–1
   dominant themes, 54
   impact of title, 62
   praise for, 63
   rejection of stock responses in, 59–60
   revised edition (2001), 62–3
   revised ending, 138–9
   success of, 117
   use of distance in, 55
   views on post-war immigration, 147–8, 152
'tyranny of distance' phrase, popularity and contextual misuse, 62

U

United Kingdom
   as destination for young academics, 19
   reception to *The Causes of War*, 90
United States
   frontier concepts, 54
   oil crisis 1970s, 242
   reception to *The Causes of War*, 90
   university students' reception to Blainey, 135–6
Uniting Church Annual Synod (1999), 3
universities
   as bastion of free speech, 154
   Dawkins reforms, 175–6
   student activism, 82
universities in 1940s
   funding, 11
   golden age, 11–12
University Gazette, 30
University of Adelaide, 47, 48
University of Ballarat, 205
University of Melbourne
   awards to Blainey, 261
   Blainey as Dean of Faculty of Arts, 136, 144
   Blainey loses re-election as Dean, 167, 172
   Blainey's undergraduate years, 10
   book commissions by, 30
   demonstrations, 158, 159
   security measures against demonstrators, ix–x
   security measures for Blainey's safety, xi, 160
   student clubs, 12
   See also Queen's College
The University of Melbourne: A Centenary Portrait (1956), 30
University of Melbourne Archives, 65
University of Melbourne Commerce Faculty, 47, 53, 117
University of Melbourne Economic History department, 50, 117
   Blainey accepts Senior Lecturer offer, 47–8
   Blainey as Professor, 74, 117
   Red Book of academic grievances, 50, 119, 176
   research funding grants, 47
University of Melbourne History department
   Blainey as Professor, 117–19
   Blainey returns to, 167
   colleagues attack on Blainey, 158
   differences in opinion between Blainey and staff, 119
   Ernest Scott Professors, 74, 117
   impact of Blainey–Parker exchange, 18
   publicly disassociates from Blainey, 155–6
   reputation and status, 11–12
   research funding grants, 119
   special leave from, 168
   supporters of Blainey, 156–7, 158
   tensions between Blainey and, 158–9, 168–70
   tutorship offer to Blainey, 19–20
   Vice-Chancellor intervenes in Blainey's return, 169, 172
University of Queensland, 159

V

Veliz, Claudio, 165
Very Short History of the World (2004), 256
Victoria and its Metropolis (1888), 8
Vietnam War, 72, 238
    activism against, 82, 86
von Ranke, Leopold, 247

W

Wadham, Sir Samuel, 31
Walker, Ron, 167
Walsh, Richard, 125
Walzer, Michael, 90
war as theme, 250–1
    in *A Short History of the 20th Century*, 253
Ward, John Manning, 208
Ward, Russel, 44, 152, 193
    The Australian Legend, 194
Warner, Lloyd, 97–8
Warrnambool *See* Rotary Conference Warrnambool (1984)
Waten, Judah, 30, 122, 127
Watson, Don, 63, 200, 250
Webb, Beatrice, 163
Webster, Owen, 71
The Weekend Australian, 172, 235
Wesley College, 8, 64–5
West, Stewart, 144
West Australian reviews, 26
What's Wrong with Anzac?: The Militarisation of Australian History (Lake & Reynolds, 2010), 231–2
Whig interpretations of Australian history, 43, 101, 193–4, 215
White, Harold, 121
White, Patrick, 161
White, Peter, 100
White Australia Policy, xii, 146, 190, 216
Whitlam, Gough, 146
    criticises Fraser's arts funding cuts, 130
    leaks details of CLF meeting, 121
    reflects on Literature Board, 126
Whitlam Government, 122
    Committee of Inquiry into the Development and Co-ordination of Museums and Collections, 94, 127–8
    dismissal of, 128, 217–18
    funding grants, 123–4
    slashes immigration numbers, 146
Wik decision, 200, 201
Wilcox, Craig, 232
William Quick Club, 15
Williams, Roy, 259
Wills, Neville, 66, 67
Wills, Tom, 178–9
Windschuttle, Keith, 171
    The Fabrication of Australian History (2002), 227–8
Wolseley, F.Y., 60
women
    absence in *A Land Half Won*, 114–15
    exclusion from mainstream history, 214
    football spectatorship, 219
Women's Weekly, 99
Woodruff, Bill, 47
Woollacott, Martin, 99–100
work, attitudes to, 212–13
world history
    growing interest and approach, 247–64
    success of books on, 256
Worner, Howard, 35
Wran, Neville, 204
Wright, Clare, 237

Y

Yarwood, Sandy, 153
Yule, Peter, 223

Z

Zika, Charles, 156